CW01215391

Styles of Organizing

Styles of Organizing

The Will to Form

Gibson Burrell

OXFORD
UNIVERSITY PRESS

OXFORD
UNIVERSITY PRESS

Great Clarendon Street, Oxford, OX2 6DP,
United Kingdom

Oxford University Press is a department of the University of Oxford.
It furthers the University's objective of excellence in research, scholarship,
and education by publishing worldwide. Oxford is a registered trade mark of
Oxford University Press in the UK and in certain other countries

© Gibson Burrell 2013

The moral rights of the author have been asserted

First Edition published in 2013

Impression: 1

All rights reserved. No part of this publication may be reproduced, stored in
a retrieval system, or transmitted, in any form or by any means, without the
prior permission in writing of Oxford University Press, or as expressly permitted
by law, by licence or under terms agreed with the appropriate reprographics
rights organization. Enquiries concerning reproduction outside the scope of the
above should be sent to the Rights Department, Oxford University Press, at the
address above

You must not circulate this work in any other form
and you must impose this same condition on any acquirer

British Library Cataloguing in Publication Data

Data available

ISBN 978–0–19–967162–5

Printed in Great Britain by
CPI Group (UK) Ltd, Croydon, CR0 4YY

Links to third party websites are provided by Oxford in good faith and
for information only. Oxford disclaims any responsibility for the materials
contained in any third party website referenced in this work.

To my grandchildren—Megan, Jack, James, Luke, Henry, and Billy—and those that Rosie and Owain may yet will to form.

Acknowledgements

This book has been gestating for a very long time and has proved difficult to bring into the world. As befits its title, two very different organizations should be thanked to begin with. First, I need to acknowledge the support of the University of Leicester in allowing me a year's study leave in 2008 to begin work on the book. Second, I wish to thank the staff of Kettering Hospital who in 2009 combatted the streptococcal bacteria which had attacked my immune system and produced an aneurysm of my abdominal aorta. There is nothing like a near-death experience to bring some sense of priorities into one's life, so I am genuinely grateful to those tiny little bastards (the bacteria, not the hospital staff) for what they attempted. But since I *have* finished the book I must have returned to some sense of distance from impending mortality. That distancing is because of what Karen has done, is doing, and hopefully will continue to do for me every day. She had an *annus horribilis* in 2009 and I thank her for supporting both Owain and me through our illnesses that year, and for just being there, before and since. Several indulgent friends who read the book in embarrassingly primitive draft form need a mention. These include Alan Whitaker, Karen Legge, Martin Parker, Barbara Townley, and Robert Cluley. I thank them sincerely for their extreme patience and efforts on my behalf. Readers for, and colleagues at, Oxford University Press also need to be thanked for their exceptionally helpful and supportive commentaries on the proposal. Colin Williams and his colleagues in a seminar at the University of Sheffield forced me to contemplate political economy much more than I had done previously, and consequently I would like to also incriminate them.

At the EGOS Conference in Helsinki this year, I lovingly revealed a list of those people since 1971 who have been interpersonally and professionally horrible to me. I update it constantly so it is a long, long list. But I have been fortunate in the last 40 years in having a small number of close friends whom I would trust with my life. They know who they are and the way perchance to the Great Western, still snuggling warmly underneath the railway arches of Wolverhampton.

The reader will note that the book is dedicated to my granddaughter and five grandsons. This gang of six may not be the last of my grandchildren to have to

Acknowledgements

be told about the importance of Northumberland to the world, but it increasingly appears as if adding to that number is now up to Rosie and Owain. I hope sincerely to see and hold any new additions that come into the world, and to welcome them into what the family modestly call 'Big Burrell'. At least it will enable me to bore them rigid too, with the same old stories that in my dotage only I find amusing.

Gibson Burrell, Lancaster and Leicester, autumn 2012

Table of Contents

Preface   x

Part I. Form

1. The Will to Form   1
2. Geometry and the Will to Form   21
3. From Protean Shapelessness to the Cube   41

Part II. From Form to Content

4. The Complexity of 'Style'   59
5. The Stylistic Features of Organizing   75

Part III. Content into Form

6. Lines of Fight   95
7. Points of Opposition   121
8. Organizational Reflections of Corner Living   143
9. Planes of Agreement   173

Part IV. The Will to Form Content

10. Interior Design   207
Conclusions: The Face of the Other   243

References   261
Index   275

Preface

You will be asked to undertake a number of small tasks throughout this book—over and beyond the work necessary in any reading. In the style of a monthly magazine, let me ask you at the outset to contemplate the following little quiz. Please look at this list of design images and decide which of them appeals most to you.

> Design patterns for organization theorists
> (*pace* Morgan 1986)
> A. Sinuous intertwined leaves
> F. Decorationless perfection
> B. Explosive alteration
> E. White-painted picket fence
> C. The collapsing tower
> G. Geodesic domes
> D. Sunlit poppies
> H. The hidden grotto

I will explain the reasons for the apparently haphazard lettering system later. There is a 'point' to it. If you have made a considered choice, then your answer reveals the design you prefer, not only in aesthetic imagery, but also across a wide variety of ideological, political, and economic positionings that we all face in forming our personal realities. We have choices, yet these are by no means unlimited. In fact, they are very heavily constrained. This book is about choice and constraint in styling 'organization' and how we arrive at the design parameters of large parts of our lives. Look to the Conclusions if you wish to know immediately what, based on your choice of options above, you will tend to prefer as your style of organizing. Otherwise, dear reader, if you postpone gratification, the quite long and somewhat challenging introduction awaits.

Part I
Form

1

The Will to Form

> By 'style' is meant a unity of form governed by a few basic principles. In this book these principles will be clarified by examples.
>
> Paul Frankl, *Gothic Architecture*, 2000: 33

> As yet, the social sciences have not even begun to consider the implications of such an approach for the study of social life. When they do so, they will have to take their cues from literature, art theory and philosophy.
>
> Bob Cooper in Robert Chia (ed) *Organized Worlds*, 1998: 157

A design envelope for styles of organizing

In the Preface to the English edition of *The Order of Things*, Foucault (1970: xi) argues that he was 'attempting to uncover the deepest strata of Western culture' by asking what was common to the naturalists, the economists, the grammarians. His answer was they employed the same rules to define their objects of study, to build their theories and to form their concepts. They were subject to the same rules of *form*ation which he had attempted to uncover. It is clear to any reader of his book that it was a truly ambitious project—an awfully big adventure—despite its shortcomings. He had sought to abandon well-accepted divisions within human knowledge and to take risks. As one surveys the contemporary scene, 40 years on, one might well ask 'Where are the big adventures and risky undertakings in Organization Studies?' It is, in truth, a quiescent, unthreatening vista which holds many a disappointment.

In this book I ask that the discipline to which I belong flirts more with danger than with safety. That it ventures forth on an adventure towards difference. In a recent analysis by Vogel (2012), a diagram is presented which shows that a journal with which I was somewhat involved stands out on a limb from the other six journals which 'represent leading scholarship in MOS (management and organization studies)' (Vogel 2012:1022). I do not object to the peripheral place in which 'Organization' is located in this article.

The Will to Form

Far from it, for it is at some distance from the Atlantic gravitational centres of the discipline and not moving in thrall to their orbit. Indeed, this sort of positioning makes one much closer to things characteristic of the Other—interesting, challenging, indeed risky, things—towards which I hope to seduce the open-minded reader.

When I began these musings my initial interest lay with a dangerous question indeed: Where are the origins of organization theory? I now think that one part of the answer lies in mythology and the ways in which human societies deal with existential angst. For organization theorists and the population as a whole, always and everywhere, the abiding horror is the abysmal hellish void which they cannot 'fathom'. The Book of Genesis and the Mesopotamian creation myths reflect this human terror starkly. Faced with a real 'Chaos', such mythologies perform an ordering function extremely well, and emplace a people snugly in space and time. They are 'stabilizing practices' within a 'strategy of a-*void*-ance'. Creation myths then are about construction and coherence and building a home—erecting, as it were, supporting plat *forms* above the pit. In this way, terror is tamed briefly and in part, whereby form and content are imposed upon a world of unpredictability and an obvious lack of human control. It is the desire and the need to per*form* this organizing of organization that I term here '*the will to form*'.

At the beginning of Genesis, we are told:

> Now the earth was formless and empty. (Genesis, 1: 2)

In the very earliest lines of the Bible, the writers of the King James version identified that there are two organizational principles that govern the human world. These are the need to find form and the need to find content. The writers play with these twin concepts, laminating them within Genesis Chapter 1, so that God is seen as moving in his six days' labours between creating the *forms* of night and day, waters and sky, land and sea whilst interspersing these with a concern for the *content* of vegetation, great creatures of the sea and sky, livestock and wild animals, creatures that move along the ground, and humanity itself. Under Christianity, then, and the Judaism upon which it is based, the essential nature of form and content is outlined by divine design at the outset of the belief system. To produce both earthly form and content is to organize—and their role is nothing less than to put an end to the reign of fathomless Chaos.

Chaos and the will to form

The organization theorist, Haridimos Tsoukas, like the chaologists within mathematics, wishes to place chaos in the realm of order when he tells us of 'the classical Greek insight of chaos as the gaping void, the abyss, the apeiron from which cosmos—form—arises' (Tsoukas 1998: 305). Alongside this taming of chaos through its formative role, we also have Castoriadis (1987) seeking a function for the void. What chaos does for him is to provide for the *ex nihilo* creation of new forms. From chaos comes order. And so we are presented with both states in the form of *chaosmos*. Chaosmos gives us both creation and the void to give birth to it. Chaosmos makes life patterned yet indeterminate. Chaosmos gives the human mind a role in the infinite. Quoting favourably from Castoriadis (1987: 341), Tsoukas (1998: 291–313) says that disorganization 'is a concept which strictly speaking makes no sense' for 'all coherent discourse and all action would be impossible' (1987: 309). Later in the text, it is claimed that 'we, as sentient beings, have no choice but to organize our world and our actions in it. The interesting questions are how we do it; what we do it for?' (Tsoukas 1987: 292). Whilst this set of questions is precisely what *Styles of Organizing* will attempt to answer, there are problems in his Athenian approach.

For my Spartan purposes, it is crucial that organization theorists retain Chaos precisely *because* it is without form or content! It is important that a group of scholars keep a strong hold on the notion of Chaos in its proper sense because this is the idea, found in many civilizations, that order comes to the world late. That before order there is no space, no time, no end, no beginning, no up, no down, no sides, no things, and no patterns. It is time-space before the Big Bang. It is the state of the universe 14 billion years ago in which no order existed because there was an absence of content and an absence of form. This does not imply that chaos is 'badly organized', for that is to remove Chaos from our lexicon as an *opposition* to order, and place it as knowable and containable somewhere on the *spectrum* of order.

Typically, however, if there exists anything outside the spectrum of order, humanity would then seek to destroy it by giving it a name and number. The dread fear of shapeless vacuity with no end to this nothingness, over eternities of time, means we seek to in-*form* it. Byatt (2011: 157) claims that 'Nietzsche in *The Birth of Tragedy* sees myths as dream-like shapes and tales constructed by the Apollonian principle of order and form to protect humans against the apprehension of the Dionysian states of formlessness, chaos and gleeful destruction' (Nietzsche 2003). This human desire for a creation myth, with a telos that has a future of meaning and purpose for our life, points to the ordering function of many religious systems. The neutering of 'Chaos' holds what Chomsky would call a 'high ideological serviceability' for numerous social groups, many of them in dominant or elite positions. The population welcomes just such 'orders'.

Precisely because of this connection between power and myth, I do not want life-affirming *chaosmos* to be all we have. Is it not better that we recognize the realm of reality where non-organizing might well prevail? For beyond humans, beyond our will, beyond humanism and beyond conventionalism, does lie a non-world of nothingness that we cannot hope to reach or fathom. In other *words*, there are other *worlds* and that is an 'l' of a difference. Let us keep 'Chaos' out of the hands of mythologizers and mathematicians. It is too precious to think about.

In the land between the Rivers Rhine and Danube lies another 'Mesopotamian' creation myth, much more rooted in Idealism and a strong sense of survivalism. The notion of a 'will to . . .' comes from a Germanic world, so that Schopenhauer's 'will to live' (*Wille zum Leben*), Nietzsche's 'will to power' (*Wille zur Macht*), Freud's 'will to pleasure' (the pleasure principle), and Frankl's 'will to meaning' (logotherapy) are all derived from a rather narrow and constrained philosophical axis. It would be foolish to equate these perspectives, of course, but nevertheless the commonalities between an underlying pattern of searches for those supposed forces that drive human beings in particular ways are worth discussing briefly. One issue is the locus of the 'drive': where does this 'will' come from? Their points of origin are not at all clear. Debates raged about whether the source of any such 'will' was to be found at the molecular level, with cells being driven towards some *telos*, or at the level of the individual psyche and its composition, or from a desire to find meaning at the level of the mind, or from violent social forces pushing towards collective interpretations. The biological, psychological, cognitive, and sociological disciplinary engines have all been fired up in the search to illuminate the origin of a 'will'.

And a second issue is how we might recognize any such 'will' when it appears. The question is usually addressed in the empirical world of 'manifestations', so that these wills are believed to show themselves in human behaviour towards other humans and towards other animals. Once identified, it is made quite possible to find such wills all around us. All behaviour might be interpreted through such lenses so that altruism, for example, can always be explained away as something fundamentally egotistical. Thus, the attitudes and behaviour of human beings can be portrayed as epiphenomenal effects of certain 'drives' derived from our nature and coloured 'red in tooth and claw'. These drives to kill, survive at all costs, and dominate the Other, are sometimes seen as reflective of the need for a Leviathan within a Hobbesian vision. On the other hand, the fact that humanity is perceived to be related in one way or another to the animal world is of course derived from the huge power of Darwinism and the developing need to address the interface between human and animal worlds.

Now it was within this inter-species context that Karl Marx began to outline a will to form rooted in the labour process when he talked of architects and bees and their differences:

> A bee puts to shame many an architect in the construction of its cells; but what distinguishes the worst of architects from the best of bees is namely this. The architect will construct in his imagination that which he will ultimately erect in reality. At the end of every labour process, we get that which existed in the consciousness of the labourer at its commencement. (Marx 1974: *Capital*, volume 1: 174)

As I shall seek to show, it is this imaginative act of pre-designing the object to be worked upon which I am calling here a component of the 'will to form'. And of course, within German Idealism, one might expect an emphasis being placed upon imaginative consciousness. But for me, it is important to conceptualize some forms of labour as just being necessary for survival too. The valorization of imagination in this Marxian passage partially hides the fact of bare necessity. Unlike Richard Sennett, who has addressed this notion in *The Craftsman* (2008), where he says that there is a basic human instinct—'the desire to do a job well for its own sake'—my view would be that the valorization of 'desire', of doing something 'well', and the non-utilitarian underscoring of 'for its own sake' all mask basic necessity and survival. There is a romance attached to the skilled crafts*man* who is seen by Sennett as being at work today in the role of doctor, programmer, parent, and citizen, all using tools, thinking about materials, and organizing their work. Yet the will to form is made manifest not only in the organization of work for craftsmen and craftswomen. It is made manifest in the daily (proletarian) lives of those who undergo seamless drudgery for hour after hour. They need to survive the elements as well as engage in creativity. Living on some unforgiving shore, on a blasted heath, with the rude wind's wild lament and the bitter weather, finding the ways deep and the weather sharp, humans require shelter (Bachelard 1964). Shelter, protection, security come before the Renaissance goldsmiths and Enlightenment printers can start their work and indulge in craft ethics.

The will to form shelter

The workshops of which Sennett speaks so eloquently (Sennett 2008: 54) have functions that are more important than just what happens within them. He defines them as 'a productive space in which people deal face-to-face with issues of authority'. What he ignores about workshops is their offer of containment, of security, of boundedness, of protection. Put simply, they provide first and foremost a roof over the workers' heads. Heidegger noted the importance of 'dwelling' and I interpret this to mean above all a safe place—a safe house. The novelist John Le Carré makes much of 'safe houses', precisely because of the confidence they give to their inhabitants in a highly threatening world of spies and spooks: 'Safe houses I have known, thought Guillam, looking around the gloomy flat... smelling of dust and drains, with a three-foot fire extinguisher in the pitch dark hall' (Le Carré 2011: 353). Security then does *not* have to mean comfort. Shelter does not free one from seamless drudgery. It is a constant struggle to prevent the elements from reducing human organization back into earth, wind, water, and fire. And even worse: it is often about what happens when the wind stops blowing, the waters dry up, the fires are extinguished, and the earth disappears. In short, the will to form is the desire to hold entropy at bay.

It is always possible that living naked under the stars is allowed in the big country; that there are times and places which obviate the need for shelter and *al fresco* living is enjoyable when the corn is as high as an elephant's eye. Arcadia, conceptualized as freedom from effort in a land of plenty, is a key part of Utopia. Yet, the 'will to form' an environment in which everyday survival is possible is the more normal state of human affairs. It may well be a very ancient tendency, for there is always a need within *homo sapiens* to find shelter from the elements and from those predators that will take men, women, and children. So whilst the 'desire to do a job well', lovingly identified by Sennett, may indeed exist, so too at some other, more basic level does the will to form a shelter. This is true, even if that sheltering is through the creation of the notion of 'mother Earth' within the cosmos itself. Setting up a shelter, be it material or ideational, is often invested with huge significance because of its centrality to survival.

Put swiftly, form forms formations in an effort to order the world into meaning. Deities are ascribed key roles in sheltering us from life's slings and arrows. Above the entrance to the apartments where the architectural critic Nikolas Pevsner was born in Leipzig was inscribed a legend from the Torah. It said:

Every house is prepared by someone. All are prepared by God. (Harries 2011: 3)

'Having a roof over one's head', provided and protected by some divine being, is a recognizable if not universal human desire. Nathaniel Owings, a founding partner in one of the world's largest architectural practices, claimed of Skidmore, Owings and Merrill, that *'we deal with the oldest forms of man's concern: his shelter'* (Owings 1973: ix, my emphasis). Without shelter little else is possible for human groups. A recent BBC series, 'Frozen Planet' (first shown 30 November 2011), shows how the nomadic Dunga people of North Eastern Siberia rely upon their shelters more than anything else. They form encampments, albeit on a temporary basis, and because of the hostile Arctic conditions, the group arrange their shelter as their first priority on ceasing their trek. Thus it is the 'emplacement' of shelters in an organized form which is a key to gaining a sense of meaning in human life. Form saves lives. The lack of form can kill you.

In the contemporary world of supposed 'terrorist threat', there is an obvious predilection to valorize security-based terms such as homeland, locale, habitat, fixity, neighbourhood, hearth, and so on. These terms are based precisely on finding a place of shelter—a place of safety (Ingold 2000: Chapter 10). This search for safe anchorage is also what is meant here by the 'will to form'. It can be characterized then as a desire to assert and insert form and structure into places where the existing form and structure are deemed insubstantial, inaccurate, inconsequential, inefficient, or unsafe—or where there is none at all. Constraint, re-structuring, per-form-ance are all that stand in the way of angst, anomie, and alienation. We are told to in-form, re-form, per-form, and con-form. Ordering processes such as these hold uncertainty at bay. However, the reader will wish to note that the 'will to form' is not only reliant upon idealism and notions cognate to the zeitgeist, but is also somewhat rooted in a set of formative materialist notions.

Design and the will to form

According to Mike Cooley (1987: 54–6) (a craftsman whose work Sennett does not cite), around the 16th century the word 'design' or its equivalent entered the European languages. Designing was not a new activity but it came to be recognized as something separate from construction and productive activity. About this time, the building of a church and the design of a church became discrete activities reflecting Braverman's (1974) notion of the separation of mental from manual labour. Cooley (1987: 55) maintains of this separation that:

> Dreyfus locates the root of the problem in the Greek use of logic and geometry, and the notion that all reasoning can be reduced to some kind of calculation. He suggests that the start of artificial intelligence probably began around the year 450 BC with Socrates and his concern to establish a moral standard. He asserts that Plato generalized this demand into an epistemological demand where one might hold that all knowledge could be stated in explicit definitions which anybody could apply.

Thus, instead of 'feel' and 'intuition' and artistic flair, the emphasis came to lie on the 'rules for design' and their systematic exploration. Logic, formulae, and geometry began to replace feelings. However, the 'will to form', so far as I am concerned, does not necessarily favour design rules over intuition and feel. It includes both (Plato 2006). There is the basic requirement for human beings to find spaces and construct places where biological needs for airborne oxygen, water (though not floods), warmth (though not excessive heat), food, and light are met (Gustafsson 2006: 225). The envelope where these requirements *are* met usually excludes humans from living atop high mountains, in dry deserts, under the sea, in Arctic and Antarctic wastes, inside volcanoes, and so on. It concentrates human life around places where clean air, clean water, warmth, and building materials are available. The will to form is constrained by the natural environment—but within that bounded arena, huge variability is possible.

The will to form, then, offers 'stabilizing practices' which allow for certain constraints and certain mobilizations to occur more than others. There is a reproduction of order with a tendency for 'many to become one' as forms come to be more durable and thence to predominate. In other words, *there is deep within the will to form nothing less than the constant organizing of organization*.

Perhaps the first articulation of the never-ending organizing of organization is in Aristotle (1998), who appears to believe that there has to be a power, an active force which drives 'Becoming and Being'. Science is about the discovery of the *aitia* or cause behind these forces and in this search 'essences' are crucial. In the later chapters of *Metaphysics*, essences are re-termed 'eidos' or *form*. Now it is not a static vision that *eidos* represents. Rather, it is a dynamic organizing of the organization of reality. What makes a house more than a pile of bricks is the plan, the pattern, the organizational chart of the basic *materiel*. 'Form' then is an active, organizing principle which drives a process. For Aristotle, it is perhaps much more of a (re)orientating plan. This underlines the notion which I seek to develop throughout this book that the will to form is the organizing of organization, and that what unites economic systems, architecture, design, and organizing is a shared orientation to a base definition: 'a deliberate plan and purpose that deal practically and functionally with the coordination of elements into an orderly structure that is in working order'. And this commonly held definition points to the production of the Becoming of Being, as well as Being itself.

If I may express it this way, whilst Sennett's concern is with the organization of production, mine is with the *production of organization* at both the micro and macro levels. Anthony Giddens (1989) has articulated this general sort of process as 'structuration' but, as we shall see, he is by no means the only writer to alight on the problem of 'producing' organization. Cooper and Burrell (1988: 103, 106–7) and Burrell and Dale (2002) have both sketched out this notion, so I will be brief here. Organization is produced in the vortex, in the face of self-recursion, impending threat, and doubt. It lies within existential gaps in a state of confused complexity. It seeks to obscure these doubts whilst securing some semblance of order. Whereas 'Form' for some non-Aristotelians is a static, fixed, completed structure, overall 'the production of organization is the articulate securing of moral principles and axioms whilst obscuring the imperfect grasp held by humanity of what to do for the best' (Burrell and Dale 2002: 109).

What I want to suggest is that organization is about security in both the structure and the process of organizing. And because of self-imposed moral constraints to produce feelings of security, design itself is hemmed in. Design is channelled, straightened, and tidied into recurring patterns. Only a limited number of 'pattern books' (which have an interdisciplinary utility) exist. These are an exceptionally useful way of understanding the will to form and the particular styles of organizing that emanate from it.

Pattern books

The will to form is not only about the desire to bring structure, order, and pattern to particular situations. It is also about that patterning taking specific, repeatable shapes of a limited number. It is as if there is a pattern book in the construction of form, and these basic patterns are repeated time after time. This is not to say that there is an identity of each and every pattern, of course, for variations are visible for all to see. My argument is that every organizational form is understandable as part of a patterning discernible in the 'will to form'. And each form contains understandable, recognizable, and repetitive elements.

We must look outside organization theory, however, for help in pattern recognition. The term 'pattern language' was developed by the architect Christopher Alexander and a team of colleagues at the Center for Environmental Structure in Berkeley in the late 1970s. In *A Pattern Language*, they use the following definitions of several terms, which I have found useful:

> A pattern is a careful description of a perennial solution to a recurring problem within a building context, describing one of the configurations which brings life to a building. Each pattern describes a problem which occurs over and over again in our environment, and then describes the core solution to that problem, in such a way that you can use the solution a million times over, without ever doing it the same way twice.

A *pattern language* is a network of patterns that call upon one another. Patterns help us remember insights and knowledge about design and can be used in combination to create solutions' (Alexander et al. 1979: xvi).

Their motivation in this work was to improve building design and it has been picked up in quite diverse fields to do with school architecture and so on. In parallel developments in the analysis of software construction, patterning has been used to improve programming techniques. In *Design Patterns:*

The Will to Form

Elements of Reusable Object-Oriented Software by Erich Gamma et al. (1995), an attempt was made to provide solutions to common software problems using the concept of 'design patterns'. They too utilize some concepts which I wish to plunder for the present task. For them, 'structure' is an arrangement of basic elements such as lines or shapes. 'Formatting' is the construction of one particular instance of a structure in movement while 'embellishment' adds material to the format without changing the structure itself. Putting these two sources together, my approach to design 'structure' is to conceptualize it as fixity, size, and shape, to conceptualize 'formatting' as the encouragement of certain pathways and processes and the discouragement of others, even to the extent that they are prohibited, and 'embellishment' is a seeking to encourage the system user that specific meanings arise from particular structures and formats. I shall make some limited use of these terms later in the book, in a hybridized form.

What I want to do, then, is to suggest that 'pattern books' are a way of understanding the will to form and the styles of organizing that emanate from this. Pattern books are to be found in the design arenas of engineering and textile manufacture and again relate to the ways in which enduring structures are to be found in the arrangement of human objects. Primarily, however, they are seen still in the world of knitting and sewing and have a utility for my purposes because of this. A book of patterns is the collection of possibilities that exist to address recurring problems and is often to do with sewing, stitching, and tying strands together. It is the opposite of dissection. Dale (2001: 202) showed that the 'anatomizing urge' can be seen to permeate natural science and quite a lot of social science too, through the 'culture of dissection' which represents a 'narcissistic phallogocentrism'. She argues (Dale 2001: 206–7) that 'weaving' threads together is *the* alternative to the slicing of the scalpel found in the hands of most social scientists. If the culture of dissection encourages penetration to the level of separate organs in the search to get quickly to the heart of the matter, patterning, on the contrary, is concerned with connecting tissues and fabricating an interwoven skein within which organization of the whole is clear. If the stylus wounds through severing, the pattern heals through suturing. *Styles of Organizing*, then, is meant to be a book of patterns for sewing together fabrics in human knowledge which have been rent asunder. For through patterns, understood and collected in one place, organization is organized.

Some patterning manifestations of the will to form

We are sutured into our everyday existence. Look around the room in which you are reading this book. Please consider the patterning of organization that

Some patterning manifestations of the will to form

is to be found. There is architecture there, and there is design. It may not be 'architecture' in the sense of a fine art, and the design may not be yours, but it surrounds you nevertheless. It has an effect upon your mood and your consciousness. It moulds how you think and sometimes even what you think. It organizes you—in both your mind and your body. The building in which the room is located also has an effect. It has been designed by professional architects to achieve something in the form of behaviour modification. Whilst we are makers of our own history but not under circumstances of our own choosing, we are also makers of our own surroundings but not under circumstances of our own choosing. Our lives can be organized for us by dedicated followers of fashion (Barthes 2009: Czarniawska 2011). We are, for the most part, the victims and beneficiaries of some forms of environmental planning and our lives are organized according to basic 'styles'.

Please look out of the window and survey the manifestations of the will to form 'out there'. Something may be learnt there about the organizing of organization, perhaps, from the complex relationships between gardens and cities, gardens and the countryside, and gardens and the wilderness. This will to form the 'natural environment', Burrell and Dale (2002) have termed 'utopiary' and have sought to analyse its links to the production of organization. Nietzsche comments (in his notebook of 1880: Autumn; 6: 206) that the 'will to power' looks as if it is mindfully absent in the comfort of the rural idyll. For here live the weak. 'They bury themselves in a garden house', no doubt for soft, fearful protection. The ways in which humans have protected their gardens from the wilderness are most interesting, for here the will to form is amenable to being closely observed. The wilderness can seem to be the antithesis of the home garden. Untamed and unpredictable, it stands in stark contrast to the managed garden. If Utopia is to be found in the cultivation of life and livelihood, the wilderness threatens it all. This sometimes creates the desire for highly managed cultivation under forms of 'utopiary' where all is formalized, counted, and measured, and then trimmed into submission. If 'Man' (not 'humanity', you will note) seeks Utopia, utopiary of this kind is often deemed necessary in the closer control of women (Plumwood 1993: 161), or in the eugenics of the Nazi 'gardening state' (Bauman 1991: 26–39) where people were 'brought into line'. Less monstrous in formation, the wilderness is kept at bay through the use of 'bay'. Civilization is boxed in by the use of 'box'. You are made safe through 'yew'. The creation of the *'termes'*, the boundary marker, to keep in the good and exclude the bad, is part of the construction of hearth and home—of a protected place in space. 'Utopiary', then, is a word used here to suggest that the attempted control of nature is sought to such an extent that there is much use of the espalier, of pruning, of hoeing, of formalized design, and of high walls, the better to keep out the wilderness and the more to produce 'organization'.

The utoparian injunction for formalization is: 'Make the bent straight. Hoe. Hoe. Hoe.' But we must bear in mind the ideological excesses that might accompany this task. When the three forming principles of concern to humans, of *recognition*, of *manifestation*, and of *coherence,* are all in evidence, there is nothing to say that any formation will be to our political or ethical taste. Indeed they may be anathema. So, whilst this book lays out my boundary terms in an orderly fashion for the undertaking of some utopiary in fashioning styles of organizing, the highly relative nature of our own 'Utopias' has to be remembered. In an equally relativistic way, styles may become private 'idioms', each with a peculiar property, seeking individual expression. What I seek to portray, instead of the idiomatic, are shared, collective, and characteristic modes of expression—albeit that they may be positively dystopian to some.

In the face of humanity's imperfect grasp of what to do for the best, attempts are made to bring predictability, regularity, and pattern into the lives of *homo sapiens*. We seek to establish *'termes'*—markers of our natural territory. In this section I wish to consider, in brief, some further examples of the will to form in operation, as it produces regular organization for both human survival and exploration. This is by no means a complete listing of methods for getting by, but it should at least suggest to the organization theorist a sense of the range of techniques for willing form into being.

The most significant of these dynamic 'formings' to discuss here, perhaps, are mapping and the relevance of the Arabic notion *'intizam al-manzar'*, grids, recipes, writing, separations, standardizations, and di-visions. Let us deal with each in turn.

First, there is **mapping**. We know from geographers the cognitive, political, and economic importance of maps (Stewart 2006) and their role in permitting coordinates to coordinate the location of defensive weaponry. But Ziauddin Sardar (1998: 28–9) points to something more idiomatic than the Ordnance Survey:

> During the colonial period, European visitors to the Middle East were particularly perplexed by the lack of perspective of Muslim cities... Visiting Cairo in 1856–7, Herman Melville complained that it had no point of view; to appreciate the city he wanted a plan... Since it was not built according to a 'plan', a 'picture', the city did not represent anything.

Hausmann's Paris had been planned to do a particular job in allowing easier military control of the city through the building of wide boulevards (Harvey 2003). This outline became a model of metropolitan development, since Paris was held up as 'the capital of modernity'. Because, however, the Middle Eastern city had not been built as a representation of something else, it seemed to the Western eye to be a maze, a labyrinth designed not for the visitor but knowable only to the local. It was a place in which even Indiana Jones would get lost. Thus, 'Colonialism required the creation of a plan or a framework that would transform non-western cities and cultures into representations, make them legible, and hence amenable to political and economic calculations' (Sardar 1998: 29). When the reverse visitation took place, Egyptians were amazed by Paris and the fact that it was all 'impression management'. They were amazed by the ubiquity in Europe of the *'intizam al-manzar'*—the organization of the view—which Hausmann's example had imposed upon more than just the French capital.

Europe was a continent of visual arrangement and discipline. Everything was organized to call forth some greater meaning. Everything was arranged to represent an image or a model of something else placed before the observing subject as a signifier of the signified (Mitchell 1991: 12). These non-European visitors baulked at the huge calculative and rational load placed upon the organization of the city and the view. It was not a familiar principle of organization to them. It did not allow them to enjoy recognition, manifestation, or coherence of the 'form' which Europeans saw in front of them.

Alongside maps, **grids** are also important in terms of the representational power that they have. Sennett, whose *Flesh and Stone* (1994) deals with the importance of grids in human society, acknowledges in that book the impact of Michel Foucault upon their joint work. In *The Order of Things* (1970), Foucault had announced that 'An episteme is, very roughly, a conceptual grid that provides conception of order, sign and language that allow a sense of discursive practices to qualify as "knowledge"' (Gregory 1994: 21). This relates to the sense of the grid that is a key part of 'abstract space', as Lefebvre characterizes the social construction of capitalistic space. The gridding of space was undertaken by the Western imperial nations throughout the 18th and 19th centuries because it was an easy and rational way, thereby fitting in with Enlightenment thinking, to allocate land dispossessed from others. Parcels of land within a grid system were allocated on a variety of bases but the key thing was the grid system arranged around cardinal points of the compass and right-angled alignments. The freedom from the meanderings of ancient land rights found in Europe was welcomed by almost all who came to colonize Southern Africa, North America, and Eastern Australia. The Rocks district of Sydney alone seems to have succumbed to urban planning by goat track.

Next, let me consider the will to form as related to the act of eating food produced to a **recipe**. All humans require food for the stomach as well as food for the mind. Claude Levi Strauss (1948) saw the foundational craft as being cooking rather than weaving, potting, or carpentry (Sennett 2008: 129). His triangular model is of the raw, the cooked, and the rotted where the first refers to nature, the second to culture, and the third to something like entropy. Cooking is the essential part of this triangle, for it gives humans their culture.

Warm food creates warm feelings and warm housing. The fire and its location in the hearth then become the centre of the home. From the will to eat comes a form of living based around the culinary world.

The notion of the recipe, either remembered by the cook or held in some written form, is central to much of management. It allows the predictable recognition of a coherent manifestation of a particular reproducible form. Mrs Beaton's *Book of Household Management* contains many (plagiarized) recipes where ingredients are recorded in particular proportions for particular portions in a classic demonstration of the linkages within Rationality between portions, proportionality, ratios and rations. J. C. Spender (1989) has also pointed to the importance of business 'recipes' in understanding differential approaches to knowledge management across the globe. Taste and fashion become products of the rise and fall of recipes and the availability of major ingredients. Indeed, Bachelard, Levi Strauss, and Sennett all show some intellectual commitment to a particular bourgeois recipe for domesticity. They conceptualize a proportionate, commodified, privatized world wherein there is a valorization of the 'family unit'. We, however, must note that the hearth need not sit within the domestic home but may well be placed within much more communally based living, such as in the household.

Turning now to the will to form as unquestionably manifest in the keeping of **written** records (Ingold 2007: Chapter 5), organization theorists should note the importance of writing to the state bureaucracies of so-called 'hydraulic societies' (Wittfogel 1959). These predate the fully developed bureaucracies upon which Max Weber concentrated (Gerth and Mills 1948: Chapter VIII). Also important in the history of written records is the medieval 'house' in which both production and reproduction take place. According to C. M. Woolgar in *The Great Household in Late Medieval England* (1999: 1), the households of the great were the most potent forces in the Western middle ages. Households like this required records—form filling—in order to keep control of the sustenance of large numbers of people. The 'house' is the site of daily worship, a location of consumption, of course, but it is also a repository of goods and services, a locus of the production of food and metal and leather and wool, and a site of work allocation. But, notes Woolgar (1999: 202), 'A most striking transition in the 16th century was the growing female presence in the household, both in terms of servants and service, and female control of domestic arrangements.'

As the Enlightenment gathered pace, the will to form may also be conceived of as '*Dichtung*', almost a *desire to divide* (Cooper 1998) and to differentiate. Once again this created a gender separation. One manifestation of this is the **separation** of home from work. The dislocation to social life which occurs when the household is no longer the centre of political and economic life is hugely significant. The trend to produce goods in large workshops exacerbated the break-up of the household and led to the rise of the factory. The intensification of the division of labour led to its counterpart in the labour of di-vision. Consequently, there came a separation of home—the locus of reproduction and small-scale production and consumption—from work, the locus of large-scale production. This separation, about which much has been written, creates the classic division between work and home, work and leisure, work and consumption, work and reproduction, a locus for rationality, and a locus of emotion. In other words, the factory trans*forms* the social landscape.

Of course, much has been written about the transformation of the Western world that is consequential upon the development of the large modern factory. Shenhav (1995) speaks of the way in which the 'chaos' of practices in small engineering shops gave way, under the auspices of the American Society for Mechanical Engineering (ASME), to 'Progressive' rationalization in which systems, standards, and schedules all came to the fore. The move to **standardization** through formalization in this particular variant of the 'will to form' was widely welcomed, partly because it appeared to save lives. For example, many needless deaths had occurred because fire hydrants were of different diameters in neighbouring areas. But this irregularity was also supported in part because engineers saw this as a way of progressing their move to secure professionalization. On the other hand, small engineering firms saw standardized pattern books as meaning 'extra clerks' (Shenhav 1995: 565) and therefore as a useless expense. This was the period of Progressivism, then, in which a new ordering of the United States was to be accomplished by systemization and widely utilized patterns—and not only on the shop floor. It was the period of the rise of corporate strategy, using elements of what Mintzberg (1979, 1992) calls the 'Design School' to analyse that which Chandler (1965) described as the links between strategy and structure (Butler and Carney 1986), using, in part, his own family's history as owners of the Du Pont Company.

A century later, however, this separation of work from home, at least within the West, is now in *reverse*. New di-visions at the global level have reorientated its direction of travel. As post-industrialization replaces the reliance on the secondary sector of the economy, factories disappear from the 'developed' world and are translocated to the 'developing world'. Here, 'old' relationships are rendered afresh in 'new' labour markets and in factories massive in size, impact, and output. As 'knowledge work' develops in the former manufacturing economies, offices are to be found increasingly in the home, and not the organization. The corporation cuts its accommodation costs, transfers its reprographic, heating, and electricity expenses to its staff, and offers 'home working' to its employees. This is a new 'will to form' affecting the atomized home. It is designed *for* you, not by you—which brings us back to where we started.

The '*termes*' under which we operate

In laying out our boundary '*termes*' as the conditions of possibility for the tasks ahead, the first collective ordering notion to deal with is architecture. 'Architecture' is the art or science of building or designing edifices for human use, taking both practical and aesthetic factors into account; it is something built; it is a style of building; a mode, manner, or style of construction or organization; it is the conceptual structure and logic of a computer-based system; it is the action or process of building (all from *The Shorter Oxford English Dictionary*). I shall use the term in all these meanings. In another volume of the dictionary lies the definition of 'organizing'. This term is taken to mean connecting or coordinating parts; putting into a systematic form; the attainment of orderly structure and working order; forming into a whole with mutually connected parts; coordinating into an orderly structure. All these usages will figure throughout this book. 'Design' is elsewhere described as a deliberate plan, scheme or plot; a plan or pattern from which something can be made; the action or art of planning and creating in accordance with appropriate functional and artistic elements making up an object; to form a plan; to create for a specific purpose. The lexicographers' definition of 'system' also follows a very similar path indeed. It means 'a unity of a complex whole; parts organized for some special purpose; a comprehensively and methodically arranged conspectus; parts having a similar structure within a prevailing political, economic and cultural order'.

Arising from this necessary articulation of some key terms comes a clear picture of the overlap between these terms 'system', 'architecture', 'organizing', and 'design'. Such is the congruence that one starts to think that each of the terms is almost defined by the use of words contained in the definition of another term. They appear to be self-referential in their commonality. Where all four notions seem to agree in the full umbra of their overlap is something like the following 'base definition':

> a deliberate plan and purpose that deal practically and functionally with the coordination of elements into an orderly structure that is in working order.

Within this book, then, my analysis shall seek to integrate four disciplinary areas around the notion of styles of organizing. Indeed, it will be my argument that these four terms are best seen as tautologies and as such we need to see and investigate not so much their interrelations as their '*intra-actions*'. They are connected from within, not without. By arguing for analysis of their intra-actions arising from their 'rules of formation', I hope to show that the connections between areas of scholarly activity devoted to these terms are myriad. For example, this shared definitional base means that hybridization of their terms is remarkably easy, e.g. as in 'organizational design', 'system architecture', and so on. It is my contention that there is a set of growths from the base definition which erupt in different places in different ways and to different extents—but they are connected rhizomatically. These following areas of knowledge are analysed hereafter as outgrowths of the same underlying expressions, sharing certain intra-actions:

Politico-economic systems
Architecture
Organization
Design.

But, of course, organization theory would see itself as much wider than the definitional constraint I have placed around it, as would architecture, as would macro-economic theory, as would design. Organization theorists in many places across the globe might wish to add so much more to the base definition, say from the wider 'organicist' definition about 'forming a whole from parts'. Architects, as diverse a group as organization theorists for sure, might wish some focus to be upon 'edifices for human use' over and beyond the base definition, whilst many designers would presumably wish the aesthetic concerns within the design discipline to figure prominently in an amended base definition. Political economy would certainly not see itself as reducible to such a definition in that it makes no mention of capital and profit and labour, for example. In other words, across these disciplines, there is a contingency to their connectedness.

Hence, I do not presume professional homogeneity here, for that would make the task of thinking and writing about architecture, design, and organization theory in a holistic way far too easy. *Styles of Organizing* would become an undemanding romp around cognate disciplines that shared much in common on a shared campus. But as architectural reviewers of my book proposal showed, one crosses the fences that constitute academic fields at one's peril. The full force of discipline may well be brought to bear against interlopers, as Foucault foretold at the beginning of *The Order of Things* (1970). Nevertheless, I shall attempt to cross these boundaries because it is my contention that styles of organizing have elective affinity with styles of architecture and styles within design and even styles within politico-economic theory. My argument is that the shared base definition that I assert exists at the overlap of the four 'disciplines' does suggest something deep that lies there, which constitutes common issues, common concerns, and maybe even shared solutions. In other words, we must set off in search of shared patterns.

2

Geometry and the Will to Form

Elementary geometry as organization

W. B. Yeats said:

> Measurement began our might:
> Forms a stark Egyptian thought,
> Forms that gentler Phidias wrought.
> (*Last Poems*, 1939,'Under Ben Bulben' part 4)

In the beginning, after terror and because of terror, was 'form'. And 'forming' was based in many places and at many times upon geometry. Geometry, the measuring of our world, is a key component of the will to form, for it is often described as the ultimate rational form of knowledge, the place where those twin components of rationality, ratios and rations, meet ratiocination and where human thought seeks for and finds the music of the spheres. The creation of form, I have argued in Chapter 1, results in 'a deliberate plan and purpose that deal practically and functionally with the coordination of elements into an orderly structure that is in working order'. But it is not supposed to be a place for the pursuit of meaning and feelings. Geometry is literally about measurement of the world and is thus a part of the *naturwissenschaften*. Supposedly, it does not belong to the *geisteswissenschaften*—the spiritual world of art history and the humanities. In this chapter, however, I shall attempt to discuss both basic geometry and basic symbolic connotations as another step on the way to looking at particular styles of organizing. For it is through elementary geometry, seen as the understanding of forces acting upon shapes and structures, that the will to form becomes more obvious in organization theory and beyond.

Geometry emplaces our perceived world within the World itself and creates the basis for the measurement of humanity's home planet. Ranging from birth to death, the size of our shelters, and the radius of food from our encampment, metrification is undertaken. As Ingold (2000: 46) argues, this calculus can be seen as the necessary 're-arrangement of nature'. It is here where the home and the economy come together in the original meaning of *economics*. Derived from two Ancient Greek words, *oikos* meaning dwelling and *nomos* meaning laws or management, the composite term suggests that, in deep history, it was clear that the household was an economic unit (Woolgar 1999). Production and reproduction in a fixed domestic location were the bedrock of economic thought. My point is that the household, the national economy, the global system, are all embedded in a social geometry originally to do with a centring around a fixed triangulation pillar whether it be hearth, harvest, or homeland.

And it is at this point that I should point to the need to outline the schematics of the geometric design of economics. In her discussion of macro-economic thought, Dow (1985) recognized the existence of something she called the Cartesian/Euclidean mode of thinking. Both Euclid and Descartes were concerned to develop a closed axiomatic system and this is central to modern economics because 'both were path-breaking mathematicians who, through their geometric method, had a profound influence' (Dow 1985: 12). Similarly, Klamer (2007) maintains that the economists Samuelson and Arrow paid close attention to changes in art, by those such as Mondrian, and this encouraged them to place 'X' diagrams of supply and demand curves in their textbooks. For Klamer (2007: 136), 'In the late 1930s an abstract representation was becoming meaningful. It resonated with the Zeitgeist. And it furthered the conversation among economists.' Although Klamer goes on (2007: 142–4) to produce a thoroughly unconvincing argument that the geometries of the square and of the circle produce very different approaches to knowledge within economics, he, like Dow, sees economics as embedded in elementary geometry.

Meanwhile, Peter A. Hall (1993: 279) argued that 'policy makers customarily work within a framework of ideas and standards that specifies not only the goals of policy and the kinds of instruments that can be used to attain them but also the very nature of the problem they are meant to be addressing'. Central to this idea is the tension between the Keynesian and Neo-Liberal 'paradigms'. Buckley and Casson (1993: 1035) maintain that 'Economic theorists are by nature system builders' and their architectural bricks are evident in the emphasis upon statistical data, the hypothetico-deductive method, and mathematical modelling. In most texts on research methods this constellation of factors is presented in a hierarchical way (Bryman and Bell 2007: 155). Similarly, there is a definite hierarchical relationship predicated in the rational 'individual' being seen as the building block of the economy. Visible across much of the homeland of economics was 'a utilitarian, rationalist and individualistic paradigm. It sees individuals as seeking to maximize their utility, rationally choosing the best means to serve their goals' (Etzioni 1988a: 1).

Furthermore, it is 'tied to a particular ideology, that of laissez-faire conservatism' (Etzioni 1988b: vii). In fact, there was some acceptance up to the 1980s that a typical arrangement in the thought of conventional academic economists was that laissez-faire micro-economics were supported alongside Keynesian interventionist macro-economics (Dow 1986: 58). But with the rise of Neo-Liberalism, the structure of dominant economic thinking changed. Keynesianism was rejected precisely because it did require a role for the interventionist state and with that, welfare rights and labour rights were undermined. The emphasis upon achieving full employment was dropped. Monetary supply became seen as crucial. State intervention was expected only in regulating the money supply and in the development of the defence industries and associated emergent technologies which had a military potential.

This is the overarching structure under which many people across the globe live in the 21st century. It provides a new social geometry of innovative circulations, reconstituted triangular or pyramidal relationships, and increased enclosing solidities—of which more later. In many branches of academic life, and not just economics, elementary geometry guards the entrance to understanding—but at a significant cost.

'Organization' and geometry

Upon my bookshelves stand many management and organization texts that publishers have planted upon them. One is sent these books as freebies. Without wishing to reveal those textbooks that I would not have paid money for, there is a nigh universal presentation of design as 'the setting of appropriate structures within which decisions are made and executed' (Butler 1991: 2) or an ensuring that 'all the parts fit together. These parts include not only strategy and culture but human resource management, size, technology, and structure' (Daft 1989: 513). Design then is a 'configuration in which all organizational components fit together to enhance organizational performance' (Daft 1989: 513). Whilst many think that Weber articulated the iron cage of bureaucracy, a glance at organizational design books would suggest he was talking in fact about the iron *triangle* of bureaucracy. These texts abound with charts of designed structures and of triangles to represent them more graphically (e.g. Martin 2005: 629). In particular, many writers refer to Henry Mintzberg's *The Structuring of Organizations* (1979) where his use of boxes and ovals and triangles in his articulation of the five basic parts of the organization (Mintzberg 1979: 20) are subsequently played out, right across the literature, in the form of differing expressions of one elementary geometry.

The iron cage of simple shapes

The widespread referencing to Mintzberg's book focuses particularly on page 301, where he identifies 'five structural configurations for organizations'. These design suggestions are:-

1. *Simple structure* where power is centralized in a small organization
2. *Machine bureaucracy* where some decentralization of decision-making takes place in a very hierarchical structure
3. *Professional bureaucracy* where expertise leads to some decentralization but coordination is built around shared professional values
4. *The divisionalized form* is a composite, loosely coupled organization where the middle managers play a key coordinating role
5. *Adhocracy* is where project teams form and then disband and the organization is held together by liaison devices.

More recent in-house articulations of 'newer' organizational forms, such as that adopted by motor bike company Harley Davidson (Teerlink and Ozley 2000: 139; Gordon and Suzuki 1991), use the representation of three overlapping circles. These are termed 'leadership circles' wherein 'shared ownership' and the notion that everyone in the organization is a leader become reflected in overlapping Venn diagrams (Scott 2008: 133–4). Willmott (2011: 266) has used the notion of a move from the 'fixed' geometry of bureaucratic organization with formal control mechanisms to the 'variable geometry' of 'streamlined' and 'hollowed out' forms of organization. Am I alone in yet again seeing the fixed geometry of the triangle being confronted by the 'variable' geometry of the circle here? But the utilization of organizational charts by almost every department of almost every organization emphasizes the geometrical figure of the rectangle. Of course, one could demonstrate this dependence in great detail but my point is that across swathes of literature we are imprisoned as much by representations of elementary geometry as we are by bureaucracy itself.

Indeed, many oscillations are detectable in the fortunes of 'bureaucracy'. Pro-bureaucratic and anti-bureaucratic strands are quite clear in the realm of organizational thinking (Burrell 2003; Clegg et al. 2011). However, long after organizations were supposed to have entered a post-bureaucratic phase, their containment within elementary geometry continued. This was a period in which discussion had focused on the very utility of the concept of 'bureaucracy' and to what extent the structural reality was different between and within organizations. In the early 1980s the issue of 'culture' emphasized a more subjective approach to organizational life, where 'subjective' was interpreted as an alternative to rationality's objectivism. But, of course, the subjective (we were told) could still be managed by appropriate techniques.

The iron cage of simple shapes

After the publication of Peters and Waterman's *In Search of Excellence* (1982), issues of 'style' were raised as part of the concern for the symbolic realm inhabited by the managerial classes. For example, Schein (1984) describes two organizations with two very different cultures. Organization A has open-plan offices, few closed doors, intense conversations, and people thronging about in 'public spaces' with a general air of informality. This comes to mind as being like the portrayal of The West Wing in the TV series of that name. Schein's description of Organization B points to a space where all office doors are closed, there is a sense of hush, and people meet by prearranged appointment. Formality and deference to those in authority dominate. The central administrative building of my own university has this sort of feel. These are 'common sense' portrayals of organizational life offered by Schein (1984), but such a dichotomy helped people to differentiate one organization from another and it helped remove the complete emphasis on 'structure' which had followed on from the post-war rise in the Warfare and Welfare states.

The interest in the concept of 'organizational culture' (e.g. Handy 1985, Schein 1984, Martin 1992) led to the development of Harrison's work, which was originally published in the *Harvard Business Review* in the autumn of 1972. 'How to describe your organisation' speaks of four main types of culture which, once in Handy's grasp, (1985: 187–96), are given a strong spatial and architectural feel to their descriptions. A 'power culture' is represented as a ***spider's web***, using the elementary circle within which other circles are contained. The figure represents a central source of power with rays of power extending out from that figure. The key individual controls the web through personality and personal power, and the selection of significant individuals to be placed throughout the web is a prime task for the survival of such a system. Also crucial are the financial links which hold the web together. Little faith is placed in committees and these cultures tend to be abrasive and tough places in which to work.

A 'role culture' is associated with bureaucracy and is represented by Handy as a ***Greek temple***. This culture depends on logic and rationality and its strength comes from its 'pillars', which are its main functions and specialities. These functional areas are controlled by the 'pediment', the triangular-shaped structure above the columns, which contains senior management. Power is based upon one's position, not personality, and the rule book is large and well thumbed. Rules and procedures are key to its continuance. These organizational cultures offer stability and predictability to their staffs.

A 'task culture', according to Harrison and Handy, is best seen as a ***net***. Some strands of the net are thicker and stronger than others and come to form nodes or 'knots' at their interstices. The matrix organization is an example of such a net-based organizational structure. The emphasis therein is upon task completion, and power is based on expertise in achieving some technical solution to a project. Individuals tend to identify with this objective, and differences are usually subsumed by similar goal orientations. Judgement of performance is based on results and there is toleration of different skills and orientations. Control of such nets is difficult because of their dispersed structure. Employees tend to enjoy such structures more than other possibilities because of the relative autonomy they enjoy.

The final culture identified by Harrison was 'the person culture' and it is represented by the ***cluster*** or 'a galaxy of stars'. This is a structure based upon high levels of individualism and a collective protection of these orientations. Barristers' chambers, families, and 'hippy communes' are given by Handy as examples of person-centred cultures. Mutuality and mutual consent are seen by supporters as the only coordinating mechanisms that will work. Cooperatives are seen as seeking to achieve this 'person culture' but so too are individuals like hospital consultants who pursue individual careerist objectives within organized places of work. Handy argues that these people are difficult to manage.

For present purposes, my argument is that we must note carefully the elementary, two-dimensional geometries used in Handy's/Harrison's articulation of culture. Spiders' webs, Greek temples, grids, and clusters are drawn quickly and easily. Circles, straight lines, triangles, and grids are used to represent different sorts of cultures because of the flat nature of the technology of books—and, of course, their planographic nature *does* offer quick visual imagery. These Harrison/Handy categories then are generalized 'design geometries'.

At the end of the relevant section in *Understanding Organisations*, Handy (1985: 196) declaims that 'The cultures have been described in impressionistic and imprecise ways. They have not been rigorously defined.' Yet his book was a guide to many a business and management student for many years, and university staff were subjected to easy and simplistic renderings of it in many an essay. It spoke to employees in some ways as a moment of recognition in what they saw around them and, in part because of this act of recognition, it sold in large numbers as a set text. It perhaps spoke to them most eloquently because it used simple spatial metaphors to which were attached much meaning.

Here is not the place to undertake a full critique of Handy's book but we should note its casual assumption that managers are male, its lack of referencing, its failure to distinguish his ideas from those of Harrison, its perhaps self-revelatory assumption that expressions of collectivism must be really based on individualism, its easy conflation of culture, structure, and style, and its very understandable neglect of the internet and the organizational consequences of that particular form of organizing the worldwide web in the 21st century.

The popularity of Handy's imagery draws upon the very materiality of the built world so as to give it a sense of concreteness to the observer's eye. Some of the impressionistic imprecision that he claims to worry about may be overcome in part by the evocation of the role of the 'mass' in his imagery. This is not a remark of any religious note but refers to Handy's tendency to draw the reader's attention to solidity. After all, the words architects use professionally do pander to this sense of being rooted and fixed. 'Weight', 'density', 'bulk', 'mass', 'solid' all are words of great substance attached to the client's endeavours.

And so too in organization theory is it normal for the 'thrust' of arguments to reflect the importance of concretization and mass. The fixation with size and shape in organizational design is found across the literature, to the extent that writers, and the CEOs to whom they pander, appear to think that size and shape are all there is. We must remember Northcote Parkinson (1957: 10), who in looking at the size and structure of the British navy, constructed his famous Parkinson's Law, which states that 'work expands to fill the time available for its completion'. In fact the relevant chapter of his book has the subtitle 'The Rising Pyramid', and this phrase is the clearest expression of the weight attached by chief administrators to solidity and what gravitas it has to offer. My main point here however, is that *Understanding Organizations* is replete with drawings of circles, lines, squares, and triangles, the better to deliver its titular objective. In Handy (1985), Figure 10 (page 208) has them all.

If simple spatial diagrams can allow us to undertake 'understanding organizations', the reverse is also true. The spatial and architectural arrangements of any organization need to be described, analysed, and theorized before we can understand the ways in which 'organization' works. As Hillier (1996: 373) has noted, 'organization can be described without reference to space, and therefore without reference to buildings, but the way in which the organization works usually cannot'. Thus my text also seeks to take the arguments outlined in Cragoe (2008) and in Chapter 7 of Hatch (with Cunliffe, 2006) as a starting point.

According to Hatch with Cuncliffe (2006: 246):

> An organization is a designed and decorated physical entity with a geographic extent and a layout of workspaces, equipment and employees. These physical elements of organizational structure and their relationships have important implications for the behaviour of people who are associated with the organization.

What lies behind this assertion of 'important implications' arising from physical elements is a set of underlying assumptions about architecture, design, aesthetics, and the built environment. *Styles of Organizing* will seek to explicate what these assumptions are, suggesting a 'design envelope' within which organizational decorative and material design might be thought to exist, pointing to what is contained centrally within this envelope and what possibilities exist at the extreme margins of it. In searching for some level of understanding of our hyper-organized, heterotopic world, it is unfortunate that we find that our analytical frameworks, both inside organization theory and beyond, tend to be hypo-organized. In other words, the complexity of today's living is not matched by the complexity of our mechanisms for thinking. In the search for 'building complexity', one key problem is the simplicity of our models, theories, and concepts. Straight thinking and straight talking are valorized. Parsimony of phrasing is often seen as offering a stripped-down version of life's twists and turns. The convoluted shambles of illiterate 'pointless' peasant life is seen as ill fitting the wide boulevards of straightforward bourgeois linearity. But in getting straight to the point, there is a loss. Straight lines, rectangles, and cubes are the work of rationalists. And for present purposes I am one of them.

I have found Francis Ching's book *Architecture: Form, Space and Order* (1996) an exceptionally useful text which helps considerably in the 'straightforward' task of opening up the conceptual space of organizing. The book is published as if it is handwritten, contains no photographs, and relies upon many hand drawings by the author through which he seeks to explicate the first principles behind architecture. It is said to be a 'collage' of different styles whereby the reader is persuaded to look for likenesses in unlike constructions which 'span time and cross cultural boundaries' (Ching 1996: vii). The author seeks to establish new connections, meanings, and relationships between forms and shapes in architecture that appear heterotopic.

Ching begins with a quote from Paul Klee:

> All pictorial form begins with the point that sets itself in motion...The point moves...and the line comes into being—the first dimension. If the line shifts to form a plane, we obtain a two-dimensional element. In the movement from plane to spaces, a clash of planes gives rise to a body (three-dimensional). (Paul Klee, *The Thinking Eye: The Notebooks of Paul Klee*, 1961)

In some senses, what we have here is akin to the articulation of two interrelated themes familiar to many a social scientist: structure and process. The first contains issues of space, structure, and enclosure. The second relates to movement in space-time. Ching says that:

> A **point** indicates a position in space. A point extended becomes a **line** with properties of length, direction and position. A line extended becomes a **plane** with properties of length and width, shape, surface, orientation and position. A plane extended becomes a **volume** with properties of length, width and depth, form and space, surface, orientation and position. (1996: 3; emphasis in original)

The elementary forms of organizational life

These simple terms in bold will form a key structural motif in *Styles of Organizing*, for 'architecture' relies upon shapes—and shapes create volumes. According to Ching (1996: 18), these shapes have organizational consequences. Much of their force is concerned with finding stabilizers for the process of organizing and for bringing predictability into human structures. The circle stands for stability and a self-centring in its environment. The triangle also stands for stability, especially when standing on its base. When standing on another vertice, however, it can represent precarious instability. The square, meanwhile, represents the pure and rational. All other rectangles, according to Ching (1996), are considered as variations upon the square and as deviations from the norm. He then goes on to discuss the architectural forms of basic organizational arrangements to which we now turn. It is worth noting perhaps, just before we proceed, that very few geometries problematize ordered stasis.

The elementary forms of organizational life

Within Ching's architectural interpretation (1996), the 'point' is the centre of a field within human vision, it often demands attention and is sometimes marked by a column, a tower, or an obelisk. It is static in nature. A 'line', however, can be seen as describing a direction of motion and of growth. Its orientation affects our perceptions of its meaning so that a vertical line often expresses commemoration of the past, stasis, and an oppositional relationship with gravity, whilst the horizontal line represents the human body at rest and the possibilities of the horizon. Lines create 'planes' that have height and length but conceptually have no depth. Shapes are the ways in which planes are primarily known to us, so that circles, triangles, and squares become key elements in the vocabulary of architectural design (Ching 1996: 18).

'Form', for Ching, is what we call different volumes, and the classic ones, obviously, are spheres, pyramids, cubes, cylinders, and cones. These geometric shapes can be empty and are therefore known as *voids*, or they can be filled and thereby become *solids*. The composition of the same forms into a new unity is possible, whereby additions of the basic form into new arrangements create the following possibilities: the *centralized* form clustered around the parent form; the *linear* form arranged sequentially in a row; the *radial* form comprising the linear form moving outwards; the *clustered* form whereby geographical proximity or a shared visual trait unifies the composition; and the *grid* form whereby the form is regulated by and related to a three-dimensional grid (Ching 1996: 57). Of course, a number of composites of these basic forms is possible and are by no means unusual. The students of the famous Bauhaus design centre in Germany experimented with a *composition*

Geometry and the Will to Form

of nine squares in which they developed different ways in which the same form might be laid out in space and asked what consequences this might have for its organizational arrangements.

According to Ching (1996: 189–97), the basic forms he identifies become differing types of 'organization', where organization, not untypically, means fixed arrangement in space. We shall deal with each of these fixed forms in turn.

1. *The centralized organization*

This is a central dominant space about which a number of secondary spaces are grouped. The central space unifies that which surrounds it and is generally regular in form and is large enough to gather secondary spaces around. Secondary spaces may be equivalent in shape and function to one another, and create an overall configuration which is symmetric. On the other hand, they may be differentiated from each other because of the environmental requirements of the site. Entrance to the centralized site must be organized by conditions of approach and of entry, and therefore a secondary space develops this function. The flow of people around and within such architectural forms usually terminates in the central space. Leonardo da Vinci around 1490 developed plans for an idealized church which look very similar to a centralized organization of this kind. Indeed, according to Ching, many major churches and mosques have adopted such forms over the centuries.

2. *The linear organization*

A linear organization essentially consists of a series of repetitive spaces which are alike in form, shape, and function. Particular spaces of importance in function or symbolic value can be located within the linear form but may have a position at the end of the line, or be offset from the main line, or be pivotal points of a segmented linear form. This organization of space is flexible and adaptable. It can run horizontally across a site, or diagonally up a slope, or vertically within a tower. It can be straight, curvilinear, or segmented. Examples given by Ching (1996: 200) include the longhouse of the Iroquois Confederacy of North American people around 1600 and an expansion of residences at St Andrews University in the mid-1960s.

3. *The radial organization*

This form of organizing space contains elements of both centralized and linear forms. It has both a central space and lines radiating from it. Whereas the centralized form is introverted inwards towards itself, the radial form reaches out. The arms may be both similar in form and function or may differ markedly. The 'pinwheel' pattern is a popular example of such radial forms and is best known to us perhaps in its centrality to prison design. Featherstone Prison, a brand new penitentiary nearing completion north of Wolverhampton in the UK perhaps expresses the radial organization extremely well.

4. *The clustered organization*

This form requires proximity in order to function. It is flexible because the integrating principle is merely a juxtapositioning, although it may be themed on similar lines of shape, or function. There is no particular place of overarching importance and so the patterning is crucial. The Palace of King Minos at Knossos in Crete, according to Ching (1996: 217), is one such example.

5. *The grid organization*

The importance of a three-dimensional grid pattern or a field is key to this form. Regular points are established at the intersection of right-angled lines and if done in the third dimension, these present a set of modules in space. This produces a grid of predictability and control where patterning is well understood and allows control of self and of movement. Whilst some grid references will be viewed as positive, this also entails that some spots will be seen in a negative way. Zoning of this type is often found in grid systems. The Great Temple of Rameses II at Abu Simbel is just such a grid form of organization (Ching 1996: 226).

For Ching (1996: 178), these particular organizational arrangements show the basic ways in which spaces can be 'organized into coherent patterns of form and space'. These patterns are configurations of structures which represent elementary forms of organizational life. What I take from Ching (1996) reinforces my strongly held view, then, that both architecture with design on one hand, and politico-economic systems and organization theory on the other, share common overlapping interests in patterning and its component structures of emplacement. To 'organize' is to place in a structured way, as any organizational chart would show. To 'organize' is to design some sort of human and material edifice. To 'build' is to manage a project in space-time through pre-planned and sometimes spontaneous organizing. To 'construct' is to create an order through and in materials. To organize is to think, through an 'architecture'—as many texts on systems design would attest. To engage in architecture involves a modicum of organizing—as analyses of architectural practices, both large and small, show. In other words, organization is a type of constructed design. A constructed design requires organization.

In Ching's drawings and musings, his views on hierarchy (Ching 1996: 338) also stand out. He argues that real differences exist within and between spaces based on the degree of importance the building is held to possess by the planners, designers, owners, and city officials. It may be given exceptional size, or a unique shape, or be placed in a strategic or symbolic location. Its importance is thus established by its breaking of a norm; it is an anomaly in an otherwise regular pattern. But regular patterns and norms do exist, as Ching shows so well, in the geometry of structures.

Becoming design

So, whilst the fixed geometry of the organizational form, identified by Ching above, constrains movement and flexibility, there are design methods for enactment by which movement can be encouraged and controlled. And it is the dynamism that one finds in much organizational life. For example, Frederick (2007: 69) states that 'a floor plan demonstrates the organizational logic of a building: a section embodies its emotional experience'. He argues (Frederick 2007: 47) that squares are inherently non-dynamic and do not naturally suggest movement. Non-square shapes, he suggests, 'more naturally accommodate patterns of movement, congregation and habitation', yet these are more difficult to develop into harmonious spaces because of the emotional experience that architectural geometry creates.

Here, then, it is important for us to remember issues of movement and circulation. Again following Ching very closely, we can learn something of generic processes of organizing activities in space, dealing with what I termed 'formatting' in the previous chapter. In terms of this enacting of patterns in space, he argues (Ching 1996: 229) that we move through a sequence of spaces in time. Thus, we have a sense of where we have been and we anticipate where we are going. He identifies the following elements to circulation: 'approach, entrance, configuration of the path, path–space relationships and forms of the circulation space'. I shall address each in turn—but very briefly.

The *approach* to a building involves the distant view. Here we prepare ourselves, and the building prepares us, for the experience of using the building. A frontal approach is along a direct, axial path and the target entrance is clear and visible. An oblique approach allows the path to be delayed and prolonged, and can permit different views of the structure at different points. A spiral approach emphasizes the 3D nature of the building as we move around its perimeter and the entrance may be constantly hidden from view throughout.

The *entrance* to a building involves penetrating the 'inside' from the 'outside'. It may be marked by a 'threshold' to introduce a vertical dimension to the entrance. The form of the opening may be a simple hole in that wall or an elaborate, articulated gateway within the perpendicular plane. A 'flush' entrance leaves the plane of this wall intact. A projected entrance marks out a transitional space, as does a recessed entrance. Each entrance marks out the space within as different, and as a 'place'. Visual reinforcement can be undertaken, with entrances being larger, smaller, or more ornate than might be expected.

Configuration of the path implies that all paths are linear, although of course not necessarily straight. Linearity allows and encourages the movement of people, their modes of transport, and their goods. Important differences follow from what is being moved. Cars require different paths from those needed by human pedestrians. The places of intersections where paths meet are difficult spaces to negotiate, and require some decision-making. Intersections may reflect the spatial organizations we discussed above (i.e. they may be linear, radial, grid, and so on) or they may contrast sharply with them in order to make a differentiation.

Path–space relationships involve a consideration of how paths relate to the spaces they link. Thus, there are pass-by spaces like a closed office, pass-through spaces such as a corridor, and terminate-in spaces such as really important spaces that mark the end point of the processing through the building (the headmaster's office).

Finally, *forms of the circulation space* for those in the building are crucial. People may walk, rest, stroll, pause, or promenade through public spaces and, therefore, corridors do not fit this function well. Large spaces for circulation are not uncommon for this reason. Circulation spaces may be enclosed in a private space or they are open on one side or both sides. Stairs are also important circulation spaces in most buildings. Wide shallow steps are invitations to ascend. Narrow steep ones are discouragers of ingress. Going up them can reflect feelings within the user of privacy and aloofness, whilst descending stairs are often accompanied by feelings of renewed confidence and security.

Ching (1996) has served a really useful purpose in presenting architecture as a series of forms that organize our everyday lives, by emplacing and enacting us, allowing certain things not to happen and certain things to happen constantly. But it is time to move to some philosophical issues underlying his concern for form.

Becoming organization

By seeking to comprehend the systematic organization of politico-economic systems, architecture, aesthetics, design, and artwork—as this book does—it might appear as if there is necessarily a focus upon gravitas, upon fixity, structures, objects, and solid materiality. In other words, a concentration upon organization as Being. This fixation on fixity is often the case in architecture and if we look at more typical textbook definitions, not only of design but of 'organization' itself, they too emphasize a definite and designed structure and function. For example, 'organizations are social entities that are goal-directed, deliberately structured activity systems with an identifiable boundary' (Daft 1989: 9–10). Readers will note the 'deliberately structured' component of Daft's definition. In relation to his emphasis on 'boundaries', it must be marked well that the very word 'organization' comes from the Greek word '*organon*' which was used to signify the distinguishing differentiation of the body's internal organs one from another (Morgan 1986; Hoskin 1995).

In organizing 'organization' we should note here that a major role is given to the metaphor of the body within the functionalist approaches to organization studies which dominate my field. Thus, we have corporate headquarters, brains of the firm, lean organizations, factory hands, and so on. Even a Foucauldian analysis, which in *almost* every way differs from a functionalist one, places the *organon* at the centre of its analysis in a metaphorical as well as literal sense. In the historical development that Foucault calls an 'epistemic break' there is a move from 'nothing more than the nomination of the visible' (Foucault 2008: 144) towards 'organic structure' (*l'organization*) 'as a foundation for ordering nature' (Foucault 2008: 251). Indeed, bodies and body parts litter the stage of organization studies—but many analysts trample over them as though they did not exist. The consequences of seeing organization as the 'bounded body of organs' is recognized by some, of course, but more often is blithely assumed in the structures of analytical formulation (Dale 2001). The 'architecture' of the body is seen as being made up of fixed structures arrayed in predictable—and geometric—ways. Da Vinci's famous 'Human figure in circle, illustrating proportions' (c.1490) demonstrates this view perfectly (Sennett 1994: 102–6). Structures became centred on and around the human body, understood rationally.

But this detailed knowledge of the human form was dangerous. The anatomizers of the human body had taken great risks when cutting open the bodies of all those they could get their hands on, in their quest to reveal an ordered world. It was a formal world of organs, differentiated from each other with recognizable functions and forms. The skeleton, muscles, blood vessels, nerves, and so on were understood in terms of the arrangement of organs which they connected. The 'system' was organized by and through the organization of fixed parts, seen as an assemblage of formed predictability allowing a comprehensible, human-centred, geometry.

But this notion of 'organization' as being equivalent to 'structure', which the translators of Foucault's notion of *l'organization* in *The Order of Things* unnecessarily adopted, is not enough. Their translation, like that of many an organization theorist, appears to be located in the static 'present'. It is

Becoming organization

today's structure rather than an ongoing process that appears to fascinate them. As Giddens (1984) has pointed out, however, the 'present' is but a fleeting moment where the past and present forever intermingle their lights. So, the movement of time between past and future creates the 'present' as but one instant...and then that 'present' has gone. Put crudely in a form of reverse aphorism, the future is always coming. It's the present that never comes.

Organization is also then a verb, a word of movement and process and fluidity. Writers such as Robert Chia, Bob Cooper, and Haridimos Tsoukas (Chia 1998a; Chia 1998b) have articulated a world of process within organization. Using the distinction between 'Being' and 'Becoming', they have spoken of the need to look at 'becoming' as much as at 'being'. It is an approach which usually follows Heidegger and concerns activity and dynamic interplay in a field of forces. Predictability is not its focus. It seeks to understand movement and speed. Boje, Gephart, and Thatchenkery (1996: 2) argue that 'For us, the meaning of organization is problematic. Rather than conceiving of organizations substantively as concrete facticities embedded in artefacts such as policies and buildings, we regard organizations relationally...as a concept of social actors that is produced in contextually embedded social discourse and used to interpret the social world.' Similarly in Clegg's *Modern Organizations* (1990) it is maintained that we live in an age in which organizations are undergoing rapid change, in both environment and form. In terms of the significance of this shift for organizations, Clegg argues that we must look towards boundary-less organizations and networking. The Third Italy of Emilia Romagna and the 1980s phenomenon of Silicon Valley have both been used by organization theorists to show that some successful organizations do not resemble the bounded large bureaucracies of the Fordist era. There is a supposed need to look at 'previously untranslated organizational forms' (Clegg 1990: 23) which do not originate in what many call the world of 'organizations', as usually understood within the boundaries of organization studies as a discipline. Thus, bearing in mind these pointers to process and to some variant of Becoming, it is less easy to accept a standardized Daft definition of 'organization' any longer without a willing suspension of disbelief.

Styles of Organizing will seek to be aware of the need to have a *twin* focus; as concerning itself with both structures and processes; with both Being and Becoming. Helpfully, Weik (2011) has written recently upon this topic. Her approach 'recognizes the fact that something permanent—call it forms, eternal objects or whatever—is needed right from the start because it cannot be logically inferred from continuous change. In other words, organization cannot be conceptually developed from the sort of ontology that Tsoukas and Chia suggest' (Weik 2011: 667). She produces a helpful table (Weik 2011: 669) which shows the likelihood of conflations around the being–becoming duality. For her, 'Being' is sometimes treated as 'Substance', sometimes as 'Existence', sometimes as 'Stability'. 'Becoming', on the other hand, is sometimes portrayed as not-Being and at others as 'Change'. Her work seeks to sensitize readers to the terminological differences here (Weik 2011: 669), so I will seek to be clear on these terms throughout.

Outside the organization theory of the typical business and management school, this play of Being and Becoming is clear in the ideas of Deleuze and Guattari (1988). Their attempt to undertake the disruption and overthrow of the organ/organization goes some way to helpfully problematize the concepts of structures, boundaries, and wholes. Their concept of the 'body without organs' begins this process of destabilization. Deleuze and Guattari argue that 'the body without organs is real inorganization', suggesting in the text of *A Thousand Plateaus* (1988: 150) that there is nothing more useless than an organ. Following Artaud, they declare war on the organs of 'sucked dry, catatonicized, vitrified, sewn-up bodies' and seek instead the value of emptying ourselves, thereby creating a 'body without organs' (Linstead and Pullen 2008). What this says to 'organization theory', by way of making problematic the notion of boundaries and structures, has not been fully explored. Neither has their insight that organization theory is misplaced in its focus on what they call the 'arboreal'. That is, against a focus upon the obvious and towering tree of knowledge, they pose instead the underground stirrings of the subterranean—what they call the 'rhizomatic'.

In a language of geometry that we are about to explore further, Deleuze and Guattari say that the arborescent system foregrounds the '*point*' at the expense of the '*line*'. Points are static and fixed and, full of *being*, stand proud from their blank surrounds, so that an arborescent system typically stresses two distant points. But because of its inability to connect these distant pinpricks, a point actually prevents *a philosophy of becoming*. Lines are different, however, from points, because 'a line of becoming has neither beginning nor end, departure nor arrival, origin nor destination... A line of becoming has only a middle. The middle is not an average; it is fast motion, it is the absolute speed of motion. A becoming is always in the middle; one can only get it by the middle. A becoming is neither one nor two, nor the relation of two; it is the in-between...' (Deleuze and Guattari 1988: 293). The rhizomatic then looks for the 'zone of proximity', 'the no-man's land', 'the line-block' that unites *between* points. The rhizomatic is all about lines and their middles.

Becoming through 'middling'

From their emphasis on linear 'middles', Deleuze and Guattari indicate a way forward for *Styles of Organizing*. They argue that they are in favour of the non-privileging of sides, of the *co-presence* of antimonies, of not seeing one of a pair of terms as always being subordinate to the other, of not seeing one term as prioritized in the face of the other's 'lack'. Here, they follow Derrida's deconstructionist invitation (Derrida 1972; cf. Cooper 1989; Kilduff 1993) for giving priority to 'the supplement' over any original and originating presence. If we can avoid a sense of one side of any conceptual pairing being subordinate to the other and develop a real feel for co-presence across any line of argument then that would be a genuine move forward.

However, despite the advocacy here of the *middle* and of the '*co-presence*' of object and subject, Deleuze and Guattari continually resort to the dichotomy as the defining way of analysis. Claims that the terms they use are *not* oppositional to each other (for example, Day 2001: 447; Goodchild 1996) have some truth in them—but not much! Even if the quote above (Deleuze and Guattari 1988: 293) does advocate the zone of proximity, one has to recognize that this is very much located within the rhizomatic approach which is distinguished by its *superiority* to the arboreal. Followers of Deleuze and Guattari are encouraged to 'break' from the grasp of the arboreal, and the no-man's land between the arboreal and the rhizomatic is *not* to be crossed. It is not to be countenanced because in the arboreal regime 'becoming' is ignored. So, the co-presence of both states seems to be undermined by their imperative injunctions, and in my view such hierarchicalization holds us back from moving beyond structure *versus* process, internal *versus* external, and change *versus* stability.

Thus, despite their protestations to the contrary, the pairing rely very heavily upon slicing dichotomies. Of course, they are by no means the only writers to do this. The practice is very widespread. Indeed, in my own field, the two-by-two matrix based upon polarized positions is a typical analytical device. I have used this approach myself (Burrell and Morgan 1979), whilst Cooper and Law (1995), for example, continue this dichotomizing tradition in their discussion of proximal and distal approaches to organization. But even the slicing dichotomy, the slash, has as its ultimate aim a healing process. The line separates, of course, but it separates *something*. The slicing dichotomy, the di-vision, is an act of creation for it represents the will to form. It is an existentialist act of hope—a desire to find that there is something there to cut in the first place. And just as I shall use the slicing stylus remorselessly, I have in the other hand a needle and thread.

In search of 'co-presence'

I would hope in the present text to develop some notions of 'co-presence' on several fronts. First, nascent in the book *Sociological Paradigms and Organizational Analysis* (Burrell and Morgan 1979) is a key concept of co-presence—the issue of 'the identical subject-object' as a possible solution to some philosophical problems. In seeking to address how it might be conceived of as a solution to deep-seated philosophical antinomies and the issue of 'lack', I will engage in a discussion of Hegel, Lukacs, and Zizek to point to the possibility of a 'rescue' of the notion. Second, I also have ambitions to build up some arguments first developed elsewhere (Burrell 2003) on the dangers to organization theory of accepting an unthinking linearity. Notwithstanding Deleuze and Guattari, lines can lead us astray because of their direct flatness. Let us note an artist's observation on linearity's connection to flatness:

> The main thing wrong with painting is that it is a rectangular plane placed flat against the wall. (Donald Judd, *Specific Objects* 1965: 1)

I am not opposed to the construction of a 2D framework (having done so with Gareth Morgan), for it has utility in 'painting a picture'—but one increasingly finds a contemporary need to see the social world in more depth than is offered by a flat and featureless approach. For one thing, planographic representations in geography—maps, if you will—are sometimes associated with 'cartographic violence' within a triumphalist geography (Shapiro 1999: 159). So, many forms of mapping may not escape this violence against those excluded and subordinated by the chart, but there is one way of providing a richer picture.

If we write about architecture, aesthetics, design, and artwork in relation to organizing, we must recognize early on that this requires thinking and appreciation in three dimensions (at least). It is suggested in this book that the 'design envelope' which is being constructed has to be seen as a three-dimensional (3D) figure and is not reduced to a two-dimensional (2D) approach which is more typical of, and more limiting to, organization theory. There needs to be the co-presence of the third dimension.

It is instructive, therefore, to consider Max Boisot's book *Knowledge Assets* (1998) where the author develops a 3D approach to understanding information flows in the 'I-Space'. Through the extensive use of diagrams of a cube formed by three dimensions of 'codification, abstraction and diffusion', Boisot creates a space in which to place issues and debates within 'knowledge management', and thence to take these further. He argues against the allegedly 2D approach of Nonaka and Takeuchi (1996), which he describes as 'intuitive and somewhat loosely formulated' (Boisot 1998: 56). For many commentators, their two-by-two matrix is posited upon an unclear distinction, and Boisot wishes in his book to increase clarity through increased complexity. However, as Spender notes in his comments at the beginning of *Knowledge Assets*, this 'framing increases the degrees of freedom and makes the analysis potentially richer, but *also more difficult to handle*' (page ix) (my emphasis). One moves on then, encouraged by the previous utilization of a cube of conceptual space in

In search of 'co-presence'

understanding debates in the organizational theory area, but mindful of 'handling difficulties' when one seeks to delve *beyond* the 2D world of the flat page.

Yet what you are reading here is essentially in two dimensions. How is one to move 'beyond the 2D world of the flat page' and think non-planographically? I appreciate, of course, that the paper this is printed on is the third dimension and without it the medium of printing is impossible, but at least in terms of common sense in the act of reading, this third dimension to paper is lost to us. And in dealing with space and that which lies within it in the world, the loss of this third dimension in the printed medium creates huge problems. Now these problems have not stopped great writers on design, architecture, and style articulating classic material via books, but it has acted as a limitation to our comprehension of their depth (sic) of understanding. Yet in looking at some of these beautifully produced books on art history, architecture, and interior design, one cannot help thinking that a certain flatness still prevails and that the untutored reader is asked to put themselves into a 3D world via what for most people is an inadequate mechanism. This is also true, of course, in organization theory, where examples of contemporary organizational life may be raised by well-placed writers, when many a reader has not experienced—nor has any hope of experiencing—that detailed case at first hand. This issue of access can be quite crucial. Access to particular business and state enterprises is much easier for some in privileged positions. In other words, these works of aesthetic or social scientific comprehension already presume that the readers, members of some cultural elite, can render the 2D world of a tasteful book into the 3D world which *they have already visited* or seen in the flesh. It is often joked that art historians have to own their own private collections in order to undertake the role they enjoy professionally. What I have sought to do in this text is to develop a (rudimentary) 3D way of understanding the links between style and organization that might begin to offer some parallels with those of the elite, nuanced, lived, and experiential aesthetics of style.

In a simple text which the cultural elite hate yet which has sold in large numbers, Stern and Dietsch's *Architecture for Dummies* (2002: 2) states that 'this book can't capture a building in three dimensions', so that it encourages experiencing great architecture for oneself. 'No photograph can capture the thrill of stepping into the cavernous space of an ancient temple or mosque, or of ascending to the top of a skyscraper for a breathtaking view' (Stern and Dietsch 2002: 13). So for the authors there is no option but to either consider plans and line drawings in 2D or to visit the building itself.

However, new computer-aided design (CAD) technology does allow an intermediate position to be adopted. If one has access to this sort of technology, it is possible to look at a screen powered by such software, whereby one can explore the recesses and spaces of real and imaginary buildings throughout the world. One can take journeys through buildings to find new spaces revealed as one takes this virtual trip. It may not give one the smells and sounds of such spaces but a trip of this kind stimulates one's senses much more than drawings and plans are usually able to do. But written text does not allow for this computer-generated experience either. One has to have specific programs designed for architects and available on powerful yet still resolutely 2D screens.

Without the embodied human in real physical space the structures of meaning upon which the person draws cannot be known to us. But Ching (1996: 374) reminds us at the end of his fascinating book that, apart from all of his very understandable emphasis upon the 'visual aspects of physical reality', architectural forms:

> also have connotative meanings: associative values and symbolic content that are subject to personal and cultural interpretations, which can change with time. The spires of a Gothic cathedral can stand for the realm, values or goals of Christianity. The Greek column can convey the notion of democracy, or, as in America in the early 19th century, the presence of civilisation in a new world.

The desire to place meaning upon our world is a key part of the will to form— and we need not be an inhabitant of that space to form its connotations. In Chapter 3, I shall attempt to consider the basic geometrical elements which make up human attempts to subdue shapeless protean space and bring form to the world through connotations.

3

From Protean Shapelessness to the Cube

From Chapter 2 the reader might assume that geometry had captured organization theory and is to be found across the landscape of many a textbook. Our teaching has become imprisoned in the 2D boxes and circles that make our material digestible. Indeed, it is difficult to find a first-year text anywhere that escapes from the geometer's craft. In this chapter my quest is the reverse of that in Chapter 1. Might we capture geometry for our own specific purposes and use it to advantage inside organization theory so as to open our discipline up rather than close it down?

'Organization' is complex. Czarniawska (1997; 2003: 240) says that we can see 'organization' as synecdoche; in other words, that which is organized becomes an entity named after its attribute. Here, in this book, it is understood as being about both structures and their design within organizations *and* the processes of organizing more generally. The aim of the book is to utilize both structural and processual approaches to organizing and, once woven together in a materialist garb, reveal the fabric of a mutual interrelationship of 'organization theory' with key features of politico-economic systems, architecture, aesthetics, design of the built environment, and associated artwork.

This fabrication will not be an easy task. Greek mythology has Proteus, as Neptune's herdsman, living in a vast sea cave. To capture him, one had to enter the darkness of the cave and sneak up whilst he slept after feeding his sea cows. This was the only time he would not be able to change his shape at will. Proteus was a shape shifter of immense gifts who had many secret lives. Ovid (2004) tells us in Book 8 (lines 730–6) of *Metamorphoses* that Proteus could take the form of handsome youth, ravening lion, savage boar, bull, pair of menacing horns, serpent, stones, trees, flowing water as a river, or fire. Shape shifting on this scale is the enemy of pattern books.

When speaking of patterns in architecture, Edward Hollis claims that: 'more often than not, the confident *dicta* of architectural theory are undermined by the secret lives of buildings, which are *capricious, protean, and unpredictable*; but all too often the contradiction is treated as the object of interest only to specialists' (Hollis 2009: 9–10, my emphasis). The secret lives of buildings, then, are not amenable to simple geometry. If we put alongside Hollis's articulation (2009) of any building's multiple histories the supposed rapidity and depth of change within organizations, then the world is indeed complex and may well appear as a melange of differing, shape-shifting styles. Is there an elementary geometry that will allow us to reflect this complexity and dynamism? Circles, lines, triangles, ovals, and squares will only get us so far in our understanding of the 'ecology' of contemporary organizations. And one suspects that geometers, who by definition are interested in features of the surface, would be unable to transfix the Protean. So the question for the present chapter is, do geometrical beginnings permit any understanding whatsoever of the ever-changing and subterranean 'protean'?

Geometers seek *form*ulae whilst aficionados of 'population ecology' and similar quantitative orientations within organization theory also seek in numbers and mathematics what they cannot hope for in reality—the making stationary of that which is mobile. In effect, they desire the capturing of Proteus. Bill McKinley (2010: 63), for example, seeks to encourage empirical testing, and 'repeated testing and replication should take place to converge on the explanation that has greater empirical validity'. For years, McKinley (2010: 48) has proved himself to be a keen proponent of 'the production of standardized measures for operationalizing variables contained in theories' and for using these to test the theory's validity. His piece *Managing Knowledge in Organization Studies through Instrumentation* (McKinley 2007) gives away in the title the pursuit of positivistic methods and of the holy grail of 'replication' and 'validity'. In order to do any of this, of course, stasis is assumed for the purposes of making measurement possible. A census date for the collection of data freezes the ongoing liquidity to make metrics meaningful. We must note, however, that McKinley is but one example of those who assume they have the power to stop the world and measure it—which, after all, is what geometry is. These geometers, or 'statistico-organizational theorists' as Donaldson (2008: 135–45) would have it, know that 'managers sit atop a vast pyramid that produces at its top data with large sample sizes from which most of the random variation have [sic] already been extinguished' (Donaldson 2008: 142). The protean is thus conquered by the pharoahic priest standing atop the pyramid, with formulae in hand.

If only it were that easy.

The geometries of process

There is no formula for survival. The number of business organizations that survive a hundred years has been estimated to be one quarter of one per cent of any given population. Once the 'death' of organizations is rendered fit to conceptualize (and this is a thanatocentric facet of organization theory that MBAs tend to hate), one can begin to speak about fundamental existential change and thence mortality rates. The aforementioned 'population ecology' (Hannan and Freeman 1977; 1989), for example, is a theoretical approach drawing upon biological science, which centres upon this demise of organizations within a given population. Yet demise is only one extreme form of change. Organizations change management, they change location, they change ownership, they go out of business, they restart in new markets or with new goals. But what they do not show is stasis and continuity. The management of change literature is so vast (and for the most part so poor) that one can show that these concerns are well recognized within practising managers at all levels. Yet the models are simple, two dimensional, and assume for the most part that change itself is predictable, manageable, and open to rationalization. The real issues of organizational 'crisis' and 'revolution' are not properly integrated into the theoretical approaches adopted, although these attention-grabbing hyperbolic words might well be, in order to sell very mainstream books.

Paul du Gay (2007) has called this sensationalist approach to the management of change an epochalist one. 'Epochalism' for du Gay (2007: 137–8) means 'an overdramatic dichotomization' or a 'periodizing schema' in which a fundamental shift is claimed to have occurred, and that the evidence is incontrovertible. His nominations for the epochalist pantheon include Lash and Urry (1987), Tom Peters (1987), and Anthony Giddens (various). These schemas offer easy solutions to which routes to transformation should be taken by governments and organizations, and in my view, reinforce the individualistic notion that because we live in times of massive change, we must be massively important ourselves. Yet, as du Gay (2007: 154) points out, 'epochal theorizing tends instead towards an unattractive admixture of self-referentiality, teleology and circularity'. Precisely the confection, we might assume, that leaders of organizations, facing change, often want. We might wish to call this 'Royal science'.

Somewhat typically, Deleuze and Guattari (1988: 363–70) see no simple relationship between geometry and organization. Geometry, for them, differs between Royal science and Nomad science. In a difficult section of *Thousand Plateaus* they maintain that the former concerns itself with stasis and the prevention of movement (as, for example, in McKinley 2007) whilst the latter, of course, favours continuous variation and movement to the limits. Royal science fixates upon 'the static relation, form-matter [which] tends to fade into the background in favour of a dynamic relation, material-forces' (Deleuze and Guattari 1988: 364). They speak of a medieval 'monk-mason' named Garin de Troyes who revolutionized the mason's craft of building cathedrals but at great cost to himself. Rather than using equations to create good forms that organize matter, he attempted to create 'forces of thrust' that are 'generated' by the material. This approach becomes a triumph for 'minor science' over Royal science, but the sponsors of his 'nomadic' approach are the Knights Templar. And, as is well known, the Templars were to be despatched in a wave of executions by the French state, bringing nomadic and dynamic geometry to a bloody end. Deleuze and Guattari (1988: 365) claim that the attack upon the Templars, in part, is because of de Troyes's approach to geometry which threatens the state's control over construction. Architects under Royal science constructed metric planes on paper in offices, and advocated the use of templates to cut stone. Journeymen, on the other hand, constructed ground-level planes through human 'organization' on site, and undertook stone cutting by 'squaring'. This, for Deleuze and Guattari, is 'operative geometry' of a kind advocated by, for example, de Troyes. Royal science, on the contrary, favours 'projective' or 'higher' geometry.

In part, they recognize the possibility of an intermediate position between these two geometries, such as Husserl's notion of a 'protogeometry' which deals in the *'vague'* notion of 'roundness' which is an essence rather than a figure. With such interests, protogeometry thereby stands in a role somewhat akin to non-science. But Deleuze and Guattari find their own deep dualism much more satisfying than Husserl's middling articulation of the intermediate notion of protogeometry, and continue to build up Royal science's implacable opposition to Nomad science. So whilst they do point out the limitations of Royal science's attempt at stasis—at stopping the world of fluidity and movement and unpredictability—organization theorists of a Weberian bent tend to believe it is through reason and rationality that good order might emerge.

The protean 'liquidity' of the social world may well need to be 'reasonably' frozen so that we can appreciate what shape it has at any particular point in time. But what can we put in the place of the geometer's magical staff that is so highly placed on top of a pyramid that it holds the world in stasis by fiat? How might organization theory seek to solve the nomadic riddle of constant flux in the world, in its organizations, flux in architectures, flux in styles of organizing, and flux in design? My perspective is that design styles reflect some very basic human choices and from deep within this act of choosing comes an ongoing dynamic equilibrium for long periods of time. In other words, there is patterning discernible within the flow. Describing this is fraught with difficulty, but elsewhere Karen Dale and myself (Dale and Burrell 2008: 213–15) have attempted to develop a 'riparian metaphor' which provides something of what is intended as foundational to the arguments contained in this book. Put simply, one cannot stop 'flow' from the top of a pyramid. One has to get down into the mud of the river bank.

What we argued (Dale and Burrell 2008) is briefly as follows: theorists of liquidity like Bauman, Castells, Virilio, and indeed Hollis, tend to focus on flow at the expense of structure. They look at liquidity more than at materiality (Dale 2005). Our position was that one has to look at both, within a mutual enacting, and in order to do this we suggested the use of riparian imagery where the notion of a river contained by a riverbank stands for our sort of approach. Hydrodynamics suggest that the conventional image of a passive set of structures in the form of riverbanks shaped by the intense and dynamic flow of water against them is not correct. The banks themselves shape and form the flow so that mutual enactment of bank and river takes place. But we are not content to allow an easy equation of materiality with the bank and liquidity with the river's liquid. There is no easy distinction between river and bank. They are held together as an emulsion, a solution, a suspension (Dale and Burrell 2008: 214). There is a mutual exchange of molecules, of fixity and movement, of solid and liquid, and together, as one, they move down the river. This situation is less like the predictable world of hydrologists measuring river flows in times of flood, and more like Mark Twain announcing that the Mississippi river was 'unknowable'. Yet the riparian approach to social materiality (Dale 2005) does allow us seek solace rather than despair in coming to appreciate both the movement and the fixed solidity of systems, buildings, and organizations.

I believe that this 'riparianism' allows us to move away from the more elementary forms of approaching the question of styles in organizational, architectural, and artistic life, and permits us to reflect its complexity in more robust ways. It also allows us to contemplate change in organizational styles of living which is not protean because the same processes might be seen in operation in widely disparate cases. Earlier, I called this patterning the 'contingency of connectedness'. But connectedness has to be dynamic. How then to engage in something akin to de Troyes's geometry, used in a dynamic way which brings out both structure and process? My answer is through the approach of 'synthetic cubism'.

Synthetic cubism

Sigfried Giedion's book *Space, Time and Architecture* (1967) maintains that architecture has an obligation to reflect the spirit of the age—the *zeitgeist*. He argues (Giedion 1967: 434–50) that the 'modern' age is characterized by a new conception of space-time and this was first reflected in the 'synthetic cubism' of Picasso and Braque, so that 'the method of presenting spatial relationships which the cubists developed led to the form-giving principles of the new space conception' (Giedion 1967: 434). Whilst Picasso was hailed as the inventor of cubism, Giedion says that cubism is not the invention of any one individual but was a generalized reaction to the end of a 'decadent epoch'. Decadence was reflected in the dominance of perspectivalism, which since the Renaissance had seen the outer world in terms of three dimensions—yet had painted it in two dimensions. According to Giedion (1967: 435):

> The three-dimensional space of the Renaissance is the space of Euclidean geometry. But about 1830 a new sort of geometry was created, one which differed from that of Euclid in employing more than three dimensions. Such geometries have continued to be developed, until now a stage has been reached where mathematicians deal with figures and dimensions that cannot be grasped by the imagination.

Artists too, particularly the cubists, came to recognize the limitations of conventional understandings of space, and saw from its many-sidedness that one point of reference could not lead to a full understanding of that object upon which we gaze. Cubism allows a relativism in perception, seeing objects from dissimilar positions and allowing none to have primacy. By adding time into their viewpoint they developed the notion of 'simultaneity' so that all faces could be seen at the same time. This process of developing cubism took place through experimentation and in different stages. To begin with, objects were 'dissected' and the surfaces of natural forms were changed into angular facets. Colour disappeared and what arose out of this was the *plane*. There was no single focal point. In the second stage of cubism's development, Giedion (1967: 438) points out that planes were given a new appeal by the use of unusual material like textiles and sawdust, and collages were created. In the third phase, colour was reintroduced and curvilinear shapes employed, having been taken from guitars and bowls. Here Giedion (1967: 446) claims that the cubists were passive and not vocal about their work nor about that set of ideas upon which it was based. Indeed, 'they kept to their *ateliers*, preparing quietly and without fanfare the symbols of our artistic language'. They did not paint movement itself but they painted still-life objects from a perspective of movement. And it is for this reason that they were taken up in architecture—and subsequently offered to organization theory (Carr and Zanetti 2000).

As his book progresses, Giedion maintains that cubism is subject to aberrations and that its symbols were not rational: it also becomes clear that Giedion wants to find sources of representations of movement in architecture which allowed the appearance of interpenetration and simultaneity, yet keep buildings as immobilized movement (Till 2009: 84). Cubism allows a little of this. Another way of accomplishing this time suppression is to take photographs in 'a freezing of time into a set of instant aesthetic moments' (Till 2009: 85). Architectural photography *freezes out* time rather than freezing time itself and

Three-dimensionality

lifts any building out of liquid time, thus proffering architects a stable platform from which to look down upon time. This is an appeal, says Till (2009: 83), 'to stability, constructional, cultural, and temporal (and) is another of architecture's defenses against contingency'. The reader should note, however, that what is important for my purposes in looking at styles of organizing is to *celebrate contingency whilst problematizing stability*.

Three-dimensionality

The task of developing a 3D model of 'styles of organizing' has taken me years of work, characterized by periods of disinclination to carry on, largely because of this fluidity of the categories in use. A price has had to be paid. But I believe that an appreciation of three-dimensional space, and all 3D objects within it, has to be portrayed in a way upon the pages of a text in ways which speaks of a 3D perspective. The main thing wrong, we have been told, with 2D approaches on the printed page to styles of organizing, is their flatness. Yet developing a 3D approach is difficult, for obvious technical reasons to do with the structure of the printed page itself. This difficulty, I now believe, can be resolved by asking a price, not of myself, but of the reader. I do not make this request lightly—for alienating one's reader is never a good idea. When I come to present my 3D 'model' in a later chapter, be forewarned—you will be asked to work at the model too. But of course it will require a subtly of presentation on my part that only the reader can judge if it works.

Why, however, should a 3D approach be the end point for the escapist thinking I advocate? The effect of three-dimensionality upon *Styles of Organization* may be to produce another form of 'boxing in' which is counterproductive. Once rid of 2D limitations, why not aim for a 4D approach or even an N-dimensional one? Certainly, some architects would claim that they are not limited to a 3D approach but see a building in many dimensions, constantly coming back in time to look at their structures afresh, building up a design, layer upon layer. David Hockney, for example, is someone who apparently manages to produce N-dimensional art by just using two-dimensional artefacts. And so, if art and architecture are capable of this N dimensionality, so the argument might go, styles produced by artists and architects cannot be reducible to a 3D framework. The scaffolding of a 3D approach may not withstand the weight of complexity offered by politico-economic systems, architecture, design, and organization theory.

First, let me deal with the issue of N-dimensional space. The limitations of the embodied human being mean that we cannot appreciate fully the view from the side of the 'other', especially if the 'other' inhabits a different space. E. A. Abbott, in his book *Flatland* (1962), envisages a world in which the narrator lives within two spatial dimensions only. His aim in writing to the inhabitants of another dimension is to stir up a race of rebels who refuse to be confined to a limited dimensionality. It is this attempt to radicalize space which offers much of interest. In science, rather than the 'novel' world, there is an ongoing search in astrophysics for the secrets of antimatter. Here, the escape from three-dimensional space to multiple dimensions is one that is being advocated. We humans need to look at a world removed from the limitations of everyday observations, so we are invited to visit *superspace*, which is 'the greatest invention since the wheel' (Stephen Webb 2004: 134). Superspace with its N dimensions has to be the place, we are told, where all this antimatter has been lost—or is hiding. It has slipped down the back of a very large N-dimensional sofa.

As Webb (2004) indicates, Theodor Kaluza wrote to Einstein in 1919 with equations consisting of four dimensions for space and one for time. The idea of higher dimensions at this point began to enter physics. Oskar Klein (Webb 2004: 142–52) argued that this fifth dimension was a real physical dimension and it was circular. Put somewhat crudely, he asserted that 'lines' as we know them are, in fact, 'hosepipes' and contain within them circular spaces invisible to the human senses. The radius of these pipes is small and may be at $10^{(-18)}$ meters making them undetectable even today. It has been argued that perhaps the universe expanded with five compact dimensions straight after the Big Bang, but one dimension stayed small whilst the rest grew large. The numbers asserted here are that the universe is $10^{(26)}$ metres wide but the fifth dimension is 10^{-33} metres small. This tiny width is known as the Planck length, making the phrase 'as thick as a planck' not very meaningful. After this, it was argued that perhaps hosepipes such as this fifth dimension can be metaphorically stood on, decreasing the width at that point but increasing it via ballooning at another point. In 1981, Edward Whitten stated that both the maximum and minimum dimensions that the universe could tolerate were 11 and, after much contention about whether it is 10 or 11, some consensus has been reached that it is best seen as 11 dimensions. N-dimensional space, indeed. The assumption was made that all the dimensions we do not experience were all curled up on the Planck length at 10^{-35}. However, this too came under contestation, so that they became seen as not as compacted as this width would suggest. Arkani-Hamed-Dimopoulos-Dvali (ADD for short) suggested that these dimensions could be as large as 1mm without violating anything we knew from experimental evidence. Not a huge space, perhaps, but one considerably bigger that Planck's thickness.

Eventually it was agreed these dimensions could be the thickness of a pen nib and we would be totally unaware of them because they live happily within a different (mem)*brane*. This is not a parallel universe as currently seen in popular science fiction where something different has occurred from events in our own. Rather, it is a place where dark matter and an alternative reality exist (Pullman 2011) and/or reside. Or perhaps it is just a repository for dark matter. For without these extra dimensions and their load potential, particle physicists cannot explain where all the matter of the universe is. Of course, it may be that the universe has a number of folds in it which cannot be perceived but which are voluminous enough to hold the majority of universal matter. It might be that galaxies exist a fraction of a metre away from us in the *brane* but billions of light years distant in the dimensions we perceive. But wherever this discussion goes, we know it is going to cost the taxpayer a lot of money to undertake the experimental work deep inside the caves of CERN.

As for the alleged recursive approach of architects to space and their constant return to the dimensions of their buildings, this may be correct, but as we shall see, there are limitations in the increasing use of CAD-based systems to facilitate this recursion and it may be that technology has replaced some of the imaginative conceptual work that used to be undertaken by architects. The architect's solution to this need used to be the balsa model which would be taken to clients in order to render their project more visible and understandable than would be possible showing 2D plans to the untutored eye. Often these models would be a thing of beauty in themselves, and would be treasured by clients as a bright, shiny reflection of their own foresight and skills in planning. Today, of course, the possibility of CAD programs to allow one to undertake a virtual tour of a building and its contents has been realized by some architectural practices and the software houses that supply them. Frank Gehry (in the *Guardian* G2, 6 July 2011: 21) is quoted as saying in response to a question from Jonathan Glancey about cost: 'It's all the 3D computer stuff we've developed. Fifteen percent of construction cost is usually wasted in design changes on site, caused by the fact that architects are still doing 2D drawings for 3D buildings. We do 3D modelling that shows exactly how the whole building fits together, and we don't need many design changes. That way we come out on budget.'

So some architects are still locked into 2D world views, perhaps. But even 3D virtual tours are not without their problems. Till (2009: 86) argues that clients, on viewing such tours, often take too seriously the notion that 'what you see is what you get (WYSIWYG)' and are disappointed when their building is opened and taken possession of, for the screen offers a mirage. It is a *'promenade architecturale'*, offered from a linear point of view following space in preordained sequence and not that of the daily experience of the building's real user. One architect has remarked that 'she will not believe in virtual reality till they learn how to put the dirt in' (Till 2009: 87). And others note that the latest forms of CNC (computer numerical control) machines allow 3D models to arise from 2D drawings, but that the new architectural shapes allowed by these digital developments in design tools cannot actually be built using the

From Protean Shapelessness to the Cube

Victorian building methods which still prevail in the construction industry! But whatever their strengths and weaknesses, this form of CAD-CAM (computer-aided design; computer-aided manufacture) representation is not possible outside an electronic medium.

Third, the notion that Great Art is transcendent and cannot be reduced to the mundane is, of course, in some ways, true. What I am concerned about, however, is organizational life, which certainly includes those who live the life of independent atelier artists but also centrally involves the organizations that ordinary men and women live in. Alongside the soaring heights of dazzling artwork, known to and seen by very few, there is the rooted quotidian. I understand that more elevated positions are possible than a limited 3D approach to design and organization but that is enough for me—and the reader—to be getting on with for the time being. I seek only to offer 'categorization', which Adam Smith (1775: 65) said is 'but one single quality, that is common to a great variety of otherwise different objects'.

In effect, then, my 3D framework is being used here in the book as a 'flotation device' to stop your author from drowning in a sea of complexity. But my hope is that it will save you, the reader, from a similar fate. And as for a 4D approach, of course all 3D images and frameworks have a temporal dimension to them. The one I seek to develop (sic) is no different—for schemas change over time. So my intention is to build a three-dimensional model of design space, given that it may offer more than 2×2 matrices and the like. And this 3D framework will take the form of a 'cube'. Therefore, it is a defence of this 'Royal' geometry that I must now mount.

Dicing with style

This part of the current chapter will attempt to build upon Ching (1996) and Deleuze and Guattari (1988), showing how organization theorists can enter a world of design provisioned with the elements of *points, lines, and planes*. My argument consists in part of an outline of three key dimensions which may be identified within a geometry of design possibilities and which I consider to 'form' an enclosed volume of intellectual space. It will be presented in the form of a *cube*, recognizing that within a cube there are three dimensions, eight extreme points, and six planes or faces.

I shall attempt to use these elementary terms to unravel the mysteries of 'styles of organizing', building up a multifaceted, perhaps 'cubist', picture of the design envelope in which organizing takes place. This attempt at cubism might allow us to approach that impossibility for perspectivalist thinking—an all-round understanding of a mobile yet solid three-dimensional volume. Through the use of a 3D shape, it becomes possible to recognize the

Dicing with style

positioning of particular styles of organizing within the 'design envelope'. Gridding and mapping of this kind allow location in conceptual space, through which one can ascertain likely relationships within, and between, different and differing styles of organizing. Thereby, the book seeks to provide 3D imagery of a complex 'surface' of interlocking design styles and an 'intermediate' level of organizational effects with a 'depth' of philosophical dilemmas.

As already mentioned, one 3D approach has been carried through to fruition in recent organization theory. Max Boisot's book *Knowledge Assets* (1998) develops a 3D approach to understanding information flows in what he calls the I-Space. Through the extensive use of diagrams of a cube formed by three dimensions of 'codification, abstraction and diffusion', Boisot creates a space in which to place issues and debates within 'knowledge management', and thence to take these further. This is exactly what *Styles of Organizing* will attempt to mimic by creating a cuboid space within which design can be seen in all its abundant colourful flowering—and yet as bounded by all the philosophical constraints of an iron cage.

The overhead, wall, and base planes of this cage together come to define the 3D world of volumes that we know as rooms and buildings and fields and landscapes. Whilst conceptually volume has the three dimensions with which we are familiar, 'form', for Francis Ching (1996), is what we call different volumes, and the classic ones of course are spheres, pyramids, and cubes. Alongside them, we face a parallel geometry of cylinders and cones. These geometric shapes can be empty and are therefore known as *voids*, or they can be filled and thereby become *solids*. Obviously, irregular forms exist but the human eye attempts to find the regular shapes of geometry in what it views by filling in the gaps, or subtracting any added solids and voids from what is being viewed. The socialized human eye seeks out the elementary forms of organizing life.

The reader may well be asking why the *cube* has been taken as the 3D solid which we are taking as the way forward. Cubism does not have to rely upon the cube. Why not a sphere, or a pyramid, or a cone, or a cylinder? My answer (somewhat presaging the chapters to follow) is that because we will be dealing with three isomorphic dimensions, each has to be given equal weight. And because equal weighting of these elements has to be expressed spatially, the cube allows this perhaps better than any other solid. But, of course, it does suggest a space of controlled and patrolled good order, where deviance is not allowed. It is cage like. It is the shape often found at the base of thrones. According to Chevalier and Gheerbrant (1996: 268), cubes are 'symbols of wisdom, truth and moral perfection'. Certainly, if one looks at the Hajj and images of the Ka'ba, the Muslim Holy of Holies in Mecca, this can be clearly seen. This stands in the Great Mosque and, as its name suggests precisely, it is a cube. It enshrines the 'Black Stone' which is held to have been given to Abraham by the Archangel Gabriel. Indeed, Chevalier and Gheerbrant (1996: 268) claim somewhat rashly that the cube has been regarded as a symbol of perfection since the dawn of civilization.

As for my cube, there are plenty of imperfections but there are no outsiders nor outliers possible within a 'grid of intelligibility' such as this dice. All is to be contained, all is to be disciplined, all is to be straightened out within its uniformity. I regret this use of the 'iron cage' even if it is made of paper (but, after all, that is precisely what Weber's iron cage of bureaucracy was made of)—yet believe that those multiple outliers that have escaped from my net will be found by the reader.

To ease the discussion, throughout *Styles of Organizing*, the 3D solid akin to the 'dice' will be taken to represent the solid design envelope of possibilities in which humans organize themselves, in and through material and conceptual space. The cube has the capacity to suggest those key architectural questions and solutions regarding form versus function, light versus shade, and inside versus outside. By using the dice in the way I intend, one can speak of its form having a function that it serves imperfectly, of the issues of what is lit up and what lies perpetually in the penumbra, of how we can use the cube as outsiders to view its structure. Yet the assumption that we can escape its gravitational pull—of not being incorporated within it—is a mistaken one.

The key function of the material form of the dice is to be a hand tool allowing the reader to manipulate a solid in space. The dice is meant to have a use in acting as a 3D adjunct to the argument written and presented in 2D. The photographs in Figures 3.1 and 3.2, taken by Simon Eling, problematize the issue of understanding a 3D figure using conventional photography, by presenting us sequentially with two images that we cannot hope to replicate in any real-life viewing of the dice itself. They are opposite faces of a three-dimensional solid.

In Figure 3.1 the high numbers on a dice are visible to the viewer. These three faces represent the limits of human perception of a three-dimensional object, in that from this view no low numbers are visible. Half the dice is invisible. From some views, five-sixths of the dice are missing from sight. But placed in this way, Figure 3.1 indicates the maximum field of vision for any observer. In organizational terms, the implication is that we see a *maximum* of 50 per cent of all possibilities for 'styles of organizing' within the design envelope.

Figure 3.2 shows the low numbers of a dice. This is the view of the three faces that cannot be seen from the perspective of Figure 3.1. It is the 'dark side of the moon' to those comfortably settled upon Figure 3.1. The design envelope used by humans in constructing organizational spaces also hides many

Figure 3.1 The high numbers of a dice

Figure 3.2 The low numbers of a dice

facets of possibility from themselves. Indeed, many designers of organizations are aware of only one facet, never mind three.

But as photographs on the page of a book, these two figures merely hint at depth. What is needed is a 'real' dice, in one's hands and carefully observed in its manipulation by inquiring eyes.

From Protean Shapelessness to the Cube

Concrete cubism

In the absence of any form of computer simulation within the 500-year-old technology of book publishing, if one wishes to undertake *simultaneity*, one is forced to return to the insights of the cubists. In order to gain a 3D perspective on a 2D page, one either has to embrace the cubists' notions of simultaneity in time or reinvent the book. With regard to the latter, reinvention would be achievable if the book contained a pocket for a 3D object outside its highly conventional shape and structure. One hoped that it might have been possible to persuade the publisher to supply every reader with a cube by which the author might address the world of 3D. Let us call this cube a dice, and let us imagine that the reader has this dice in front of them for the discussion to follow. It would make things much easier. By attaching the book's two-dimensional text to points in and on a six-sided conceptual shape, it might be possible for the reader to conceptualize, in real space, this third dimension to a model of space, systems, architecture, design, and style. However, the costs of this might be seen by publishers as prohibitive, particularly with low print runs, and so we have to conceive of a way of getting a 3D object into your hands.

Figure 3.3 shows a do-it-yourself paper technology 'cube' that I would be very grateful if you were now to consider making.

You will need scissors for this task and there will be a need for glue. Trace the shape onto a sheet of paper, please, then cut around it and label the extreme left face with the number 1. The 6 on this dice thus becomes the opposite face to the number 1, for, as we all know, opposite faces of a dice must add up to 7 in total.

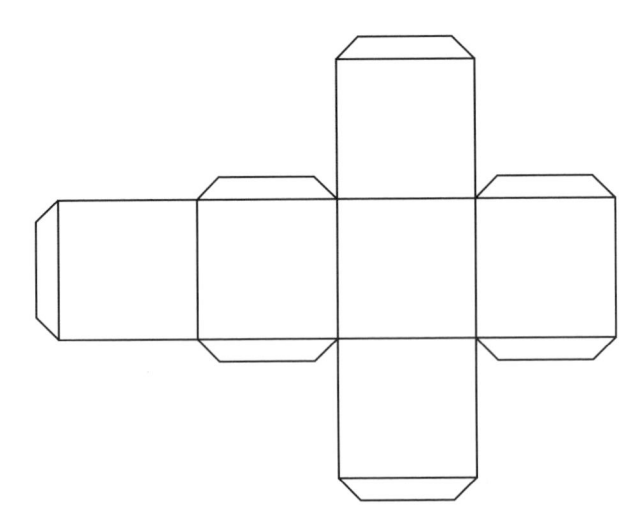

Figure 3.3 A self-assembly cube

Once you have cut out the shape, please secure the sides of the dice together with glue of some description. We now have in front of us a dice which takes a cuboid form, and with this in hand, we are ready to begin to develop our model of styles of organizing.

The parameters of the model

What this book seeks to do in the chapters of Part II is to explore the patterns that 'the will to form' takes. This analysis will take place on two fronts. The first is at the level of the politico-economic system and the organizational world. The second is in the realm of architecture and design. Part II seeks to understand the spaces available for organizing both our built socio-economic environment and the building up of our lives as organized social beings.

In order to comprehend 'styles of organizing' we must recognize that these both create, and are channelled by, certain possibilities. There are limits to what is possible in the design of buildings and in the design of organizations. My argument is that the will to form does not permit an infinitude of possibilities. Rather, the will to form is constrained. Whilst these are biological and chemical limits, often created by physical laws, there are other cognitive constraints emanating from the mind of the designer and their 'clients'. In some ways, then, styles of organizing are constrained by possibilities drawn from within the humanities as well as the natural sciences. And I have chosen to express these constraints in a way consonant with the humanities, the social sciences, and the natural sciences in equal measure. The way in which I have sought to play fairly with knowledge from such a broad spectrum is to emplace it within a cubic formulation drawing upon simple, well understood geometry.

The next chapter moves away from the issue of form and looks for the first time at *content*. What shall we emplace within the cube? The answer lies in Chapters 4 and 5, which comprise Part II of the book, where there is consideration of the issue of style itself.

Part II
From Form to Content

4

The Complexity of 'Style'

In this first Chapter of Part II, I wish to begin the task of filtering content into the form of the cube and to suggest that we fill the void with varieties of 'style'. For 'style' is of significance both in furthering our understanding of the organized life that we lead and in appreciating the process of organizing and how it is achieved. However, it must be noted that 'style' is a rather complex notion.

The importance of styles comes from their power base in furthering principles of inclusion and exclusion. Because of this power, particular styles have intellectual appeal to specific individuals, organizations, states, and transnational entities. 'Style' often means a particular, characteristic way of performing, producing, or presenting the results of a creative task in which appearance, expression, and distinctiveness are valorized—all within a material context. 'Idiom' is the word I will use to describe highly particularistic and personalized forms of creativity characteristic perhaps of 'genius' (as befits its Latin derivation from the 'id'), but 'styles' is taken to mean more patterned, predictable, and routinized forms of creativity. Given this, organization and systematization are central to my concerns but so too are architecture and design (both widely conceived) where idiosyncratic idioms are often described as 'art'.

Umberto Eco (1986: 165) sees style as a 'way of forming' but for him, 'style' is a literary issue and is to do with creating arguments in a persuasive and elegant way. Barbara Cziarnawska (2003) follows the same path in her article, 'The Styles and Stylists of Organization Theory', seeing style as 'a way of executing a task' (2003: 239). She claims that style has been fully discussed in literary theory, aesthetics, and even in history but is a stranger to organization theory. A style for her is a 'technique of making a thing' and is specifically about how writers construct well-crafted arguments. Yet 'style' may well not be about elegant adornment but concerns itself rather with incision, a wounding, a cutting, an excision—with the *stylus*. It is not that the pen is mightier than the sword. The pen *is* a sword. The pen is nothing but a weapon—a sharp blade 'de-*forming*' via an 'execution' of a specific kind. Styles

The Complexity of 'Style'

are destructive at the same time as they are creative. By marking out a form, they fail to mark out all other forms. By a process of exclusion, a 'style' cuts off certain connective tissues. The Microsoft Word package reflects this centrality of excision in the creative process by the superior symbol of the scissors and the word 'Cut'. Style then is driven by a sense of aesthetics *but* also by excavating a deep bloody materiality.

The word 'style' is taken to mean in this book a mode or manner of living or behaving; a characteristic way of producing a thing and of executing a task; a distinctive type of architecture; a particular shape and structure of artefacts; and as a customary procedure for undertaking activities. This is quite a broad approach to 'style' wherein two things are important, the first of which is how something looks at first glance. This has to be a key part of the task. So style is an ordering, a containment of difference, a stifling of originality, an ethnic cleansing of plurality—an act of violence. It places limits on imagination and heightens awareness of such features whilst simultaneously deadening our eyes to other features. It attends to 'how' and 'what' questions. But appearance is not all. The second task is to consider the *construction* of appearance as being as important as the surface 'look'. The substructural aspects of style must be given due consideration. This concern for construction is what Crossley (2000: 13) is getting at when he says, 'Frankl never shook off the notion that style (and its principles) is a force inherent in the forms themselves.' We are told that Frankl saw this construction of appearance as being inherent in the style itself, as a reflection—a manifestation—of its own underlying 'aesthetic will' (Crossley 2000: 13). Style, in this view, is a cognitive structure in which we are often required to live out our lives. Indeed, we may be imprisoned by our style. By understanding a style's aesthetic will and the wounds that come with that power effect, we can perhaps come to transcend it and sew up our self-inflicted wounds.

Styles of organization have consequences, some intended, some not, for how the perceptions and behaviour of employed staff are modified. Morgan (1986: 19) quotes from a story told by Chinese sage Chuang-Tzu about an old man's views of new irrigation techniques. 'I have heard my teacher say that whoever uses machines does all his work like a machine. He who does his work like a machine grows a heart like a machine, and he who carries the heart of a machine in his breast loses his simplicity. He who has lost his simplicity becomes unsure of the strivings of his soul.' My argument in this text is that all styles are machines which, as we live through and within them, have consequences for our work, our hearts, our souls.

In my undergraduate lecture on bureaucracy I am fond of using a quote from the novelist Julian Barnes (2009: 15): 'on death, the heart assumes the shape of a pyramid'. This is the observation that human hearts after death contain blood which has coagulated at the cardiac base, creating a pyramid

Histories of organizing

form from the organ's rigor mortis. Yet, more poetically, it might also mean that once the heart is dead the classic bureaucratic geometrical form may insinuate itself into rigorous existence. In other words, the classic pyramidal shape only arises when all the heart's emotions have died.

And organizational design, of course, is often equated with the rise of 'bureaucracy', a word traced back to its etymological origination around about 1756. So the unwary reader of a book called *Styles of Organizing* might make the assumption that we need *not* look at styles prior to that date because they are not necessarily going to have a 'formal organization' anywhere near them. But, of course, state apparati existed long before that year and time within the Ancien Régime, and the existence of pyramids today in and around Giza marks enough for many people to say that bureaucratic forms of organizing existed in hydraulic societies, millennia before they did in the France of the Sun King, Louis XIV (Mitford 1994). As Wittfogel (1961) argued in a beautifully elegant thesis, along the major river valleys of the world arose powerful 'hydraulic societies' which saw organization of the populace on a massive scale, with an architecture to match. So, given that formal organizing of a population goes back perhaps 10,000 years to control floods and allow irrigation of crops in the Tigris-Euphrates valley, is it necessary to span all human time and all human space to see what forms of organizing are associated with all human building projects? The answer to this is 'yes'. But it is not a realizable objective.

Histories of organizing

In cultures where writing was not widely developed or not developed at all, the reliance on oral history makes any understanding of their styles of organizing much more difficult. The predominant wills to form in the West valorize formulae—maps, grids, and recipes wherein writing has huge significance. Without paper or vellum, the record is much more patchy. Many buildings in many parts of the world were made of wood or other organic matter and have long deteriorated in oxygen—much as humans do themselves. Archaeologists in the UK are left with post holes, marked by changes in surface colouration from the surrounding soil, to indicate where large Anglo-Saxon timbers once stood. And where and when scholars dig successfully have often required drought conditions to show the positioning of buildings through their parch marks. We know the building types and the organizational types of so few societies over the millennia because the ravages of time have swept them away. Thus, we know something about some structures in some societies through stone but very little about their social and organizational processes.

The Complexity of 'Style'

It is primarily stone which 'signals' to us from the past. It is not wood, nor thatch, nor skins, nor paper that preserve our understandings of the designs of the ancients. Civilizations that chose wood with which to build are much less known than those which chose stone and marble, for these still often appear on the surface of the contemporary world. The presence of a record in fashioned stone indicates to us something of the past and the present—and possibly the future. Neil MacGregor, in his book *A History of the World in 100 Objects* (2010: xv) points out that Shelley's response to seeing the ruins of Rameses II was the poem 'Ozymandias':

> I met a traveller from an antique land,
> Who said: Two vast and trunkless legs of stone
> Stand in the desert. Near them on the sand,
> Half sunk, a shatter'd visage lies, whose frown
> And wrinkled lip and sneer of cold command
> Tell that its sculptor well those passions read
> Which yet survive, stamp'd on these lifeless things,
> The hand that mock'd them and the heart that fed;
> And on the pedestal these words appear:
> 'My name is Ozymandias, king of kings:
> Look on my works, ye Mighty, and despair!'
> Nothing beside remains. Round the decay
> Of that colossal wreck, boundless and bare,
> The lone and level sands stretch far away.
> (Percy Bysshe Shelley, 1994)

MacGregor (2010: xvi) is keen for us to believe that objects speak of the messages which they were, in some ways, designed to communicate across time. For him, such 'signals from the past—some reliable, some conjectural, many to be still retrieved—are unlike any other evidence that we are likely to encounter'. In my terms, he seems to think these signals usually allow insight upon social processes as well as on material structures. MacGregor still sees the written word as highly desirable in his search for meaning but he wishes to add to that the history afforded to us by objects. For *things* give us a voice, even if we are illiterate. Objects endure and carry culture with them (Edensor 2005). They are part of the archaeological record and open up past lives to some form of historical examination when previously reconstruction of the past was on the basis of the written word which skews history so much in favour of the literate victors.

The stones of Rameses II had survived to 1818 when Shelley saw them, and will continue to endure, we might imagine, for yet more millennia. And it is this 'monumentalism'—the deliberate creation of large objects, buildings, and statues to commemorate the life and existence of the powerful in and through durable stone and marble—which was not lost on Adolf Hitler and the Third Reich's architect, Albert Speer. They were so aware of the importance of thinking ahead that they planned their imperial building of the '1,000-year Reich' with its future ruination in mind. Instructions went out that 'steel and ferro-concrete could no longer be used in the construction of official Nazi buildings because they were too perishable. The use of marble, stone and brick alone would ensure that, at the fall of the 1,000-year Reich, they would resemble their Roman models' (Woodward 2002: 29). Hitler argued that his monumental architecture should be built by slaves—just as that of the Roman Empire, for that made future generations aware of the power required to produce such edifices. Architect and Fuhrer attempted to control their image in history, many generations into the future, envisaging Nuremberg as an ivy-clad ruin after the eventual collapse of the Third Reich.

However, MacGregor points out that the meanings of 'things' change with time and that things take on meanings that could never be envisaged at the moment of their creation. Later periods come to alter the 'original' and thus document their own time, as well as that of the object retrieved. What we must also consider is something that MacGregor is keen in places to *under-state* and that is in the conflict of cultures—*Kulturkampf*. Whilst he does talk, as one might expect in any history of the world, of war and weapons and warfare, this is seen through the lens of the maintenance of property and power. This bias is clear when he speaks of the Standard of Ur, which is a wooden box, constructed around 2500 BCE by the Mesopotamians. It is decorated with stones from Afghanistan, from India, and from the Gulf region. On one of the sides of the Standard is to be seen a large collection of human figures shown variously as paying tribute to the king, being defeated by him in battle and in all cases reflecting the power of the military in their lives. What is not discussed here by MacGregor are the reasons for, and causes of, a conflict of cultures between Ur and its near neighbours, because that often requires the written word to bring the battle of ideas into our consciousness. It also makes it much more difficult to tell *the* story of an object rather than *a* story of the object, for there has to be some assumption of homogeneity and oneness in a narrator telling the tale of an object that is recorded for a specified number of minutes and is for broadcast. The objects are straitjacketed to tell one story rather than many, to reveal one culture rather than many, and to demonstrate homogeneity, not heterogeneity.

But heterogeneity is only one of a number of deep problems we face before moving on.

Nine issues in organizing styles

In relation to 'organizing' styles for the reader, a number of points need to be made at this juncture.

First, my approach to these issues is, in some measure, tendentious and partial. I am not some addled adherent to the 'Design School' identified by Mintzberg (1990), where the CEO is seen as 'the rational architect' (Zald 1981: 125) who always achieves their design choices through intellectual reasoning. And whilst Starbuck and Nystrom (1981) and Barzeley and Estrin (2009) articulate the world's need for a school of science for organizational design (Galbraith 1973), I am less sanguine about such an undertaking. For it is not clear to me that the politics of design are as central to any 'design school' as they should be. Latham and Dale (2012: 1) say that 'Design itself is often treated as if it is linear in process, singular in its expression as a plan, and homogenous in its implementation. Here [in their paper] we conceive of design as contested, multiple and ongoing.' And, of course, design, whether of buildings, objects, organizations, or of the world economy itself, *is* subject to all sorts of political processes, often involving subordinate members of the structure engaged in a constant struggle with senior management about the ways in which design is formulated, implemented, and reformed. Design may also be highly contested between senior members of a client organization and the consultant design team. We might even note that no design survives its first shock with organizational politics and I would have no wish to deny this glaring organizational reality. Indeed, enhanced analysis of this contested arena of design styles needs encouragement (Kornberger et al. 2011). But here my approach is focused upon a post-settlement situation where a design is in situ.

Second, I do not mean that we should be simply attending to the fixed organized places where many of us spend our *working* lives. Attention here in this book is upon the organization of our everyday experiences at hospital, home, school, university, company, cinema, restaurant, theatre, museum, zoo, theme park, beach, pub, night club, football ground, on the way to work, on the way back from work, and a myriad other places and journeys where we confront organization. And that means everywhere. For as individuals (in the UK, for example), even in the privacy of our own beds, we confront a world organized for us by Swedish furniture manufacturers, Japanese television makers, US producers of media content, UK duvet producers, German publishers, News Corporation, Chinese light bulb makers, carpet manufacturers based in Belgium, and an environment in our room governed by the suppliers of Russian gas, French electricity, and Scottish water. Even from before we are born, our prenatal lives are organized by state health services and the bureaucracies surrounding our mothers, and fathers.

Third, how does this multiple and myriad world that surrounds us, drawn from all parts of the globe and operating upon us in so many different ways, open up the possibility that we are subject to specific and knowable 'styles of organizing'? How can such an 'intermediate' notion of 'style' fit with the vast

Nine issues in organizing styles

array of influences from many organizations located in many different cultures that organize us on a daily basis? I have indicated earlier that processes of 'recognition, manifestation and coherence' are involved in forming styles of choice. In what ways then do the forces acting upon our lives become arranged, ordered, and organized into integrating and intelligible 'actants' that carry out this set of roles? Without embracing actor–network theory in any serious way, my answer is that this ordering is achieved through the differing ways that they are assumed to address key human choices in *ideational antinomies*. As Jenks (1998: 5) puts it, the early sociologists saw their work as about morality and values, and tended, because of this, to deal in core binaries or dichotomies. Here 'two strong and opposite positions' each with its own strength of argument is pitted against the other, allowing each to speak for itself and against the other.

My view is that core antimonies, by being actants upon us, have a material effect, informing our design choices by processes of inclusion and exclusion. We select styles of organizing but not in circumstances of our own choosing.

Fourth, if in this book I am 'organizing styles' for others, then even within one culture (that of the UK, for example) one must recognize that different subjectivities are in play. Michel Foucault's concept of *heterotopic spaces* may have some theoretical purchase here. The complexity of the world is reflected in the city as a heterotopic space (Foucault 2000) in which meaning is loosened and the 'order of things' is actively disrupted. Old certainties disappear. If this is correct, and it is by no means clear that it is (McLeod 1996), then any model of styles of spacing must reflect the ambiguities in the life of urban spaces and the multiple interpretations allowed and encouraged in their users. This suggestion of a heterotopic spatial quality, in which the subjective interpretations of the city dweller differ markedly, itself profoundly problematizes the notion of style because it brings into question the capacity that we have to describe and analyse the 'same' phenomenon. Men and women, for example, may experience space quite differently. Grosz (1995: 47) argues that there is a link between the very concept of architecture and the 'phallocentric effacement of women and femininity'. If human users of space cannot agree on the object of our theorizing and its outline and content, then there is little conceptual purchase in attempting to explain this supposed 'theoretical object'. What styles are perceived by you may not be the ones that I see before me. 'Styles' differ perhaps in the mind of the beholder. But these minds too are subject to processes of structuration that pattern our perceptions. It is perhaps the same for concepts of 'beauty'.

Fifth, then, the question of aesthetics and the differential appreciation of 'beauty' will run throughout this book, so perhaps it is as well to deal with it briefly here (for a fuller discussion, see Dale and Burrell 2003). Wolfgang Welsch (1997) maintains that 'the aesthetic' is a polysemy in that there is a

The Complexity of 'Style'

wide variety of usages of the term. These include callistics, cosmetics, harmoniousness, sensuousness, perceptiveness, cultivation, appreciation, phenomenology, and artistry. This listing demonstrates the complexity in coming to an understanding of styles from 'an aesthetic viewpoint' because it depends upon one's definition of aesthetics and one's negotiation of the conceptual minefield.

Lefebvre insists that we understand space through an embodied experience in which *all* our senses are involved. Once we adopt a corporeal understanding of the nature of space it becomes clear that the noise and the smell and the taste of urban life often demarcate it from the supposed 'peace of the countryside'. This is further complicated by the issue of 'anaesthetics'. In one or two isolated spots within his text, Welsch (1997: 25, 72, 83), raises the issue of the 'double figure' of aesthetics and anaesthetics by arguing that continued excitement leads to indifference. Over-stimulus gives way to the nervous system shutting down. To the extent that one or more of the senses is stimulated through an aesthetized stimulus, it is implied that one or more of the remaining senses is anaesthetized. Anaesthetization thus can become one way of surviving the terror of partial stimulation or overstimulation of the senses and of perception (Dale and Burrell 2003: 160–6). A similar point is also made by Antonio Strati (1999: 81). Aesthetics, says Strati, is the knowledge given to us by our sensory organs and is related to the Greek verb '*aisth*' which means 'to feel'. He maintains that '"anaesthetics" . . . is the means whereby the sensory facilities are blunted, and one of these means may be art'. By art making the ordinary extraordinary, 'these are ways to "anaesthetise" organizational actors and thereby render them insensitive and entirely unable to comprehend organizational life' (Strati 1999: 81). So for Strati, whilst aesthetics sharpens the sensory faculties, anaesthetics dulls them. Political economies, architecture, design, and organizations are all implicated in the process of anaesthetization.

Sixth, please notice here how the literature looked at so far embraces the valorization of 'the city space'. Now it may be that it is fine for the metropolitan dweller to believe that the city is where the action is, and where all of human life is to be beholden, but even in the UK significant numbers of the population live in small towns, villages, and the countryside. Of course, the rise of the megalopolis *is* of great significance to the powerful in the state, local government, business, and the media but not all people live in conurbations where space is heterotopic and the order of things is constantly threatened. Changes in styles within the non-urban realm may well reflect the existence of different rhythms—in capital city, regional conurbation, suburbia, and countryside—within the same nation state.

Seventh, in working towards a model of style, I think it helpful to suggest that issues of style are 'above people's heads'. Clearly, this is a dangerous formulation, suggesting the very thing I wish to avoid, and that is the notion that non-elites cannot come to appreciate the aesthetic and artistic content of what surrounds them, how they are organized, and what effects they have upon the population. I make no such assumption since it will undermine my enterprise. My point is that the way in which aesthetic styles are often backgrounded means that we miss them as we negotiate everyday reality. The clues to architectural and design style are often above eyeline, so that literally, rather than metaphorically, they are over people's heads. The construction of the modern townscape is to draw the line of sight of the shopper to the shop windows that they are encouraged to pass. The eye is drawn by shop displays to a spectrum of space that is perhaps at most four metres above ground level. The inclusion of the shop's name and its branding devices keep the eye's horizons fixed at this point. How often do we look above this level in the urban high street and contemplate the upper storeys for their architectural devices and their style of construction? Today, even if we are more aware of Walter Benjamin's characterization of the 19th-century Parisian 'flâneur' (Benjamin 1999) with time on their hands to take the air and to look around, taking in the sites, sights, and sounds of the city, how often do we ask ourselves, as tourists, about the fabric and construction of the world? The assumption is made that its understanding lies beyond our reach. Rather, we are absorbed by the lower images of contemporary consumer culture (Featherstone 1991; Lury 1996). And for this reason we must contemplate the style of politico-economic systems which, for the most part, keep our eyes cast downward in an accepting state of anaesthetization.

Eighth, this contemporary assault upon our senses can encourage the development of what Simmel (1991; 1995: 24) calls 'the blasé attitude'. Cities create a concentrated stimulation for the individual, resulting in 'the highest degree of nervous energy'. In the face of this urban assault which is so intense, city dwellers 'retreat into inattention and reserve' (Cronin 2006: 626). In this sense also, city dwellers find that issues of style are 'over their heads' because they switch off in order to survive the daily rigours of metropolitan life. Minds are numbed in order to manoeuvre through densely packed streets where threats of eye contact exist only in order to discommode the commuter. Eyes are cast down in pursuit of a Simmelian blasé attitude. Again, this numbed unquestioning of what lies over our heads raises issues of the organizing of contemporary politico-economic systems. We become blasé about the economic woes of others, even if they sit on a rug outside a shop, asking us for the price of a cup of tea.

Ninth, and finally, in his book *Whispering City: Rome and its Histories*, RJB Bosworth (2011) shows how the grand architecture of Rome is staged by popes and politicians for the visitor interested in its classical, Renaissance, and Baroque architecture. But the reality is one of multiple histories, multiple

The Complexity of 'Style'

architectures which do not shout out their origins, lives, and fates, but rather whisper them. Some buildings, of course, owned by the elite, might well shout out their positioning on issues of design politics into the faces of those who work in or walk past them, but many merely murmur them (Bosworth 2011), signalling quietly their designers' intentions. So in this book, styles and their effects on organizational lives are to be traced in whispers as well as through shouts. One has to look and listen and sometimes even *lip-read* the silence of a 'style' in order to fully comprehend how styles organize our lives for us. Patience is to be required, skills are to be acquired, and time is to be allowed to pass. For in some senses we are always, already, imprisoned by basic design assumptions, and these become 'institutionally embedded' (Scott 1995), meaning that we need time and energy and insight to begin to recognize just how embedded these assumptions are in our own psyches.

It is to the issue of the effects of the passing of time that we now turn.

The passing of styles as periodization

There is a periodization of styles in organization theory, in economics, in architecture, and in design. The periodization of styles in organization theory is of course discernible if one wishes to look through that lens. Shenhav (1995) is but a more sophisticated version of what is typically presented in textbooks: namely, scientific management is the start of it all. Thereafter, a variety of styles of management is discernible. Even Clegg and Dunkerley (1980: 72) insist that 'the analysis of organizations begins to emerge in the last years of the nineteenth century as precisely that practical and analytical individualism which characterised marginalist economic analyses of the sphere of distribution'. Yet despite the early closure of their temporal interests, they do start to show here the interconnections of organization theory and economics (Perrow 1990; Rowlinson 1997). Writers such as Pfeffer (2008: 147–8) see such a relationship as bad for organization theory because it suffers from 'economics envy'. He claims that we cite economics at an increasing rate, we 'buy in' to its behavioural assumptions and we stop asking questions that should be raised. Most important perhaps, is his claim that this interest is not reciprocated by economists, so in facing a one-way traffic, organization theory should not be co-opted by the methods, assumptions, and topics of this Other. Despite this warning, I intend to enter the domain of the economists and see what might lie there of a useful nature. Immediately, one sees that chronological segmentation is also clear in the writing up of the history of economics (Dow 1986; Galbraith 2000), wherein schools of thought are presented as subject to a rise and fall. Galbraith's book has 22 chapters, each dealing with a phase in economic thought 'through an awareness of its history' (Galbraith 2000: 1), following strict chronological order, and divided into major schools of thought. In architecture too, 'styles' is a word that is irrevocably linked to periodization. Yet in seeking out patterns we must be careful not to expect to confront linear sequences.

When it comes to the issue of architectural styles, 'There is a tidy and misleading analogy between history and human life which proposes that architectural movements are born, have youth, mature, and eventually die. The historical process which led to the creation of... movements in architecture had none of this biological inevitability, and had no clear beginning which can be pinpointed with precision' (Curtis 1996: 21). So the search for 'origins', then, perhaps has to be avoided. But architects and designers often see the world as made up of 'periods' defined by the time's victorious styles and the well-accepted accompanying component stylistic indicators. Hence we are told that the Romanesque gives way to Gothic, Baroque gives way to the Rococo, Art Nouveau gives way to Modernism.

Amy Dempsey begins her book *Styles, Schools and Movements* (2004: 5) with the disconcerting notion for those seeking simplicity that 'Styles, schools and movements are seldom self-contained or simply defined; they are sometimes contradictory, often overlapping, and always complicated.' Nevertheless, she presses on and claims that 'The 300 styles, schools and movements collected in this guide bring together the most significant developments in Western painting, sculpture, architecture and design.' She draws a time line from 1860 to 2000 and places upon it these differing artistic styles, separating them into 'Art for the People', where designers and architects have sought to 'create a total living environment for the modern world' (Dempsey 2004: 6); 'Art and Style', where the 'avant-garde' search for new styles capable of expressing modern life; and 'Art and Mind', wherein the function of art was to represent 'the inner worlds of emotion, mood and sensibility' (Dempsey 2004: 6).

From my point of view, this search for completeness is understandable but, of course, it is never completed. She chooses to look at 'Western painting, sculpture, architecture and design', which immediately gives her approach a geographical set of blinkers. Left outside her field of vision are whole libraries of 'Eastern', 'African', 'Aboriginal', 'Latin American', and many other classifications of the art of the non-Western Other. Second, Dempsey (2004: 9) chooses to concentrate upon material 'within the bounds of painting and sculpture', and although there is content on architectural style, it tends to be seen as the accompanist to interior design stylistic movements such as in the Arts and Crafts Movement's notion of 'total design'. Third, by starting her classification only in 1860, she has nothing to say of the major architectural movements that predate that year. There is nothing on Gothic, Baroque, or Neo-classical stylistic movements. Yet there is a sociological patina here as

The Complexity of 'Style'

attempts are made to look at styles in terms of how they speak at a societal level and not necessarily always through an elite voice.

On the other hand, Emily Cole's edited text, *A Concise History of Architectural Styles* (2003: 7) assumes that architecture is of and for the powerful. It deals with the chronological ordering of architectural styles which 'begins with Egyptian architecture' and ends with 'the latest style covered in the chronology...the Picturesque movement of the late eighteenth and early nineteenth centuries'. Cole et al. (2003) are much more historicist and globalist than the vast majority of classifiers and identify the following world 'styles' up to the advent of the Picturesque:

Ancient Egypt
Babylon, Assyria, Persia
Early and Classical India
Early and Dynastic China
Classical Japan
Pre-Columbian
Pre-Classical
Ancient Greece
Ancient Rome
Early Christian and Byzantine
Islamic
Romanesque
Gothic
Renaissance
Baroque and Rococo
Palladianism
Neo-Classical
Picturesque.

Ten elements, common to the architecture of almost all periods, are illustrated and discussed. These ten elements are: columns, towers, arches and arcades, doorways, windows, pediments, gables, roofs, vaulting, and stairways. So here we have a breadth of historical time which is absent in Dempsey's approach, beginning as it does in 1860, whilst Cole et al. obviously stop their discussion around 1730. Cole et al. are conscious of the need to discuss architecture across the globe whilst, as we have seen, Dempsey concentrates on design styles in the Western world.

From this description of a few styles, and recognizing the way in which architects and designers tend to see their passing, it is in the alleged supersession by new styles in some hypothesized linear way that one can see a number of problems. First, Jencks (1987: 13) argues that the suppression of styles often takes place on the assumption of a theory that there is a 'single strand' in architecture and design which assumes dominance. This, he argues, is akin to Zeitgeist theory which posits that one design style fits in with the spirit of the age at the cost of all else. In place of single-strand and Zeitgeist assumptions, Jencks wishes to articulate '*a series of discontinuous movements*' (italics in original). He argues, in other words, for pluralism. If this is so, it certainly complicates matters. But it is the route that I shall attempt to take in approaching all four disciples of architecture, design, political economy, and organization theory!

Second, all styles involve engagement with what has gone before, even if it is as a pure antithetical reaction of hatred and opposition. The tensions in architecture and design mean that there are constant repetitions of styles over long historical periods, so that a Neo–Gothic period arose in Britain in Victorian times, as indeed did a Neo-Classical revival. Historically-based ideas reassert themselves in the hands of those who wish to make a point for their own epoch by deriving old ideas from the past and representing them as 'Neo-'. Neo-Liberalism is a good case in point.

Third, it would be foolish to suppose that styles ever die out entirely. Often there are pockets of particular styles that remain, even when that style has supposedly been totally slain by what succeeded it. Companies and individuals continue to design in this style to which they became accustomed, and become backgrounded more than they do become extinct. Thus, as Jencks argues, any modern epoch contains a plethora of styles lying alongside one another, with one, possibly, being in dominance.

Fourth, the history of a style is also the history of ideas in politics, economics, and in social thought. Architecture and design are art forms, which means that whilst transcendence of the everyday may well be sought, these aesthetic pursuits are locked into prevailing debates and thought about power, money, and the human body. They are also linked closely with views on nature, human feelings, and the importance of history (Lowenthal 1985). Art and design as material texts need to be con*text*ualized. 'Style' and 'organization' both inhabit the social and human sciences—but they are not the same, of course. It cannot simply be asserted that when one speaks of style, one speaks of organization, nor that when one speaks of organization one speaks of style. However, this book will attempt to bring them closer together in a web of connectivity and speak of both at one and the same time. It sees organization and style as both being representative of the 'will to form'.

Frederick appears to point in this direction when he says: 'true architectural style does not come from a conscious effort to create a particular look. It results obliquely—even accidentally—out of a holistic process. The builder of an American colonial house in 1740... built sensitively with the materials and technology available... The colonial architecture that resulted from these considerations was uncalculated. Early American houses were colonial because the *colonists* were colonial' (Frederick 2007: 82). In other words, the will to form does not start and end with appearance, but also with the material constraints of organization—and with a particular set of social and economic arrangements.

When it comes to speaking of heterogeneity in our organizational arrangements, Du Gay (2007: 140) remarks: 'After all, techniques of economic and organizational management rarely come ready-made; they have to be invented, implanted, stabilized and reproduced. This involves much hard, frequently tedious, work whose success and effects cannot be taken for granted "in advance".' Also important is how we are to understand periods that do not share our own particular conceptions of space and culture if Moholy-Nagy (1947: 56) is correct in his view that 'Every cultural period has its own conception of space.' And if it is difficult enough to understand other periods, what are we do in understanding change within our own? Kenneth Clark, the art historian, said that he could tell much more about a civilization by its architecture than by anything else it left behind. Thus he opined that 'Painting and literature depend largely on unpredictable individuals, but architecture is to some extent a communal art' (Clark 1969: 330). If, as I have already said, this book is an attempt to discuss these issues of taste and style in relation to styles of organizing, we must ask how, if at all, and to what extent an artistic, architectural approach to design creates, reflects, or mimics the organizational life that it en-houses.

In this task, we must recognize, of course, that someone living in a modernist tower block may not, in any way, embrace the tenets of modernism. Rudofsky (1964: 1) argues that architecture is 'an anthology of buildings of, by, and for the privileged'. Le Corbusier and Mies van der Rohe both recognized this when the former said that architecture should be a 'profound projection of harmony' and the latter that there was a need to 'create order out of...desperate confusion' (both quoted in Clegg and Kornberger 2006: 148). These notions suggest that architects have no desire to shoot themselves in their fee. Yet a factory worker in a Neo-Classically facaded wool mill may not wish to contemplate the Neo-Classical world at all, nor that of the Ancients upon which it is supposedly based. Owings (1973: 47) complained that in the USA by 1900 'the whole country was suffering aesthetically under the domes of pseudoclassic Rome'. What is more likely is that the owners and controllers of the buildings saw in these styles certain elements which they desired. Thus, and bearing in mind the base definition with which the book began, I am not so much seeking to 'study down' the work hierarchy within the corporate and non-corporate world but more to 'study up' and look at the activities, achievements, and motivations of designers, architects, chief executives, and owners in constructing the world for their staffs—although I also recognize that such 'vertical' discussions privilege the concept of hierarchy from the outset (Child 2009).

My invitation to a readership in 'business and management' has itself a vertical dimension. It is to look upwards at the buildings that they inhabit—but to think foundationally. It is to look up into the economic system but think foundationally. By this is meant the requirement to consider lofty issues of philosophical debate, understand systems of aesthetics, and examine that which is so much more than the mere 'container' of social and business life. Above all it is to contextualize social life within a political economy. The architecture of our thought systems, by which we undertake the ideational organizing of ourselves, resembles in no small measure that solid material architecture in which we walk, work, and sleep. There can be no room within an 'embodied materiality' (Dale 2005) for a Cartesian split between mind and body. We are brains but with bodies, material flesh with cognitive ability, we occupy space but we also create it.

It is even more important, therefore, for organization theorists, and students of business and management more generally, to listen carefully, look intensely, and examine in detail what is to be found around us on a day-to-day basis—were we only to look as if for the first time. Awareness of the environment built for us by economists, senior managers, architects, and designers is often at surprisingly minimal levels, so that it is accepted as the sea in which we swim. We cruise, without problematizing its origins, construction, and potentialities. Look around today and ask yourself if there is anything new that you can see.

5

The Stylistic Features of Organizing

Anything new to see?

I ended the last chapter with a request to the reader to look around. I do not ask at this point that we peer into the wood-panelled corridors belonging to our vice chancellors and chief executives to see how they decorate their executive suites and letter headings. Sitting in an office of your own or on a train is as good a place to begin as any. So I want to suggest an unshakeable interest that we should have in the *mundane* ways in which our lives are organized.

At first glance, a car park is a car park is a car park. It is merely a silo for containing pieces of metal. Simon Henley in *The Architecture of Parking* (2009: 15) disagrees. 'Car parks could be explained as the cold realization of the engineer's criteria: the car is a certain size and it is parked in a space with prescribed dimensions, with a predictable turning circle and ramps and floors that must not exceed a given pitch. *But somehow these criteria do not give rise to the inevitable*' (my emphasis). For example, the typical parking space in the USA is 2.8 metres wide and 5.8 metres long. In Europe it is 2.4 metres wide and 4.8 metres deep. Clearly there are issues of scale at play in designing these structures (just as there are in designing the size of paper used in each continent). But car parking is much more than intercontinental engineering.

A silo for storing pieces of metal in the form of cars is exactly what each of the 19-storey, glass-clad car towers of the 'Autostadt' in Wolfsburg, Germany is, but these are glass display cabinets—personalized cocoons—awaiting the new owners of their high-value contents. Here the car park is to display branded products which have been personalized and lovingly stored with your name on it. It is anything but featureless. The style antithesis to the 'Autostadt' is the dark storage room constructed of concrete, buried underground and smelling of urine and danger. In the movie *Get Carter* (1971) the Trinity Square car park in Gateshead features, as Carter throws the developer Cliff Brumby from the top. One architect says to the other as Brumby's body hits the ground, 'I have an awful feeling that we are not going to get our fees on this job' (Henley 2009: 63). Trinity Square was demolished around 2009 despite claims that it possessed 'iconic status' as a result of its filmic appearance.

A key figure in late 20th-century architecture who always got his fees was Gordon Bunshaft, a leading partner in the huge architectural firm of Skidmore, Owings and Merrill (SOM), and it is interesting to note that his last-ever design was for the six-storey circular car park of the National Commercial Bank in Jeddah. Here SOM's 'international style' is given an Islamic twist in terms of its window decoration, and there were separate areas for females and males to arrive in, before and after they did business in the bank. So, even though most car parks offer only 'an architecture of compression', the styles in which this compressive architecture can be expressed are many and varied. When we deal later with 'monumentalism' as a style in architecture and organization, a car park was the first thing to draw my attention. Just as Breugel the Elder perceived the Tower of Babel to be a great helix, Bertrand Goldberg saw Marina City built in Chicago in 1962 as just such a shape (Henley 2009: 225). Two 'corncob'-shaped towers of forty storeys of apartments each rested upon nineteen storeys of car parking. From the entrance, a driver needed to travel one full kilometre up the spiral in order to park on the nineteenth floor. Vertiginous views across Lake Michigan awaited them on every turn. Over 450 spaces were available in each tower for those drivers who managed to hold the steering wheel at full lock all the way up the ramp. 'Compression' indeed. This is an example of monumentalism in the service of the automobile, which was a style to be found across continental Europe and the UK (especially Coventry) in the early 1960s. Considering the range of possibilities here, we have one architectural structure for storing cars, found in many places across an industrial world, and expressed in many stylistic forms.

At the other end of thinking about styles, in contradistinction to seeing many styles reflected in the construction of a single building type, all across the planet, one is able to witness a singular, particular building, expressing many styles over much time. The Town Hall of Arras in northern France is somewhat remarkable for its wide range of architectural styles. When Louis XIV visited Arras, it was the capital of Artois and the Hôtel de Ville was famed for its Flemish take on Renaissance styling. For his royal visit, Baroque styling was added to the edifice and, a century later, Neo-Classicism, which was very much in vogue, was used in the design of the town hall's wings. Art Nouveau designs, often associated with 'the Low Countries', were added to the internal decoration of the building in the early 20th century. In many respects, then, the Hôtel de Ville represented the changing architectural and design styles of those centuries it had overlooked on the site upon which it stood. This melange of styling worked well both aesthetically and as a reflection of the town's fortunes in the shifting landscape of north European politics and statecraft—until the First World War, when the Hôtel de Ville was shelled into oblivion. Its high tower made it an observation platform for espying the troop movements of the enemy during the Battle of the Somme and it therefore became a legitimate target for German artillery, which duly destroyed it. In the 1920s it was decided to repair and restore the town hall as it had been in the summer of 1914, save for some internal reorganization of room sizes and so on. What the visitor sees today is a replica of a set of styles reflecting the history of a town once famous across Europe for its tapestries. On the face of the building is etched a political and commercial history, fully reflecting the changing fortunes of nation states, old and new industries, not least of which was the support for continued labour employment during the Depression, a civic desire to reflect and enhance architecture and thereby the standing of the city, a perceived need to build upwards across a very flat landscape and thereby dominate it, a wish to offer continuity as well as change in the appearance of the urban setting, and a commitment to extract full reparations in the face of a defeated enemy. It is a story as richly embroidered as any one of the town's own tapestries. It is a tale of a complexity in which patterning is very difficult to discern amongst the twists and turns of its creation.

Because of the possibilities of such enfoldings (Deleuze 1993), fauxness, and over-codings, I have necessarily been selective in my choice of what patterning in the organizing of the world to consider. This book seeks to show that styles of 'organizing' illuminate our surroundings and speak to us of past, present, and future. And 'organizations', in their turn, come equally to show their socio-economic context in the systems, designs, and architecture that they employ. Few buildings have the layers of stylistic complexity that the Hôtel de Ville at Arras does, but we should not assume that an absence of 'over-coding' means it is an easy task to speak of styles and their meaning in the organizational context. It is decidedly not. Folds of meaning are themselves enfolded one upon the other (Deleuze and Guattari 1988). The inhabitants of any architecture may see it very differently from those who see it from the outside; functions change, decay sets in, and weathering takes place, rendering the rendering quite different from that envisaged by some architect. Yet there are patterns that are discernible, similar motives to be found amongst the thinking of a building's financiers, an identity of values and attitudes between generations, the use of similar material and furnishings, and a set of common human requirements to do with shelter, adornment, and symbolic reflection. Buildings are highly particular but sometimes they share universalities. And perhaps that universality is to do with the distribution of power.

The Stylistic Features of Organizing

Styles as opposition or integration or differentiation?

Issues of style are contested in time and space, so 'styles' may reflect social and organizational processes of *opposition* to, or *sameness* with, or *difference* from, the Other. This distinctiveness in the uses to which 'style' is put in the social realm allows one to fruitfully explore the links between styles and politics. Hereafter, how styles are organized and in turn how they organize our social and organizational relationships will be discussed in the text by the use of examples of sameness and differentiation, but especially in terms of opposition. All three are involved in political tension. Changes in style can be fruitfully seen as a product of a play of forces between opposition, sameness, and differentiation in which outcomes are never certain. The book will contain examples of these dynamic plays of forces in the heterotopia of organized forms.

The major articulation of today's 'will to form' lies largely in the hands of the elite who are keen to emphasize *difference*. That is, style may not be about 'Oneness' nor about 'Otherness' but may be about 'Difference' in a plurality of styles. Many would argue that this is the predominant sense of 'style', in that it is meant to show differences between human beings that allow some sense of separateness to come to the fore. Thus, differentiation between classes, age groups, between gender, between sexualities, between ethnicities, between religions, and between 'orientations' are allowed, encouraged, and shaped through the mechanism of style.

Styles as pluralistic politics

What we find in looking at styles is increasingly high levels of colourful differentiation. Elsewhere (Dale and Burrell 2001) it has been argued that every move towards the aesthetic is also dependent upon an equal move of an-aesthetization. Within organization theory, there has been attention to a set of aesthetic issues about the design *content* of organizational architecture. For example, Hatch and Cunliffe (2006: 230–2) note that 'when you hear the words landscaping, design and décor, you probably think of the artistic side of architecture and the decoration of an organization's buildings and grounds. Façade, focal point, furnishings, lighting fixtures, ceiling and wall treatments, floor coverings, use of color and form, displays (e.g. of foliage, art, advertising or technology) and countless other details contribute to the landscaping, design and décor of an organization's physical structure.'

When this panoply of design opportunities is added to the dress requirements of organizational employees, more possibilities exist for different colours of fabrics and fashion choices to be expressed. These are thought to convey 'values' and to reflect cultural choices. Hatch and Cunliffe (2006: 232) maintain that 'physical elements associated with landscaping, design and décor offer important clues to the organization's culture and its image to outsiders'. They give some examples of the symbolic nature of the architectural appearance of buildings, including the colonnade by Bernini in St Peter's Square which Eco described as 'an immense pair of arms, open to embrace the faithful' and of the symbolic value of geographical locations such as Ellis Island, New York (which also embraced the faithful newcomer to the USA). Symbolic objects such a cross in a Catholic church invoke the behaviour of kneeling in most of the congregation, whereas a counter in a McDonald's outlet conditions us to queue. Styling of, in, and by space then are seen as crucial to a few pioneers in organization theory who would encourage us, no doubt, to look around.

But if we place ourselves in the hands of the architect Charles Jencks, we might expect some increased depth of analysis. Jencks (1987) provides the notion that there are six traditions in *politics* and architecture which form 'the evolutionary tree' for the period 1920–70. These six traditions are:

logical
idealist
self-conscious
intuitive
activist
unconscious.

He argues that fusions of these styles are always possible and 'the best architects are the least classifiable' (Jencks 1987: 29). What is so useful about Jencks is the way that he ties these architectural traditions into politics, allowing us perhaps to see what organizational principles are being conjured from these six styles. For the *'logical'* approach, Jencks (1987: 72) turns to Buckminster Fuller and his geodesic domes which were designed to use technology to put an end to politics. Here, there was an emphasis on 'systematic planning, continuous growth and the cybernetic revolution' where 'within ten years it will be normal for man to be successful... Politics will become obsolete.' Jencks immediately compares this view with that of Positivism, where Saint Simon advocated the triumph of the professional manager over the state official. Buckminster Fuller places the 'Universal Architect' in the stead of the bullying politician, to the advantage of all. The successful search by managers for technological, technical, managerial, and functional efficiency would provide lost beauty and majestic eternity to all architecture. Jencks maintains that the Japanese 'Metabolists' and the New Bauhaus based at Ulm from 1955 until 1968 are heirs to this tradition, and that living in societies characterized by fast technological innovation, a political philosophy of

The Stylistic Features of Organizing

meritocracy, and a belief in managerialism, there were fertile architectural grounds for the logical tradition.

For the *idealist* tradition, Jencks (1987: 31) argues that the bedrock is 'humanitarian liberalism, reformist pluralism and a vague social Utopianism'. There is an obligation to provide alternative visions to the prevailing orthodoxy and to develop 'a spirit of construction and synthesis'. Le Corbusier was part of this tradition, it is maintained. The limitless potential of the machines of the assembly line was to be the destroyer of class and the creator of boundary-less, democratic brotherhood. He was characterized inaccurately as offering flat roofs, reinforced concrete, homes as machines for living in, and communism. Architecture in the idealist tradition was to be the pursuit of politics by other means.

The *'self-conscious'* tradition of architecture in the 20th century was represented by Hitler's 1,000-year Reich. For Jencks (1987: 46), 'The politics of the self-conscious tradition...are conservative, elitist, centralist, and pragmatic with an occasional element of mystical fundamentalism thrown in.' Hitler opined that the house with the flat roof was oriental and therefore Jewish and therefore Bolshevistic. The pitched roof of Germanic architecture, on the other hand, was good, upright, and true. In Italian Fascist architecture the same political conservatism based on the glory of the Caesars also led to civic monumentalism, the creation of monuments to short-lived despotic regimes.

The *'intuitive'* tradition is represented for Jencks (1987: 59) by Art Nouveau and the Catalonian work of Gaudi, both drawing upon anarchism, anarcho-syndicalism, guild socialism, and ideas of 'mutual aid'. Walter Gropius's manifesto for the Bauhaus in 1919 is a clear example of these tenets, and a form of small-scale organizing based on the 'soviets', then being discussed and implemented in the newly emerging Soviet Union, was commonly advocated. Architects of the intuitive tradition sometimes dislike the straight line and advocate free-flowing curves perhaps exemplified by the Sydney Opera House and Gaudi's Barcelona architecture.

The tradition of the *'activist'* is exemplified by those who take action to deal with issues of housing and accommodation. Engels demonstrates this approach, says Jencks (1987: 81), where the emphasis is to be in the socialist state upon communal housing, palaces of labour, and other 'conductors and condensers of socialist culture'. Collective facilities would liberate women from individuated drudgery. This became known as constructivism: the construction of the communist future through social and architectural engineering. In the post-war world it was squatters in Arizona or the *barriada* of Peru who developed a constructivism in some ways reminiscent of 'soviet' (in its original meaning) architecture.

Finally, the *unselfconscious* tradition was meant to relate to, and work for, large building programmes and mass housing in the post-World War II world

(Jencks 1987: 76). It was an architecture of and for the Welfare State that was to be 'restrained, dignified and anonymous'. However, whilst this architecture was designed to be a simple response to present-day requirements for many, it would be fair to say no new iconic architecture appeared as had been promised.

Jencks's description of these models is very useful because he does make a serious effort to tie together politics, organizational principles by which society might be articulated, and architectural ideas. Thus one style rests upon a triad of technological innovation, meritocracy, and managerialism; the next on humanitarian liberalism, reformist pluralism, and utopianism; the third style is fascist and is based on a conservative, elitist, centralist world view with the occasional element of mystical fundamentalism; the fourth has anarchism, anarcho-syndicalism, guild socialism, and ideas of 'mutual aid' at its heart; the fifth sees the importance of communal housing and 'palaces of labour' to socialist culture; whilst the sixth advocates large building programmes and mass housing.

According to Jencks, then, architects and designers, perforce, are creatures of politics, organizational arrangements, and economics. So we must assume that they are also in thrall to the marketplace. In Glancey's introduction to *C20th architecture* (2000: 6), he announces

> Architects, as Phillip Johnson, a very clever US architect said, 'are whores': as members of one of the world's oldest professions, they get paid for doing what other people want. And that means the design of banal office blocks and brainless shopping malls as well as beautiful private houses and churches that have the power to reduce the noisiest citizen to silence.

Whilst some architects have been dreamers who tried to put their utopian thoughts into practical form, for Glancey (2000: 6) the architect was 'on the whole, a willing collaborator with governments, property developers and the moving spirit of the times'. He argues that the role of the architect was marginalized as 'society' wanted more buildings but for less. 'In order to preserve their role, architects had to become "imagineers", shaping and guiding the look of buildings and the way they related to their settings.' Thus, 'architects try in their different ways to create order and would-be perfection from an imperfect world' (Glancey 2000: 7). Historically, this seems a little too glib, for Glancey does not define that reification, 'society' and, as social scientists, we also know that many early industrial buildings never did involve architects, for it was engineers and industrialists who led the construction efforts. In other words, Glancey says a lot more about the professional identity of architects and how they define themselves and their role than he does about the social processes of what is going on *outside* architectural firms. However, given that Glancey's book is about 'the structures that shaped the twentieth century', it might be expected that his focus would be upon the 'Art Architects'—that group of 'signature architects' whose work is seen as representing a high art form. On the other hand, the generalized social processes within ordinary architectural practices that help explain the replication of building types and forms lies unexplored. It must be recognized that architecture—and design—are professions of diversity and heterogeneity.

Julier (2000: 1) tells us that 'Design is a highly entrepreneurial profession... Few industries in the West have grown in terms of economic presence and cultural import as design has in the last two decades.' He says that designers no longer differentiate themselves by the visual style they have created but by their approach to business, in which strategies of differentiation are the major driving force (Julier 2000: 2–3). Since its organization and aims are often multi-layered, there is no single model of design consultancy. A key component echoes that of some architecture, however, when it was asserted by the Design Council in 1986 that within the UK 'the design process is a planning exercise to maximize sales and profits'. Clearly, some design firms take a different perspective from this but there is a tension in the field of design which mirrors that in architecture. Design has been classified by Bourdieu (1984: 359) as a 'minor profession' and designers are seen as part of 'the new petite bourgeoisie' which deals in presentation and representation. In order to create and maintain their jobs, they must become 'cultural intermediaries' and creators of taste. They build art colleges which foster notions of marginality and edginess, allowing Julier (2000: 36) to maintain that:

> It is important to reinforce here that designers draw on this system to differentiate themselves from other professions and educations, to identify and distinguish themselves and their skills. But they are also involved in constant manoeuvrings to differentiate themselves from each other.

Styles therefore are about differentiation and are articulated by professions which themselves are differentiated. The idea of segmentation is crucial here. Markets are segmented, professions are segmented, careers are segmented, lives are segmented. In organization theory, differentiation is our bread and butter too. Reed (2005: 115–16) articulates this desire to segment when he identifies through very close labelling that:

> a neo-liberal management theorist such as Bennis, a neo-liberalist economist such as Schumpeter, a social democrat such as Schumacher, a neo-corporatist such as Elias, a technological determinist such as Bell or Castells and a theorist of radical participatory democracy such as Illich can all agree on the underlying currents of history.

And just as Glancey berates some architects for their incorporation into capitalism, adherents of critical management studies accuse those outside that camp of being servants of power. In later chapters, I shall attempt to build upon this helpful contextualization of design, politics, and architecture, albeit in a somewhat critical way. Nevertheless, the approaches taken by Jencks and Glancey to 'design' are a useful starting point and it is helpful to consider organization theory in their wake. Unfortunately, Guillen (1997, 2006) is a rare example of a writer who has looked at Taylorism in the light of its design aesthetic, and has sought to explain its originatory role within much of American corporate life. In my view, this argument is not a complete success, precisely because of its failure to treat origins carefully enough, but nevertheless it is an intriguing attempt (which we consider in a later chapter) to bring the production of organization to the fore. For present purposes, it is enough to note that for Guillen, Taylorism represents an important integrational design aesthetic right across the organizational world.

Styles as integrational

Elements who occupy elite positions may well believe in 'One Nation', whereby design becomes a way of articulating social integration around core values. One only has to look at flags to see the importance of design to national unity. Many maintain that they are protecting a shared national heritage by promulgating the merits of certain cultural artefacts. Sutton (1999: 7) tells us that:

> Nikolaus Pevsner began his classic *Outline of European Architecture* (1943) with what he thought was a statement of the obvious: 'A bicycle shed is a building; Lincoln Cathedral is a piece of architecture.' In the event, no sentence in the book proved to be more controversial. Today, nobody would dare say such a thing. Architecture is no longer seen as a series of isolated great buildings, monuments, works of art: it is the totality of the 'built environment'.

Pevsner, like F. R. Leavis, believed that a canon existed of great artistic work which unified and edified the human soul and which must be protected at all costs. Today this is seen as elitist and unrepresentative, but more importantly for our purposes the artistic has come to be seen more in relation to the social. Instead of the idea of great men (sic), who created out of their individual genius some sublime representation of the human spirit, architecture has come to be seen as a social practice embedded in systems of power. Creations are seen not as timeless but as interrelated to their times: to cultural, social, and political movements, whether in tune with or in counterpoint to any supposed zeitgeist.

Whilst Pevsner did claim (1964; 1975) that Lincoln Cathedral was 'architecture' but a bike shed was not, for me *each* reflects 'organization' in the economic, political, and social spheres as much any 'major' architecture does. In 1311, Lincoln Cathedral had surpassed the height of the Great Pyramid at

The Stylistic Features of Organizing

Giza and was the first building to do so anywhere in the world in almost 4,000 years. So it does merit some attention! However, bike sheds too are rich in meaning and what happens behind them has reached the level of cliché. Originating, by definition, no earlier than the last quarter of the 19th century they have become places of 'vulgarity' in the original sense of the word. They may be made of wood, or metal, or asbestos, or brick, giving us material clues to the designers' intentions. Durability and cheapness vie alongside each other. What size are they? What size are the people who use them? It is important for designers to note that 'Summer people are 22 inches wide. Winter people are 24 inches wide' (Frederick 2007: 96). Do the dimensions of a bike shed reveal an expectation of large numbers of users relative to the population, or it is a minority location? In Amsterdam today, next to the central station, there is a huge bike 'shed' more akin to a multistorey car park, reflecting in part, perhaps, the transportation opportunities opened up by the flat topography of the Netherlands. It is a bike shed that is usually full and may reflect a nation unified by its basic topographic dimensions. Elsewhere, the functions of the bike shed may have changed over the years, so that whilst illicit smoking and sexual activity remain enduring features of a building placed at the end of the social and architectural spectrum, in many places its use for storing bicycles may have declined in the face of widespread smoking bans and the increasing use of the car. In other words, the humble bike shed may speak as loudly of social life, and the changes to it, as an empty and decaying church.

In fashion, too, style also becomes a way of identifying *Oneness through Sameness* so that through the use of visual and cultural cues, identity is established. And since identity is related to id-entity (the wholeness of the self, conceptualized as pure in some form), oneness is central to its formation. Another way of expressing this is through the notions of sameness and thence of course to the concept of uniformity. And once we reach this point, the wearing of uniforms is not far behind. Style, then, can be about uniformity, wholeness, oneness, sameness, and identity. Fashion stylists such as Punks or Goths or New Romantics express a group identity and a cohesion that may not be offered by conventional social structures (Vermorel 1997). Style is about belonging to a Oneness and in Chapter 9 I attempt to deal with 'planes of oneness' where belonging and shared identity are crucial to menageries of strange bedfellows.

Styles as oppositional

In Baz Luhrmann's movie *Moulin Rouge!*, a battle of styles—an *opposition*—is shouted out. Whilst critics made much of the Bollywood-ish musical

Styles as oppositional

numbers, my interest is in the film's use of 'style' in architecture, in dress, and in decoration to make clear a dramatically tense differentiation. Whilst she did not receive that much attention, Catherine Martin's work as art director is outstanding. The heroine, Satine (played by Nicole Kidman), is being courted by the Duke of Monroth in the face of Ewan McGregor's character, Christian, and to make clear this conflict of perspectives and possibilities, a dramatic differentiation is made between the Baroque lusciousness of the eponymous theatre itself and the lodgings of the Duke, which are shown to be very 'Classical' in style. In cutting from an image of the Moulin Rouge to the Duke's quarters we see, immediately and starkly, that we are dealing with relationships of opposition. Satine is attacked under the Duke's Neo-Classical roof, where the aristocracy is presented as surrounding itself with classical forms of empire, of dressing formally and expensively, whereas the avant-garde clientele of the theatre tend to adopt extravagant and colourful modes of decoration and demonstrate living a life dedicated to excess. Style becomes a way of distinguishing oneself from the Other. In pursuing such a way forward, the oppositional approach will be adopted in large parts of this book where conflict is seen as a way of creatively recognizing the existence of difference in design.

Architecturally, there are cases of buildings shouting out their styles as oppositions, reflecting political differences within a fractured elite. One such example (discussed in Simon Jenkins in the *Guardian*, 8 July 2011: 35, quoting Gavin Stamp) is that of 'the Battle of the Styles' occurring in the UK about 1858. Lord Palmerston and the (partial) Gothicist Sir George Gilbert Scott argued fiercely over the design for the Foreign Office in London's Whitehall. Palmerston, prime minister at the time, was in favour of imperial classicism which he saw as best reflecting the power and longevity of the British Empire. This is a Mediterranean approach based upon military conquest. Against this was pitted Scott's city state medievalism in which it was north-*western* civilization which was supposed to stand out. Born in 1811, Scott was crucial to foundations of Britishness, having produced over 800 buildings right across the Empire, from Newfoundland to New Zealand, and these ranged from churches to schools to hospitals, asylums, workhouses, and vicarages. He was a devoted follower of Pugin, who, as we shall see later, articulated the importance of the Gothic style, and he had built the Albert Memorial and Edinburgh University. In India, Bombay University was constructed in Venetian Gothic, whilst medieval churches were 'restored' to a condition they had never seen before—but which he assumed their builders had really wanted. Scott emphasized the vertical line ascending upwards in a search for spirituality, whilst the pointed arch and the soaring turret were meant to offer people reassurance, comfort, and continuity in an age of rampant industrialization.

Differing dramatically from this design approach of Scott's, operating at the level of a design pattern, was William Morris. He was Scott's implacable enemy and proclaimed Scott's demise with the phrase 'the happily dead dog'. Put simply, if Morris had sought an authenticity in material, which was the aim of the Arts and Crafts Movement to which he belonged, Scott's Gothic Revival sought an authenticity in style derived from 500 years before. This was a clash of vitriolic proportions (Simon Jenkins 2011, 8 July: 35) precisely because it was the pattern's structure that was so different in the respective cases of Morris and Scott.

In order to progress beyond the exact particularities of the 1858 Battle of the Styles, I wish to briefly outline the uses of the analytical terms outlined above. One can get some sense, I hope, of the utility here in understanding oppositional wills to form. At the level of 'pattern language' a battle is supposedly under way within the case, so a *network of patterns* is called into being by the existence of the competitor position in a political confrontation. Linguistic forms are utilized in a discourse of apparent ideological competition when in fact there is much agreement about the pattern to be used. For present purposes we must note that there is deep agreement amongst the creative classes about the need to differ from each other.

To remind the reader, 'A *pattern* is a careful description of a perennial solution to a recurring problem within a building context, describing one of the configurations which brings life to a building. Each pattern describes a problem which occurs over and over again in our environment, and then describes the core solution to that problem, in such a way that you can use the solution a million times over, without ever doing it the same way twice' (Alexander et al. 1977: xvi). The pattern in use here is to do with a core solution to an enduring problem; namely British imperial power and the best way to project this within the heart of the capital city. There is huge agreement about this objective and its legitimacy. What is shared is an acceptance of the political importance of the objective of showing the Foreign Office in the best possible light. The core solution to that problem involves architectural dominance through large expenditure and public demonstrations of political support. The pattern in the Battle of the Styles, then, is one of assumed superiority and it is often at this level that choices about material for the outside and the inside of the design are made.

The 'Structure' within this pattern is the arrangement of basic elements within its design, and often involves a basic linearity in geometry and associated charts, diagrams, and plans. Here one speaks of organizational types and specific functions. It is a level concerned about emplacement where this term is taken to mean 'the construction of certain places for certain activities and certain people. It also involves the processes of inclusion within, and exclusion from, specific spaces' (Dale and Burrell 2008: 48). Structure produces boundaries, cells, and compartments, leading to fixity. Put very simply, design organization at the level of structure tends to be about divisions, rooms, and how they will be arranged.

The 'Format' is to do with the forming of the design object into a working arrangement where enactment is permitted. Enactment is taken to signify 'the ways in which social lives are lived, are processed through, are experienced through mobility and what power effects this brings about' (Dale and Burrell 2008: 48). It is where one concentrates upon corridors, passageways, barriers, and entrances; it allows for who might see whom, when. Design organization here is at the level of the processing of people.

Embellishment is where 'enchantment' comes in (Dale and Burrell 2008: 47–8). For me, this term implies the linking of meaning and matter, the symbolic and the material, in ways to produce power effects. Adornment is key to its understanding. Clearly, it is often at this level of embellishment where style is thought to reside. But this easy assumption tends to mask the importance of politics and the 'higher' levels of patterning. For example, the emphasis on the vertical line can be seen as all about embellishment but it also in-forms formats, formulae, and structures. Indeed, the vertical line in the Gothic style (Ball 2009) is often seen as the essence of the pattern itself.

In comparing the Neo-Classical and the Gothic approaches to the design of the Foreign Office we can perceive that certain design features operate across pattern, structure, format, and embellishment, creating major style differentiation. And if there were to be a battle between them, featuring the leading architects of the day, over which style was most fitting to represent Empire, we might expect full contestation on all architectural and symbolic fronts.

Once style is conceptualized as a process of identification and of marking out oppositional difference, we confront its *economic dimension*. The marketing textbooks are full of the importance of branding and the economic advantages that this provides in competitive markets. Branding is the establishment of stylistic differentiation of 'self' from competitors and their products. Style here could mean design of the product through its colour, its shape, its packaging, its touch, its feel, its smell, and its sound. The whole human sensorium may well be involved in the appreciation of style and stylistic difference. The famous case of Apple and its relationship to IBM is replete with the significance of issues of stylistic differentiation. IBM was huge and bureaucratically formal and used a particular shade of blue to identify itself, its staff, its advertising, and its products. It became known from the 1960s and 1970s as 'Big Blue'. Apple decided in a self-conscious way to design itself around the inversion of this. Its product and corporate designs were meant to be colourful, the company was to be small and non-bureaucratic in its managerial 'climate', and instead of producing mainframes it was to focus on designing and making small personal computers. Stylistic inversion of this kind is a well-known principle throughout business life in the building of a company from the start. Virgin's original formulation as an airline clearly had British Airways as its Other because it was its domestic competitor but also it was conceptualized—structurally—as its design antithesis.

Once style is conceptualized as opposition to Other and/or as identification of Self, we confront its *political dimension* too. Power is to be achieved, maintained, strengthened, and lost by adopting a 'style' which supports or confronts those in positions of domination. Clearly, empires have risen and fallen in which certain aesthetic styles have dominated. For example, Simon Schama (1988) seeks to interpret Dutch culture in the Golden Age, when the Dutch economy was 'hegemonic'. He asks if bits and pieces of culture can be put together to make a coherent whole. Schama (1988: 292) discusses the rise of handsome villas in the Italian Palladian style, modified by a Dutch take on 'classicism', built outside the commercial towns. Clusters of such villas arose, surrounded by parkland and offering hunting to the patricians and cloth manufacturers. However, he spends most time on the house of a West India Company director, designed by De Keyser. Bartoletti's house was a three-storey building on the Herengracht (Gentlemen's Street) where the most impressive rooms were on the ground floor. Maps of the territories controlled by the company greeted the visitor and there was a plurality of paintings—even the maid's room contained seven paintings upon the wall. The 'great hall' of the house was used for formal receptions and gatherings and was adorned with furniture and paintings. According to Schama's description of the house (1988: 313), 'Its family name does not, in fact, announce an alien Mediterranean presence on a northern canal, for its decorative richness was purely a Dutch affair.' Dutch Protestantism was strong and had stopped the full embrace of Renaissance architecture and of the Baroque too, in the main because of the association of these styles with Catholicism. So religion is a key component in the assessment of the value of styles and what comes to be valued. Styles may well reflect an opposition of *religious beliefs*.

Yet, most surprisingly, Schama speaks not of the Dutch East India Company, the *VOC* (Verenigde Oostindische Compagnie). There is no reference to the company in his mammoth *The Embarrassment of Riches* and where trade is briefly discussed, it is in terms of the nation state. In other words, by focusing on individuals and the state as the key levels of analysis, Schama ignores the world of organizations. As organization theorists, we are fortunate that Law (1986) and Cooper (1992) have spoken of the *Portuguese* East India Company from which we might learn something of the VOC. An organization such as the Portuguese East India Company enacted 'control at a distance' (Cooper 1992: 258–60). This is where control is exercised either through the substitution of a 'symbol' for direct human involvement or by bringing that which is cut off by a boundary nearer, yet still holding it at a remove, or by both of these means. As for the latter, the construction of astronomical tables of solar declination (Law 1986: 252) kept the sun at a distance but allowed much better navigation by having those tables on board the ship. As for the former, let us consider the use of symbols by that major competitor to the Portuguese East India company—VOC—and seek to add something to Schama's decidedly non-organizational analysis.

Styles as weapons of, and against, empires

According to Harm Stevens (1998: 6–7), the VOC was:

> a complex organization with many different facets. It was both merchant and shipowner, as well as shipbuilder; in some parts of Asia it was regarded as a kind of sovereign; at sea, but also on land, the VOC was powerful and feared; moreover, as a transport company, the VOC was the principal intermediary between Europe and Asia, bringing goods and people—and with people, ideas—from one continent to another. The VOC was a multinational *avant la lettre* with trading posts spread throughout Asian and Africa.

The artefacts created, manufactured, and transported to Batavia, VOC's HQ, were designed to bring Dutch life to Asia and to emplace therein 'what it was to be Dutch'. The aim was to ensure that the essence of Dutchness was in a position of dominance within Batavia, and the chosen mechanism was the company. In effect, then, the VOC was 'the exponent of Dutch culture' (Stevens 1998: 7) and fulfilled this function (as the British East India Company was to do later, and elsewhere), by concluding treaties with foreign rulers, building fortresses, appointing governors, maintaining an army, and upholding order in the interests of trade (Stevens 1998: 17). Its vehicle for 'action at a distance' was the 'armed merchantman'. Most important, however, was the portability of Dutch culture so that, once en-lightened by the Enlightenment, it could be packed up, taken in these armed merchantmen in the form of clocks, clothing, weapons, tools, and ceremonies to be deposited in Batavia and beyond. This emplacement of understandings took the form of language, of course, but of architecture too. In Batavia, one would have seen 'European' buildings (for that, read Dutch), where factories, civic buildings, churches, the orphanage, and the council house all looked as if they might have been brought from Amsterdam. The styles of the empire reflect the power of the military and their use of a cultural might in the production of subordination against opposition.

Yet cultural might is always, everywhere, inadequate. We must remember that in contemporary Afghanistan, stylistic differences between US troops and Afghan citizens create mutual distaste and disgust. The American troops are reported to find the Afghan lack of 'cleanliness' revolting whereas US troops urinating and swearing in public create equal feelings of distaste. The English are viewed throughout Europe by many as cruel to their children and generally unclean. So we are dealing here with stereotypes which play a significant role in styling differences.

Styles have reflected the political interests of the elite in making sure their grip on power is demonstrable, on an everyday basis, for slave and citizen alike. But the slave retains some base level of stylistic control. The uniformity of controlled behaviour that is sought is achieved by indicating a 'taste' that is imperial and which is unchallengeable. Indeed, imperialism often entails subjects wearing a uniform. But once opposition is able to articulate itself, it often embraces stylistic differences to demonstrate this political differentiation. Opposition tends at first to be small scale, meeting in private and in secret, communicating in code and argot, adopting mechanisms for identifying members that are not known personally, and for preventing ingress by the agents of the powerful. In this set of tasks, such an oppositional group seeks to develop a stylistic inversion from the Other it opposes. Starting in small ways, symbols, artefacts, and encoded design items come to reflect opposition. As confidence in opposition forces grow, distinctive patterns and colours are adopted for flags, team strips, uniforms, and standards to make the comparison clear and bright.

When looking in the UK at the rise of Punk fashion in the 1970s, for example, the concept of opposition is essential. The distinctive principles of organizing that those engaged in 'the war of the flea' tend to adopt in direct opposition to bureaucracy render up quite distinctive principles by which they operate. The state does not find these easy to comprehend, and, by not understanding them, often fails to overcome the opposition. Similarly, the guardians of high street fashion found a youth movement of the kind represented by Punk very difficult to deal with, let alone understand. In the beginning of hostilities, guerrilla units of this type tend to go 'underground' in reality as well in metaphor. They are units of the darkness, not of the daylight. They are designed, in other words, to be opposed through their differences with the powerful. Opposition in style creates, reflects, and is created by opposition along many political and economic dimensions at the level of design structure, format, and embellishment. Yet, of course, we know how incorporation works. Fashion is appropriated; guerrilla armies are decorated and become the key apparatus of the fledgling state.

In drawing this chapter to a conclusion we are faced with a world of Difference and of Opposition. How can it still be maintained that 'style' remains comprehensible in the face of so many idioms? The answer to this lies in finding, within 'style', universal questions that most societies attempt to deal with in one way or another. There is not one design structure, then, but nor is there an infinitude of them. Here is where the notion of pattern books might come to the fore, because a book of patterns is the collection of possibilities that exist to address recurring problems of a material and ideational kind. This is not to embrace the search for some universal *'zeitgeist'* but is rather to understand the plurality of *'problematiques'* in which styles pit themselves.

The concept of *problematique* raises the issue of the generality of the sorts of questions that stand the test of time, and which are deeply embedded in many idealist philosophies, as well as those of a more materialist bent. My argument is that the questions remain really quite similar, but it is the answers that differ dramatically. These questions revolve around deep existential anxieties. What is nature? What is humanity? What is time? What is space? My claim is that it is in the answering of these sorts of questions undertaken by humans that we can distantly perceive patterns. It is these patterns that the present book seeks to explore through the linear geometry of the cube. The 3D nature of the cube means that it is imperative that I lay out each of the three 'lines' which create each of the dimensions. This I will do in the next chapter. But looking at lines is only part of this task.

Thus, I intend in Part III to look at the key principles behind design that are dependent upon using the geometry of a cuboid space. I shall sequence the subsequent three chapters on *lines*, *points*, and *planes* in that order. This part seeks to put *content into form* by bringing material dealt within Parts II (content) and Part I (form) respectively, into the context of cuboid geometry.

Part III
Content into Form

6

Lines of Fight

Chapter 5, as the last chapter in Part II, attempted to lay out the stylistic content of organizing. I turn my attention in this part to putting that content into a geometric form. The creation of the particular geometry of the cube will be achieved through specific attention to *lines*, *points*, and *planes*. Devoting a chapter to each of these three elements in turn, Part III moves incrementally in building up a cubic volume. As we proceed, the material developed in Part II will be decanted into the cubic void of the chapters which form Part III. In this way I hope to say something about the location of, and interrelationships between, fundamental styles of organizing.

Beginning here with the 'line', I seek to *out*line the basic parameters of the '*design envelope*' in which system and organizational structuring, processing, and design take place—both in time and in space—and show that this 'design envelope' can also be observed and analysed through attention to the variety of architectural design 'styles'—both in time and in space. I hope to demonstrate that whilst there is a huge range of possibilities through which humans might organize their lives, the constraints of the human body, our cognitive limitations in space and time, and our relationship to nature mean that these arrangements for organizing ourselves are necessarily limited to an 'envelope' of possibilities.

Please note that here I shall deal with architecture and design first, then look to organization theory and politico-economic systems, but not because of any acceptance of a hierarchy of knowledge and a belief that the second always depends upon the first. This ordering is simply to build upon material in Part II whilst it is fresh in the reader's mind. I might have just as easily begun with organization theory and shown how its concerns for an order of patterning are mirrored in architecture. It should be clear by now that it is my view that all four disciplinary areas share common overlapping interests in patterning, and because of their component parts they are overlapping endeavours intersecting in a number of interesting places.

Lines of Fight

In Deleuze and Guattari (1988: 202–7) there is a discussion of the notion of 'lines of flight'. These, we are told, are the most difficult lines of all. Florence Julien had extracted 'lines of flight' from photographs and, within the blur, the observer is able to see that children leaving school have a different line of flight from demonstrators being chased by the police. Autistic children have 'lines of drift' rather than 'customary lines'. Deleuze and Guattari (1988: 204) say that there is nothing more active than a line of flight amongst humans and animals. Yet a line of flight lies dormant, it pre-exists social interaction, and awaits the human before it explodes. So lines of flight are immanent in the social field awaiting an explosion.

This notion, then, is seen a key conceptualization in Deleuze and Guattari's theoretical development. Since their advocacy of 'nomadology' is based upon movement, particularly in relationship to its extremely powerful opposite, Royal science, it is not surprising that they speak of 'flight'. In the face of overwhelming odds, that response is how one survives. Here, however, I want to talk about lines of *fight* between styles, where the contestation between perspectives is made clear, even though it is contestation only across the horizontal plane, between powers of creative equivalence. It should be obvious here that by speaking of 'fight' I am pursuing the notion that styles reflect, perhaps above all, the politics of opposition.

As Ingold (2007) shows, 'lines' have a history all of their own. The line is, according to Chevalier and Gheerbrant (1996: 610), the symbol of intellectual and moral rectitude. Thus, the 'line' represents a threat to the labyrinthine, the twisted, the coiled, as well as to opponents drawn up across 'the lines'. Everywhere, since the bent are seen as enemies of the straight, linearity is dangerous. It brings on many changes. The line in the shape of the wide boulevard is antithetical to the convoluted 'shambles' of plebeian life. The front line in World War I was an articulation of the principles of linearity and invoked the industrialization and mechanization of war on a massive scale (Pick 2001). The line therefore is a creature of rationality and, if driven straight, often carries all before it. It is, perhaps, the essence of Royal science. Violence, cruelty, and injustice await the non-aligned.

We have already seen that the notion of 'battle' is often invoked in discussion of competing styles where opposition between stylistic expressions is represented as hostile and bloody. But I do not simply wish to draw upon dichotomizing slashes. Of course, philosophical antinomies are important and 'lines of fight' do involve other discussions that have an edge to them. Yet battle lines can be drawn up in places where philosophical dualities have *not* yet trodden. For example, Henri Bergson said in *Creative Evolution* (1907): 'In reality, life is a movement, materiality is the inverse movement, and each of these two movements is simple... Of these two currents, the second runs counter to the first, but the first obtains, all the same, something from the second. There results between them a *modus vivendi*, which is organization' (quoted in Roland Recht, *Believing and Seeing* 2008: 49).

For Bergson then, 'organization' is the name of the *modus vivendi* between the counter movement of materiality and movement. For him, it is *not* a battle line because he speaks of a *modus vivendi*, an agreement to live together, via negotiation. However, let us recognize that any *modus vivendi* comes out of struggles and contestation. Without them to begin with, no ways of coexistence would be necessary. In fact, 'organization' was a concept of hard-won liberation from the Ancien Régime. It suggested the end of ineffectual aristocratic rule and a drive to understand how the organs of state could and should interact for efficiency and good governance. Saint Simon had picked up this idea a century before Bergson, and portrayed it as a key concept for the management of the new post-Revolutionary French state (Clegg and Dunkerley 1980). One hundred years later, in a France again racked by social unrest, Bergson claimed there is a mode of existence which stands in a counter movement to its own self. Since he was a philosopher of 'becoming' more than of 'being', the search for movement and change in a situation of political conservatism exercised him considerably. This tension he identified, between vital movement and materiality, runs through this part of the current chapter.

Alongside this particular tension lies another contradiction; that of 'rationality' on one hand and of 'feeling' on the other. One person who attempted to tie both these particular contradictions together was Paul Frankl, whose quote below begins this book. He said, 'By "style" is meant a unity of form governed by a few basic principles. In this book these principles will be clarified by examples' (Paul Frankl, *Gothic Architecture* 2000: 33). And of course, *Styles of Organizing* also seeks to show that a few basic principles lie behind a unity of form. And I intend to incorporate Frankl's duality within my geometry, presenting it as but one strand of three.

In order to present his 'few basic principles', Frankl worked out an extremely sophisticated system of stylistic interpretation using this dimension of rationality/feeling, called *Das System*. He died at Princeton in 1962 whilst working on *Zu Fragen des Stils*, which was not published until 1988. Within it, he argued for the use of 'membrology', which is the study of the 'membra' that are to be found in each style. In ways not totally unrelated to the 'branes' now being invoked in the search for the missing seven or eight dimensions that hold antimatter, Frankl sees membranes as relevant and having explanatory value. For Frankl, each membrum was saturated in one of two polarities and each style could not be understood 'exhaustively, either by description, denomination, or classification of the membra alone, or by recognition of their stylistic polar oppositions alone: each must be grasped jointly in their reciprocal relationships. Each membrum, even, is saturated with one of these two polarities' (Frankel 2001: 15).

Lines of Fight

This is a complex argument, resonating in places with contemporary physics, but what I take from it is this. These particular ideational antinomies, as identified by Frankl, represent polarities along a line of contestation, each saturated in difference from the Other. He presents these tensions between positions as the basic principle by which style may be identified. It is this idea from Frankl of the 'saturation of polarities' in dealing with styles that I find extremely helpful, and one I hope to elaborate upon.

The saturation of polarities

My ambition in this book is to clarify, in part through a detailed and saturated analysis of polarities, how humans organize themselves in space according to a large but finite number of ways of addressing their relationship to understanding in what ways *types of knowledge* are valorized, what *relationship to Nature* they enjoy and how they see the competing relevance of the *past*, the *present*, and the *future*. In this chapter, I turn to a consideration of these major dimensions of the design cube, each conceptualized as a line of fight. Each dimension is conceived of as a straight line and is analytically placed here to emphasize the centrality of these elements for a human understanding of their position in space. The human's place in space may be conceived of as an intertwining of nature and nurture, of phenomena and noumena, of subject and object, of the built environment and the given environment, of aesthetics and anaesthetics. Every positioning provides for us a way of organizing *and* a way of not organizing. The ways in which this understanding is conceptualized I here call upon as indicative of styles of organizing.

I represent 'styles' as occupying particular positions in debates which, and it is important to note this, *social* scientists would recognize. I try not to ignore the natural sciences and the humanities on these issues but my positioning is obviously going to be that of a social scientist. These debates will be characterized in this chapter as occupying 3D linear spaces with a myriad of intermediate positions being possible. Because this is a chapter based upon the 'line', it is crucial that we see the possibility of many 'points' being occupied along the constraints of containment upon the straight line. So, bearing in mind Deleuze and Guattari's (1988) indication of the importance of middles, within these lines of fight many intermediate positions are possible.

Three key debates which are significant to social scientists and those in the arts and humanities, but which appear to be rarely surfaced by everyday working architects for discussion and debate, seem important to discuss. These are why, how, and when the style expresses any respect for and level of detail about:

A. human feelings and human rationality
B. the relationship between past and future time
C. humanity as a part of Nature and humanity as apart from nature (NB upper case and lower case are deliberately different).

These, the reader will note, are not totally at odds with those identified in *The Order of Things* as three 'epistemological regions', namely biology, economics, and philology (Foucault 1992: 355). But readers will be asking themselves, no doubt, what could be gained by such a drawing up of these particular lines of contestation. It is my argument that each style has these three hidden assumptions built into it, and is necessarily derived from, and is productive of, its positioning in relation to these elements. Each style has to take a position, whether it is aware of it or not, to the questions of human understanding, to times past and to nature. Rather than use the word 'naturalism', which has a particular meaning in epistemology, I am going to employ the term 'Naturality' to express more succinctly what constellation of meaning I seek. In this chapter, because I am dealing with lines of fight, I have chosen to concentrate upon these lines of fight as articulating contestation between extreme polar positions upon the lines as thus:

Sensibility	Rationality
Sedimentism	Rupturism
Naturality (a part of Nature)	A-naturality (apart from nature)

Before going on to articulate these extremities of each line of fight, let me reiterate the importance of all those intermediate points upon these lines. So, for example, it may be that 'bounded rationality' or *'wertrationalitat'* exists in intermediate positions on the first dilemma. On the second line of fight it is possible to conceive of varieties of evolutionism being possible in the intermediate spaces of that line, whilst on the third dimension human cognition can be seen to put us in, and yet separate from, nature in its rawness. Please note that I do not see these intermediate positions as being necessarily superior because of their 'middlingness'. The 'golden mean' for me is by no means the same as the German Idealist's search for an 'identical subject-object' that I will attempt to seek at the close of this book. That is much more complicated a notion than occupation of the middle ground.

Strand A

Turning first to the extremities of these dimensions, it is suggested that each artistic style finds it incumbent upon itself to adopt a position in the writings of its adherents to the question of whether human feelings in the sense of the world of emotion should be relevant to our human understandings. This means not only a commitment to a search for understanding ourselves, but also of the world in which we live. In English we tend to call this *sensibility*. For those committed to this 18th-century notion of sensibility, the world of feelings is the one aspect of the real world which makes meaningful experience possible (Bragg 2002, Radio 4). Diderot described 'sensibility' in his *Encyclopaedia* of 1755 as 'the moving spirit which animates belief' and it became associated with a keen appreciation of the natural world and of deep capacity to feel. Thus, in Laurence Sterne's *A Sentimental Journey*, written in 1785, the lead character Yorick speaks to the reader thus:

> I sat down close by her, and Maria let me wipe the tears away as they fell, with my handkerchief. I then steeped it in my own—and then in hers—and then in mine—and then I wiped hers again—and as I did it, I felt such undescribable emotions within me, as I am sure could not be accounted for from any combinations of matter and motion. (I am positive I have a soul; nor can all the books with which materialists have pestered the world ever convince me to the contrary.)

Here then, Sensibility's main concerns appear to be the importance of 'undescribable emotions' and the soul—and directly in the face of 'matter' and 'motion', and the materialists who speak of them. In 1808, the German educationalist, Niethammer, described the study of Greek and Latin as *literae humaniores* and showed how the Renaissance had been centred on the revival of this interest in human-centred learning as opposed to God-centred learning. The opposition of secular humanism to Christian theology allowed the questioning of clerical dogma and set up the possibility that the views and feelings of human beings had a value in and of themselves. Furthermore, that respect for the basic humanity of people underpins all other human rights. It allows also the rejection of the view that human beings are merely depraved animals, or the view that they can make no free choices of their own, or that there is no meaning to human life. Feelings and emotions are seen as remarkably unique to humans and as differentiating them from the baser animal kingdoms. Art which allows the expression of emotion and is then shared with others is seen as the highest cultural form. The sharing of pain and passion, enjoyment and frustration, the agony and the ecstasy, are all encouraged in this high respect for emotion and feelings. Jane Austen's contribution to this issue comes, of course, in *Sense and Sensibility*, published in 1811, wherein it is by no means clear that sensibility is to be highly valued.

We are talking here, of course, of more than emotions and feelings. 'Humanity' is a huge concept as suggested by that notion of the 'humanities' and obviously involves a number of elements over and beyond the issue of emotion. Not least, there is the issue of *selfhood*. We have an 'identity' parade for our consideration, of notions that are related but different. For example, 'self', 'I', 'me', 'individual', 'ego', 'id', 'us', 'we' are all aspects of selfhood which share similarities but they also hide differences. And these differences are often glossed over by theorists of the subject. 'I' and 'me' are distinctive in that one suggests the 'I' is the prime mover and is active and dynamic. 'Me' suggests a passive recipient of actions and encourages the notion of reaction. Furthermore, the individual need not be a 'self', for in many branches of psychology the individual is a reactive, passive, unreflexive respondent to external stimuli. 'Identity' is also a weasel word, suggesting either a plurality of subject positions or an entity of the 'id' which is complete, whole, and unfragmented. When it comes to 'we' and 'us', what is meant by selfhood is the human's self-conceptualization of their place in relation to other humans. This differs enormously across cultures. In Southern African Ubuntu philosophy (Necku Nyathi 2009), for example, the conceptualization of selfhood depends upon recognition by others. The self exists only in relation to being seen appreciatively as one of a community. The central greeting is the key to understanding this culture of collectivism, for it is 'I see you.' Your existence as a full member of the collectivity is recognized in this greeting. In, let us say, Californian approaches to the self, there is no requirement for large collective recognition since a narcissistic self -regard (Lasch 1979) will suffice. Self-help books propound the virtues of individuated bootstrapping, whereas in many cultures such egocentric strategies for dealing with life would not be understood or valued.

Whatever one's orientation to selfhood, however, it is clear that it is an issue locked deep into the heart of sensibility. The rise of the 'individual' as a concept within the Enlightenment has to be seen as part and parcel of this concern for 'ego' rather than the state, the clan, the tribe, the village. Individuality thus became a concern for the burgeoning middle classes of the Western world. Meanwhile, it has been argued, scientific research was able to escape from dogma without the notion of individualism. Science developed through a new professionalism and the protection of the collectivity offered by the company of others in the likes of the Royal Society and the Lunar Society. However, the rise of Darwinism, Utilitarianism, marginal economics, psychology as a science, and so on, all push for an individuated approach to social understandings.

Rationality

Much has been written on the rise of rationality. Townley (2008) offers a good overall picture of its complexity. Wilson (1970: xii) argues that it involves 'systematic observation, the conscious process of creating well defined categories and employing them in in accordance with equally conscious logical principles'. He goes on to say that rationality seeks to order knowledge systematically 'in value-free, emotionally neutral, abstract propositions' (Wilson 1970: xii). Clearly, this involves some sense of humanity's difference from both the animal world and from a world of superstition and magic. Rationality is associated with the rise of science, calculation, and logic. It is seen as essential to civilized debate because of its valorization of reason and the full use of the 'mind' by all humans.

Put crudely, rationality relates to a method in which the criterion of the truth is not sensory but intellectual and deductive. In most views, it stands opposed to 'faith' and to the Church, which rests for its power and prestige upon blind belief. 'Sight' is crucial to rationality in terms of how the Enlightenment (sic) approaches an end to benightedness. Rationality is profoundly anti-clerical and anti-traditional. It tries to seek means by which to achieve ends in this world, not the next. So religion's claim to faith through emotion is seen as deeply problematic. The positive conceptualization of feelings which is at the core of aesthetics is thus questioned in rationality's first flush of vitality. Rationality seeks to use ratios and ratiocination, numbers and deep thought, in an attempt to open up 'Nature and Nature's laws [which] lay hid in night' to the blinding light of inspection. Rationality, of course, is not usually thought of as a 'style' at all but it places the human being as subject to well-known mathematical and natural laws in which individuals have no right whatsoever to assume they can escape from these underlying forces of nature. What we feel—our sensibility if you will—is irrelevant within the constant struggle for the survival of the fittest.

The only part of the human body Cartesianism recognizes as important is the mind. And whilst this may lead to scientific developments which the world had not dreamt of, this emphasis on the power of thought, untrammelled by feeling, is a difficult position to adopt with any happy consequences for meaningful discussions of aesthetics and sensibility. Rationality is cold and hard-hearted—indeed, it has no heart at all. Valverde's famous picture of the anatomized man shows him holding his own skin which has been flayed off in one hand, whilst the knife which he has supposedly used in this process is in the other. The skin, the site of pain and feeling, once stripped away, allows rational contemplation of underlying structures by the viewer who feels no pain whatsoever. The in-compassionate viewer is placed as central to rational linearity because they are permitted 'some sense of perspective' over those who are emotionally involved. The rise of rationality therefore throws up the likes of Reverend Malthus and the allied, if crude, notion that people who breed like rabbits deserve to die like flies. Mathematics can show that death is rational and is not to be grieved. It also gives us Dean Swift's satirical reaction to a faux rationality, based on his deep sensibility, that the people of Ireland should eat their own children, thereby solving both the problem of rural overpopulation and the Irish famine (Swift 1991).

Rationality's success in creating a scientific and technological 'revolution' meant that its approach spread across the globe. It gave rise to approaches built variously upon determinism, nihilism, and fatalism, in which human emotion and feelings became seen in a somewhat reductionist way. Sensibility was seen as derived from the animal origins of our species and as the product of our mammalian physiology. Once treated as no different from other species, and as subject to the same laws of nature, humanity can be seen as an economic resource to be exploited as are any other animals in the field. Humanity's beastly pain and suffering have no more relevance than the cries of animals entering the slaughterhouses. Once subject to the gaze of rationality and the apportionment of value that comes through 'rationing', everyday human consciousness becomes seen as a product of socialization, propaganda, and education, particularly if it is provided by the church. Therefore any products of it, in the form of the arts, say little about the 'real' human condition and much more about its conditioning by pre-Enlightenment purveyors of faith. Feelings, then, are incidental and get in the way of international progress. They should be dispensed with by great thinkers.

It is believed by some philosophers that any good rationale must be independent of emotions, personal feelings, or any kind of instincts. In universities we tend to support notions of value-free objectivity and the whole Enlightenment enterprise. Any process of evaluation or analysis, that may be called rational, is expected to be highly objective, logical, and 'mechanical'. If these minimum requirements are not satisfied, i.e. if a person has been, even slightly, influenced by personal emotions, feelings, instincts, or culturally specific moral codes and norms, then the analysis may be termed non-rational or even irrational, due to the injection of subjective bias. However, it is evident from modern cognitive science and neuroscience studying the role of emotion in mental function (including topics ranging from flashes of scientific insight to making future plans) that no human has ever satisfied this criterion of rationality, except perhaps an insane person with no affective feelings whatsoever. Thus, such an idealized form of rationality is best exemplified by computers, and not people.

Notwithstanding the weaknesses of idealizing rationality as a point of reference, the power of the concept of rationality is such that we live with it every day. We are asked to produce arguments, to debate, to provide evidence, to think for ourselves, and to question, to read, and to write. Without rationality and the rise of reason, the world would be a different and much more scary place.

The *intermediate* positions associated with the likes of 'bounded rationality' allow us to perceive rationality as, at least in part, infused with something like emotion. Following writers such as Simon (1950), the ways in which decisions are made cannot be anything other than partial because complete information is not available to us as human beings. We have a partiality that comes from the position in which we stand and the time at which we make a decision. And speaking of time, we are often time constrained in decision-making so that we make decisions without the 'full' facts being available. The weapons of mass destruction have not yet been found—but let us decide as if they will be. We know 'in our heart' that it is the right decision anyway.

It is certainly possible for rationality to be seen as a certain type of sensibility. Julian Huxley's analysis of the Tennessee Valley Authority, *TVA: Adventure in Planning* (1943) is indicative of this 'intermediate' perspective on rationality. In the foreword by John Winant, US ambassador to the UK at the time of publication, there is an extraordinary outburst against private enterprise that jars with today's contemporary easy acceptance of corporate capitalism's involvement in everything. Winant says (Huxley 1943: 6): 'In spite of the fact that private enterprise had neither envisioned this project nor was implemented to carry it through, vested interests in the United States fought it with a bitterness that has seldom been equalled in any controversy involving private property and the public welfare.' The sensibility, then, that drives Winant, and to some extent Huxley, is a 'welfare' and 'warfare' rationality, where the state is driven by concerns for the public good (Reed 2010: 561–4). It is easy to forget that this was the post-war climate in which organization theory grew and flourished, and that one of its first interests was in the TVA and the 'type' of rationality that the state utilized in the UK and the USA in the 1940s (Selznick 1949). In particular, the Columbia School (Haveman 2010: 586) used the research there as a launch pad for developing the critique of Weber's work throughout the study of organizations.

Huxley's book begins with an organizational chart of the huge set of enterprises involved in the TVA and points out that whilst the English Lake District comprises 25 square miles of water, the TVA produced, through planned rationality in the service of the 'New Deal', lakes of 1,100 square miles in area. He goes on to look at the architecture of the dams built, the electricity-generating facilities, the housing for the workers that was required, the construction of highways, lookout buildings, and petrol stations. The chief architect of the TVA was a Mr Wank. His belief was in 'good, honest, efficient structures and never mind the mayonnaise' (Huxley 1943: 74)! Part of this drive to the utilitarianism of good structures was the 'demountable house', which was mass produced in sections as 'war emergency housing'. This may seem a very natural form of corporate rationality but it was a product of *wertrationalitat*—driven, rather, by the corporatist values of a wartime struggle. To quote Mr Wank once more (Huxley 1943: 75), the TVA 'consciously adopted architecture as one of the instruments of policy in building up a sounder, more vital civilisation in the Valley'. One must note that it was in a book published by The Architectural Press that Huxley (1943: 77) waxes lyrical on the TVA. 'Here is architecture on a scale dictated by the age,' yet 'It is in the design of detail that the architect, as the great humanizer, has played a magnificent role' (Huxley 1943: 94). It is precisely this tension that marks out an intermediate step on the sensibility–rationality line of fight. And it also shows quite graphically how organization theory and architecture closely hold hands in extreme social conditions.

Let me now go to a discussion of the next line of fight—the saturated polarity of Strand B.

Sedimentism

This is one end of a saturated polarity where time is crucial to space. It is famously the fourth dimension. The particular meaning I wish to attach to this gnostic statement (that time is crucial to space) goes beyond the mere notion that it is the fourth dimension. My point is that respect for time, for its passage, and for its richness leads to a particular set of styles of organizing—a pattern book of possibilities. It is, of course, the essence of political conservatism that the past is seen as well worth preserving, and that all change is or should be gradual, and that 'at the end of the day' all is for the best in the best of all possible worlds. Good men and women have struggled hard to get a society to how it is today and nothing else beyond their constant efforts could have been done to improve it. Otherwise, it would be different from and worse than the way it looks, feels, and functions.

On the other hand, of course, the defence of tradition and what appears to have been laid down in the originating myths of a society can create dystopian environments. Those that seek to use the Bible, for example, to defend a policy regime which is hostile to the place of women in the Church, or of seeking to punish homosexuals for their orientation, tend to reflect the importance of tradition to 'our' way of life. The literal, unquestioning use of laws enshrined in the deep past can lead to societies in which social progress has been held back for centuries. From this perspective, severe human problems originate from accretions of power effects.

Sedimentism is the name I wish to attach to the idea that social structures and systems lay down patterns in the sands of time and, through such accretion from low bases, we have reached today's heights. Looking back allows one to see how layer upon layer of social interactions has been accreted one upon the other over decades and centuries. The future will be made up in exactly the same way, by exactly the same processes.

Surprisingly perhaps, Althusser's work on structuralism (1969) comes close to something akin to a strong version of sedimentism. Writing in part to explain the failure of the Parisian 'events' of 1968 to radically change French society, Althusser turned his back upon explanations based on direct action by students and the workers. For him, it is not humans who make history but particular configurations of structures which arise at given points in time. Based upon a notion of the 'totality', his 'structuralism' does not see the totality as simply made up of parts, but that each part has the totality contained within it. Generally speaking, the economic 'practice' acts as the 'structure in dominance' but on occasions this may be replaced by one of the other three practices (political, ideological, and theoretical/scientific respectively) and it is they which become the structure in dominance. Economic factors, then, are not seen as causal in all circumstances. But it is nevertheless deep and hidden structures which govern surface social relations, albeit separated as they are, by many layers of a structured 'reality'. There is little place for the political activist here, for they are put in a difficult position. Althusser claims that real objects, and reality itself, are so sharply separated from the theoretical world of the activist and scholar that empiricism is not worthwhile. It can tell one nothing of note about deeply hidden structures.

And why is this categorized as sedimentism? It is because (to use a geological metaphor) the surface and the deep are differentiated one from the other. Behaviour and structure are very different strata, located at quite different levels. And most importantly, each 'social formation' has to be understood as a separate 'case study' in which different conjunctions of practices, beset by different contradictions, play out in specific historical events. Surface events bubble away as a result of a deep play of forces far below—but as humans we can never predict these 'events' or fully comprehend them. We can certainly not control them. For Althusser, then, structuralism offers a way of comprehending stability and the absence of change. Through it, one can envisage the totality as ongoing and unstoppable and as a social formation built for survival, despite all the efforts of members of the society to bring about change of it and within it.

Although less severe in his sedimentism than Althusser, it appears to me that the work of the mid-career Anthony Giddens is reflective of such an approach. In his writings in the 1980s, especially where he focuses upon 'structuration theory', we see some discussion of these processes of sedimentation. For example, he says that 'the rules agents draw upon to produce and reproduce their activities organize practices that are deeply sedimented in space and time' (Giddens 1989: 256). He goes on: 'As reproduced across time and space, systems of interaction and social relationships have a "fixity" deriving from their institutionalized character.' Moreover, 'structural constraint' for Giddens (1989: 258) means that 'Examining the nature of such

Sedimentism

institutionalization is inseparable from analysing the recursive characteristics of structure.' Thus, 'study of the "everyday" or the "day to day" forms a basic part of the analysis here, many seemingly trivial or mundane features of what people do being the actual "groundwork" of larger scale institutions' (Giddens 1989: 298). Sedimentation here is in the form of 'groundwork'.

According to Gregory (1989: 187), Giddens focuses upon the theorization of 'the problem of order as in large measure a problem of pattern'. Clearly this is of interest to a book such as this one, committed as it is to understanding patterns. To do this pattern work, Giddens deals with time-space routinization and time-space distanciation, both in the context of 'system integration' at a conceptual level of the whole system. Time-space routinization is to do with the 'patterning' of social practices in time and space which draw upon structures of rules and resources. In this way through patterning, time and space enter into the most stable forms of social reproduction (Gregory 1989: 192). This stabilization is also brought about by the self-assurance allowed by routines, the ontological security they offer, and the cementing of the institutional–individual linkages through repetition. Sedimentation, for Giddens, then, is the routinization of patterning through 'repetition and cementing'.

Giddens sees the separation of synchronic and diachronic approaches—statics and dynamics—as having little utility, and he rarely uses the word 'crisis'. Gregory (1989: 202) makes the point that even 'the process of continuous transformation ... is barely registered in existing formulations of structuration theory'. Also, by taking on board some of Hagerstand's ideas on time-space geography, Giddens apparently becomes embroiled in a 'suspended animation' where stasis is seen as the norm. He minimizes the volatility of time-space distanciation wherein social relations are stretched across time and space. He sees everyday and mundane settings as being 'drawn upon' and as having a 'substantially given character'. In short, according to Gregory (1989: 213), 'it is easy to see why structuration theory is sometimes mistaken for a reproduction model in which power freezes routines in place'. As for his view of the past, Giddens (1989: 278) himself admits that 'it sounds as though I was proposing a romantic view of the past, in which people lived in harmony with one another in the local community and in harmony with nature'.

Now the characterization of the work of Giddens as representing sedimentism may come as a shock to some readers but the major clue is in the very name of his theory of 'structuration'. It is not a theory of 'activation'—for surely he could have expressed the choice to start from that 'end' of the duality and he certainly does not. Indeed, action is given a low priority from the 'off'. For as we have seen, he says (Giddens 1989: 256) that 'In my usage, structure is what gives *form* and *shape* to social life, but it is not *itself* that form and shape.' Thus, it is structure that provides the 'fixity' in which action can take place, but fixity is pretty much what it is all about. Sedimentism is clearly reflected in such an overview statement of his own work.

Opposed to this position on a line of fight is *rupturism*. Here, disrespect for the past and its achievements leads to another disparate set of approaches. The cult of the new, the revolutionary, the detotalization of what existed, the pursuit of progress, all lead to an embracing of an ahistoricism. Now 'historicism' is a difficult term—so difficult, in fact, that I have chosen not to use it here when some might think it is that of which I speak. But I have found it so full of contradictory meaning that an exposition of it as a term in use seems unhelpful. Rupturism appears to fit in with Henry Ford's misquoted aside, 'History is bunk,' which reflects such thinking very well. As a member of the 'Progressives', Ford had a particular orientation to the future and its relation to the past. Like many Progressives, he embraced efficiency, science, and control of the population's health and behaviour through state intervention and intrusive organizational means. Until very late in his life, he turned his back on what had gone on before in the USA, and embraced a progressive view of industrialism.

Now interestingly, both Althusser and Giddens are often seen as dealing with rupturism more effectively than most social theorists. As we have seen, Paul du Gay (2007) has Giddens down as an 'epochalist', nominating his 1994 and 1998 tracts on 'The Third Way' as suggesting the arrival of a new epoch. This schema in certain ways was taken up by the UK's incoming Labour government. But such is the concern in Althusser and Giddens (mid-career) to explain the *lack* of change that they focus upon the stabilizing effects of deep structures. If we are to find theorists of ruptures, we can do worse than gaze upon the later work of Zygmunt Bauman, whose attempts to make 'liquid' almost all forms of social formations demonstrate rupturism in action. According to Bauman (1995: 111), industrial labour seems to perform in the 20th century a 'disappearing act'; mass armies are no longer mobilized; regimentation of the population has ended; individuals' identities become under-defined, floating, and disembedded; privatization has replaced collectivization; de-institutionalization of processes of self-formation has occurred so that 'inadequacy' is more important now than 'deviation'; the modern individual is no longer the purveyor of goods but is a 'sensations-gatherer'. People move from handling objects which possess a mass and a solidity to being 'tasters' who lick and stroke ethereal impressions. The human body is now private property and is not part of the body politic. In short, everything changes.

The metaphor of movement is everywhere in social theory, literary criticism, cultural theory, and geography. As Cresswell tells us (in Benko and Strohmayer 1997: 360), 'Mobility is the order of the day. Nomads, migrants, travellers and explorers inhabit a world where nothing is certain or fixed.

Tradition and rootedness have the smell of death. Diaspora is everything. Monumentalism, the edifice, the rooted and the bound are firmly placed in the museum of modernity.' The romanticization of the 'nomad' concept in postmodernity, according to Cresswell, is a central part of the recent theorizings on all things mobile. That there has been huge interest in the last decade on the introduction of movement into considerations of space and what goes on within it seems undeniable. This shift has severe implications for organization studies because leading thinkers like Manuel Castells (1989: 142) claim: 'There is a shift, in fact, away from the centrality of the organizational unit to the network of information and decision. In other words, flows, rather than organizations, become the units of work, decision and output accounting.' Castells (1989: 171) further provocatively states that there has been a 'transformation of the flows of power into the power of flows'. This transformation—if it has occurred—surely means that much of organization studies is locked into studying theoretical objects and processes from outdated worlds. Whilst Luke (1992) has argued that there has been a shift from place to flow, from spaces to streams, and from organized hierarchies to disorganization, with one or two exceptions where the vortex has been invoked (for example Tsoukas 1987; Cooper and Burrell 1988; Chia 1999), organization theory has failed to pick up much on such supposed shifts.

This rapid movement in space and society is sometimes called fluidity, liquidity, or nomadism, or dromomania, or disorganized capitalism, or fast capitalism, and so on. What is apparent is that this movement is associated with activity, change, dynamism, and progress. It is associated with being on top of things in the sense of having one's finger on the pulse of the changing social world. It is therefore not at all unlike futurology, and many of the leading social theorists of change are in demand as pundits. What changes fast, then, is the object of the newly fashionable 'rupture' in which a caesurist break is identified with what has gone before. All this is in an effort to identify the shock of the new. Since the late, great sociologists at the end of the 19th century are always lauded for their ability to recognize the signs of newness in capitalistic industrialization at that time, there seems to be a pressure on today's leading sociologists to also lay claim to such insight in such an epochal way. It is shocking not to be new. Readers might wish to nominate their own aged candidates in the social sciences searching after a rupture—and an honour.

Evolutionism is a *middling point* on this line of fight. This is usually defined as 'the process by which structural reorganization is affected through time, eventually producing a form or structure which is qualitatively different from the ancestral form'. In this way it is an approach or set of approaches which allows qualitative change alongside quantitative change. Such theories tend to look to technologies, social structures, levels of energy utilization, values, and norms and ask when these become 'step functions' allowing changes to lead to new 'stages' of development. As such, evolutionary theories tend to become enmired in issues of 'progress' where inter alia the complexity of the division of labour, class structures, and intellectual sophistication are seen as indicators of increasing complexity and therefore of progress. They often seek to provide road maps of history. Eric Olin Wright (1989) argues that there are three elements to a theory calling itself 'evolutionary'. These, put crudely, are a sense of direction, a sense of 'improvement' (or at least 'stickiness downward'), and a mechanism permissive of 'upwards trajectory'.

Giddens (1989: 262–4) has accepted that his own typology of social forms is evolutionary, even if he wishes to avoid being labelled as a provider of a 'general theory of (historical) development'. Of course, Wright wishes to play upon the political consequences of such a view, with evolutionary notions of progress being steeped in occidentalism and besmirched with the taint of imperialism. These evolutionary ideas appear to be justifications for a despoiling colonialism and the patronizing of a more 'primitive' social organization than one based on capitalist industrialism. And the existence of two world wars, led by such civilized societies, further raises questions about progress as a telos behind social evolution. Talcott Parsons's later work (Parsons 1969) falls short of his earlier forays into social theory and seems to the 21st-century eye to be crass evolutionism of the worst ethnocentric kind. The apex of all human attainment and a model that we will, or should, all mimic (Bell 1974) appears to lie directly out of Parsons's window.

Today, neo-evolutionism offers something not associated with the notion of progress, nor of Western domination, nor of stages with a telos of industrial capitalism, but does allow for counterfactuals in 'evolution' and celebrates alternative pathways. So the intermediate positioning of approaches to rupturism and sedimentism is obvious and popular (Tonnies 2011; Sahlins 1960).

Let us now turn to Strand C and consider its saturated polarities.

Strand C

The question here is: 'Are members of humanity apart from nature or they are a part of Nature?' For dramatic and expositionary purposes in this section, if Nature is capitalized, then humanity is assumed to be a part of it. If nature is in the lower case, then the assumption is held to be that humanity is different from nature and is apart from it. Which position on this line of fight we might adopt is also a choice we face. Let us consider the latter issue first.

A part of Nature (Naturality)

The location of humanity in an environment provided by 'Nature' (with the 'n' fully capitalized in recognition of its importance) is a crucial element in considering styles. The modern cosmopolitan city dweller may assume that they live in an unnatural world where harnessed electricity means access to perpetual light, piped gas implies perpetual warmth, filtered water leads to no thirst or waterborne infestation, and refrigeration means no heat exhaustion. Nature is kept at bay through civic, metropolitan major public works. Yet, for 5.5 billion people on the planet, such luxuries are less available, and nature is less controlled. In the majority of places and spaces across the world, dehydrated, fly-infested, open-sewered communities predominate. Here, desert encroachment, rising sea levels, intensifying monsoons, new infestations of uncontrolled insects, hydro-politics, and exploitative aid programmes are much more common features. Nature has not been de-naturalized for 70 per cent of the world's current population.

Where there is a high respect for Nature, I am going to employ the term 'Naturality' wherein humanity is seen as part and parcel of the natural world. Here, humans are conceptualized as animals sharing the planet with the myriad other species that have developed, but this state of 'naturalness' is to be welcomed, rather than deplored, as it might well be by humanists. Since we are but one species on a planet of finite resources, there is emphasis on seeing humanity as sharing the eco-system, and on each generation being a custodian for the next one to come. It leads to approaches which seek to be non-exploitative. In architecture this means thinking about CO_2 emissions, particularly in the uses of concrete, recycling of materials, emplacement of buildings in the landscape, and landscaping. Green architecture has become popular—one is close to saying it has become big business—and even university buildings seek easy prizes for their greenness. John Urry (2011) has claimed that key to understanding the problems of university greenness is the termly migration of students across the planet, emitting huge amounts of carbon dioxide from the con trails of their flights back home, and then returning again to their universities across the globe at the same cost to the environment when terms restart. In a place like Tasmania, the Greens are currently active and strong and a section of the voting population is concerned to conserve and protect the environment. But another section of the island's population wishes to exploit its natural resources in mining, logging, and hydroelectric power for economic development. Styles of organizing adopted by Greens and Browns tend to differ—as we shall see.

With regard to the wilderness and its treatment from within this perspective, one finds a naturalistic version of the untamed wildness that is typical of

Romanticism. Here the human dread of, and unwillingness to tackle, the dangers of nature, raw in tooth and claw, produces a very different response to matters of taste and style than one finds at the opposite point in this line of fight. Simon Schama (1995) points to the very distinctive Roman and Germanic attitudes to the boreal forest and its consequences for thought. If one comes from the open grassland plains, or terraced olive groves, it is unlikely that the same aspects of nature will be held in regard as someone who emanates from small clearings in the closed forests. Tacitus saw Germania as being for the most part 'bristling forests and foul bogs' (Schama 1995: 76) and that the indigenous peoples were therefore 'children of nature'. Can there be, then, a style of organizing associated with the wilderness that in some way or other is 'authentic'? What would an aesthetic of unpredictable wildness look like? High respect for Nature, and the non-human world as repositories of unobtrusive enjoyment, as rendered visible in 'green architecture' and some attempts at gardening, will be dealt with when we look at organizational forms in relation to their basic assumptions in a later chapter.

Apart from nature (A-naturality)

Lester Frank Ward (1841–1913), a geologist and paleontologist by training but a sociologist by choice, theorized that the 'law of nature' had been superceded by the 'law of the mind' (Ward 2012). Humans were no longer subject to nature, having invented themselves through pure cognition. He stressed that humans create goals for themselves and strive to realize them, using modern scientific methods. In 'nature' there is no such intelligence and awareness guiding the non-human world. Whereas plants and animals adapt to nature, humanity *shapes* nature. So the relationships humans have with nature are also reflected in the tensions between the natural sciences and the humanities. The 19th century saw the scientists' and industrialists' attitude to 'nature' taking a dramatic form. Nature was presented figuratively as a secretive, veiled, female body which natural science should reveal unclad to the eyes of the scientific observer, and thus render Nature's body for malleable use by Progress's penetration. This imagery and attitude lead to a familiar world of gravity-defying skyscrapers, the megalopolis, and the welfare/warfare state wherein the pursuit of massive state-sponsored science and technology projects leaves the environment as a very low-status issue. Such a low respect for nature means that the place of humanity in the landscape is seen as legitimately exploitative, and sustainability is not seen as an issue of any note. And such an aversion to living in harmony with nature is evidenced, for example, in the Baroque period where nature could be and was 'controlled' through human artifice. Water is the best exemplar, perhaps, where it was to be used through intensive hydraulics as an item for stately decoration and not as a 'natural' force to be respected. In this view, derived from the Baroque, and found in the 17th century, but evident in many more besides, a building is emplaced to make as much startling impact on the environment as possible, and that is what its function is meant to be. The view that the resources of the planet are at the disposal of the builders is a long one and the rivalling of God in seeking to make buildings as shocking as possible goes back at least to the notion of the Tower of Babel. If the wilderness is to be tamed, rendered tillable, cultivated, and built upon, then that consideration of the built environment as exploitative is to be expected.

The choice exists for styles to reflect upon how and where the natural is going to be subjected, on one hand, to constant assault or, on the other hand, where the 'Natural' will be respected as outside human control or wilful interference. Schama (1995: 7) is quite clear that the wilderness is as much a product of human craving and human framing as any garden. The wilderness does not name itself, nor does it venerate itself. Human beings do that. So again, we must recognize the existence of many *intermediate* positions where the notions of *stewardship* and sustainability attempt to keep both short-term economics at bay, sometimes with some success. Under the practice of 'stewardship', farmers receive extra payments for protecting watercourses, preventing soil erosion, preserving archaeological sites, and providing public access.

In the following quote by a Canadian environmentalist, we get some sense of the way in which stewardship is seen as straddling the ground between 'apart from nature' and 'a part of Nature'. 'Our choices at all levels individual, community, corporate, and government affect nature. And they affect us' (David Suzuki). This suggests that the middle ground to the debate lies in recognizing mutual interactions between humanity and nature but that they are separable entities. The rise of corporate social responsibility (CSR) also seeks to take a middle ground between the right of a corporation to do what it does vis à vis the environment, but also to respect its duties to the environment at the same time. We might debate where CSR ends up on these issues but in theory, it is an intermediate perspective on this particular line of fight.

Three lines of fight

What we have seen so far, then, are three key and separate dimensions to understanding stylistic difference. Now I understand that there are other lines of fight that exist in debates surrounding stylistic issues. In my view, these operate particularly at the level of embellishment but I am concentrating here upon patterning and 'pattern books'. Whilst the proponents of styles may not identify themselves with particular positions on these three dimensions of pattern structure, my argument here is that they *must* do so in one way or another—even if it is only at the level of their meta-theoretical assumptions. In other words, it is possible to discern the extent to which these elements of regard to human feelings/rationality, regard to the past, and regard to Nature are held by *any* particular style. At the level of its deep pattern, each style has to address these questions, however briefly, however reluctantly, however constrained. Any style has to demonstrate, whether it is aware of its values on this or not, what its stance is with regard—or lack of regard—towards sensibility, sedimentism, and Naturality.

Dicing with style—again

I have presented three lines of contestation above, with the clear probability that intermediate positioning in many pointed places is possible on each dimension. How then to progress from these lines of fight? My answer is by developing a 3D model of the interrelationships between the three dimensions—the three lines of fight—identified above. These issues, represented as conceptual continua, form three dimensions which each and every style in organizing, and each and every style in construction, must relate to in some way or other. At the end of each line of argument there is an end *point* which represents the extreme view of each and every position.

The three lines of fight I have suggested, we now know, are:

Sensibility	Rationality
Sedimentism	Rupturism
Naturality	A-naturality

And upon them are to be found many intermediate points. Allow me to be provocative. These three lines may be conceptualized as dealing with separate and distinct issues, so at the risk of gross simplification one might suggest that Strand A is more of an issue for the humanities and arts, Strand B is likely to exercise social scientists more than other areas of the academy, and Strand C is of most pressing concern to natural scientists. Clearly such a trichotomy is likely to raise many hackles and, at the margins, it would not work very well at all, as there is much of 'interstitial' interest going on. Interdisciplinary politics would make acceptance of such positioning difficult. However, I am reminded of Cooper's epigraph (Cooper 1998: 157) with which this book begins, suggesting the social sciences take their cues from 'literature, art theory and philosophy'. So I am keen not to constrain *Styles of Organizing* as to be active only on the terrain of social science, so the three dimensions adopted here are a gesture, not least towards a more 'inclusive' approach to architecture and design and organization. The 'will to form' is not the exclusive province of any of the branches of knowledge—but is deeply embedded in all three.

Since there is a distinct logic behind each of the lines of fight and, moreover, there is a factual separation between the three dimensions identified, they may be placed within the dimensions of space separable in normal vocabulary as height, width, and depth. In other words, by placing these three analytical lines at right angles to each other in 3D space, one creates a straight-lined design envelope.

As such, it carries with it many dangers. Please remember that the straight line is the tool of choice for the imperialist map maker and the stabilizer of movement. It also marks the trajectory of the anatomizer's scalpel, that can destroy as it goes through the body. Yet, my argument is that this conceptual envelope, made up of lines, is also an instrument of suturing. It offers a weave and weft as well as a deep cut. It is a woven fabric of value, for it contains within its folds all the tensions creating the range of design structures. It encapsulates in one piece a whole range of creative styles for understanding human approaches to organizing space. If every style must have an attitude to human feelings and their relationship to ratiocination, must have a view as to the utility and force of history, and is bound to take a stance on humanity's relationship to nature, then a deep purse of design possibilities has been formed.

Of course, I hear you say that every style does much more than that, and the details and the stylistic minutiae uniting and separating them remain crucially undifferentiated in this schema now before you. Of course, their attitudes to ornamentation and decoration do differ. Yet styles have much more to do with differentiated approaches to nature, thought, and history than with tiny details of ornamentation. Specificities are crucial—but not that crucial here—and not that crucial now.

Once we have our three finite dimensions and place them at right angles to each other, six faces appear in the cuboid form. As already indicated, this conceptual space of six faces, eight extreme points, and three dimensions, thus defined, attempts to deal with certain issues within the arts and humanities, in the social sciences, and within natural science. I have made choices here in labelling these faces, and the numbering is crucial to navigation. So I would be grateful if the reader would contemplate the dice world at this moment (Figure 6.1).

The cube that the reader may have constructed earlier in the book becomes useful here. If you have not yet labelled the faces of the dice with numbers, please do so now. Since it has six faces, I am labelling the faces on the basis of the number of dots or the number on the face. Face 1 either has one dot or the number 1 upon it, and so on. Face 1 is directly opposite Face 6 because opposite faces on a dice must add up to 7. Thus Face 2 is opposed to Face 5, and in similar logic, Faces 3 and 4 are also opposed. Human eyes and their

Lines of Fight

location on the human head limit the number of faces we can see at any one time. Sometimes you can see one face, mostly two faces, and sometimes three faces. No human can see more than three faces simultaneously without the aid of cameras and an elaborate visualization technology. No human can see the base face to the dice unless a camera is placed below a transparent surface upon which the dice has been specifically placed for the purpose of observation. So, whilst techniques can be developed to look at all the faces of a 'real' dice in 'real' time by a single observing human being, it is expensive, complex, and problematic to do so. And it does suggest that the observer of the dice is only too well aware of the problems in everyday usage of the cube.

The cube positioning system (CPS)

Face 1 is a flat space in which all theories of style placed there subscribe to the view that humans are *a part of Nature* (*Naturality*). It is a plane in which this assumption of 'oneness' with nature is shared by all that live upon it.

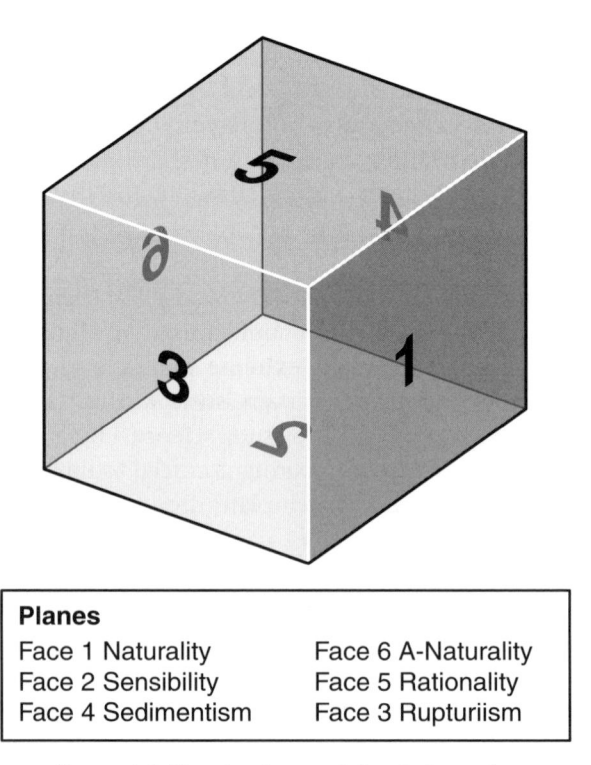

Planes
Face 1 Naturality   Face 6 A-Naturality
Face 2 Sensibility   Face 5 Rationality
Face 4 Sedimentism   Face 3 Rupturiism

Figure 6.1 The six planes of the design cube

The cube positioning system (CPS)

Face 6 represents the dark side of Face 1 since they can never set eyes upon each Other in their everyday world of assumptions. Face 6 then is the plane or flat space upon which dwell all styles that take the view that humanity exists *apart from nature* (*A-naturality*). Here, humanity is differentiated from nature and from 'natural' species through our unique and specific capacity to escape from its terrors and mitigate the risks of living in this world using thought, communication, and technological apparatus.

Face 2 is the plane of *sensibility* and here all theories discussed agree that human feelings, emotions, and the forces of the id are crucial to understanding human life. There exists a duality (a two-ness) about irrationality that we are able to study as human beings but can never come to control. Our sensibility always ends up by controlling us.

Face 5, on the other side of this argument, is the dark side to sensibility. Here it is assumed that we live on a plane of *rationality* in which it is possible to use scientific and mathematical techniques to understand the material world of things but also the ideational world of the mind. Nothing exists that is not capable of being subjected to ratiocination. 'Chaos' itself does not exist and large mathematical problems are solvable if only we can build machines with enough computing power.

Face 4 is the plane of *sedimentism*. Every style existing upon this plane adheres to the conviction that every human design owes something to the past and its understandings. What we are is the product of the ancestral past, whether this is at the level of the genetic makeup of individuals, or the cultural milieu in which we are immersed, or language game in which we grew up, or the deep structures of the social formation in which we live. We are the 'bearers of structure'.

Face 3, however, adheres to the opposite viewpoint, assuming that *rupturism* is the way history moves, through dramatic and catastrophic shifts of seismic proportions. The past is a straitjacket to creativity, for conventional understandings teach us only the wrong lessons. We need to be geared up for cataclysmic change and not small alterations. History, the past, and what has been laid down by previous generations have to be abandoned in order to move significantly forward. We must embrace radical transformations.

We can now understand, perhaps, that those ideas that graze upon these six planes, created by three separable dimensions, share in common an intellectual territory marked out by its 2D assumptions. But as I argued above, there is a great need to develop a three-dimensional approach to any understanding of styles of organizing. Planes are not enough in understanding cubes, for they remain separate and alone, and *flat*. These six planes, somewhat autistically, pay no attention to the cuboid world which lies above and beyond their ken. Face 1 cannot sympathize with Face 6 because they are worlds of misunderstandings and conflict. Each to the Other is the world upside down. Faces 5

Lines of Fight

and 2, and Faces 3 and 4 are worlds in opposition. They are the other side of the moon to each other.

What we carry forward, then, into Chapter 7 is an analytical geometry of three lines:

Lines
Sensibility   Rationality
Sedimentism   Rupturism
Naturality   A-naturality

These three lines produce a three-dimensional space if placed at right angles to each other. They allow for multiple intermediate 'points' along these lines but end at extremities where there is a remarkable clarity of positioning. Diagrammatically, just two extreme positions are presented in Figure 6.2, which shows Point 'a' as the meeting place of Naturality, Sensibility, and Sedimentism, and Figure 6.3, which shows Point 'f' as the meeting place of A-naturality, Rationality, and Rupturism.

Of course, points 'a' and 'f' are but two of the possible extreme limits of this conceptual space. Because of the nature of a cube, there are eight points

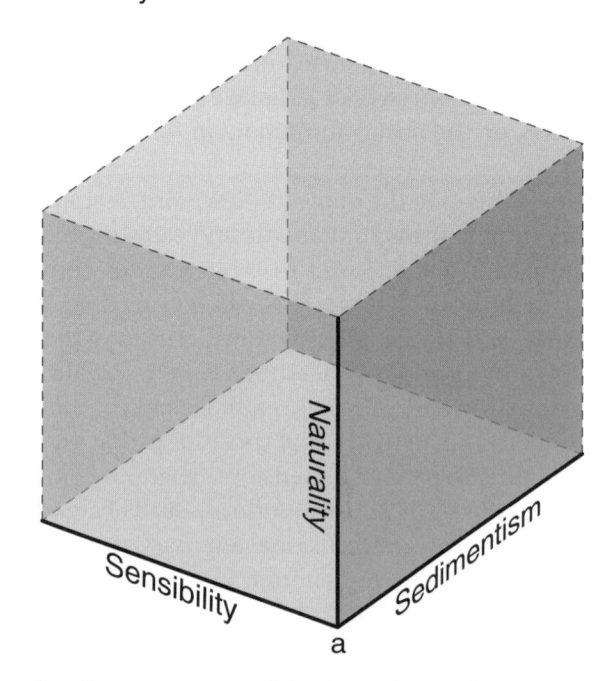

Figure 6.2 Point A as the conjunction of the three planes of naturality, sensibility, and sedimentism

The cube positioning system (CPS)

Point 'f' is the meeting place of A-naturality, Rationality and Rupturism

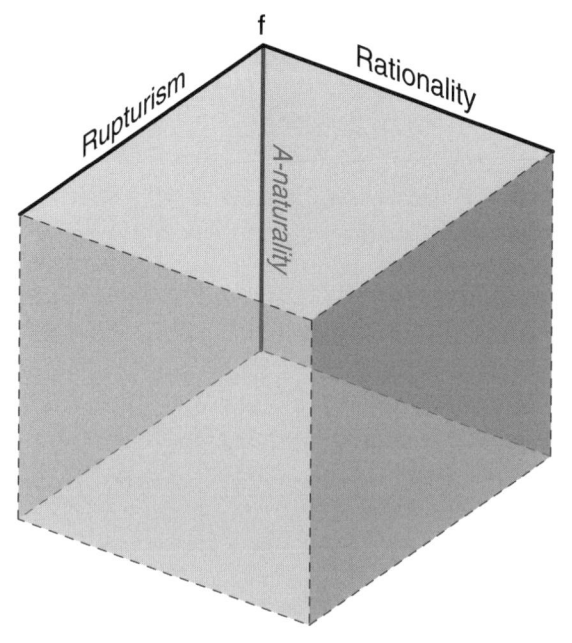

Figure 6.3 Point F as the conjunction of the three planes of A-naturality, rationality, and rupturism

created by the six sides and the cubing of end points to each line. Thus we have 2×2×2 to give us the number 8, representing the possible end points to our conceptual envelope. Here, at these extremities, I shall engage in what du Gay (2007: 155) calls *'casuistry'* or case-based reasoning. Whilst his notion is relegated to a textual footnote, it has resonances with what I seek to do here. As suggested by du Gay, an attempt will be made to provide an analysis of wider organizational issues and dilemmas by dealing with the circumstances and details of one particular case via a methodical mapping of likenesses and differences. I hope Chapter 7 will not resemble a 'grey, meticulous and documentary' form of analysis too much (Foucault 1986: 76) but will bring some colour into organization theory.

7

Points of Opposition

In this chapter, I shall stay with the theme of stylistic opposition and engage in analysis at the edge. In a sense the corners of the cube represent the places where my 'plot lines' come together. I trust that this method will allow the reader to see the breadth of possibilities that exists in organizing design choices. But also to appreciate the limits to what may be achieved when humans are faced with deep philosophical problems. I shall concentrate upon the eight points in the cuboid conceptual space which demarcate, severally, the limits of our spatial envelope within which styles might exist. The extremities are marked as the eight locations at which three particular faces meet. Thus, the following points are labelled A, B, and so on, and relate directly to the eight *corners* of the cube where the extreme points of my three dimensions meet. Thus, each point marks out an extremity, recognizable as a three point coordinate. Figure 7.1, which is entitled 'Eight Points of Opposition', presents these co-ordinates.

It is here in each corner where one sees 'pure' idealized design in the sense that the designers have taken a risk and pushed the envelope as far as they can in developing a style of organizing. What we will find in the corners is, by definition, outside the 'normal range' and it may be a little scary.

Figure 7.2 outlines the dimensions and labels attached to the cube.

The vehicle for presenting my analysis here will be 'fast cornering'. That is, I shall give very brief attention to each of the eight corners, suggesting in the first instance what the politico-economic system is that pertains in each style. As already stated, I shall use the method of oppositional conjuncture in which to bring out the force of the posited differences. Therefore, opposing pairs of conceptual orientations will be discussed in *juxtaposition*.

In terms of these diametrically opposing positions, which are important for our discussions, we should note that:

Point A is opposed to F
Point C is opposed to G
Point D is opposed to H
Point B is opposed to E.

Points of Opposition

Eight Points of Opposition
A Sensibility, Sedimentism, Naturality
C Sensibility, Sedimentism, A-naturality
B Sensibility, Rupturism, A-naturality
D Sensibility, Rupturism, Naturality
E Rationality, Sedimentism, Naturality
H Rationality, Sedimentism, A-naturality
G Rationality, Rupturism, Naturality
F Rationality, Rupturism, A-naturality

Figure 7.1 Eight Points of Opposition

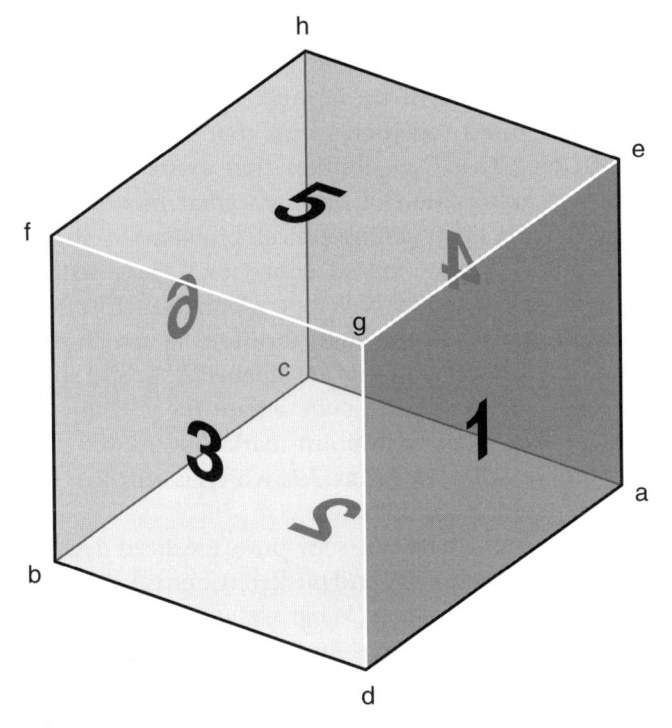

Figure 7.2 The location of the points of the design cube

Fast cornering in the world of management

There are great dangers in taking the eight points of greatest difference in the design cube and seeking to match each up with a particular politico-economic 'system'. Some commentators would no doubt argue that economics is a social science that is locked into relatively specific political forms so that, for example, there is a widespread assumption that all economics is derivative of a generalized capitalist system. That is not my assumption and in the discussion below the reader will come across some quite different and sometimes startling forms of politico-economic organizing. Out of these economic and political approaches come quite different approaches to management. For my purposes there is not a generalizable form of management that arises only with capitalism, nor is it that all previous forms of 'managing' that pre-existed the Industrial Revolution have been small scale and isolated. Management is not a uniform entity—indeed, it is particularistic in its composition—and differs in the eight corners of the design cube. Economics, too, is particularistic in its approaches and offers distinct differences in the corners of the design cube.

My task, then, is to demonstrate the full range of alternatives that exist in the choices humans face in designing politico-economic systems and the managements that come with them. These choices, as I argued before, are severely limited by our assumptions.

What I seek to do is to attach a useful label to each of the extremities; a label that encompasses the sort of politico-economic approach that one associates with that corner of thinking. I shall, of course, outline in a little detail what each of these labels means below.

Bearing this in mind we arrive at the following 'extremist' options (Figure 7.3). This may be further represented by Figure 7.4, which emplaces these Politico-Economic Systems within the design cube.

The extreme points to the design cube then are marked by the following major antagonisms:

Green Environmentalism versus Neo-Liberalism
Potlatch Economics versus Bright Green Environmentalism
Schumpeterianism's 'Creative Destruction' versus Heritage Economics
Pol Potism versus Keynesianism.

Let me now turn to a brief description of each of these systems, bearing in mind that, in the same way that Barley and Kunda (1992) argue that macroeconomic explanations are available to explain differences in styles of

Eight Points of Opposition

A Sensibility, Sedimentism, Naturality	Green Environmentalism
C Sensibility, Sedimentism, A-naturality	Potlatch Economics
B Sensibility, Rupturism, A-naturality	Schumpeterianism
D Sensibility, Rupturism, Naturality	Pol Potism
E Rationality, Sedimentism, Naturality	Heritage Economics
H Rationality, Sedimentism, A-naturality	Keynesianism
G Rationality, Rupturism, Naturality	Techno-Environmentalism
F Rationality, Rupturism, A-naturality	Neo-Liberalism

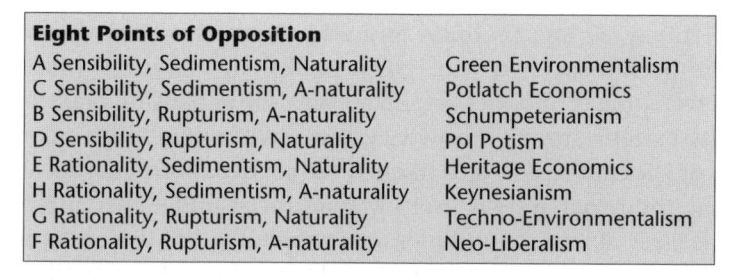

Figure 7.3 Eight Points of Opposition in Politico-Economic Systems

Points of Opposition

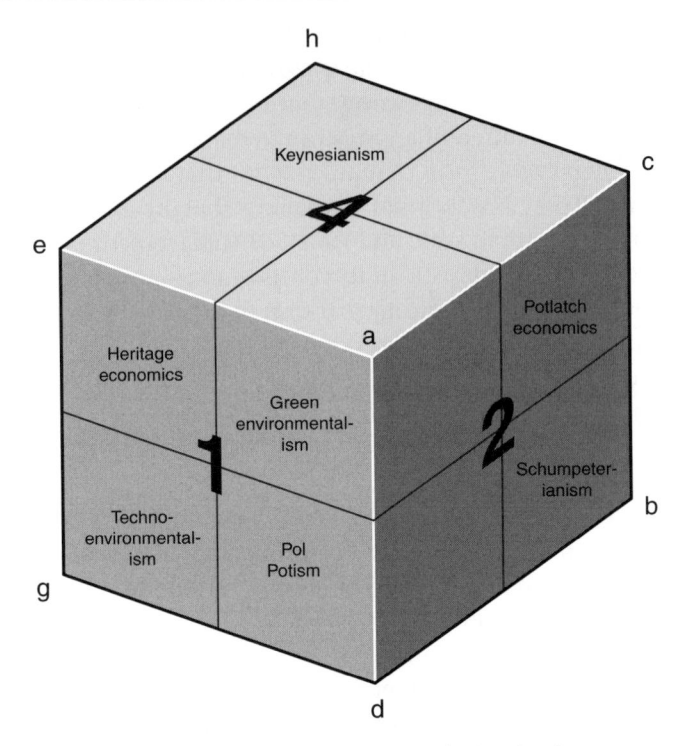

Figure 7.4 Politico- Economic System choices in the corners
Note: The 'hidden' face in this cube is Neo-liberalism

managing, I shall attempt to link these politico-economic positions directly with assumed models of managerial roles.

Green Environmentalism tends to assert that technologies are usually in the hands of those that wish to exploit the planet and that the development and use of any and all new technologies will be driven by the profit motive in the majority of cases. The early activities of German Green Party *die Grunen* and Jonathan Porritt's book *Seeing Green* (1985) are perhaps good examples of this approach when it has a particularly strong politico-economic orientation. Environmentally benign products and ethical practices with regard to suppliers have been associated with green banks, and financial practices that support developing economies are linked with the possession of green credentials. In its extreme form, however, green environmentalism takes on the approach of Dickson (1974) and Illich (1973), where both question the existence of the industrial system itself. Management under this anti-industrial system has clear objectives and measures which are not driven by return on investment, nor the creation of a malleable workforce. It is usually based on participative management and has a local, almost parochial orientation. Overall one could say that it is not pro-capitalist.

Opposed to Green Environmentalism is Neo-Liberalism, which is a politico-economic ideology that advocates the liberalization of trade, open markets for labour, capital, and money, and the privatization of nationalized industries (Hay 2004). The central pillars of these ideological assertions are Neo-Classical Austrian economics built upon 'the market' and 'the individual' as the basic units of analysis. There is a belief that the 'nanny state' has created a culture of dependency amongst the population and that the state needs to be rolled back to allow entrepreneurialism to flourish. Harvey describes it thus:

> Neoliberalism is in the first instance a theory of political economic practices that proposes that human well-being can best be advanced by liberating individual entrepreneurial freedoms and skills within an institutional framework characterized by strong private property rights, free markets and free trade. The role of the state is to create and preserve an institutional framework appropriate to such practices. The state has to guarantee, for example, the quality and integrity of money. It must also set up those military, defence, police and legal structures and functions required to secure private property rights and to guarantee, by force if need be, the proper functioning of markets. Furthermore, if markets do not exist (in areas such as land, water, education, health care, social security, or environmental pollution) then they must be created, by state action if necessary. But beyond these tasks the state should not venture. (Harvey 2007: 21)

Similarly, Hay (2004: 511) argues that Neo-Liberalism is a political rhetoric of the anglophone democracies wherein there is a presentation of the non-negotiable character of external economic imperatives, the powerlessness of domestic action to do anything in the face of such constraints, and the transfer of power to supra-domestic authorities like independent central banks. Management herein is seen as global and driven by 'shareholder value', with little attention being paid to national economic policies. Risk taking is encouraged in the senior managerial cadre, where the 'financialization' of all sorts of relationships is the norm. It is exceptionally pro-capitalist and seeks the end to barriers to the free movement of capital. Whatever its full conceptual composition, it is a powerful rhetorical device that is a contemporary structure in dominance.

In another corner of the cube we find a politico-economic system of a somewhat different hue. First analysed in newly opened-up areas of the United States by anthropologists such as Franz Boas (1897), potlatch ceremonies were found to be a feature of certain tribes in the Pacific North-west. These events were and are associated with the distribution of tribal wealth. The interest in gift exchanges as a form of politico-economic system was then taken up by Marcel Mauss, who saw this relationship as a different form of economic exchange (1954). Leaders of these tribes hosted gift-giving and gift-receiving ceremonies in their homes during the winter months. Dancing and ceremonial feasting are part of the ceremony. A key feature is the destruction of wealth, often in the material form of food, blankets, and ornaments. The holder of the potlatch may even lay down a challenge for others to match their destruction of goods and chattels. To the state authorities this politico-economic arrangement was seen as 'worse than worthless' and was banned for decades. What the missionaries and agents found so distasteful was the burning of objects and wealth in order to impress the population. Debord (1996) argues that the potlatch ceremony still exists today in the fetishism of commodities and there are those who thought the 'Moon race' of the 1960s between the USA and the USSR looked suspiciously like an attempt to burn off state surpluses rather than redistribute them to the wider population. The potlatch may also be thought to link to Veblen's notion of 'conspicuous consumption' in his *Theory of the Leisure Class* (Veblen 1899).

The approach to management in this corner of the design cube is that of the separation of ownership from control and that the managerial cadres are there to maximize the personal wealth of the owner. Management here is the servant of capital and of power, and functions in order to serve its 'magnificence'. David (2008), in his 'The Historical Origins of Open Science' (*Capitalism and Society*, 3(2), article 5), argues that a distinction must be made between two categories of employee in the service of the noble households and dynastic families. These are 'savants and virtuosos' and respectively had utilitarian or ornamental purposes (David 2008: 34). Engineers of weapons of war and the constructors of irrigation and flood defences were brought to the court for their utility, but virtuosos were called to court for reasons of adding to the 'magnificence' of their employer. At this particular point, it is very much management virtuosos serving the owners' magnificence that I have in mind. And that magnificence may well be enhanced by showcasing the consumption of wealth in the form of, for example, the Vanderbilts' housewarming party where dinner guests were asked to take their jewel-encrusted gold cutlery home with them. In 1897, the Bradley Martins threw a party at the Waldorf Astoria that cost $369,000 (Diggins 1999: 6). This is a form of potlatch economics.

In the contemporary world of management, the potlatch is to be found in East London today; and was present four years ago in Beijing. Broudehoux (2007) looked at the Olympic Games 'legacy' in China and itemized the money spent on 'prestige' architectural projects. It was a project much more associated with state managerial prestige than it was with economic or financial payback. She argues that as a direct result of the Barcelona games, that city is now the most gentrified in the world, the working classes having been relocated. In Montreal, the Olympic games are still being paid for and have to date cost 25 times their original estimate. For all we are told that management is driven by a rationality of means–ends calculation, under potlatch economics we must learn that the ends may well be the survival and enhancement of political power—and those that manage on its behalf.

On the other hand, Bright Green Environmentalism (Steffen 2003) believes that technology and improved design can solve many of the problems of overconsumption that the environment currently faces. Unlike 'dark' green environmentalism, this new branch encourages radical change by embracing technology such as bio and nano technologies, dense urban settlements, electric cars, and so on. What is required is the use of existing tools, models, and ideas rather than their rejection. This is styled 'techno-progressivism' and is about the research and adoption of environmentalist design through more widely distributed social innovations. The idea of Bright Green Environmentalism has been taken up by the city of Vancouver, for example. It stands opposed to the conspicuous consumption of excessive consumer society and the burning-off of the national surplus in high-prestige projects. Management herein is a driven by technological innovation and consists ideally of trained, liberally minded engineers. 'Technocracy' is the favoured form of management, where expertise is encouraged and rewarded. In this corner, I have in mind that there is not the drive to 'magnificence' but to problem solving in an efficient technique-driven way by recognizable 'savants'.

In another different area of the design cube, located at Point B, we come across Schumpeterianism, which is associated with the notion of 'creative destruction' and the gale that blows across capitalism from time to time.

In *Capitalism, Socialism and Democracy* (1942), Joseph Schumpeter spoke supportively of the role of the entrepreneur rather than the state in the march of capitalism. Inveterate risk takers such as Henry Ford would always take gambles on the future, and they both reflected and created what we might call unpredictable 'churn' in the existing system. This unpredictability led to 'bust' in the economic cycle, which would be driven back to 'boom' by the next wave of entrepreneurial activity. Thus Schumpeter argues that:

> Capitalism... is by nature a form or method of economic change and not only never is but never can be stationary. The fundamental impulse that sets and keeps the capitalist engine in motion comes from the new consumers' goods, the new methods of production or transportation, the new markets, the new forms of industrial organization that capitalist enterprise creates... The opening up of new markets, foreign or domestic, and the organizational development from the craft shop and factory to such concerns as U.S. Steel illustrate the same process of industrial mutation... that incessantly revolutionizes the economic structure *from within*, incessantly destroying the old one, incessantly creating a new one. This process of Creative Destruction is the essential fact about capitalism. It is what

capitalism consists in and what every capitalist concern has got to live in. (Schumpeter 1942: 82–3; Becker and Knudsen 2009)

Sawyer (1989: 9) maintains that the 'Austrian approach' had a 'generally favourable attitude towards capitalism and particularly towards the benefits of competition'. For Schumpeter, capitalism's demise would be brought about by the end of entrepreneurialism and the rise of the state bureaucracy which he must surely have seen, looking out of his window in wartime America. Obviously, the manager is conceptualized here as 'entrepreneur' and risk taker—someone who adds value by innovative approaches to making money. There is an aversion to the concept of state bureaucracy having large areas of influence, so managers struggle to avoid the label 'bureaucrat' and may indeed take to themselves the epithet 'executive'. There is a long tradition in business and management in separating out the free-thinking entrepreneur from the bureaucratic manager (Clegg et al. 2011). The view is typically held that the former serves capitalism, the latter the organization (or themselves).

In the face of creative destruction, I wish to place its opponent at Point E as prosaic 'heritage sites' or more widely perhaps 'heritage economics'. This looks at first glance as if it, too, may be a form of creative destruction in that from the ashes of industrial sites come museums and themed visits but for me it is the opposite of destruction. It is the maintenance of the declining, despite their imminent demise. For once the industrial or cultural site has been allowed to turn to ash or face ruination, then it has gone. What I am conceptualizing here is the continuity of sites based on their 'authentic' heritage and not their wilful destruction. 'Authenticity' is always a difficult term here, for as Julier (2000: 131–2) tells us, Leeds has the site of the Royal Armouries museum but no history of armaments production. Yet Sheffield steel and Stoke pottery have produced museums that have an authentic connection to their site and locale and which make an economic impact. Heritage sites, of course, rely upon 'cultural tourism'. The National Trust for Historic Preservation in the United States (2012: 1) defines heritage tourism as 'traveling to experience the places and activities that authentically represent the stories and people of the past', and cultural heritage tourism is defined as 'traveling to experience the places and activities that authentically represent the stories and people of the past and present'. Both are involved in heritage economics.

Obviously the Grand Tour undertaken by British aristocracy in the 18th and 19th centuries was a form of cultural tourism that relied upon heritage sites such as Venice long after the Arsenale had closed its doors for the business of building a trading empire. The notion of 'the tourist', of course, has come under much scrutiny. For some (Chaney 1993: 165), a tourist is 'a distinctive type of stranger, collaborating in the spectacle being performed'. The tourist is thus a member of an audience rather than a member of a crowd, which raises the whole question again of authenticity. Yet heritage sites and the tourism built around them and the 'Tourist Gaze' (Urry 1990) represent a politico-economic system of a kind that is heavily dependent, as we shall see, upon Romanticism. The manager in this corner of the design cube is part historian, part marketing expert. They have expertise in local culture and must produce 'multiple local enthusiasms' (Urry 1995: 2). They seek to invent a past and a future which has 'dramatic' possibility as the creation of a theatrical experience for the customer. The orientation is protectionist and localist and concerned about employment.

A final pairing of opposites begins with what I am calling here 'Pol Potism'. This is the ideology and management approach taken by the Khmer Rouge from 1976 in Cambodia. Once in power, they abolished money and private property, outlawed religion, and undertook a number of other extreme reforms. These involved the reordering of the calendar as Year 0, the destruction of all American factories and distribution centres, and the forcible evacuation of the population from Phnom Penh into the countryside. Existing homes were burnt and national self-reliance was the order of the day. Humanitarian offers of help were all refused. The Killing Fields is the name given to the execution of thousands of people who spoke different languages, adhered to different religions, or were well educated. These were allocated lesser rations than full members of society and were then subjected to systematic violent attention. The approach was a politico-economic system of a remarkable kind, reflecting the Maoism that dominated China in the 1960s via the 'little Red Book' (Kiernan 2004; 2008). Managers in this system were banished if they held technocratic expertise. The 'twin circulations' (King 1977) meant that managerial cadres were replaced by peasant-worker decision-makers, who rotated in this role. There is no place given in this corner for expertise in management or for bureaucratic management as a whole. As soon as the cities were cleared of population the central state apparatus was made redundant. Just as the Red Guard across the border in China had been given licence to break all existing norms of respect for tradition, the Khmer Rouge questioned any power that came from age, education, experience, or position. Social harmony was not valorized in this restructuring.

Opposed to this, I have placed Keynesianism, which, of course, sees the state as playing a key and constant role in economic life and is thus very different from Pol Potism. Social harmony, money, and private property were to be defended, not abolished. Having witnessed the slump of the 1930s, John Maynard Keynes saw the business cycle as the most difficult of economic problems because it created large-scale unemployment. He saw the role of the state as being to create an economic policy which stabilized high levels of employment and thus maintained social order. One way of doing this was a high level of investment by government in infrastructure, thereby injecting a

Points of Opposition

stimulus into the economy. The 'multiplier effect' thence ensures that the benefits of this injection become widespread and continue to grow. His belief was that there was no automatic mechanism that would move the economy but that government action was required. The concept of 'equilibrium' for him did not hold up as a defensible notion, particularly when expressed in the form of 'monetarism' (Morgan 1978).

Here, under Keynesianism, the manager is the repository of social responsibility to offer employment and to manage the human resources of the firm as a crucial part of the task. Whilst efficiency is important, management of the state, for example, carries heavy social responsibility to the population. Legitimacy resided in giving the voter the right to employment. So too does the legitimacy of the organizational manager. Both have a 'duty' to maintain social harmony.

Having laid out the basic politico-economic and managerial elements of the design cube, I now seek to overlay on top of them some parts of architecture and design which fill the *same intellectual space*.

Fast cornering in the world of architecture and design

What, then, in terms of architecture and design, demarcates the presence of these eight spaces as extremities? Again I shall be brief here in articulating the corners of the design space, which explains the repetitive title of this section of the chapter—fast cornering. Please note that whilst I shall pay attention to several organizational issues in the architecture/design corners, it will be in the next chapter that major attention will be given to specific organizations.

In this part of the chapter I am pushing the design envelope as far as it can go, so it will come as no surprise to some readers to find the work of well-known 'signature' architects being discussed here rather than 'ordinary art'. Their radical designs often exemplify extreme articulations of 'outlandish' notions, and as such, much has been written about both architect and design. The reader will also find in some corners the identification of one or two classic styles of building by which I hope to make my point more clearly. But there cannot be a serious attempt at deep analysis of each corner in any detail. All I seek to do is to mark out boundaries, establishing the *termes* of the debate.

Given these are the corners, the far-flung outposts of the architectural design space, it follows that I would argue that all other architectural attempts fall, in stylistic terms, within these outposts. Since they are extreme examples and as such mark the conceptual limit of the envelope, the act of drawing boundaries helps mark out the edge of the space that is inhabitable. They also serve another purpose. By focusing upon polarities between extreme positions, I seek to show the organizational theorist that these design types bring a 3D richness to the organizational world that we do not generally comprehend. My net is a wide one. There are inbuilt tensions in my examples between contrasting campus designs for university accommodation, between cathedrals and mass-produced housing, between socialist building complexes and royal palaces, and between communal housing and one private house. Organization theory can illuminate much beyond the world of business—and it should do so. Organizing is going on all around us in so many ways that 'business and management' as an epithet just cannot capture.

Let us begin with ***Point A*** at the edge of our conceptual space. It is, of course, the politico-economic system of Green Environmentalism. Point A is a tight place marked by a commitment to sensibility, sedimentism, naturalism. The design space to begin this part of my analysis of points of opposition might be with the expression of Romanticism that is associated with Gaudi and his particular brand of Catalan Romanticism. There is a Green Environmentalism of sorts in this approach, for there is an overwhelming interest in organic nature so that animals and plants are to be found throughout his designs. It has connections with Art Nouveau but most importantly, one must remember that Barcelona at this time was a centre for Spanish industrialization, and that a concentration upon the protection and understanding of the natural world was not widespread.

A building that best sums up Gaudi's amazing creativity and represents for me his location at the extreme end of the envelope of possible spatial designs at Point A is the Casa Milà in Barcelona. It was designed and built between 1905 and 1911 for a wealthy couple as a show of their opulence—but through the medium of a housing development, in the city centre. It has the appearance more of a sculpture than of a building. Lifts were placed only on every second floor so that residents would get to know each other better. Not a single straight line is used and the floor plans are all different, being supported by pillars and columns. The roof offers the opportunity to see surrealistic and colourful chimneys. It is organic and visceral in its style, representing to some a set of caves in a natural rock formation. It suggests it is alive and that it is in constant movement. Balconies are made from ornate ironwork that takes the shape of fantastical natural formations. It appears as if humans have moved into a natural cave system, rather than this being designed by a human with functionality in mind. Fireplaces appear to be carved out of the walls. Gaudi wished to use many religious elements in his final design but was prevented from doing so by the local authorities, concerned with political unrest at the time and the fact that the building was higher than municipal building regulations allowed, and that pieces of its structures jutted out into the streets. In surveying this building, the reader might note the elements in the building which show it is not for use by a private family but is a block of apartments for a society in which collectivism was and is strong. Notable too is the lack of a single straight line, the use of highly decorative ornamentation, and the organicism throughout, the use of religious symbolism in this ornamentation, and the surrealism that is often implied. It is the work of a phantacist decorator.

It is said that Gaudi was motivated by architecture, nature, his Catalan nationalism, and a deep religiosity, yet was interested in utopian socialism in his youth. He was a person of extremes. In later life, Gaudi was prone to fasting, which sometimes injured his health, and he adopted an unkempt appearance which proved to be his undoing. When knocked down by a tram in 1926 at the age of 73, he was not recognized. No one came to his aid because he looked like a down and out. Yet he was alleged to be a dandy in his youth, dressed in costly suits and attracted to a gourmet lifestyle. He remained unattached throughout his life and was described by some as 'unsociable and unpleasant'. After his death, his work was regarded for a period as 'excessively imaginative' and he went out of fashion. His papers and 3D models, which he used extensively, were destroyed. Salvador Dali, a fellow Catalan, helped rescue his reputation in the 1950s and his work achieved World Heritage status in 1984. The Casa Mila is now a World Heritage Building.

In the next chapter I shall consider this particular form of adorned space in relation to the styles of organizing of which it speaks, but the reader should be forewarned that my organizational example is *not* an obvious one.

Let us now consider **Point F**, the extreme opposite in our cubist conceptual space to Point A. Point F is a corner marked by rationalism, rupturism, anti-naturalism and sees nothing of value in Point A whatsoever. As already prefigured, this is the location of Neo-Liberalism as the dominant politico-economic system. Here then we are set in Austria—which some claim is the home of Neo-Liberalism. It was certainly the home of 'logical atomism' and the belief in the value of mathematical language as the basis for all understanding. At this extreme in the conceptual envelope in the design cube, we will find not a set of families, but a single occupant for whom the house is designed (Leitner 2000). All is straight lines, nothing is decorated. Nothing is organically alive but all is controlled and rigid. Comfort has been dispensed with in the pursuit of ascetic minimalism. Its enemy is the Art Nouveau of Vienna and its designer is one Ludwig Wittgenstein (1889–1951).

He designed and built this grand villa in the period 1926 to 1928 for his sister, Margarethe (Gretl) Stonborough-Wittgenstein. The original plans that were drawn up were for a classicist design but Wittgenstein took over control and purified it of all classicism (Leitner 1976). Some have said this building represents the house of an autistic person and I have chosen it as one extreme end point for this reason. There is an 'idiom' here of a very specific and individuated kind. It is an outlandish conceptual space of and for all styles of organizing. In its severity and simplicity, perhaps, the structure reflects the logical clarity of some of Wittgenstein's thinking; but also, perhaps, it speaks of some problems of his own psyche.

His plan cleansed the original of what the philosopher thought was superfluous and he made sure its proportions were optimized. Like most lovers of rationality, he used ratios throughout the planning and building phases. He preferred the 3:1 and 4: 1 ratios as aesthetically most pleasing. The façades were freed from all adornment. Everything relating to proportions was minutely planned and perfectly manufactured, for Wittgenstein had a large budget and lots of time (Leitner 2000).

Because Wittgenstein was struggling with depression, his family of brothers and sisters, to whom he had given away his vast fortune inherited from his father, offered him a new role—architect. The job of designing the Wittgenstein House came as a rescue for his creative talents. According to Stuart Jeffries (*Guardian*, 5 January 2002) Wittgenstein's sister, Hermine, wrote: 'Even though I admired the house very much, I always knew that I neither wanted to, nor could, live in it myself. It seemed indeed to be much more a dwelling for the gods than for a small mortal like me, and at first I even had to overcome a faint inner opposition to this "house embodied logic" as I called it, to this perfection and monumentality.'

The philosopher's work on the design of the house focused on the windows, doors, window locks, and radiators. Each window was shaded by metal screens instead of curtains, with each weighing about 150kg, but they were easily moved by a pulley system designed by Wittgenstein himself. Bernhard Leitner, author of *The Architecture of Ludwig Wittgenstein* (1976: 2), said that 'There is barely anything comparable in the history of interior design. It is as ingenious as it is expensive.' He also took a year to design the door handles, and another year to design the radiators. When asked by a locksmith working for a specialized company that he employed to realize his designs in steel and brass for the window latches, he claimed that a single millimetre meant everything to him. This injunction may be thought to parallel or even reflect the interest elsewhere in Vienna, and within 'modernist economics', for formal, reductionist, and axiomatic representations that showed a preference for logic and geometry (Klamer 2007).

It was not a cosy home and the amateur architect would not contemplate carpets or curtains. Apparently, Wittgenstein hated curtains, so his sister was never allowed to use any. His room in Cambridge University, some time later, contained only a deck chair and an electric fire. Located in the unfashionable Kundmanngasse district of Vienna, the Wittgenstein House contained rooms that were to be lit by naked bulbs, and the door handles and radiators, over whose design Wittegenstein had also slaved for years, were left unpainted. The floors were of greyish polished stone. As a whole, the house was a stark cubic mass devoid of any external decoration whatsoever. In fact, this house could be seen as a reaction against the decadence of Art Nouveau which was a style in the ascendancy at the time. Wittgenstein's close friend Adolf Loos had written a paper called 'Ornament and Crime', in which he argued for the suppression of decoration, as this was necessary for regulating human passion. For Wittgenstein and his sister Gretl, there were no curves, no *joie de vivre*, and no passion (Leitner 2000).

Gretl lived there and found the place to her liking. Like most of the aristocratic Von Wittgensteins, she loved art and was a patron of leading artists, including Gustav Klimt, who painted her portrait, whilst Ravel composed a piece for her brother, Paul. Post-World War I Vienna was said to be a city of aesthetic and moral 'decay' and the reaction against that decadence had affected many intellectuals. For example, whilst Loos's architecture raged against decoration, Sigmund Freud simultaneously argued that the unconscious 'id' heaved below a purportedly ordered society, and Schoenberg's atonal music turned the musical world upside down. So Wittgenstein's architectural foray has to be put into this socio-political context as well as his own psychological one.

Of his time as an architect Wittgenstein said:

> You probably imagine that philosophy is complicated enough, but let me tell you, this is nothing compared to the hardship of being a good architect. Back when I was building the house for my sister in Vienna I was so exhausted at the end of the day that the only thing I was still able to do was to go every evening to the cinema. (Jeffries 2002)

The Wittgenstein house exhausted the architect, perhaps, but it is its logic, its form, its clarity, and its functionality that prevail. It is the home designed by a single-minded person who wished at the time in all things to remove emotion and replace it by measurement, to suppress the humanities in the search for *decorationless perfection*. Klamer (2007: 184) maintains that a group of French students of mainstream economics have set up a website to underscore what they see as the *autism* of economics, wherein clarity and function have replaced resonances with everyday human activity. What this sort of architectural and economic concentration upon 'decorationless perfection' has to show to us in relation to styles of organizing will be outlined in the next chapter. My example chosen there is one that should not shock or scandalize the organizational analyst too much.

Let us now consider **Point B**, marked by a commitment to sensibility, rupturism, anti-naturalism. It is the location of Schumpeterian 'creative destruction'. At this extreme point within our cube what do we find in terms of architecture and design? It is Frank Gehry's Stata building at MIT, which was opened in 2004. It is meant to represent 'deconstructionism', which for some is a synonym for 'creative destruction' (Glancey 2003). It is an academic complex with lecture theatres, in what is known as Building 32. Two nine-storey towers on the top—Gates Tower and Drefoos Tower—stand above these lecture theatres and contain, amongst others, one Noam Chomsky and one Tim Berners-Lee, who both have offices within it. It cost $300 million and looks like 'a party of drunken robots got together to celebrate'. Somewhat typically for this period (Dale and Burrell 2010), the architect uses the notion of a 'neighbourhood', a 'town centre', and a connecting 'street' that winds around the ground floor. It was paid for by two married alumni—the Statas—who graduated in the 1960s. On its opening, many commentators were extremely complimentary. According to Robert Campbell (2007), 'the Stata is always going to look unfinished. It also looks as if it's about to collapse. Columns tilt at scary angles. Walls teeter, swerve, and collide in random curves and angles. Materials change wherever you look: brick, mirror-surface steel, brushed aluminum, brightly colored paint, corrugated metal. Everything looks improvised, as if thrown up at the last moment. That's the point. The Stata's appearance is a metaphor for the freedom, daring, and creativity of the research that's supposed to occur inside it.'

Nicos Salingaros, (2004: 40), however, writing as both an architect and a mathematician, signified an issue that was raised earlier about 'chaos theory' and its relationship with deconstructionism, reflecting perhaps a mathematical versus an architectural sensibility. He severely criticized the building thus:

> An architecture that reverses structural algorithms so as to create disorder—the same algorithms that in an infinitely more detailed application generate living form—ceases to be architecture. Deconstructivist buildings are the most visible symbols of actual deconstruction. The randomness they embody is the antithesis of nature's organized complexity.

Just as Wittgenstein's house was based on a harmony of mathematical forms and ratios, Gehry had created a construction that contradicted these notions of functionality. More criticism ensued. In terms of its users, it was alleged that people get vertigo inside, because of the lean of the buildings. MIT also paid an exceptionally high price for it, its glass panels offer its inhabitants no privacy, and there is no sound insulation. Built on the site of the old Radiation Lab, which was a very flexible building, it was seen as lacking this ability to shift in its functions. Gehry was paid $15 million for the plans but the building started to show leaks, not least in its pipes for soiled water, ice and snow kept falling from its roof and blocked its exits, mould had grown up alarmingly quickly, and masonry had cracked. All this meant that MIT sued the architect in 2007 and the case dragged on for three years before it was resolved. In his defence, Gehry said that the building had seven billion pieces of connective tissue in its fabric, so it was bound to have problems. He added that MIT should have paid

Points of Opposition

more for 'value engineering' and paid for these problems to be sorted out during the build. From today's standpoint what Gehry's high-prestige building does is to use deconstructionism and create a design with twists and tilts suggesting *'explosive alteration'*. And we shall see later what 'explosive alteration' tells us about a style of organizational design that is currently being constructed.

Juxtaposed with Gehry's creative destruction in the form of architectural deconstructionism, let us now consider **Point E**—where the design cube comes to a point at the juxtaposition of rationalism, sedimentism, naturalism. The politico-economic system here is that circulating around the tourist gaze and heritage sites.

Opposed in design terms to MIT, we find another university building, namely the Neo-Palladianism of Thomas Jefferson, who considered the founding of the University of Virginia to be one of his greatest achievements. Undertaking the project toward the end of his life—after a long career that included serving as a colonial revolutionary, political leader, writer, architect, inventor, and horticulturalist—he was closely involved in the university's design. He planned the curriculum, recruited the first faculty, and designed the academical village, a terraced green space surrounded by residential and academic buildings, gardens, and the centre point known as the Rotunda. As the most recognizable symbol of the university, the Rotunda stands at the north end of the Lawn and is half the height and width of the Pantheon in Rome, which was its primary inspiration. The Lawn and the Rotunda have served as models for similar designs of 'centralized green areas' at universities across the United States and beyond.

American architects in no small measure attribute the roots of their profession to the 'Sage of Monticello.' Jefferson had studied the structures of Europe and read extensively on the great architects. Possessed by a penchant for Palladio, Jefferson set out his architectural masterpiece in the wilderness of Virginia. He believed that architecture was crucial to the creation of an American civilization. For him, the building of the university was a metaphor for American ideology, to express the American desire to break cultural—as well as political—ties to Europe. American architecture, for Jefferson, would and should represent the civic life of Americans, and he sought to establish the standards of a national architecture, both aesthetically and politically. Yet the university is in part a homage to European architecture as an architectural 'bricolage' of Italian, Greek, and French influences—all cast in American building materials.

The assemblage of historical designs present in the university symbolize the construction from disparate influences of Jefferson's own New World Order, both architecturally and intellectually. This order was nothing less than a reorganization of academic life where:

> The rooms on the Lawn were to be occupied exclusively by privileged young white men only, and preferably those from the south and west. Women and African-Americans had no business on the grounds, except of course, as servants and slaves to the men. Additionally, the control Jefferson exerted even over the privileged faculty and students is reinforced by the architecture. (Smith and Bugni 2006: 139)

Jefferson wanted total control over the project and in order to establish classical order within it, he utilized a very rigid structure. In the design of this 'academical village,' Jefferson envisioned a democratic (though, of course, slave based) community of scholars and students, coexisting in a single village, which united the living and learning spaces in one undifferentiated area. Jefferson organized the whole space around the open expanse of 'The Lawn', surrounded it with student rooms and central pavilions, and housed faculty members in his monument to Classicism. The effect of this design was intended to be progressive, yet rooted in classical disciplines; broad-based and elective, but still centralized; and accessible, but still reserved for the privileged elite.

There is something feudal in this image of the 'New World Order', but also an image of a society based on slavery. Classicism invites these views of imperial power, based as it is upon slave labour and patrician obligations and rights. As a style of organizing there is much to say on this later. My organizational example is also from within the analysis of colonialism, but it is from a very different part of the North American continent and is not a very obvious one for an organization theorist.

In another corner of the design cube we confront **Point C**. Here is the corner position in this design envelope where we find the location of the extremes of sensibility, sedimentism, anti-naturalism. For me this is the place of the potlatch ceremony and the burning up of resources in a search for magnificence. Here we do not find a signature architect but rather a defining trope of architecture—the collapsing tower and the overreach of the builders. Point C is the location of the Gothic style, and the space we will briefly look at is Beauvais Cathedral. The medieval cathedrals consumed huge amounts of capital, manpower, material, and ideological effort. To some commentators, they were the major effort by the aristocracy and the rising merchant class to win the favour of God, and that of the local population, but at the cost of huge conspicuous consumption.

Begun in 1224 in northern France, the nave of Beauvais Cathedral was to be 48 metres in height. But the work was interrupted in 1284 by the collapse of the recently completed choir. This collapse is often seen as an architectural disaster that produced a failure of nerve among the French masons working in the Gothic style. It is now believed that the collapse was caused by resonant vibrations induced by high winds. Originally, the High Gothic style of the cathedral was marked by great engineering expertise and architectural innovation. It has been called 'the Parthenon of French Gothic' with its Gothic pointed arch, flying buttress, and rib vault, allowing the walls of the cathedral to seem less massive than in previous approaches to Gothic building. Even though the structure was to be taller, the buttresses were made thinner in order to pass maximum light into the cathedral. However, despite all the planning that went into the cathedral, it was only 12 years after its completion that the major collapse occurred.

Centuries later, more work was carried out and eventually the transept was built from 1500 to 1548. Yet, in 1573, the fall of a too-ambitious 153-metre central tower stopped work again. The foundations of the cathedral were not well enough designed to achieve such dizzy heights. The cathedral was left alone thereafter until, in the 1960s, the cathedral's caretakers removed iron bars which were laterally connecting the buttresses, in the hope of making the cathedral look more attractive. This action caused the transept to separate from the choir, so steel rods were quickly added. Since then, throughout the 1980s and 1990s, a number of sundry modern braces have been added, and in 2001 a team of architects from Columbia University scanned the entire edifice and are attempting to save it from collapse.

This tendency of High Gothic cathedrals to collapse because of humanity's hubris is also a theme of William Golding's *The Spire*, a quote from which we will consider below. The emphasis within the Gothic on spending money and resources to achieve great height creates pressure on the masons to build upwards, when structural limitations are sometimes overlooked or are unknown. The *collapsing Gothic tower* is a theme to which I shall also return in the next chapter, and the organizational example chosen is a fairly obvious one.

Opposed to the potlatch of medieval European cathedral building is **Point G**, which is represented by Buckminster Fuller's notion of the dymaxion—which stands for 'dynamic maximum tension'. Much of his design work had little pretension towards architecture. It was all about engineering and often 'wall and roof were one' (Glancey 2000: 208). It is not fear of the collapse of the dominant symbolic structure in a given region that drives Fuller's design, but the desire for a quick-erecting, mass-produced domestic structure by which to populate the prairies. Its position in the design envelope is marked by an extreme orientation towards rationalism, rupturism, naturalism. And it was marked in the previous section as a politico-economic system of techno-environmentalism (or Bright Green Environmentalism). Herein, of course, lies a belief that sustainability can be achieved through the use of brand new technology that will have positive green implications. Renewable energy sources, sustainable resources, and the reduction in greenhouse gas emissions are clearly important technological areas for sage investment today. As too is the need for cheap housing in hostile conditions.

A century ago, Fuller entered Harvard University, but he was expelled after 'excessively socializing' and missing his midterm exams. Following his expulsion, he worked at a mill in Canada, where he took a strong interest in machinery and learned to modify and improve the manufacturing equipment. Fuller returned to Harvard in the autumn of 1915 but was again dismissed. One of Fuller's lifelong interests was using technology to revolutionize construction and improve human housing. In 1927, he designed the Dymaxion house, an inexpensive, mass-produced home that could be airlifted to its location. The word 'dymaxion', coined by a department store, became synonymous with his design philosophy of 'doing more with less'. Dymaxions were all factory-manufactured kits, assembled on site, intended to be suitable for any site or environment, and to use resources efficiently. One important design consideration was ease of shipment and assembly. The final design of the Dymaxion house used a central vertical stainless-steel strut on a single foundation. Each structure was assembled at ground level and then winched up the strut. Only two prototypes were built and one of them was installed indoors in the Henry Ford Museum in 2001.

Criticisms of the Dymaxion house's design include its supposed inflexibility which completely disregarded local site and architectural idiom, and its use of energy-intensive materials instead of locally available ones. Yet Fuller chose aluminium, for both its weight and strength, and because of the fact that since the end of World War II, there was substantial excess capacity of the metal available for non-military use. It was a design driven by a wartime philosophy and has resonances with the Tennessee Valley Authority (TVA). If 'Doing more with less' was the design philosophy of the dymaxion, it is an interesting principle behind a particular style of organizing which we will turn to below, where I will briefly assess a small-scale firm on Cambridge Science Park in the light of the dymaxion's design philosophy.

Point D is a far-away corner marked by Sensibility, Rupturism, Naturalism and we shall look here for an example derived from Art Nouveau which is characterized by a rejection of historicism, an embracing of the cult of nature, and an interest in the subconscious and the mystical. Directly alongside this, of course, I have previously placed the politico-economics of the Khmer Rouge.

In *The Shock of the New*, Robert Hughes (1991: 165) reminds us of Le Corbusier's dictum that there was a choice between 'architecture *or* revolution'. In other words, construction does not sit well with a desire to undertake destruction, and it continued to be that the poor did not have '*l'architecture*': instead they had slums. So the achievement of democratic structures in and

Points of Opposition

through architecture is not easy (Dale and Burrell 2008). Indeed, Pol Pot and the Khmer Rouge sought to put an end to mainstream architecture in order to bring about the necessary revolution. Factories and warehouses in particular were burnt down. But in terms of construction rather than destruction we might look to *fin de siècle* Belgium.

From 1895 to 1899, Victor Horta was in charge of a design for the House of the People, a major building for the progressive Belgian Socialist Party, consisting of a large complex of offices, meeting rooms, café, and a conference/concert hall seating over 2,000 people. Its demolition in 1965, in spite of an international protest by over 700 architects, has been described as one of the greatest architectural crimes of the 20th century. The building had been mainly constructed in white iron (more than 600,000 kilograms were used) and 15 craftsmen worked for 18 months on the ironwork. To make this construction possible, Horta drew no less than 8,500 square metres of plans. The building was completed in 1899 and was considered a master work. Because of the experimental combination of brick, glass, and steel, this building was considered an example of art representing freedom. Horta's construction of the *Maison du Peuple* also had a philanthropic aim: to open up an airy, light-filled space to people living in the slums. The choice of the Workers' Party also had its origins in the quest for a style that would actively deter the conservative middle classes from entering it—although they did go in eventually, in 1965, through the medium of bulldozers.

The reforms of the Khmer Rouge may not appear to correspond with Horta's image of the needs of the Belgian Socialist Party, but there was the common heartfelt desire to transform society through revolutionary means, to keep out the middle classes from this process, and to emplace the working class in airy open spaces. In keeping with the notion that 'art' is capable of representing freedom, Horta's Art Nouveau work will lay the foundations for a discussion of 'art as freedom' as a design principle. In my choice of organizational design, to be discussed below, I turn to Mexico.

Point H, the opposite of Point D, is represented within the design cube as extreme forms of the Baroque, where rationalism, sedimentism, anti-naturalism are to be found. It is the corner place of Keynesianism. Of course, I realize that some work on my part will be necessary to show the patient reader how and in what ways Keynesianism resembles the Baroque. And it will not be enough to show that he visited Louis XIV's Palace of Versailles as financial representative of the British Treasury at the Treaty of Versailles negotiations in 1919!

Versailles is one of the largest and most opulent castles in the world. It is decidedly not a socialist building and stands as a testament to absolutism. Boasting around 2,143 windows, 1,252 fireplaces, and 67 staircases, the castle is one of the most visited attractions in France and teaches us much about the

Baroque style of organizing. The Palace of Versailles was built for use from 1682 by Louis XIV, an absolute monarch who engaged in boring court etiquette to keep all the courtiers—now moved out of Paris—busy and distracted from plotting against him. Louis envisaged Versailles as a seat for all the Bourbons, as well as his troublesome nobles. His bedroom was the fulcrum around which the palace rotated and its rooms were named after an appropriate Greco-Roman deity. Most famous are the Hall of Mirrors and the enormous gardens, full of grottoes and fountains that required huge amounts of water. This was investment in state infrastructure carried out at huge expense through taxation and military conquest.

Today, many tourists see Versailles as unparalleled in its magnificence and splendour; yet few know of the actual living conditions many of Versailles' august residents had to endure. On each floor, living units of varying size, some 350 in all, were arranged along tiled corridors and given a number. Each door had a key, which was to be handed in when the lodging was vacated. Many courtiers would trade lodgings and group together with their allies, families, or friends. The Noailles family took over so much of the southern wing's attic that the corridor leading to all the lodgings on that floor was nicknamed 'Noailles Road' by courtiers of the time. Rank and status dictated everything in Versailles; not least among that list was one's lodgings. These nobles were placed within a 'gilded cage' as the Duc de Saint-Simon had it. Luxury and opulence, however, were not always in the description given to their residences. Many nobles had to make do with one- or two-room apartments, forcing many of them to buy town houses in Versailles proper, and keeping their palace rooms for changes of clothes or entertaining guests, rarely sleeping there. Rooms at Versailles were immensely useful for an ambitious courtier as they allowed palace residents easy and constant access to the monarch, essential to their ambitions, and gave them constant access to the latest gossip and news.

Here in the palace is to be found a 'reason' that is particularly Baroque (Buci-Glucksmann 1992). It is a mode of rationality that stands against the reason of the middle classes, but is in favour of reason in the service of the state and its control, through surveillance and subterfuge. The Baroque has a sense of the religious past and the need to engage in a counter reformation against the sin of Protestantism. Rationality that stands for scientific knowledge and what that brings to the population in terms of 'Enlightenment' is opposed by much of Baroque 'reason'. Yet scientific knowledge is acceptable, insofar as it is under the control of the state. Nature is to be controlled and mimicked, so that in the Palace of Versailles were to be found the largest waterworks in the world to feed lakes and fountains. It was also a set of buildings designed to fool the eye.

President Truman believed that Keynesianism itself was reliant upon a *trompe l'oeil*. 'Nobody can convince me that Government can spend a dollar it's not got,' he is reported to have complained. According to his biographer, Robert Skidelsky (2003), Keynes was of a generation that believed they should and could rule by 'culture' and not by expertise. It was a matter of 'breeding'. He was an Old Etonian, a member of Kings College and of the somewhat secretive Cambridge Apostles Society, and President of the Cambridge Union. He was a director of the British Eugenics Society as well as the Bank of England and was a member of the Bloomsbury Group of intellectuals. In short, he was a powerful man if not exactly the Sun King. Keynes remained a lifelong supporter of the Liberal Party and argued that Marxism was based upon poor scholarship. The 'boorish proletariat' were much less preferable for him than the bourgeoisie and intelligentsia. There are many ways in which his rationality was Baroque in nature, seeing the power of the state as having the first call upon what reason finds reasonable. In terms of styles of organizing, the Baroque points to an architecture and design of power through the *trompe l'oeil*. The organizational example I have chosen of this type of design is an obvious and infamous one.

Bearing these corner signposts in mind, we shall proceed in the next chapter to offer some organizational examples of each extremity of the design envelope, as it relates specifically to organizations and organizing.

8

Organizational Reflections of Corner Living

Eight points of extreme design style for organizing

To repeat what has been said in Chapter 7, put very simply one is able to find in each extreme corner of our conceptual space examples of the following approaches to politico-economic systems, and architecture, and design, and how they might be characterized. So as to remind the reader, the geometric points where these extremities are to be found in the design cube are added to the characterization of certain elements of style in the summary below, which it should be noted, is in *alphabetical* order.

Summary of characterizations

Point A is where we might expect to find Gaudi-type designs in the form of 'excessively imaginative adornment'. This is associated with a style of organizing where 'Green Environmentalism' is seen as reflective of participative environmental objectives and a defence of naturality. Point A is the meeting point of the lines of sensibility, sedimentism, naturality

Point B marks 'deconstructionism' and the work of Frank Gehry through the shorthand notion of 'explosive alteration'. It is associated with the design style of organizing via Schumpeterian 'creative destruction', where the emphasis is upon entrepreneurial risk taking and a robust defence of wealth creation. Point B is the meeting point of the lines of sensibility, rupturism, A-naturality.

Point C is the location of High Gothic in its classical form and is caricatured perhaps as the tarot card, 'the collapsing tower'. It is reflective of the politico-economic system of the potlatch, reflected in particular ceremonies concerned with consumption. Management here is the *servant* of capital and of power, mounting a stout defence of authority. Point C reflects the joining up of sensibility, sedimentism, A-naturality.

Point D is the place where one might look for Art Nouveau wherein art is seen as 'freedom' from the existing order. It is a place of the politics of Pol Potism wherein there is the twin circulation—an inversion—of expertise and skill with non-expertise and non-skill, and an attack upon traditional and modern forms of authority. It seeks revolution in cultural matters. Point D is where the lines of sensibility, rupturism, naturality meet up.

Point E is the space occupied by Neo-Classicism and Neo-Palladianism's search for a 'New World Order'. It is the location of a politico-economic system based on heritage sites, heritage economics, and the tourist gaze. Emphasis is placed upon a theatrical imperative to provide a 'show' and mount a defence of the need for presentation as well as substance. Management is nothing if not locally expert. At Point E the lines of rationalism, sedimentism, naturality come together.

Point F is limited to the embrace of Modernism and even extends to Wittgenstein's supposed autism. It is about an expression of the drive towards 'decorationless perfection'. It is an expression of Austrian Neo-Liberal politico-economic thought in its search for the 'logical atom'. Neo-Liberalism is seen as global, driven by 'shareholder value', with little attention being paid to national economic policies. It seeks constantly to offer a defence of capitalism. Point F is at the conjunction of the lines of rationalism, rupturism, A-naturality.

Point G is where the 'dymaxion' concept is to be found, and a mass production ethic of 'doing more with less'. It is close in terms of its assumptions to what is now called 'Bright Green Environmentalism'. It relies upon the importance of highly skilled technocratic management with a shift of skill and expertise towards professional engineers. Point G brings the lines of rationalism, rupturism, naturality to a closure.

Point H is the conceptual space of the Baroque where much power comes from the use of state expenditure on public works and the *trompe l'oeil*. Its expression in the Palace of Versailles demonstrates absolute power over nature and the state. It is associated in this corner of the design cube with Keynesianism, for Keynesianism seeks social order and a defence of the status quo through security of employment and the expression of social responsibility by the elite. Its major concern is defence of the state's socio-economic responsibility, often in the form of massive public works. Point H is the place where the lines of rationalism, sedimentism, A-naturality meet.

For the sake of quick and easy exposition yet again, I have paired up antithetical *opposing corners* so that the reader can appreciate the deep structural tensions which exist within discrete patterns of organizational design. As I have said already, my analytical tools in undertaking this comparison rely upon patterning, which in turn consists of the structuring, formatting, and embellishing of the basic design. Let us consider how the first organizational

Summary of characterizations

example is comprehensible using these grappling irons as a model for what is to follow. I cannot claim that any of what is to follow represents a proper case study with a level of acceptable detail. My canvas is too broad for that, perhaps. The reader would have to satisfy themselves that each of these caricatures is not too distorting. It is perhaps a form of casuistry or case-based organizational reasoning (du Gay 2007: 138) in which I seek to engage which is permissive of 'taxonomic mapping' (Jonsen and Toulmin 1988). We begin with Point A, which is located for the reader by Figure 8.1, Each separate point will be located in this way by its own figure (Figures 8.1–8.8).

A. *Sensibility, sedimentism, naturality (a part of the natural)*

THE CASE OF THE NATIONAL TRUST
Now if we begin at the beginning, my nominee in this category might surprise British readers. It would be the National Trust (NT), an organization with a huge presence in the English Lake District and evincing a particular orientation towards the poet Wordsworth in particular. This may seem a parochial place to begin our analyses but NT is a rather large organization in the UK

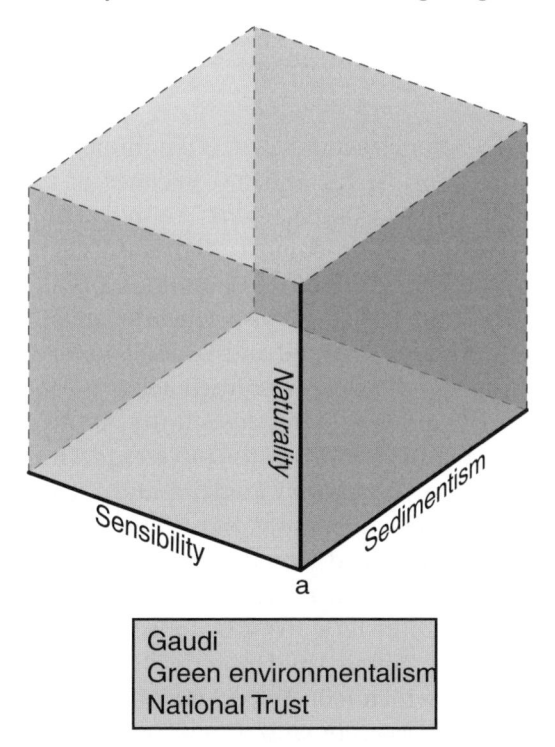

Figure 8.1
a. Sensibility, Sedimentism, Naturality—The Case of the National Trust

145

context, concerned, as Gaudi's Barcelona now is, with tourism. As we saw earlier (Broudehoux 2007), Barcelona is now the most gentrified city in existence and Gaudi's architecture is a major selling point. Put crudely, both NT and the city of Barcelona are selling a tourist experience.

It may appear obvious that there is a hint of Green Environmentalism in the ideology of this British organization but the reader will be asking just how Gaudi's architectural design resembles in any way whatsoever the National Trust of England and Wales. So this is a very difficult, yet interesting, organizational place to begin. As for 'greenness', William Wordsworth was to say that 'the passions of men are incorporated with the beautiful and permanent forms of nature', thereby encapsulating this corner of organizational thought. In terms of architecture and design, the identification of this corner of the design envelope was with 'excessively imaginative adornment'. But here, in this chapter, my concern is with organizational life reflective of this specific pattern of assumptions.

As mentioned above, I shall look to address the National Trust and other organizational examples in later sections through the threefold medium of what Dale and Burrell (2008: 48) call emplacement, enactment, and enchantment. The meanings of each these terms were outlined in Chapter 4 and these marry up respectively with 'structure', 'format', and 'embellishment'.

Emplacement in structure
By 2011 the NT had 5,500 permanent staff, 3.8 million members, and 61,500 volunteers. It was responsible for 280,000 hectares of land, 700 miles of coastline and over 200 buildings and gardens. It also had thousands of tenants in houses and farms. The Trust's income in 2010 was £406 million, with £125 million coming from the membership, £105 million from rents on the properties, and £50 million from legacies. It also generated income from the sale of items in its shops throughout England and Wales. Founded in 1895 by three Victorian philanthropists who were concerned about the rampant industrialization affecting the UK and destroying the countryside, its mission expresses a deep sensibility to romantic notions of the picturesque. It acts as protector of countryside and coastline throughout England and Wales and, as we have noted, is a major landowner in its own right. The National Trust had 100 members originally, and it is said that the first Duke of Westminster was a principal contributor at a time when the family owned (as they still do) large parts of Chelsea and Westminster in west London. They also happen to own large country estates throughout the United Kingdom. The National Trust claims to have a mission which reflects 'conservation, heritage and learning', which clearly marks it out as an organization located at an extreme position on the plane of sedimentism. It seeks to offer a 'meticulous duty of care' where all that it owns lies 'in safe hands'. It is about conservation, for it claims that

'we stand for places, for ever, for everyone'. It evinces a structure of and for natural protection, conceived of as defence of a national tradition of architecture and high(ish) culture.

Enactment of format
The National Trust has recently dropped the 'The' and moved towards using lower case in its straplines. This is seen by many members as symptomatic of the 'Disneyization' of the Trust. In October 2011, reports of dissatisfaction at attempts at 'the management of change' by Dame Fiona Reynolds and others were circulating, with calls for an extraordinary general meeting to discuss these unpopular innovations to 'liven up' properties, where staff wore costumes and role played. Enactment here means 'acting' inside the premises to bring a theatricality to the proceedings. Theming was to be taken further than ever before, so that actors were to be employed to 'bring the past to life'. The National Trust Executive was accused of seeking to become a 'dictatorship' by bringing in rules to prevent ordinary members questioning decisions made at the top. The debate is about 'protecting' on one hand and 'sharing' on the other, and the question is which side of this duality the NT member embraces more than the other. 'Protecting' suggests the whole issue of conservation and conservatism, whereas 'sharing' involves attempting to involve active participation from children and other visitors. This duality is one that the NT is currently addressing and it is likely at the time of writing that those with a 'protecting' orientation will prevail, not least because the typical member is well past child-rearing stage. The formatting of NT property is a major issue, particularly because of the need to 'process' the punter through old houses and country estates, when the properties themselves originally had quite different routes and routines.

Enchantment via embellishment
Visitors to National Trust shops or UK members of NT will know that these shops contain historically themed material with large price markups. Pictures of scenery, animals and birds, and great houses adorn various pieces of merchandise where the picturesque is in obvious profusion. Chocolate-box confectionery, calendars, and cookbooks, all decorated in the requisite NT regalia, are to be found in profusion. In other words, the NT is selling a particular form of landed heritage through 'excessively imaginative adornment'. But such a phrase would not be used to describe NT's corporate HQ.

The Trust's headquarters is at Heelas House in Swindon, Wiltshire. The name of the building comes from Beatrix Potter's married name, for she was a staunch defender of the Trust and its conservationist mission. It seeks to use open-plan offices unlike those it had in London. It is on a 'brownfield site', occupying the land where a disused railway line once ran. Cost saving has been allowed by the move out from central London of perhaps £1 million per annum. The building requires only 15 kilograms of carbon per square metre to be produced, instead of 169 kilograms in a typical air-conditioned office. About 40 per cent of electricity is generated from 1,554 photovoltaic cells on the roof, offering solar-powered heating as well as power generation. The building mimics the railway sheds it has replaced and uses timber and wool from NT properties. There are 450 people working there and we are told that very few car park places have been provided. This HQ, then, is by no means the locus of decorative ostentation. But its shops and houses are. They are decorated in ways which involve restoration to former glory and expenditure on authentic antiques and decorations. Whilst the Trust's HQ bears no resemblance to a Gaudi design, NT is protective of those Art Nouveau buildings that it owns and has developed an organization that secures the survival of the architecture and the goods within it across many designs and styles. But the reader should now come to recognize that they should *not* expect an easy equivalence of corporate HQ architecture and organizational design from this first and instructive example.

In short, the National Trust does resemble an extreme corner of the design envelope, where commitment to the past, to understanding Nature, and to developing some sense of sensibility into our understandings all come together in what is a commercial enterprise. And it has resonances with the pattern book that generated Gaudi's Catalan Romanticism and how he approached the structuring and formatting of his constructions. But at the level of embellishments within its corporate buildings, there is nothing of note. In other words, the reader should not expect the HQ of a corporation or large public sector organization to 'look' anything like the design pattern upon which the organization draws. The patterning may well operate at the level of the hidden, until one visits the organizational sites well away from one's expectations.

F. *Rationalism, rupturism, apart from the natural*

At the level of architectural design, in this particular corner was found the Wittgenstein House. Here, for my purposes in this section's corner space, is an organizational pattern occupied by the 'extremist' Henry Ford and his commitment to an autistic productivism, set within 'modern times'.

THE CASE OF FORD'S MOTOR COMPANY

Emplacement in structure
In a series of books published in the 1920s and 1930s, Ford generated an articulation of the Ford way. In his *Today and Tomorrow* (1926) we are allowed

Summary of characterizations

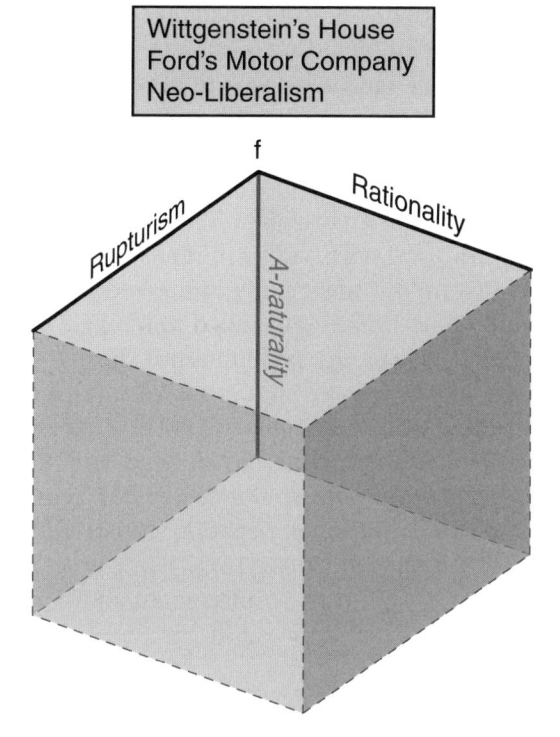

Figure 8.2
f. Rationality, Rupturism, A-naturality—The Case of Ford's Motor Company

a glimpse of his vision for the spatial transformation of America, and indeed the world, through the automobile:

> From a mere handful of men employed in a shop, we have grown into a large industry directly employing more than two hundred thousand men... Our dealers and service stations employ another two hundred thousand men. But by no means do we manufacture all that we use. Roughly, we buy twice as much as we manufacture, and it is safe to say that two hundred thousand men are employed on our work in outside factories... And this does not take into account the great number of people who in some way or another assist in the distribution or the maintenance of these cars... These people require food, clothing, shoes, houses, and so on... (Ford 1926: 1–2)

As is well known, Ford went in for 'vertical production', with the company seeking to control production from accessing raw material right through to car sales. He organized his plants into strictly segregated divisions, sometimes called 'chimneys' in which there was vertical movement of information and commands but very little lateral movement between divisions. Ford was very concerned with 'emplacement'. He listed 28 plants that the Ford family owned outside the 68 in the USA and Canada, and articulated the different related industries they owned including mining, foundries, tool making, glass manufacture, electric power, railroads, even grocers. They produced chemicals and fuel for 88 petrol stations and also for aeroplanes. If we look to Ford's approach to nature we confront his policies with regard to rubber. By 1914 the USA imported over 50 per cent of the world's crude rubber, which brought him into severe competition with British producers. By 1915, World War I had begun to show that motor vehicles had an immense military value over trains and horses and that Germany was greatly hampered by its lack of access to rubber. The USA and Great Britain continued to struggle over access to supplies of crude rubber and over the price charged during the 1920s. In this struggle, nature was the victim as huge areas of land were given over in experiments to produce viable rubber plantations. Technological developments concerning tyre manufacture meant that in 1922 longer-lasting 'balloon' tyres were launched whilst the search for synthetic rubber was launched by an inter-organizational network, consisting of Ford, Edison, and Firestone (Dale and Burrell 2008: 157). Fordism in the hands of its founder, then, concerns 'structuring' emplacement above all else.

Enactment of format
In *Moving Forward* (1937), Ford devotes two chapters to explaining how his company has been 'taking the methods overseas'. 'When the representatives of Russia came to buy tractors for their state farms, we told them: "No, you first ought to buy automobiles and get your people used to machinery and power and to moving about with some freedom. The motor cars will bring roads, and then it will be possible to get the products of your farms to the cities." They followed the advice and bought some thousands of automobiles. Now, after several years, they have bought some thousands of tractors' (Ford 1937: 7–8). Differences within the pattern were to be allowed, and were even encouraged under Fordism. His design for organizational processing was a radical one. There is a clear rupturism to his designs when he trumpets that 'We abandoned our Highland Park Plant—which was in its day the largest automobile plant in the world—and moved to the River Rouge plant because in the new plant there could be less handling of materials and consequently a saving. We frequently scrap whole divisions of our business—and as a routine affair. And then one has to be prepared against the day when a complete change may be necessary and an entirely new plant constructed to make a new product. We have gone through all of this.'

Of course, this rupturism that the Progressives shared with Ford did not mean that they *never* looked back. Ford did so when 'formatting' of his life's work was being contemplated for presentation to the world as a biographical journey. Ford and his colleagues saw residues and elements of the past in what

Summary of characterizations

they did. Near his death, Ford enacted a programme to set up a retrospective village in which the horse predominated so that future generations could see, via a working museum, the world that had been lost. Relatedly, there were elements of the past that greatly interested the Christian-inspired 'Progressives' and Ford thought could be used going forward into the future. In doing this reformatting, Ford did not work alone. A network of organizations was constructed in which like-minded industrialists sought collectively to format a world that was of more use to them.

Rationality was to be used in all variants of people processing, particularly in the 'Americanization Programs' which involved corporate classes to teach immigrant workers English. The culmination of these classes was made into a theatrical production where immigrants to the USA now working for Ford exited a large contrived 'mixing pot', wearing what was supposed to be standard US dress, having entered it in their 'traditional custom'. On exiting, the Americanized worker faced the assembled audience which had been incited to make as much noise of support as possible.

Enchantment via embellishment

As Banham (1986; 1972) has discussed, Ford's interest in 'zero architecture' approaches that of Wittgenstein quite closely, for both wished to strip out ornament and excrescences. Every spare inch of concrete is removed to give a stripped-down appearance for almost all factories and offices. This 'ruthless rationality' (Banham 1986: 86) was always attractive to cost-cutting entrepreneurs. This 'zero architecture' is a form of 'autism', perhaps, for in the construction of his automobile plants, there is a single-minded internalized rationality. Each edifice is reflective of a commitment to economic rationality, stripping out all extra cost. There is a concomitant view of the past as 'bunk' and a desire to control and exploit the natural world. To summarize, in any description of the extremities of organizational possibilities, Henry Ford usually makes an appearance, and this design cube is no exception. With his commitment to a right-wing Progressivism, a belief in the power of scientific rationality, and a desire to make nature subservient to his company, Ford fits this corner nicely.

Let us now move to another pair of oppositions in their styles of organizing, namely points B and E.

B. *Sensibility, rupturism, a-naturality*

THE CASE OF VIRGIN GALACTIC

We have seen that a useful term by which to describe some of Frank Gehry's buildings may well be a disorientation that comes from 'explosive alteration'. To my mind this ties in with the popularization of the disorientation that

Organizational Reflections of Corner Living

> Gehry
> Schumpeterianism
> Virgin Galactic

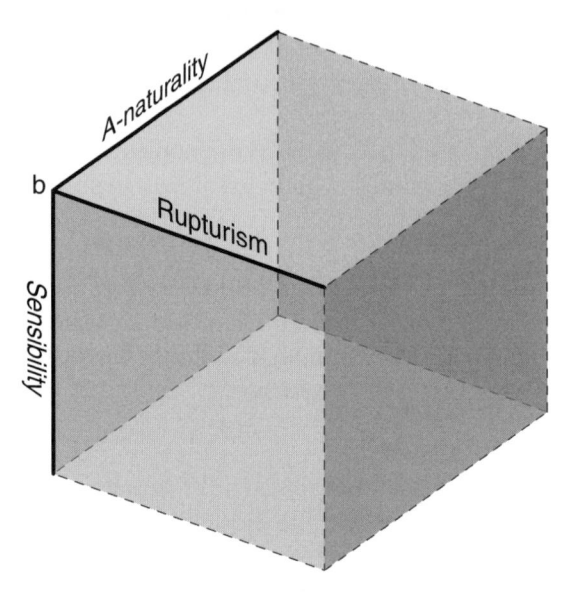

Figure 8.3
b. Sensibility, Rupturism, A-naturality—The Case of Virgin Galactic

comes through in Schumpeter's notion of 'creative destruction'. In *Capitalism, Socialism and Democracy* (1942), Joseph Schumpeter articulated the notion around that entrepreneurial figure, Henry Ford, who was seen as having developed the automobile industry via the creative destruction of existing modes of transport (for example, the railway system). Thus, booms and then busts were seen as essential to the development of capitalism because of their liberation of new energies to new entrepreneurs, through the destruction of the old. The welfare state, however (being fully discussed in that period 1935–45), according to Schumpeter would bring creative destruction to an end through the decline in entrepreneurialism. How times change. In the 21st century the welfare state is in retreat and entrepreneurialism is everywhere encouraged. It may well be that this change in the organization of parts of the business world is now being witnessed in the rise of *private* space travel and in the decline of NASA.

Emplacement in structure
According to Parker (2009: 86) there now exists a 'space libertarian community', with deals being done between various companies—the media, venture

capitalists speculating on future income, sponsors who want publicity, and so on. Parker says somewhat provocatively that:

> Dickens and Ormrod's materialist analysis of the space industries concludes that off-earth capitalism is pretty much like capitalism on earth, in the sense that it runs into periodic crises that need to be fixed by the development and exploitation of new markets. These 'fixes' are necessarily temporary, but the promise of the 'outer spatial fix' is that it (potentially) opens a variety of ways in which capitalism might be extended beyond the boundaries of the earth. Adopting some ideas from the geographer David Harvey, they argue that the commodification of space allows for various circuits of capital to be re-imagined and a hegemonic model of neoliberalism to spread skywards.

In the text emanating from the Cato Institute, *Space: The Free Market Frontier* (Hudgins 2002), NASA is seen as a huge problem for wasting taxpayers' dollars. Its fall from grace is spectacular:

> This is a dramatic turnaround from a government-funded organization renowned for its arrogance and intellectual superiority. Even the Russians have shown the sort of entrepreneurial zeal more akin to American capitalism. (Kemp 2007: 50)

As I write, it is only Russian craft, designed in the 1960s and based on battle tank designs, which are capable of carrying humans into space. NASA, with the end of the space shuttle programme, is currently unable to carry out this task, and is seen by many as an enormous failure in terms of its achievements and its cost. But out of this destruction of the state-based US space programme, new business opportunities have arisen.

According to Parker again (2009: 89):

> Sharing this vision of deregulation are a series of companies who wish to take capitalism further into space. There are now commercial proposals for flying capsules with ash or mementoes into the moon or out into space, orbital rides around the moon, moon tourism, space hotels (including a proposal from Hilton International), new methods of collecting solar energy, and even mining on the moon. Companies such as Bigelow Aerospace, Excalibur Almaz, Rocketplane, SpaceDev and Venturer Aerospace are involved in various speculative projects, most of them proposed or 'under development'. At least eleven places are also vying to become 'spaceports', seven of them in the USA. It seems that, forty years after the first man on the moon, the state–industrial monopoly that put him there can no longer protect its territory.

A leading company involved in this 'explosive alteration' is a joint venture between Scaled Composites and Richard Branson's Virgin organization. They have joined forces to form the Space Ship Company. It is better known as 'The Virgin Galactic' project and its aim is to send passengers into space for six minutes at a cost of $200,000 per person. At the time of writing, 450 passengers have signed up for this flight, with a $20,000 deposit each. This tourist flight was meant to have been available from 2009 but has been put back until 2013. Each vehicle is meant to carry six passengers and have two pilots. It is based in La Cruces, New Mexico, where the New Mexican authorities have constructed 'Space Port America' with a 10,000-foot runway to encourage this activity. Further spaceports are planned by the Space Ship Company for Dubai and elsewhere, to allow for global coverage. White Knight Two takes SpaceShipTwo on its back to a height of 53,000 feet and releases it. Thereafter, allowed to go upwards under its own power, the 60-foot-long craft passes the 100-kilometre mark above the Earth, which is supposed to represent the beginning of space 'proper'. It proceeds to 110 kilometres above the Earth's surface and allows passengers to remove their seat belts to experience weightlessness for the six-minute period. Its wings are then extended and it makes re-entry into the Earth's atmosphere, touching down at one of its spaceports.

As the master of self-publicity, Branson's company has published a book on Virgin Galactic wherein the project is described by Kemp (2007). He begins his polishing of the Virgin image by articulating in as clear a way as possible a position marked by sensibility, rupturism, and a belief in being apart from nature. First, this is clearly a hugely costly 'Enterprise' (the name of the first spacecraft to be launched), requiring development costs that usually only the state can bear. There have to be large environmental consequences too, even though it is claimed that Virgin Galactic is 'greener' than the efforts of NASA. Sinha et al. (2012: 225) describe Branson as a 'Celebrity CEO' who depends upon public attention for the continued operation of his empire. 'Celebrification' is a process which is mass-mediated by the press and TV and is designed to produce the image of 'the possibility and desirability of untrammelled human agency, power and distinction in a complex world' (Guthey et al. 2009: 12). What better, then, than to conquer space through entrepreneurship?

Enactment of format
Nationalism and bureaucracy, twin enemies of the (supra-)globalizing business tycoon, have no place in the new frontier of space. Spencer (2004: 19) is not coy about this:

> Yes, we are right at the beginning of a space renaissance. And it is happening because we are finally getting it—that this renaissance is a private show. It is fueled by you and me, not by mega-government agencies, not by skunk-black secret projects.

Virgin Galactic, then, is but one example of a Neo-Liberal organization in search of the fruits of creative destruction and seeking to enact that destruction too (Harvey 2007). Yet its organizational structure and processes are not at all clear. How it functions as an organization adopting this strategy appear somewhat inchoate, and the slippage in launch date is not a surprise, perhaps, if one believes in the values of 'bureaucracy'. The entrepreneurial zeal also produces many a failure and we shall have to await delivery of the spacecraft and its mother ship to better understand the organization that has gone into them.

Enchantment via embellishment
More interestingly, perhaps, Kemp tells us that:

> Space has become interesting again. And so much more fun. The Cold War rivalry of NASA and the Soviet cosmonauts was highly political and intensely serious. What is happening now is a space renaissance—and any renaissance is characterised by more colour and flair and a flowing of fresh thinking and activities. (Kemp 2007: 5)

Here, we see the search for sensibility in 'colour and flair' and even a renaissance, allowing, of course, for the rupturism with the present that so many entrepreneurs claim. Space is presented as exciting and as a must-go tourist destination for those of affluence.

In design terms, this is an example of a corner where structures of emplacement, the format of enactment, and the enchantment of embellishment line up with each other in both the architectural example and the organizational example. One can overdo simple connections here but both required the resources of multimillionaires to put up the money and work at the publicization of the project. Both relied upon the deconstruction of what went before. Both require huge computing power and the resources of CAD machines to hold their designs in spatial tension. Both involve high-profile celebrities in their memberships. In short, the shock of the new is embraced in how both spacecraft and Stata building are presented as 21st-century enterprises at the cutting edge of technology. But also note that both projects are monuments to their 'creators'—meaning the person or persons with the money.

Let us turn now to the opposite point in styles of organizing which is:

E. *Rationality, sedimentism, naturality*

THE CASE OF TILTING
In Jefferson's 'New World Order' there was an orientation towards cultivation of the land in order to create a (slave-based) utopian collectivism. What I have chosen to concentrate upon here is a particular New World Order based upon those fishing communities/collectives around the coast of Newfoundland. These 'outports' are the oldest European settlements in Canada, having

Organizational Reflections of Corner Living

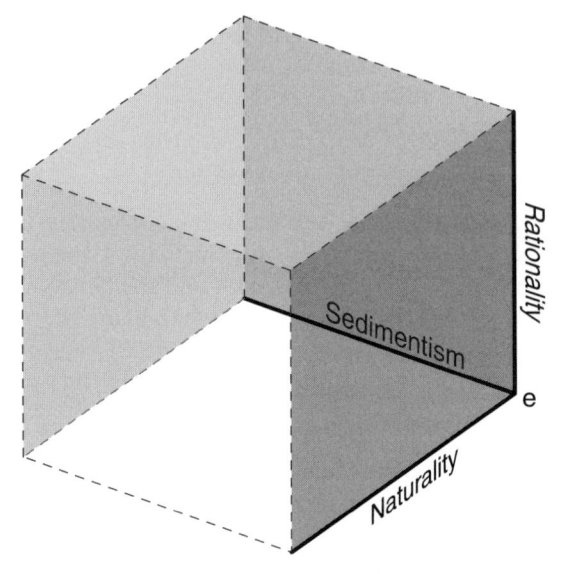

Figure 8.4
e. Rationality, Sedimentism, Naturality—The Case of Tilting

concentrations of settlers from Portugal, Spain, France, and England. 'Outports' are those fishing villages in Newfoundland and Labrador that are remote from the centres of population because of the difficulties in driving on roads across the harsh terrain. Communication, therefore, between these ports was via the sea. The main occupation was fishing for cod off the Newfoundland Grand Banks and so the economy was and is marine based. Villages in these remote areas of Newfoundland have survived both the near extinction of the Newfoundland cod stocks and the changes to social structure and employment opportunities that happened as a result of this ecological disaster. There had been catastrophic collapse of the cod population throughout the 1980s, which some have described as a 'managed annihilation' because of the use of high-technology boats taking all sizes of fish without regard to the reproduction of the shoals. It was and still is recognized that cod had been virtually hunted to extinction.

Summary of characterizations

Emplacement in structure
With the cod moratorium of 1992, some outports faced a forced relocation by the state since their economies were smashed. The Canadian government insisted that 100 per cent of the population of these remote communities had to agree in order for members to benefit from the large payments being handed out. Unemployment rates were enormous in these communities, which possessed an ethnic and racial homogeneity that is the complete opposite of cosmopolitanism. One island of particular note was Fogo Island, famous for its 'pure' Irish culture. Here, not a single resident male held a university degree since the typical lure was the mainland for those seeking professional careers. The fishermen of Fogo Island had founded a protective union many years before, and a cooperative store still functions at the aptly named 'Seldom Come By'. In the 1960s there had been an experiment with 'participatory communication' amongst the 555 people on the island. The 'Fogo Process' was the name given to this experiment, which was widely hailed as a successful attempt to introduce participation into the island. It was reflective, and productive, of an egalitarian set of communities set around the coast. And most interesting on this interesting island is the township of Tilting, found to the north. Here, Robert Mellin stayed for a decade (1987–97) to study the population and its architecture. His book is entitled *Tilting: House Launching, Slide Hauling, Potato Trenching and Other Tales from a Newfoundland Village* (2003). Mellin is a professor of architecture and what captured his interest were some remarkable practices in the town reflecting a commitment to a particular rationality based on harsh environment. Traditionally, outports are noted for their distinctive architecture of small wooden houses, associated outbuildings, and fishing piers. Tilting is treeless, the houses face the sea, and there has been a practice of utilizing the old Irish system of land inheritance, where sons build their own houses upon the father's land. This creates collectives of housing based on family ties, all concentrated in particular areas. Rooms are added on to houses when the family grows and, remarkably, *they are taken away* if the occupant is elderly and needs less space. The building materials are then recycled in other 'additions'. The Tilting villagers exemplify sustainable practices in their architecture and living, with no attempt now being made to dominate nature, not even in what little is left of the fishing industry. They represent the antithesis of a 'spaceport' (Dicks 2000). This is why they exemplify an approach to seeing themselves very much as a part of nature, with a concomitant social development, notwithstanding that they have reoriented themselves to forgoing industrial-style fishing.

Enactment of format
Look at contemporary pictures of the township and you will see there is not a hi-tech fishing trawler to be seen. That way of life has virtually disappeared, to

be replaced by heritage and history-oriented work. Mellin (2003) points out another remarkable architectural practice to do with recycling. Because the harbours freeze each winter, it is possible to move houses around, across the ice, and relocate them. Houses are specifically designed to be founded on very insubstantial brick piles, which make their 'launching' to another location comparatively easy. Houses are regularly moved across the small bay to other locations. 'Slide hauling' is the way in which other large goods are moved around by the collective throughout the winter months. In terms of sedimentism, there is great emphasis put upon Irish ancestry and the protection of Irish culture. Songs and music brought from Ireland predominate and there was great resistance to the 'cultural genocide' threatened by the Canadian government's attempts at resettlement of the populations who lived in the outports.

Now this might not seem credible to some readers, but there is an Arcadian version of the life of Tilting which resonates with Jefferson's image of a more southerly part of the North American continent. It is a similarity based on a structured attempt to live through the cultivation of a primary industry and to eschew urban living. At the level of enactment, both represent a type of collectivism enacted via a shared culture and shared ethnicity. They are communities of practice in which the community is cemented together by a Durkheimian 'mechanical solidarity' based on a deep similarity of experience and background. Both face a changing world with fortitude but the rise of bureaucratized industrialization threatens the natural resources upon which the community thrives, and the possibility of an influx of 'incomers' looking for jobs and homes might well appear to threaten both. *Enchantment via embellishment* differs here remarkably because climates are vastly different and the cultural heritage of the two communities draws upon different worlds, albeit both from corners of Europe. Yet both communities paint their wooden fences white. In Tilting, the defence of rural Irish culture is a key part of the community's raison d'être today. In the University of Virginia, it was a 'high' culture of the Grand Tour that was being promulgated in the 19th century.

We move now to a new pairing of organizational opposites.

D. *Sensibility, rupturism, naturality*

THE CASE OF THE ZAPATISTAS

The major rupture that this corner of organizational design depends upon is some form of utopian thinking where democracy comes into the world of humanity and its organizations. Whilst Parker (2002: 5) declaims that 'Peter Drucker, Daniel Bell, Alvin Toffler, Tom Peters, Charles Handy, Peter Senge and even Bill Gates have all written within a genre of book length fantasy which proposes that people will be happier, richer and smarter if the world is organized in such and such a way,' he recognizes that today Utopias are

Summary of characterizations

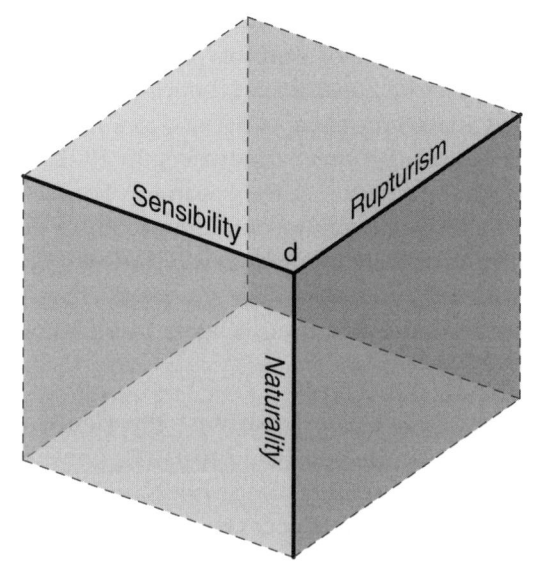

Figure 8.5
d. Sensibility, Rupturism, Naturality—The Case of the Zapatistas

written in an increasingly conservative way. The powerful form of social critique to be found in More, Butler, and Morris and Le Guin and Piercy leads to a radical utopianism—but where is one to find this in organized form (McLeod 2004)?

It might be argued that anarchism (meaning, of course, without central rule) cannot be relevant to a globalizing world economy in the 21st century. With its emphasis on small-scale, anti-state, pro-local democracy, anti-leadership, ultra-leftist views, what could be the possible use of such a stance to the contemporary world? Anarchism, however, is alive and functioning in the anti-globalization movement (Bircham and Charlton 2001: 321–8). Anti-capitalist demonstrators in a variety of recent economic summit meetings have organized themselves, using quite explicit forms of anarchist organization and rhetoric. Exploiting modern forms of communication but within a cell-like structure that emphasizes the benefits of small-scale activism and acephalism, anarchists have discovered ways, again, of circumventing opponents committed to large-scale bureaucracies. Commentators such as Manuel Castells (1997) have shown the relevance of anarchism to Mexican Zapatistas and it is clear that more widely in Latin America, it is a widely accepted organizational principle (Bethell 1984; Marshall 1993).

Emplacement in structure
What, then, is the democratic architecture of the Zapatistas? As Castells (1997: 73–80) shows, as far as the RAND corporation (of whom we will speak later) is concerned, Mexico is 'the scene of a prototype transnational social netwar of the 21st century'. The *Ejercito Zapatista de Liberacion Nacional* had been formed in the 1970s in the Chiapas province of Mexico as a peasant defence force to protect themselves against the large landowners. In 1972, some tribal groups were legally granted a 'bioreserve' in the Lacandon Forest (which appears to have been a way of allowing logging companies to enter the forest), but this act displaced families already living there. It was these 4,000 families and their supporters who formed the nucleus of the Zapatistas. They gained some help from Catholic priests who leaned towards liberation theology.

Enactment of format
One could argue that it was the Zapatistas' experience of NAFTA which brought its fermentation to the boil. The Zapatistas, however, see themselves as but part of a 500-year fight against colonizers. Named after Emiliano Zapata, who had been instrumental eight decades before in the peasants being offered agrarian reform, the Zapatistas saw these reforms being overturned by the NAFTA agreement. The priests helped organize the movement, bringing together peasants in unions based upon the community. Armed insurrection took place in the face of the NAFTA 'reforms' and the processes of 'economic modernization' that Mexico agreed to undertake. On the day that the NAFTA agreement came into effect in 1994, an uprising of 3,000 men and women, mainly of Indian ethnicity, took place. It was suppressed by superior military might but the government chose to negotiate with the Zapatistas. For the first time, negotiations were held in the Indian languages, not Spanish, and a ceasefire was announced.

Enchantment via embellishment
What has attracted so much attention is the Zapatistas' use of the Internet. They were described as the 'first informational guerrilla movement' (Castells 1997: 79), since through the use of videos, telecommunications, and computers, emanating supposedly from deep in the forest, they used the Internet to mobilize global support. Meetings in 'meat-space' also brought the Zapatistas to prominence so that they became known as revolutionary forces both through being seen on platforms and exhibition halls and through word of mouth. The fame of the Zapatistas spread in North America and Europe. The expectations of innovation in appearance, rules, and conduct, and the overall shock of the new, are also there in their organizational form in facing the

Summary of characterizations

issues of modernity and industrialization (Castells 1997: 76). They feel at home with the mystical and the spiritual and this is reflected in ceremony and art that are not rooted in a European sensibility. They draw upon 'native' and 'naïve' themes in their construction.

Clearly at the level of embellishments, animals figure in both and there is a strong naturalistic bent to the design imagery. So whilst on the surface the embellishments of Art Nouveau do not look that different from the embellishments to the organizational structure and behaviour of the Zapatistas, my argument here is that the Zapatistas in fact closely resemble in several ways the example of Art Nouveau at the beginning of the 20th century. They ride a similar wave of revolution in the 21st century. Both Art Nouveau and the Zapatistas represent spirits of optimism at the fin de siècle. They share emplacements. Both are seen as examples of novelty in organizational design and both embrace a 'spiritualism' in coming to their subject matter. Of course, their formats for enactment differ in that one was very much based around design catalogues for particular products to be sold in the market and the other is seen to rely on that 21st-century technology, the Internet, selling politics and organizational difference.

Pitted against this extremity of the design cube is:

H. *Rationalism, sedimentism, a-naturality*

THE CASE OF ENRON
I have maintained that the architectural and design style most associated with this corner of the design envelope is the Baroque and as we shall see it has a great concern for the *trompe l'oeil*, grottoes, and caves. My argument here is that an organization in recent times which approximated this Baroque set of features was none other than Enron. Both the Baroque and Enron were prone to a 'madness of order' (Burrell and Dale 2006). Much has been written on this case and I do not wish to cover old ground, so my exposition here will be brief and to the point.

Emplacement in structure
It is specifically to Enron's false dealer rooms that I will briefly turn, for Enron created an organization based upon tricks of the eye. Impression management was a key part of its armoury whilst there are also grottoes and caves in which members of the organization could hide. In Mimi Swartz and Sherron Watkins's book *Power Failure: the inside story of the collapse of Enron* (2004), the writing is replete with such imagery. Thus, 'illusory profits hid its ballooning debt', 'inside a honeycomb of financial entities'. Reminiscent of the Baroque's concern for mazes, Chinese walls were said to exist within Enron so that

Organizational Reflections of Corner Living

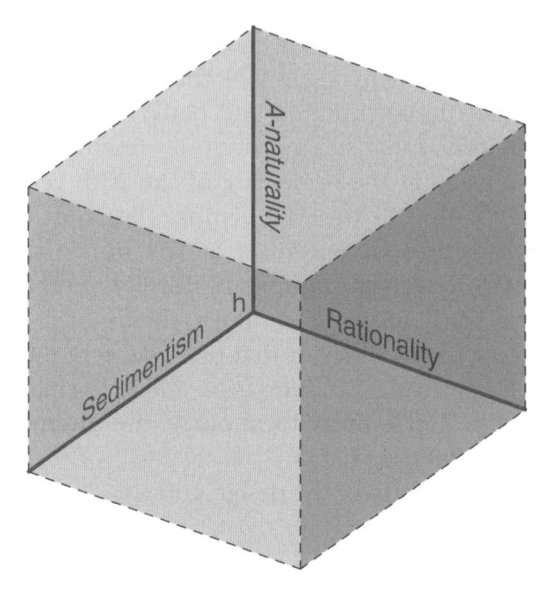

Figure 8.6
h. Rationality, Sedimentism, a-naturality—The Case of Enron

departments did not know what their colleagues were up to and competition between them was encouraged.

Enactment of format
Bethany McLean and Peter Eckland's 2006 book *Enron: the Smartest Guys in the Room* deals with similar issues. White undulating walls contained a cavernous space wherein banks and banks of computer screens were aligned in rows. There were four screens to each Enron employee, dealing not only in energy but in energy futures. Benefiting from massive deregulation of the state, and privatization, Enron brought new ways of making money to energy supply. Buying up assets that made losses, they took advantage of changes in accounting regulations so that they could claim projected profits were actually profits and in this practice they were assisted by their auditors, Arthur Andersen.

In 2000, Enron was ranked seventh in the Fortune 500 and was supposed to be worth $100 billion. In effect, it had become a bank without having any banking regulations in place to govern it. In terms of the *hidden recesses* of the company, it had developed new systems and instruments to hide what was going on. It was trading derivatives but outside any legitimate stock exchange

Summary of characterizations

and the attendant regulation; it used 'mark to market' valuations of its worth; it set up Special Purpose Entities, which were trusts in which to hide things; it used Volumetric Production Payments (VPP), wherein it loaned money to oil and gas companies in return for oil and gas; it developed Cactus funds, which were similar to traded bonds, made up of VPPs; it set up a JEDI (Joint Energy Development Investors) with the major pension fund for Californian state employees. Overall, it became the 'market maker' for oil and gas prices, which went upwards, despite the rhetoric of Enron claiming that it could drive energy prices down. In 2000 it could not maintain electricity supplies and over the summer large numbers of people died in the heat.

Enchantment via embellishment
So far as *trompes l'oeil* are concerned, the classic example from Enron is the creation of a fake dealing room where visiting analysts to Houston were shown traders acting in a pretence of undertaking transactions. These visits were carefully choreographed in the Enron Energy Services part of the HQ and these premises existed for some time, as furnished and arranged, only for the fooling of visitors. According to Joseph Phelan, who was head of EES (BBC Business News 21 February 2002), staff were brought on from other floors and told to pretend to be at work concluding trades. Phones rang constantly to suggest a highly busy trading room and the buzz in the facility's atmosphere was entirely false. Everyone, apart from the analysts, was acting.

And perhaps in a similar way we should recall the movie *The Sting*. Here, the lead mafioso who is the object of the conmen's desire is led to believe that the briefly created bookies' illegal gambling den is a real one, through actors and tricks of the eye. We see precisely the same features as Enron's EES. A hidden room, actors, a mark who is greedy, pecuniary violence perpetrated against the punter, and so on are all there as a mirror image to the much larger-scale scam of the Enron dealing room.

At the level of structures of emplacement, then, my view is that Enron looked like a Baroque organization. Certainly it seemed to utilize a form of Baroque reason (Buci-Glucksmann 1992) in which the maintenance of power is central. Their formattings of enactment too are similar, in that the pattern of enacting everyday organization in both relies upon strong central figures who wish to control imagery above all else, and place great emphasis on smoke and mirrors. If Versailles kept up a great pretence by moving water around between fountains, Enron maintained its pretence by moving money around and—as the residents of California discovered—not electricity. Their embellishments designed to enchant the auditor differed, of course, rooted as they were between Houston and continental Europe, and lying centuries apart.

We now turn to our final pairing of opposing corners of the design cube. These are points C and G.

Organizational Reflections of Corner Living

C. *Sensibility, sedimentism, a-naturality*

THE CASE OF FREEDOM TOWER

The image I am keen to play with here is the collapsing tower, both of Beauvais, as well as in myth, and found in the Gothic style of thinking. In this ludibrium, let me take a longish quote from William Golding's novel *The Spire* in order to make my point.

> 'Right Father. I've never denied your interest—even your enthusiasm. You couldn't know of course. But things have settled themselves, haven't they? And I'm glad, in a way. No. Not in a way; in every way. Things have come to a point.'
> 'What point?'
> Roger Mason laughed easily, in the dim choir, like a man at peace.
> 'It stands to reason. Now we must stop building.'
> Jocelyn smiled with his lips. He saw Roger from a long way off, and small. Now, he thought. We shall see.
> 'Explain yourself then.'
> The master builder examined the palms of his hands, knocked the dust off them.

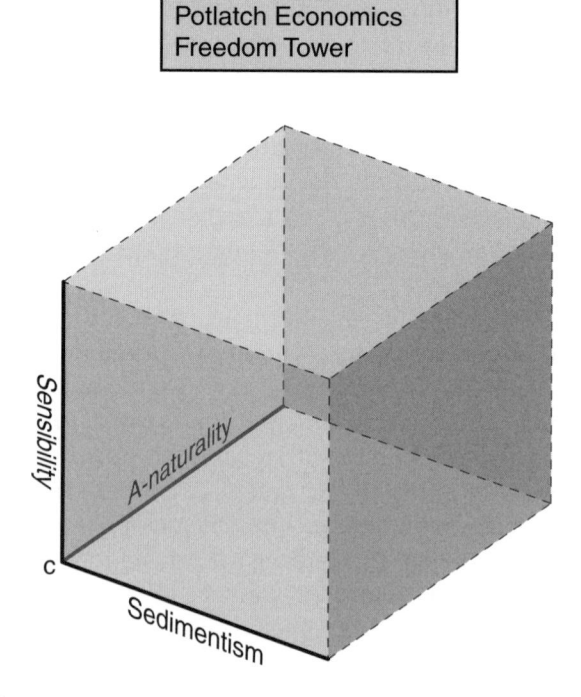

Figure 8.7
e. Sensibility, Sedimentism, a-naturality—The Case of Freedom Tower

'You know as well as I do, Reverend Father. We've gone as high as we can.'
(William Golding *The Spire* 1964: 83)

Emplacement in structure
This section from Golding's novel is as close as one can get to the clearest expression of 'the will to form', a will to form the landscape and even to defy gravity—to control 'our' world as best as we can, using all our powers of organization. Yet the spire falls. Organization can only take us so far. The Gothic builders knew this, and often sacrificed themselves in order for their cathedrals to survive. But architecture in this part of the design envelope is about fear more than sacrifice.

Parker's organizational take on 'Gothic' (2009) is far too broad for my tastes but it does raise the issue of the mutability of the term 'Gothic' and some deeply entrenched fears. Beginning as a term of abuse used by Vasari, it transmogrifies over the years to become a signifier of worlds of vampires, monsters, and haunted castles. This is not my understanding of 'Gothic' (even if it is acceptable to discuss such things as the monstrous as 'Gothic'). Of course, it can be a term used to describe sites of darkness and collapse, and there is the fact of 'gothic's antagonism to the possibility of human progress (Davenport-Hine 1998: 276) but the cathedral of Beauvais for me is a central signifier here.

Enactment of format
I have written (with Karen Dale) elsewhere about fear and the Freedom Tower on the site of the collapsed Twin Towers, so will be brief here. Yet as I write this paragraph on 11 September 2012, this is still a raw issue. The new buildings around 'Ground Zero' will attempt to be the most secure edifices in the whole world. Intensive use of surveillance cameras, huge metal and concrete barriers to traffic, and a whole panoply of identification checks at their heavily guarded and fortified entrances will make these commercial buildings, owned by the Port of New York, the most security conscious on the planet. Their construction has been marked by feuds between Daniel Libeskind's architectural practice and Skidmore, Owings and Merrill (SOM), represented by David Childs. So a contentious joint project carrying so much symbolic weight has ended (almost) in edifices built upon fear and hate on so many levels. At the level of the architects, Libeskind (2004: 255) says:

> Here were the rules of the SOM game: Nobody from Studio Daniel Libeskind was allowed into SOM's offices unless an SOM staffer with an equivalent title was present... At the beginning, I was not allowed into the offices unless David Childs was present. Yama asked why. The answer came back that I was intimidating and might gain an advantage over Childs and the SOM staff.

At other levels, of course, fear of attack and hatred of the 'terrorist' mark out this highly emotive site as a collapsed tower in the classic Gothic way. Rational

Organizational Reflections of Corner Living

organization can take us only so far in any building. Sooner or later, sensibility must enter the frame. The design logics of Beauvais Cathedral and SOM, as architectural and organizational reflections of each other, may not strike the reader as immediately obvious. Yet their structures of design are akin. Excess and transgression are to be found in both. The higher one builds, the more excessive and transgressive the activity becomes. We are told by Owings (1973: 55–6) that he married into the Otis family, meaning that high-rise buildings were designed by someone married to an heiress of a high-speed-lift manufacturing company. Achieving height was made easy. It is the design pattern of seeking height that drives the tower to collapse. Height has long been valorized and whether in the form of the corporeal, the architectural, or the geographical, it has come to be associated with the achievement of command and control. The juxtaposition of 'high and mighty' is reflective of just such an association. Countries vie with each other to control the commanding heights that separate them. Whilst the enactment may change, atop mountain chains great walls are built to both keep out and keep in those the state wishes to dominate through emplacement. Within the heavily populated river flood plains tall buildings are erected upon the mounds which there pass for high ground. In 21st-century Riyadh, rival princes preside over competing towers to press their claims for political influence with the king. Mountain, river valley, or desert matters not. Height provides help to the powerful everywhere. Towers of Babel are constructed still.

Of course, the *embellishing designed to create enchantment* differs as height is sought and collapse is feared. So whilst SOM have become masters of decorating their 'international style' in a local way, the structures and formats, the emplacements, and the enactments used are essentially 'Gothic' in orientation. It is that humanity tries to outdo their gods. Indeed, Owings is quite specific throughout Chapter 5 of his memoirs (Owings 1973) about the fact that SOM explicitly sought to be master builders in the Gothic tradition. On 12 September 2001, *Time* magazine proclaimed: 'If you want to humble an empire it makes sense to maim its cathedrals. They are symbols of its faith, and when they crumble and burn, it tells us we are not so powerful and we can't be safe' (quoted in Urry 2003: v). The link between Gothic cathedrals and contemporary corporate architecture is not a difficult one to capture.

Opposed to this great monumentalism, we find Bright Green Environmentalism.

G. *Rationalism, rupturism, naturality*

THE CASE OF ENVAL
In this far corner of the design envelope, there is affinity with Buckminster Fuller's notion of 'doing more with less'. Here one finds a confidence in

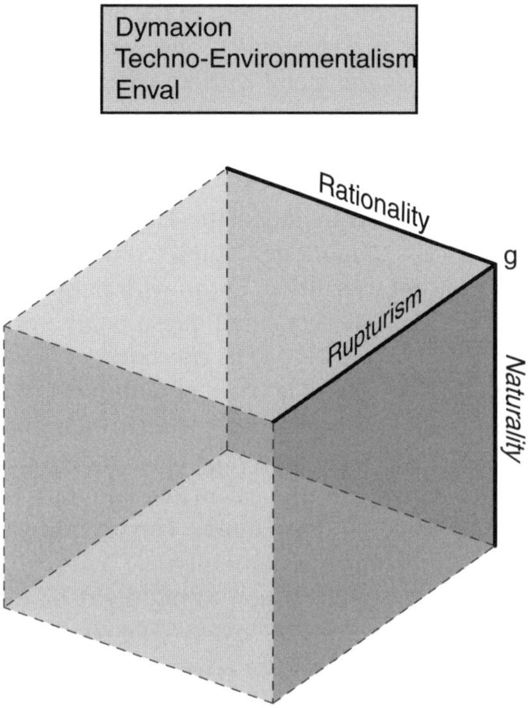

Summary of characterizations

> Dymaxion
> Techno-Environmentalism
> Enval

Figure 8.8
g. Rationality, Rupturism, Naturality—The Case of Enval

science and engineering and in the abilities of technology to solve some pressing environmental issues. These new 'green' technologies are often to be found in small-scale high-tech, university-led enterprises and I have chosen Enval as the particular representative of this sort of design corner for no other reason than its chairman has an MBA from my own university.

Emplacement in structure
Enval is based upon Cambridge Science Park, which is commercial property owned by Trinity College and has been labelled as the key part of 'Silicon Fen'. As a company, it grew out of Cambridge University's Department of Chemical Engineering when one of the professors and a PhD student developed a technique of 'microwave-induced pyrolysis' whereby aluminium recycling is permissible from waste packaging. Aluminium production requires huge amounts of energy and the recycling of it from waste saves this cost in cash and pollution. As I write this section, by strange coincidence, today it has been announced that Alcan's aluminium smelter at Lynemouth in Northumberland is to close because of high energy costs and falling demand for the metal. I know several people who work there, so their unhappy redundancy will add

to the already high levels of unemployment in the area—but the surrounding towns will become cleaner as a side effect. The patented work of Enval is a development which recycles the metal without oxygen, so greenhouse gases are not a by-product of pyrolysis. However, those oils and gases that are produced from the process can be utilized in heating and other energy-requiring processes. Enval is now a private company, backed since 2006 by a consortium of investors which included the East of England Development Agency, Cambridge Angels, Cambridge Capital Group, and Cambridge Enterprise. It has set up a prototype facility in Luton with help from the food giant, Kraft. The organization remains very small, presumably until full-scale operations of the technology are possible, so its *enactment of format* is not particularly clear. Yet it serves as an example of an organization that believes that a rupture with the past is possible in terms of the technology of recycling waste, and that new attitudes to waste are both possible and desirable. It also evinces a commitment to rationalism and the calculated adoption of new technologies based on the microwave. In these senses, it is an occupant of the corner space of rationalism, rupturism, and naturality.

Connections that I might have chosen to highlight here between Fuller's designs and the nascent technology of Enval would revolve around the use of aluminium in both approaches and the advances in the uses to which this metal is put after recovery. The design logic is built around high technology and new forms of metallurgy. The organizational *embellishments* of the two examples drawn from this corner of the design envelope are by no means identical, although one is an architecture of the North American plains and the other is of the East Anglian fens. It is a set of examples primarily drawing upon structured emplacement and enactment through formats that is reflected here.

Summary of organizational characterizations

What should the reader make, then, of these oppositions? Well, there is no easy identification of signature artists' radical building design with everyday organizational examples but the organizational design principles underpinning them are quite similar. I ask the reader to mull over these suggested strands and look afresh at deeply held foundational assumptions upon which they assume particular types of organizing take place.

As we conclude this chapter, we are faced with a pairing of the extremities of our conceptual envelope as follows:

a. The National Trust
f. The factories of Henry Ford

Summary of organizational characterizations

b. Virgin Space Shuttle
e. Tilting fishing community

d. Zapatistas
h. Enron

c. Skidmore, Owings and Merrill
g. Enval

In the corner of the cube around Point A is a conceptual extremity characterized by a commitment to something akin to Green Environmentalism, reflected in the design interests of Gaudi, and to the organizational mission of protectionist groups such as the National Trust. Volunteers make up a large fraction of the organizational structures. There is a seasonal element to the rhythm of organizational functioning. Participation by 'members' (not 'employees') is a crucial part of their functioning. The reader will know that proximity to this design corner is predicated upon a constellation of assumptions and interests based on what I have called sensibility, sedimentism, and naturality.

The corner of Point F is an extremity which is highly populated in the contemporary world. Its politico-economic system of choice is Neo-Liberalism, and its design ethic is the stripped-down Modernism liked by Ludwig Wittgenstein and carried into the world by Henry Ford's Motor Company. Its motto may well be 'zero architecture' if that means governance structures of capital flows, whilst its aesthetic dictum is 'decorationless perfection' in that such an approach strips out all superfluous cost. Neo-Liberalism valorizes flow over structure—unless of course 'system architecture' in the form of military structures is threatened. It asserts the values of globalization in the interests of shareholder value. Its highly popular assumptions are aligned around rationality, rupturism, and anti-naturality. The power of this style of organizing means perhaps that we are all f...ed.

Point C is an extreme position in the design cube which is unpopulated. Its politico-economic system choice is akin to the highly conservative potlatch ceremony where power maintenance is the issue through the use of 'magnificence'. And its architectural style commitment is to something massive and monumental like the cathedral at Beauvais. Today the prickly issue of the Freedom Tower in New York bears this hallmark of Gothic monumentalism and humanity's designs to set about controlling nature and its component, gravity. These attempts to deal with the inevitability of the collapsing tower always fail. Management's duty as servants of capital is to ensure the greater magnificence of their paymasters, and to demonstrate their closeness to god(s) whilst not drawing attention to the likelihood of foundational collapse. Its design coordinates are sensibility, sedimentism, and a-naturality.

Organizational Reflections of Corner Living

Point G is identified here with Bright Green Environmentalism as its politico-economic system choice. Its architectural style commitment is to designs such as Fuller's dymaxion, and small high-technology companies on the likes of Cambridge Science Park mean that organizations such as Enval might be thought to reflect the extremity's design choices. These, of course, are rationality, rupturism, and naturality (being a part of nature). Management's function in this corner of the cube is to come up with problem-solving solutions to technical issues. It is indicative of the 'savant' side of the dichotomy previously outlined. This is a long tradition in management thinking from Taylor's time onward; but organization theorists please note, this is not a densely populated area of the cube at the time in which this book is written.

The corner wherein Point B stands is a popular corner with supporters of late capitalism. Schumpeterian economics predominate here and the deconstructionist movement across art and design and architecture reflect the interest in complexity and the badly named 'chaos theory'. Thus Gehry's architecture in Bilbao and his MIT building come to stand for this design approach. My nomination of Branson's Virgin Galactic at this point comes from its creative destruction of NASA's work and its alleged dependence on the arts of computer technology and 3D animations for its technical achievement (if this does in fact happen). The manager here is not a bureaucrat but is much more of an entrepreneur-salesperson selling an out-of-this-world experience. This part of the design cube appeals to watchers of *Dragon's Den*. It is to be found where sensibility, rupturism, and anti-naturality meet in the corner.

Point E is a tight location where the tourists gaze upon heritage sites, and this is the basis for a politico-economic strategy for survival, protection of employment, and limited economic development. My nomination for this location is not an organization but a community, suggesting that it is organiz*ing* and not organiz*ations* that needs to be considered. So there was some presentation of material on Tilting community in Newfoundland. Management here takes the form of repackaging and marketing. It is about impression management rather than any other form of managing. This was compared to the University of Virginia which shares much in common at the level of design principles. This corner is characterized by a commitment to the principles of rationality, sedimentism, and naturality.

Point D is a corner that many find difficult to contemplate as a design choice. Its commitment to radical change in the system frightens many who would point to the design excesses of Pol Potism. Whilst this set of principles is extreme, it is an old one and architecturally we can see that in Brussels the Hall of the People was meant to include and exclude in quite rigid ways. Similarly today, that same people's socialism is evident in the work and ideology of the Mexican Zapatistas. The managerial role in this part of the extremities of the design cube is somewhat defunct since acephalous forms of

Summary of organizational characterizations

organizing are valued much more than those offering hierarchy. It has made design choices in its structure and appearance and whilst these are redolent of the choices of positions very close to sensibility, rupturism, and naturality, we must note that they do still appeal to groups across the world.

Point H is also a popular location because of its defence of capitalism and the power of the state apparatus. Its politico-economic strategy is one akin to Keynesianism with its interest in the need for full employment to control the masses and thereby restrain the power of the mob. Keynes himself was quite clear on this. Its architecture of choice is huge state-sponsored building projects like the Palace of Versailles or the Olympic Park at Stratford in east London. For through massive public works and the provision of services, the economy is thought to prosper. Hence Enron entered electricity supply and the provision of public utilities as a private company in order to take its share of this state-led demand. Unfortunately, it appears to have been more

Eight Points of Opposition	
A Sensibility, Sedimentism, Naturality	Green Environmentalism Gaudi/Art Nouveau National Trust
C Sensibility, Sedimentism, A-naturality	Potlatch Economics Beauvais Cathedral Freedom Tower/Skidmore, Owings and Merrill
B Sensibility, Rupturism, A-naturality	Schumpeterianism Gehry's MIT building/Deconstructionism Virgin Galactic
D Sensibility, Rupturism, Naturality	Pol Potism Maison du People/Art Nouveau Zapatistas
E Rationality, Sedimentism, Naturality	Heritage Economics University of Virginia/Jefferson Tilting
F Rationality, Rupturism, A-naturality	Neo-liberalism Modernism/Wittgenstein's House Ford's Motor Company
H Rationality, Sedimentism, A-naturality	Keynesianism Baroque/Palace of Versailles Enron
G Rationality, Rupturism, Naturality	Techno-Environmentalism Dymaxion/Post Modernism Enval

Figure 8.9 Elements of Design Corner Living

concerned with profits than with service provision and in order to maximize revenue it was keen, I have argued, to use as many *trompes l'oeil* as possible. Management takes the form of a concentration upon 'creative accounting' where 'accounting' means both working with numbers *and* rendering a written and verbal account of what has happened to those in authority. This populated corner of the design envelope is characterized by the principles of rationality, sedimentism, and anti-naturality. Figure 8.9 presents a summary thus far of how styles of organizing are interrelated.

In Chapter 9, we move away from the corners to consider the planes presented by each face of the design cube. Here the extremes of organizational life are left behind and life is calmer, perhaps, down there on the plains, where the world is laid out for us in pastel-shaded 2D. Therein, we will move on planes of agreement, seeking to identify where disagreements are few and far between in an open space characterized by shared assumptions.

9

Planes of Agreement

So far we have dealt with 'lines of fight' in Chapter 6 and 'points of opposition' in Chapter 7 and have considered, in each case, open stylistic hostility. These were the corners in which lurk the strange and unusual.

It is time to come out into the open.

Since lines are made up of myriad points, all reflecting a different position with regard to the relevant argument, it should be obvious that many, many intermediate positionings between extremities are possible. Life forms exist across, and upon, all the intermediate points between extremes. But I do not have the space to lay out many intermediate locations upon the three lines of fight. So in this chapter, my intention is to look for commonalities and areas of agreement. *Holism* rather than hostility is the feature I seek to reveal. The best way of doing this, perhaps, is to look at the six faces of our design cube, dealing with each plane in turn, seeking out a general description and, (given my constraints), a single organization that typically represents the major assumption of each plane. This should allow some (limited) coverage of intermediate points upon the three dimensions.

These 'cases' range from an extremely large state-controlled bureaucracy to a global environmentalist group famous for its successes, from a political party to a private army, from a research organization to a public broadcaster. Each is seen as indicative of the plane (plain) upon which it is to be found. In Figure 9.1 is an 'exploded' presentation of the six planes of the design cube. The planes themselves may be thought of as level spaces in which all who reside there share one major design assumption in common.

It may not strike the reader at first glance that my nominee, like any choice of exemplar, is a reasonable one, but I ask for your indulgence. Compared to the previous chapter, what we find here upon the planes are middling, unremarkable places—economically, architecturally, and in design terms. I shall consider each face as a plane and ask in detail what precisely unifies it internally. The reader should note that these six planes represent the arenas of debate upon which much of systems architecture, design theory, and

Planes of Agreement

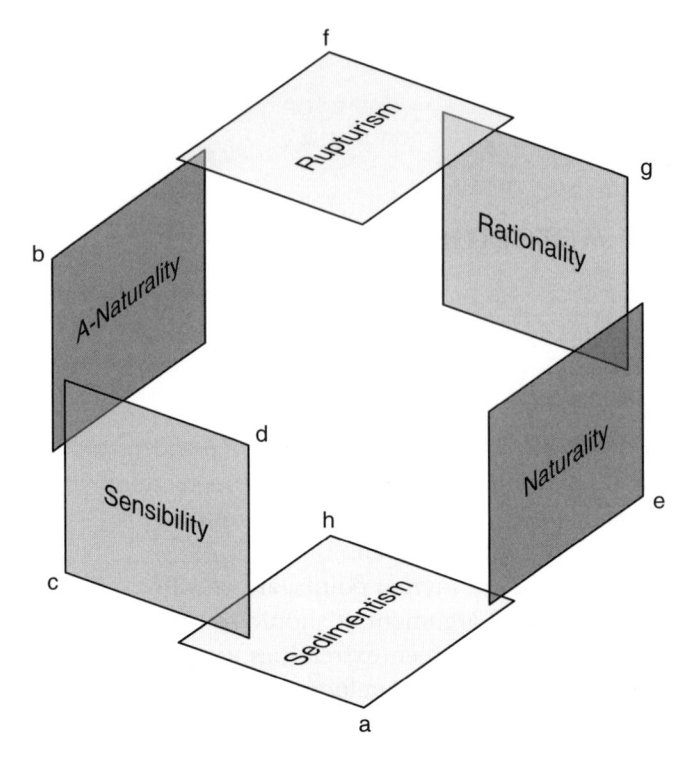

Figure 9.1 The planes of agreement

organization theory live out their ordinary existence. Their planographic nature allows us to survey the range of commonly shared issues, largely untrammelled by topographical differences.

Face 1

The plane of Naturality

In this section dealing with Face 1 of our cube, all positions upon it are committed to a belief that humanity is within Nature and does not stand outside it. Its corners mark out the space within, as do the lines of fight between the corners. Here then, the one widely held assumption is that any style by which one comes to know the world has to accept that men and women are part and parcel of a natural world and do not have the capacity to stand outside it.

These extreme points help us map out the boundaries to the stylistic content of the major approaches to politico-economic system, organization, architecture, and design, creating between them this first plane. These become points of surface tension acting as a containment device for the plane, holding it in its place as in Figure 9.2.

At the level of architecture and design, we have seen that the corner points are marked, for me at least, by certain specific building styles. At the level of politico-economic systems we can also see very great differences. Yet points A, E, G, and D outline the vessel of containment which functions to hold the plane together as in Figure 9.3.

In this plane, then, Nature and its close relationship to humanity are firmly accepted, and it is believed that Man cannot control such a powerful force. We are in the hands of Nature and must be wary not to seek to control it for our own purposes. In the Arcadian vision of this plain of plenitude, humanity lives in harmony with a non-threatening nature whose bounty offers us all. In

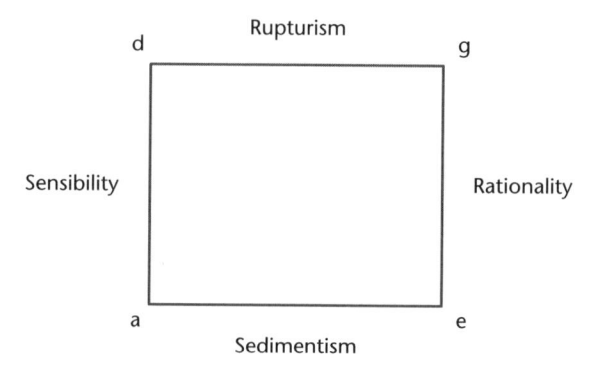

Figure 9.2 Face 1: The containment of the plane of naturality

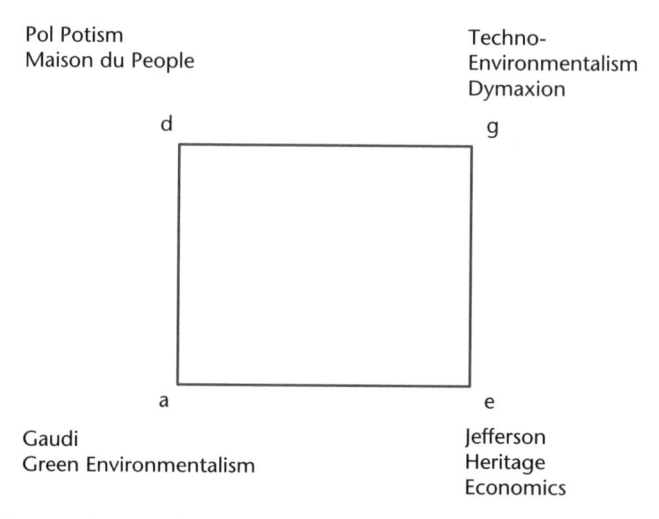

Figure 9.3 Face 1: The containment of social organization upon the plain of naturality

Planes of Agreement

another view, the world of socialism will provide for humanity and its future needs. In the land of the dymaxion, the wide, fecund prairies of America will have upon them mass-produced homes for all, whereas in Gaudi, a version of Catalan socialism provides for the collective needs of all. Nature has to be worked with, in order to produce harmony for us, but that is a possibility in some utopian visions. Only the nature of the Utopia differs—and it differs dramatically.

As we have seen, Face 1 has four points to it, one in each extreme corner. Each point will contain the assumption that humanity is a part of nature because every idea at home on this plane does so by definition. The organizational form typical of the midst of Face 1 is best looked at via a case. This case is meant to represent intermediate points upon two of the three lines of fight. The organizational design chosen as an exemplar of the whole plane because of its central positioning is Greenpeace. I shall again use the notions of emplacement in structure, enactment of format, and enchantment via embellishment as a way of analysing each case, beginning with Figure 9.4.

Few contemporary organizations across the globe are characterized by a high respect in its thinking for history and the relevance of the past, a high respect for human emotions and human feelings in what is constructed, and an equally high respect for nature and things 'natural'. But this is the one face of the design envelope where we would expect to find them. Such organizations would adopt structures and systems that valued the past and which saw the organization's place in the natural world as harmonious and ecologically friendly. This 'natural' connection might allow us to expect a seasonal dimension to its work, using a cohort of volunteers within what would need to be a participative structure. High levels of human affect would be welcomed. One thinks here perhaps of the voluntary sector and of green organizations such as Greenpeace as representative of such a position.

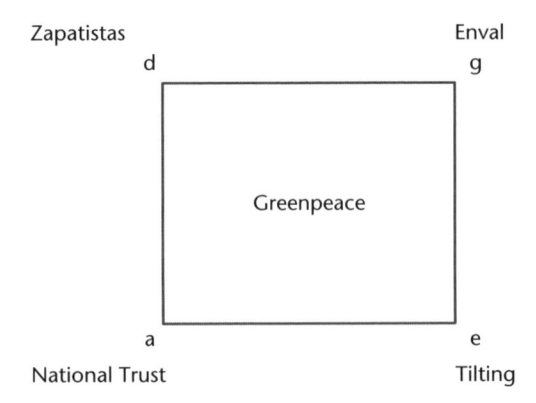

Figure 9.4 Face 1: Naturality and the organizational case of Greenpeace

The rise of NGOs and international movements such as this organization represents have made some impact upon governments and the corporate world. Yet NGOs have less status than private capitalist-based organizations and therefore, because organization theory is status driven, have been less studied (Princen et al. 1994).

EMPLACEMENT IN STRUCTURE

Greenpeace is classed as an SME in terms of European commercial law. By 2008, it had 240 staff with 15,000 volunteers and 2.8 million members, the majority of whom lived in Europe, but its board reflects, for some, a contemporary Asian orientation. Greenpeace International came into existence in 1979. Under its new structure, the local offices contributed a percentage of their income to the international organization, whilst it took responsibility for setting the overall direction of the movement. One of its founders was David McTaggart, whose personal vision was summed up in a 1994 memo: 'No campaign should be begun without clear goals; no campaign should be begun unless there is a possibility that it can be won; no campaign should be begun unless you intend to finish it off.' The placing of topics within this framework, of course, proved and continues to prove very contentious (Eyerman and Jamison 1989).

Greenpeace was transformed thereafter from a loose international network to a global organization which enabled it to apply the full force of its resources to a small number of environmental issues deemed of global significance. McTaggart went against the anti-authoritarian ethos that prevailed in other environmental organizations that came about in the 1970s by reshaping Greenpeace as a centrally coordinated, hierarchical organization. It is for this reason that I place Greenpeace centrally upon the plane. While this formalistic structure granted Greenpeace the permanence, longevity, and narrow focus necessary to match forces with government and industry, it led to the recurrent criticism that Greenpeace had adopted the same methods of governance as its main enemies, the multinational corporations. It has adopted the classical bureaucratic structure, even though its mission is very different from a corporate one.

On its official website, Greenpeace defines its mission as the following:

Greenpeace is a global campaigning organization that acts to change attitudes and behaviours, to protect and conserve the environment and to promote peace by:

Catalysing an energy revolution to address the number one threat facing our planet: climate change.

Defending our oceans by challenging wasteful and destructive fishing, and creating a global network of marine reserves.

Protecting the world's remaining ancient forests and the animal, plants and people that depend on them.

Working for disarmament and peace by reducing dependence on finite resources and calling for the elimination of all nuclear weapons.

Creating a toxic free future with safer alternatives to hazardous chemicals in today's products and manufacturing.

Campaigning for sustainable agriculture by encouraging socially and ecologically responsible farming practices.

Notice here, then, the valorization of the past by the use of such words as 'defending' and 'protecting'; the respect for nature in the terms of 'threats', 'wasteful', 'destructive', and 'ecologically responsible'; and the call to the importance of human emotions and feelings in 'peace', 'the number one threat facing our planet' and 'creating a toxic free future'. This is a very good reflection of the 'high-end' organizational principles outlined above as being typical of Face 1 (Wexler 2004).

ENACTMENT OF FORMAT

The history of Greenpeace may be well known to readers but, of course, it is a controversial organization, heavily involved in politics at the corporate and national levels. The organization is now 40 years old and has an income of around 230 million euros, mainly from donations from individuals. It enacts its commitments through this budget, so we may learn something from the details. Greenpeace claims that its core values are, firstly, bearing witness to changes and threats emanating from climate change, to forests and oceans, to and from agriculture, from toxic pollution, from the nuclear industry, and to foster peace and disarmament. To this end in 2010, it spent its income in the following ways (all figures approximate). To climate campaigns went 25 million euros, forest-related campaigning 9.7 million, oceans received 7.3 million, peace and disarmament expenditure was 2.4 million, sustainable agriculture 4.9 million, toxics 3.7 million, and 'other' 1.4 million euros. It claims that its expenditure on 'organization support' to both HQ and the regional offices was 32 million euros. Its marine operations, including the support of three ships, cost 23 million euros whilst almost 35 million euros went on public relations and media work. Greenpeace also claims to value non-violence in its conduct of campaigns, to value independence from governments and corporate sponsors, to have no permanent friends or foes, and to be keen on promoting solutions to problems. It has an organizational structure which defines the relationship of nationally based offices to the central administration based in Amsterdam, which itself is controlled through a 'Stichting Greenpeace Council'.

ENCHANTMENT VIA EMBELLISHMENT

If one wishes to look at its buildings, it is remarkably difficult to get hold of a picture of the Amsterdam HQ of Greenpeace at Ottho Hedringstraat 5, 1066 AZ Amsterdam. This may be a deliberate ploy of the organization because of its high profile in the corporate world, which is not necessarily sympathetic with its aims. The previous building—which it occupied for ten years—was styled in the fashion of the *jugendstyl* approach and was usually pictured with bicycles outside; but since we are talking about Amsterdam, this is not to be remarked upon, perhaps. After Greenpeace left, it became occupied by a variety of corporate offices. Today, the HQ occupies a building on an unremarkable commercial estate with one small plaque to mark its occupation of rather cheap rental space. Sustainability is perhaps reflected in the building's use of bicycles and its non-occupation of a prestigious HQ.

This plane is expected to be a terrain in which many environmental organizations, NGOs, and voluntary organizations operate. The value system here is driven by an approach to the issue of 'Nature', which brings in its train attitudes and behaviours that produce certain design constraints. The 'deliberate plan and purpose that deals practically and functionally with the coordination of elements into an orderly structure that is in working order' on this plane are likely to produce a plan and an order of working that are consonant with a nurturing attitude to Nature. In organization design, on this plane just such an idea will be commonplace and the defining feature of its stylistic preferences.

Face 6

The plane of A-naturality

The planar space (Hillier 2008) which we describe here has the following boundaries of points and lines, which can be seen in Figure 9.5.

This plane shares an assumption (very contrary to Face 1) that nature can be controlled and should be controlled. Humanity is more important than Nature and should be separated from it. Nature is there to be subdued, manipulated, and understood in order that man (sic) should be able to 'live long and prosper' and, in so doing, become more powerful, more dignified, and greater overall. Height should be achieved at all costs because of the sense of superiority it offers; water and landscapes should be under human control through massive engineering projects; the internal and external environment of buildings should be climate controlled. Doors should open and curtains close at the touch of a button. Buildings should be able to withstand mathematical contradiction and not resemble boxes. Above all, they should be stripped out from all ornamentation and should be places for the

Planes of Agreement

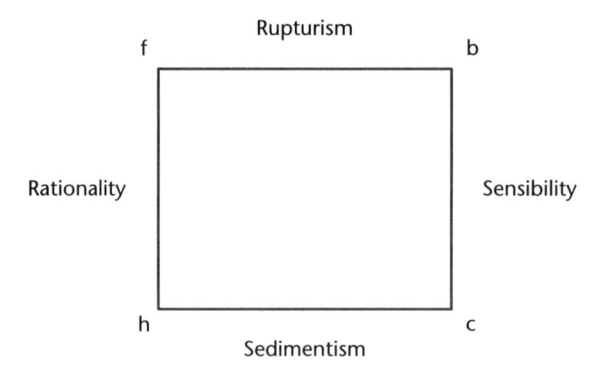

```
                    Rupturism
            f                       b
            ┌───────────────────────┐
            │                       │
Rationality │                       │ Sensibility
            │                       │
            │                       │
            └───────────────────────┘
            h                       c
                   Sedimentism
```

Figure 9.5 Face 6: The containment of the plane of A-naturality

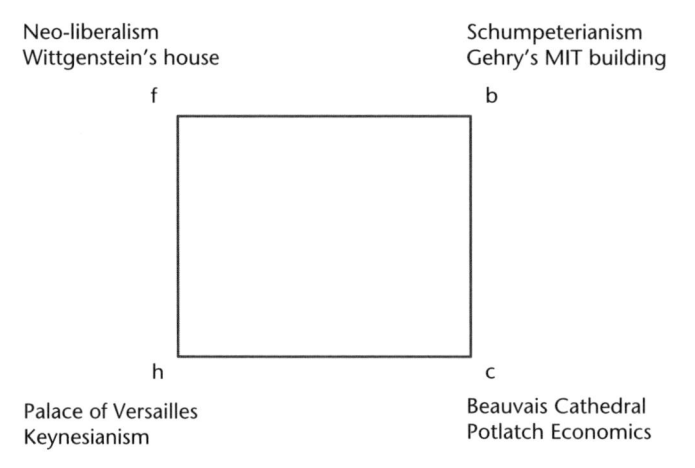

```
Neo-liberalism                      Schumpeterianism
Wittgenstein's house                Gehry's MIT building
            f                       b
            ┌───────────────────────┐
            │                       │
            │                       │
            │                       │
            │                       │
            └───────────────────────┘
            h                       c
Palace of Versailles                Beauvais Cathedral
Keynesianism                        Potlatch Economics
```

Figure 9.6 Face 6: The containment of social organization upon the plain of A-naturality

contemplative introverted individual. He, as man, should be able to look up; look afar; at nothing in particular should his gaze require it; collect nothing (as in minimalism) if he so desires, and look always and forever to the future.

The four corner points all speak of human control over some form of nature. Of 'himself' by Wittgenstein, of 'gravity' by Gehry, of his 'aristocratic followers' by Louis XIV, and of 'height' in Beauvais. Whether it is self, science, or society, this plane wishes to control all that it surveys. So what does a typical organization upon this plane, that is committed to controlling all forms of nature, look like? In thinking about this, we must note that this is a very well inhabited face indeed! Figure 9.6 indicates this.

Face 6 represents the dark side of Face 1 since they can never set eyes upon each Other and this gives us some insight into what sort of organization might

Face 6

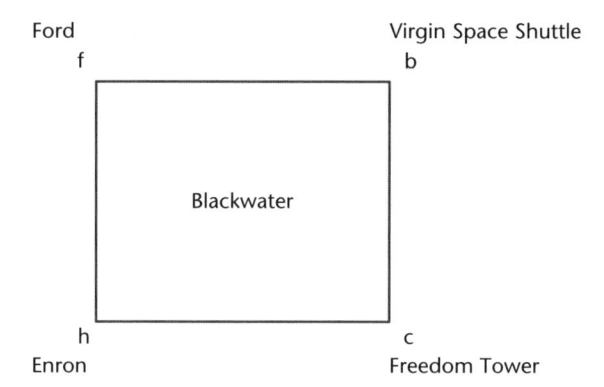

```
        Ford                    Virgin Space Shuttle
         f                              b
         ┌──────────────────────────────┐
         │                              │
         │                              │
         │         Blackwater           │
         │                              │
         │                              │
         └──────────────────────────────┘
         h                              c
        Enron                    Freedom Tower
```

Figure 9.7 Face 6: A-naturality and the organizational case of Blackwater

be opposed to Greenpeace. The exemplar chosen here is Blackwater Inc. and it is placed in the middle of Face 6 as outlined in Figure 9.7.

First, some context to this face of A-naturality. This face may look like it is the home of organization theory. Quite clearly it is American, driven perhaps by notions of the wild and lawless frontier. It is a plane in which guns and ammunition are replete. It is the locus of dominant economic paradigms and of the powerful upon their gated estates. Organization theory has been derived from a tradition of bureaucracy in which the state was taken for granted, as was its ability to utilize its arsenal of weapons against others. The barracks and the arsenal are *the* key metonyms of the organized world (Hix 2003). Furthermore, organization theory itself was an arsenal of devices to kill and maim in a shooting war (Bauman 1989). Organization theorists would be, and have been, very keen to undertake warfare in the interests of the state if so required. However, the state is in retreat, and economies built upon warfare and welfare where the state directly controls much of this expenditure are declining—at least temporarily.

Hardt and Negri (2000: 339–45), are really rather interesting on this point. In the new 'Empire' which the world faces, they tell us that:

a. in the imperial framework administration becomes *fractal* and aims to integrate conflicts not by imposing a coherent social apparatus but by controlling differences
b. imperial administration's dominant value lies in its *local* effectiveness, for local autonomy is the fundamental condition of the imperial regime.

This raises an interesting question. What form of universalizing organization theory could deal with fractals, differences, and local autonomy, and what form of organization theory could deal with these administrative contradictions within the Empire? Let me turn briefly to one possible answer to Hardt and Negri's questioning. That is, to the role of the *private army* within private capitalism run by the entrepreneur, fighting against those whose value systems are not state based but are more linked to non-industrial, ideological, and religious beliefs. The style of organizing within private armies would be quite distinct (Weber 1947).

Central to such an attempt would be a consideration first of arsenals and thence to the design of private armies. *Arsenals* were key organizational forms that dominated the state's thinking about how production should be managed (Taylor 1911). The construction of an arsenal involved some of the most skilled parts of the society and therefore those possessed of some labour market power. It has to be recognized, however, that the role played by the government's own arsenal shifts in the 20th century. With the industrialization of warfare and weapons production, a number of armaments manufacturers arise who are not part of the state apparatus—at least in ownership terms. Companies such as Krupps, Armstrongs, and Scheidners undertake much development work on new weapons. A weapons race then ensued in which these companies played a major role, not least in exporting lethal hardware around the world. The admixture of arsenals where the state controlled routine weapon production, alongside private companies undertaking research and development of new, expensive weaponry became the norm. It was this integration of public and private, state and corporation, which Eisenhower had identified in his farewell speech as president, as being crucially different. The exchange of personnel between these spheres was also evidence of the interconnectedness of go-go (government owned and government organized production of weapons) and co-co (company owned and company organized weapons manufacture) where they were becoming go-co (government owned and company organized). The hyphen between the military and the industrial in the complex gives way to a slash (i.e. military/industrial rather than military-industrial). Boeing is a classic example here of a company that operates as a hybrid. The Boeing 707 started life as an in-flight refuelling tanker that failed to win the defence contract. The Boeing 747 (Jumbo) has the distinctive hump to allow two battle tanks entry into it because it started life as an attempt to win the long-range transport role for the US army. Only after its failure to win the contract did it transmogrify itself into a long-range passenger aircraft. When you sit in cattle class next time, try to imagine you are occupying the space designed for the comfort of an Abrams tank.

Let us now turn to private military companies (PMCs), which received $300 billion from the Pentagon in the last ten years. Some of the larger PMCs include Blackwater USA; Vinnell, Brown and Root; MPRI (Military Professional Resources Inc); and Sandline International; but numerous others exist. It was reckoned that in Africa, primarily in Angola in the 1990s, over 90 such companies were operating. Although they have 'ceased to trade' (one description of such armies is that they are 'non-lethal service providers'), Executive Outcomes and Sandline spawned other offshoots. Such activity is legal and there are serious attempts being made to relax international law regulating the use of mercenaries or 'civilians authorized to accompany a force in the field'.

One serving member of the military, writing in *Military Law Review* (Milliard 2003: 5) is in favour of PMCs and opines that today's 'flawed approach ignores mercenaries' long history, their modern transformation into sophisticated private military companies (PMCs) and their increasing use by—not against—sovereign states engaged in the legitimate exercise of procuring foreign military services'. Indeed, The Foreign and Commonwealth Office of the UK in 2002 reported that it would be cheaper to use such forces, rather than seek troops from UN member states, but noted wistfully that few companies were capable of providing or willing to provide the full range of services necessary. The Pentagon believed that it could save a further $6 billion per annum by converting military support to contractor positions. The tax dollar would thus be better spent!

However, 'the US government has no idea of exact numbers, let alone individual names, of persons performing extra-territorial contracts outside of the US on behalf of the US', for the Department of Defense does 'not keep a record but such assignments are part of a growing trend' (*Military Law Review* footnote 425). Naturally there are huge concerns about the use of such forces, including questions of their motivation, their loyalty, their efficiency, and their humanitarian stance. But the return to such a system with ex-military leaders in control of small bands of *condotierri* seeking to confront its Other is a model that is certainly developing. Usually with the support of big business in confronting armed resistance to Neo-Liberal expansion. Let us consider one of the biggest of these.

Blackwater or Xe

EMPLACEMENT IN STRUCTURE

A useful organizational representation of just such a stance is perhaps Blackwater. Formed in 2001 to undertake protection of US officials in Iraq, it is made up of ex-special services personnel. By 2007 when Jeremy Scahill produced his book *Blackwater: the rise of the world's most powerful army*, Blackwater had 2,300 soldiers in nine countries and was capable of raising an army of 21,000 ex-troops and police. Blackwater personnel were sent into New Orleans after Hurricane Katrina, well before attempts to bring in fresh water and food were made, and even before rescue attempts of the population were undertaken. Their role was the security of 'property' and the prevention of looting. One operative said New Orleans was just like what they did in Iraq 'without the roadside bombs' and the company's reputation for safeguarding civil liberties was not enhanced by its efforts in Louisiana. Blackwater is a privately held company and does not publish information about its structure or its internal affairs. It changed its legal structure, name, and logo in 2006 after considerable bad press coverage over the behaviour of its staff acting as private soldiers (or mercenaries) in Iraq. It has done so again recently.

ENACTMENT OF FORMAT
The company undertakes training of more than 40,000 people a year, mostly from US or foreign military and police services, in its facilities within the United States. The training concerns offensive and defensive operations undertaken by the military, as well as smaller-scale personnel security. The technologies used and the training techniques espoused are not limited by US domestic law, although it is unclear what legal status Blackwater Worldwide operates under in the US and other countries. Nor is it clear what protection the US extends to Blackwater Worldwide operations globally. Certainly the state reacted badly to the incident at 'Blackwater Bridge', the name given to a site in Fallujah where two bodies were hung up from a four-man Blackwater team that was attacked by a crowd who recognized their organization.

ENCHANTMENT VIA EMBELLISHMENT
The company is based in a vast wetland area on the North Carolina/Virginia border, named the 'Great Dismal Swamp', near Moyock, and is described by most locals as a 'wasteland'. This site is now called 'US Training Center' since the company was renamed as Xe. This site covers 7,000 acres and is the largest private military facility in the world. The site comprises several ranges for active war training; indoor, outdoor, and urban reproductions of sites of warfare; a man-made lake and a driving track which were created by the founder, Erik Prince. Originally it taught SWAT tactics but moved into guarding diplomats in 2001. Prince is a Republican Party donor of significance and was an intern to George Bush Senior. Here, in the Great Dismal Swamp, he built this state-of-the-art private training facility, naming it 'Blackwater' after the heavily coloured water of the swamp. A new facility on the west coast of the USA faced fierce local opposition which focused on the potential for wildfire increases, the proposed facility's proximity to the nearby national forest, noise pollution, and opposition to the dubious actions of Blackwater in Iraq. In response to these environmental concerns, Blackwater West said: 'There will be no explosives training and no tracer ammunition. Lead bullets don't start fires.' So much for its environmental concerns! As for its concerns to maximize profits, on 21 July 2008, Blackwater Worldwide stated that they would shift resources away from security contracting because of extensive risk

in that sector. Mr Prince said that 'The experience we've had would certainly be a disincentive to any other companies that want to step in and put their entire business at risk.' Blackwater has earned billions of dollars from the American state for its role in Iraq, Afghanistan, and in the highly controversial security operations after Hurricane Katrina. This company, one might argue, stands against a sense of history, human feelings, and nature. It is typical of the plane of being A-naturality.

On this plane, of course, we find many organizations which are in the extractive industries within the primary sector of the world economies. Whether it is removal of coal, oil, diamonds, uranium, or timber, organizations in this sector have specific attitudes in their design features, not least of which is a deep concern for their security and the securing of land rights. They often have high security requirements because of their treatment of local populations. The typical attitude to nature is one of exploitation and slash and burn. In the Indonesian islands and in Amazonia, both western and indigenous private for-profit companies, have an exploitative attitude which is well documented. Staff are employed on contracts through which the company abrogates some of its health and safety obligations. Or in some cases labourers may even be indentured labour without rights at all, having signed these away in order to gain work (Cooke 2003). A-naturality stretches perhaps as far as slavery in activities inclusive to its style. These industries are notoriously unsafe and inherently dangerous, so organizations on the plane of A-naturality have used particular ways to overcome these difficulties. The four organizations previously mentioned as inhabiting this plane (Enron, Ford, SOM, and Virgin Galactic) have or had particular attitudes to labour flexibility and control of the unions. So whilst Blackwater is a service organization providing services to the military and quasi-military forces of the West, its attitude to the Great Dismal Swamp, irrespective of the non- attractiveness of the landscape, is one typical of the plane of being apart from nature.

We turn now to different planes. In the next section Faces 2 and 5 are compared and contrasted.

Face 2

The plane of sensibility

As we have already seen, *sensibility* refers to an acute perception of, or responsiveness toward, something, such as the emotions of another. This concept emerged in 18th-century Britain, and was closely associated with studies of sense perception as the means through which knowledge is gathered. It also became associated with sentimental moral philosophy. Its face is contained by the following lines of fight as outlined in Figure 9.8.

Planes of Agreement

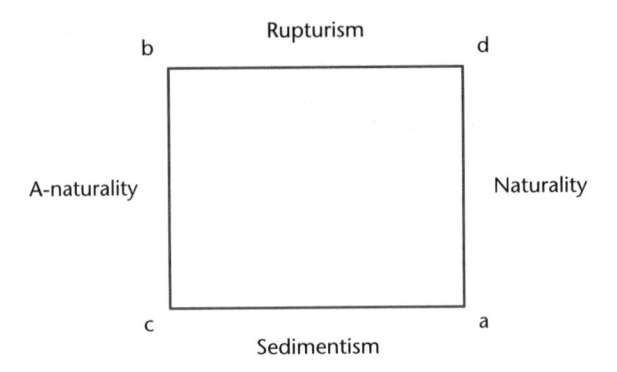

```
              Rupturism
        b                    d
        ┌────────────────────┐
        │                    │
A-naturality                 Naturality
        │                    │
        │                    │
        └────────────────────┘
        c                    a
              Sedimentism
```

Figure 9.8 Face 2: The containment of the plane of sensibility

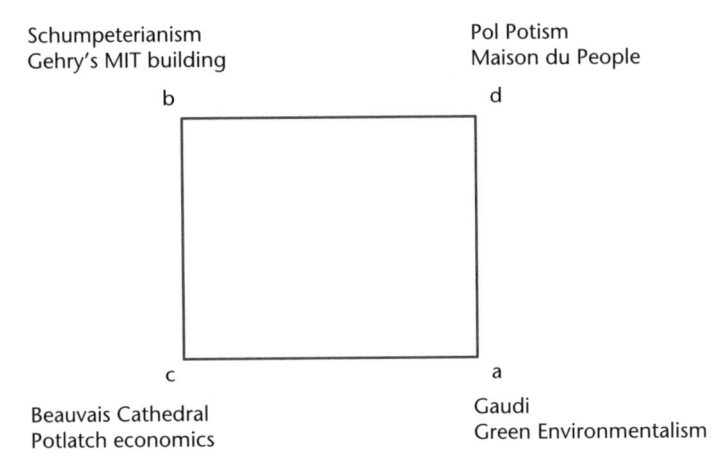

```
Schumpeterianism              Pol Potism
Gehry's MIT building          Maison du People
        b                    d
        ┌────────────────────┐
        │                    │
        │                    │
        │                    │
        │                    │
        └────────────────────┘
        c                    a
Beauvais Cathedral            Gaudi
Potlatch economics            Green Environmentalism
```

Figure 9.9 Face 2: The containment of social organization upon the plain of sensibility

The corner points that hold this planar surface in tension at the level of architectural design and politico-economic system are as in Figure 9.9.

Sensibility here means in part the rejection of Newtonian causality and the embracing of emotion as a way of understanding life. Typically, it signifies a rash boldness that motivates old and new priesthoods. This brash confidence could be found in the chaology of the MIT maths professors or the soaring ambition of the priesthood to be in some way rivals of God in the medieval cathedrals, where their use of gargoyles to keep away the devil was made obvious by the builders.

Brissenden, tracing the evolution of the 'family' of words related to sensibility and sentimentality, notes the extraordinary breadth and variety of meanings attributed to these terms in the 18th century—a linguistic as well as philosophic explosion:

Especially during this period they were charged with great and often vague emotive power—moral, sexual, political, often semi-religious. They represented or could be made to represent a constellation of highly significant general ideas and feelings; while at the same time they could be used with precision, delicacy and scientific neutrality. They operated across the broadest spectrum of thought and discourse: the same word in one context could be coldly empirical while in another it could radiate the most enthusiastic idealism. At the highest level they played a part, sometimes an essential one, in the languages of physiology, psychology, philosophy and the emerging social sciences...At the lowest level...part of what Steven Marcus, in his study of sexual literature in the Victorian age, has characterised as the 'fantasies' of a period, that 'mass of unargued, unexamined and largely unconscious assumptions' on which a society's world view bases itself. (Brissenden 1974: 20–1; Marcus 2008: 1)

At the organizational level we, too, might see these unconscious assumptions at work in the realm of sensibility (Pixley 2002; Barbalet 2002). The notion of a rejection or at least a heavy questioning of antecedent causality, the centrality accorded 'gut feel', and the investment in fantasies of a positive kind mark off the power accorded to a priestly class. The unquestioned influence that these charismatic clerics have over organizational life on the plane of sensibility can lead to some strange and exotic happenings within something akin to a 'totalitarian regime'. Heretics are banished because they think, and they do not believe. Here, all points on this plane assume that a key force in human life is sensibility, emotion, and feelings—and that styles must reflect this fundamental element in human life.

What characterizes the position of the central spot in the centre of this plane? My answer is drawn from the history of *BBC Radio 1* in the 1990s which sits nicely as a case in the middle of a sea of sensibility. Put simply, this is an example, perhaps, of a semi-religious priesthood purveying fantasies of managed change in which cherry picking was to be undertaken with no thought for the consequences on the rest of the crop. Figure 9.10 emplaces this case.

At the time of writing in October 2011, the BBC has chosen 'Delivering Quality First' (DQF) as its name for yet another round of high-profile changes. In what is meant to be the most dramatic cuts faced by the corporation, 2,000 staff have been made redundant. However, on reflection, DQF is just the most recent name for change, the previous programme of cuts being called 'Creative Futures'. Before that apparently was Greg Dyke's blunt strategy of 'Cut the crap and make it happen.' And before that was John Birt's attempts to introduce change.

In October 1993, a British DJ named Dave Lee Travis announced on air that he was leaving Radio 1, having been forced out by the changes to the organization brought about by its controller, Mathew Bannister. At the time, Radio 1 reputedly had well over 16.5 million listeners, and in 1993 was the most

Planes of Agreement

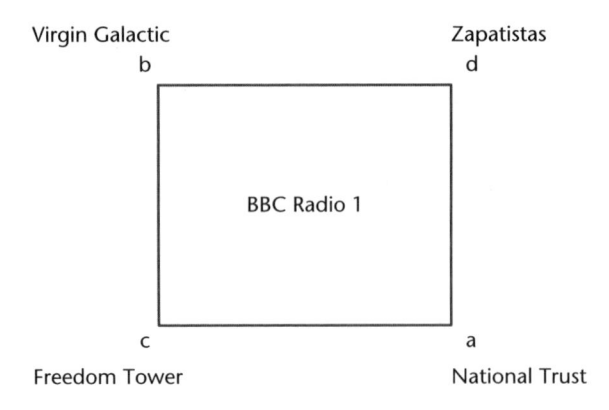

```
        Virgin Galactic              Zapatistas
             b                            d
             ┌────────────────────────────┐
             │                            │
             │                            │
             │         BBC Radio 1        │
             │                            │
             │                            │
             └────────────────────────────┘
             c                            a
        Freedom Tower                National Trust
```

Figure 9.10 Face 2: Sensibility and the organizational case of BBC Radio 1

popular radio station in the world. And for some 'reason' at this point it was decided that extensive, far-reaching changes were needed to be made. But the logic utilized was driven by sentiment and emotionally-based fantasies around the notion of 'distinctiveness'. The BBC Director-General, John Birt, thought that Radio 1 was not distinctive enough from commercial operators, and wanted to shift the target audience from the age range of 13–40 to 13–25. Bannister and his predecessors had attempted to produce a 'radio revolution' by shifting the audience of the station towards this 13- to 25-year-old segment of the market, and away from the greying population who had stayed with the station since its inception. 'It wasn't broke' but the BBC senior management decided to fix it anyway. The management of change programme that was begun, based on demographic interpretation, saw the sacking of numerous DJs and administrative staff. Bannister was assisted by Trevor Dann who was known to many staff at the time as 'Dann, Dann, the hatchet man'. At this time, the BBC as a whole was described by insiders as a 'totalitarian organization' and no more so than in Radio 1 which left no room for manoeuvre in its DJs, as its playlist was decided upon by senior staff. By 1997, there was a ban on 'old music' so that no record of the Beatles, for example, could be played. No record over five years old was allowed. Between 1992 and 1996 the station lost one-third of its listening audience, the numbers dropping from 16.5 million in February 1993 to only 11 million in October 1994. Part of the 'revolution' involved the launch of DAB radio in 1996 and, in the same year, the studios of Radio 1 were moved into the basement of Yelding House in London, formerly a car showroom. Put simply, the organization that was Radio 1 at this time was possibly 'mad', infected by the perceived need for radical organizational change (Czarniawska and Sevan 1996). The literature at the time was full of 'BPR' (Business Process Re-engineering) and this was what was attempted (Hammer and Champy 1993).

According to Simon Garfield's book *The Nation's Favourite*, from May 2001, using many former Radio 1 presenters, Radio 2 became Britain's favourite radio station, marking the changes at Radio 1 as counterproductive and change for change's sake. And despite the recovery of figures later in that decade, this must go down in the corporation's history as one of its strangest attempts at reflecting top management's sensibility and abandoning much that was excellent.

Many organizations found on this face of sensibility have been pushed into change for the sake of change. I could name a well-known business school in the United Kingdom that has undertaken and continues to prosecute precisely the same sort of change programme as Radio 1 did. It is not a rational change programme that is being undertaken, but it will be interesting to see what results from this engagement with sensibility. Over one-third of staff are rumoured to have left this institution in the last year (Parker 2012). It has been 'felt' that change was necessary, with the vice-chancellor apparently having a gut feel that complacency had set in. Evidence does not need to be presented, of course, where strong feelings are present, particularly if they emanate from senior intestines. Consultancies, of course, make fat fees from encouraging chief executives to embrace radical change programmes when they are not needed. The encouragement to act, to embrace busyness, to be seen to be moving, is in fact a form of sensibility. MBA students when faced with cases to 'solve', rarely, if ever, choose the 'do nothing' option. One might suggest that often it turns out to be the best option.

Face 5

The plane of rationality

This might be thought to represent *the* plane of organization because here one finds a calm sea of rationality from horizon to horizon. Figure 9.11 presents this face. As we have seen in previous chapters, the extreme points on this face are marked by the following parameters:

In terms of the extreme corners of the design envelope for architectural forms and politico-economic systems, the following examples seem most appropriate to me as outlined in Figure 9.12.

But what is life like across the plane of rationality and in its centre? First, I would not wish the reader to think that organizations are necessarily to be found clustered on this plane. Many organizations are imbued by sensibility as much as they are by rationality. How else could one explain the clasping of 'hierarchy' when there is little evidence for its efficiency across organizational life? Second, the relationship between rationality and political power has been studied to show that in real-life decision-making, rationality is context

Planes of Agreement

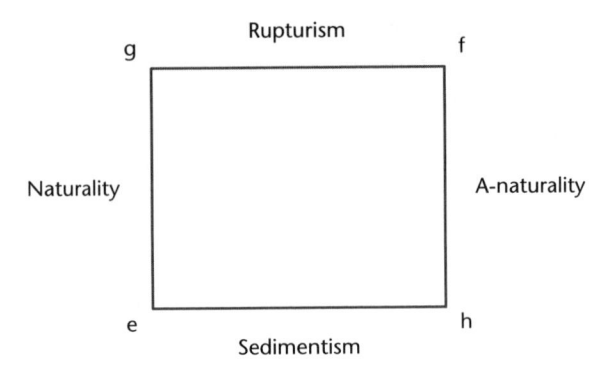

```
              Rupturism
       g                    f
       ┌────────────────────┐
       │                    │
Naturality                  A-naturality
       │                    │
       │                    │
       └────────────────────┘
       e                    h
              Sedimentism
```

Figure 9.11 Face 5: The containment of the plane of rationality

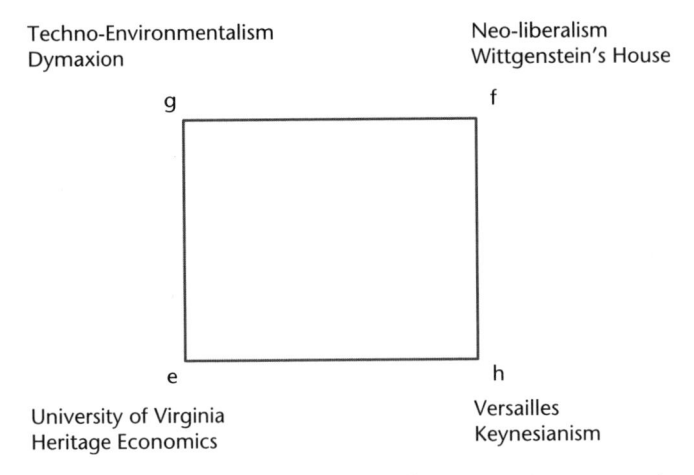

```
Techno-Environmentalism        Neo-liberalism
Dymaxion                       Wittgenstein's House
       g                    f
       ┌────────────────────┐
       │                    │
       │                    │
       │                    │
       │                    │
       └────────────────────┘
       e                    h
University of Virginia         Versailles
Heritage Economics             Keynesianism
```

Figure 9.12 Face 5: The containment of social organization upon the plain of rationality

dependent and the context of rationality is power. Thus power profoundly influences rationality, and what decision-makers think of and present as rationality is often a rationalization of power positions, according to Flyvbjerg (2002). In a paraphrase of Blaise Pascal, Flyvbjerg concludes that 'power has a rationality that rationality does not know'. And this is to be shown to be accurate perhaps in the case study chosen here.

What lies centrally beneath the centre of the plane then? The *RAND Corporation* is my nominee here, located as in Figure 9.13.

The RAND Corporation is a non-profit-making company that originally started in 1947 as part of the Douglas Aircraft Corporation. When it became separate the next year from that company, much funding came from the Ford Foundation. Indeed, it appears to have received funding from the Rockefeller and Carnegie Foundations as well as from Ford, with all of whom it shares

Face 5

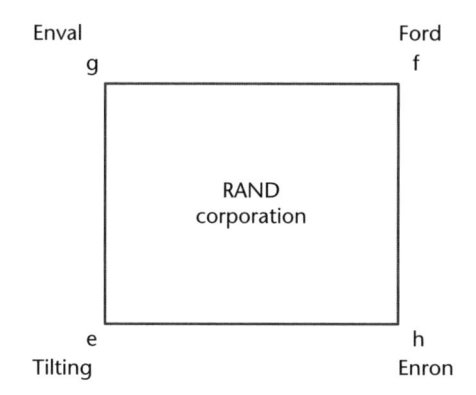

```
        Enval                    Ford
          g                        f
          ┌─────────────────────────┐
          │                         │
          │                         │
          │        RAND             │
          │     corporation         │
          │                         │
          │                         │
          └─────────────────────────┘
          e                         h
        Tilting                   Enron
```

Figure 9.13 Face 5: Rationality and the organizational case of the RAND Corporation

interlocking directors. Since then, funding has come from both the US military and the US government. It uses engineering and economics as its primary academic bases rather than history or politics or the arts/humanities more generally. It values 'independence, objectivity and non-partisanship' through systems analysis—although if one reads Selznick's (1950) piece for RAND on the Soviet Union's 'organizational weapon', objectivity is not the first word that comes to mind.

In 2004 it moved to its new offices, designed as a campus, in Santa Monica, California. It is in the shape of a stylized fish, not unlike the Christian symbol. Almost every office is an identical size of 10×14 feet. A former chairman is the (in)famous Donald Rumsfeld. Ex-staff members include Condoleeza Rice and Francis Fukuyama. It made its reputation in defence issues but is now involved in healthcare research, although 50 per cent of its work remains in 'security related areas'. Because of this, it is often difficult to assess what assumptions it has built into its models, which are often based on 'systems thinking' and 'rational choice theory'. It has about 1,700 employees 'to help to improve policy and decision making through research and analysis'. It operates out of 11 offices worldwide, and has an annual budget of $250 million. Its strap line is 'Objective Analysis: Effective Solutions'. The point, of course, is that this objective analysis rests on intense mathematicization of problems with very little apparent comprehension of cultural difference or the vagaries of the human psyche. Since this area of sensibility cannot be measured, it is ignored by the Nobel prize-winning staff whose expertise tends to be in quantitative economics. It has also been described as being full of 'Wizards of Armageddon' because of the likes of Herman Kahn who was so much the model for Stanley Kubrick's Dr Strangelove that he asked for royalties! His notion of Mutually Assured Destruction (MAD) is part of that construction.

Planes of Agreement

Famous as the originator of the use of game theory, of having had 30 Nobel prize-winners associated with it, and of developing the notion of MAD, the RAND Corporation has been a force to reckon with. For example, Monsanto made the defoliant Agent Orange during the Vietnam War and the RAND Corporation, (standing for 'R and D') evaluated its impact and went on to calculate the cost of the war in terms of deaths per $1,000. Rationality of a sort was evident in their very footsteps. Just as it had been for IG Farben 30 years earlier (Bauman 1986). In Hay (2002), the RAND Corporation, still active in military circles, produced a document for discussion on the future of US arsenals. It recommended that of the 11 contractor-operated arsenals in the USA in 2001, all be privatized and that the two government-controlled arsenals move towards this status by 2007. The largest US arsenal, and therefore the biggest probably in the world, is the Redstone site in the Tennessee Valley. As we saw in the discussion of Blackwater, arsenals and private armies are key parts of the contemporary organizational world. They are places where modernism abuts Baroque reason.

What is being advocated by the RAND Corporation report (Hix 2002) on arsenals is nothing less than a return to the days of the *condottieri* where the government subcontracted its protection to private companies driven by the motives and values of private capitalism. The report, which was widely discussed, received strong support from the business community but less from the military sector. The same is true in France of naval arsenals in this same period. And in other parts of the world, privatization of arms production carries on apace. It is instructive to see what Max Weber has to say on this relationship between private arsenals and private armies a century ago:

> The bureaucratisation of organised warfare can be carried through in the form of private capitalist enterprise just like any other business. Indeed the procurement of armies and their administration by private capitalism has been the rule in mercenary armies. (Gerth and Mills 1991: 222)

Weber goes on to show that where *condottieri* are found, the soldier is the predominant owner of the means of warfare although the state does provide some of the wherewithal to undertake (sic) his work. The regiment was typically 'owned' by the colonel, whose function was as entrepreneur and thus was an economic unit rather than a military one. Capitalism's first giant enterprises such as the Dutch East India Company (VOC) were built upon this model. And Clive of India seems to have suffered from a mismatch of state and private expectations of what was legitimate for him to expect by way of reward for undertaking his work on the subcontinent. Private armies, private capitalism, entrepreneurial warlords. These issues are coming back to haunt us upon the plane of rationality. 'Soldiers of Reason' is a title given to the members of the RAND corporation. Eisenhower's remarks about the military-industrial complex allegedly stem from his dealings with the RAND Corporation and their particular 'rule of reason'. As we noted above, it is a Baroque reason fused with modernist principles.

In terms of management practices, this sort of organization has a patterning of attitudes and behaviour which emphasize advanced mathematical techniques, game theory, and computer 'wizardry' in management's 'armoury'. Rational choice theory and systems thinking are also key parts of the technical range employed in analysing key policy concerns. Independence and objectivity are supposedly obtained from such techniques but rationality here is the servant of power. Like many consultancies, what RAND appears to offer is the answers the client has already thought of and wants legitimated.

This plane of rationality then, resting on Face 5, contains upon its surface many research-based organizations in both the public and private sector. But since rationality is seen as central to organizations and organizing, it is to be expected that this face is awash with representatives of the organized world. Indeed, almost any organization theorist might think that almost all organizations would inhabit this plane at some depth or other. But in fact, very view escape the countervailing pull of sensibility for long (Meyer 1990). Gut feel often drives the commissioners of research, which in turn drives the nature of the conclusions the consultants reach.

Face 4

The plane of sedimentism

Again, some context. Sedimentism in Europe is associated with the rise of nationalism. How, then, is sedimentism to be understood here as being different from nationalism's bedfellow, historicism? Well, historicism, in the broadest sense, means the emphasis is put on historical style, but this term is now understood to mean a characterization of designs in the second half of the 19th century, which in turn can be differentiated into 'neo-styles'. In the search for a 'national' style undertaken in many countries, historicism played a leading role, especially when fused with Romanticism and an invitation to return to the styles of the Middle Ages. Architecture was a key vehicle for this stylistic turn to historicism but different styles were chosen to represent different sectors of the built environment, sometimes reflecting class background and other times, religion. For example, the situation in England is a complicated one with different styles being used by different congregations for different religious purposes. Romanesque and High Church Gothic styles vied with each other in terms of what was required from each church and cathedral. Typical of northern Europe is Heinrich Hübsch's work, *In What Style Should We Build,* for it problematizes architecture and the sedimented

Planes of Agreement

structures surrounding and underpinning it. In painting, historicism shows up in the work of the Pre-Raphaelite Brotherhood through their thematic interest in medieval legends and literary works, and here again a design ethic was sought that resonated with their spiritual life.

But sedimentism means something different and moves beyond an historicist orientation. It reflects a concern for all the past and not just some valorized period in which greatness had supposedly been achieved.

If historicism maintains that a golden age existed in the past which we have now lost, sedimentism says that it is the *principle* of looking to the past, both recent and deep, that is the key way of offering some understanding. It is here where it relates to nationalism for in the sediments of the past we are thought to find our own national origins and genesis. But it is precisely because of this conjunction of nationalism, conservatism, and abiding respect for tradition that makes this plane unpleasant for many—including the young.

How is this principle of sedimentism worked through? Well, it lies upon a planar space constrained and defined by a surface tension between points A,C, H, and E as in Figure 9.14.

The four corners to the plane of sedimentism are marked by examples of architectural and politico-economic design as follows in Figure 9.15.

The desire to build upon tradition and to protect it is the driving force right across the plane. Here, the importance of the past, respect for history and what it has to teach, protect, and offer are paramount. The value system of the plane is often associated with religion and its observance of deep underlying values of spirituality. Echoes of the past abound, even if it is only there in Gaudi's work as a return to the caves. A-spiring to greatness was in the vaulting ambitions of the Gothic builders as they sought to climb up to their Maker. Although Jefferson was a believer first and foremost in rationality, The University of Virginia was to mimic the classical styles of southern Europe around

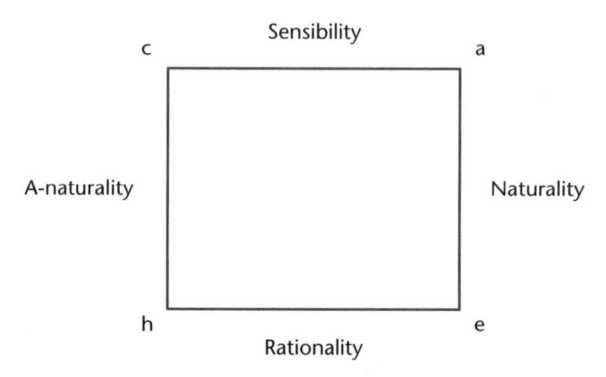

Figure 9.14 Face 4: The containment of the plane of sedimentism

Face 4

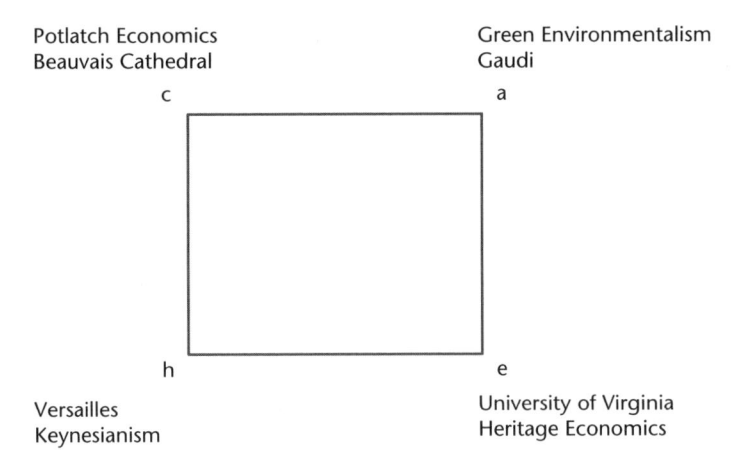

```
Potlatch Economics              Green Environmentalism
Beauvais Cathedral              Gaudi
          c                            a
          ┌─────────────────────┐
          │                     │
          │                     │
          │                     │
          │                     │
          │                     │
          └─────────────────────┘
          h                            e
Versailles                      University of Virginia
Keynesianism                    Heritage Economics
```

Figure 9.15 Face 4: The containment of social organization upon the plain of sedimentism

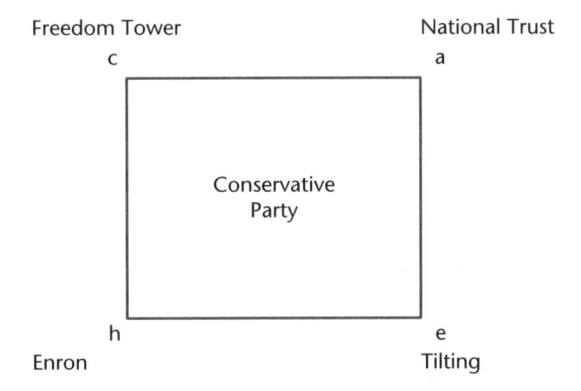

```
              Freedom Tower              National Trust
                    c                          a
                    ┌───────────────────┐
                    │                   │
                    │    Conservative   │
                    │       Party       │
                    │                   │
                    └───────────────────┘
                    h                          e
                  Enron                      Tilting
```

Figure 9.16 Face 4: Sedimentism and the organizational case of the British Conservative Party

the birth of Christ, whereas Versailles too sought a cave system reminiscent of grottoes, arbours, and some retreats from the glaring openness of the Elysian fields.

What sort of organization would you find centrally on a plane like Face 3? Figure 9.16 reveals my thinking. At the level of an organizational design typical of this plane, the 'central office' so to speak is the *Conservative Party* of the UK.

The British Conservative Party sees itself as defending the rights of private property, of protecting traditional values, institutions and practices, and the use of a strong military to protect and pursue national interests. It claimed it had 177,000 members in 2010 (Bale 2011). This has to be compared to estimates of 3 million in 1950, 750,000 in 1992, and 350,000 in 2001. The membership remains heavily drawn from the landowning and business/professional classes, although when it comes to elections, perhaps one-third of the working class vote for it on occasion. It is concentrated in rural and non-industrial areas, particularly in the south-east of England, with very little support being found in the 'Celtic fringe' of Wales and Scotland, nor in the remaining industrial areas of the UK. In 2010 its income was £20 million but its expenditure was recorded as £26 million. Its sources of funding have remained clouded in mystery but it appears to rely heavily upon personal donations, some of which may be from non-domiciled Britons. The party was founded in 1834, building upon the Tory Party foundations which themselves were laid down in 1678. The Party was professionalized under Disraeli's leadership in 1870 at a time when bureaucratization was not welcomed everywhere, since the aristocracy were deemed to know best. Its history under Thatcher was an interesting one when the party moved from a 'One Nation' approach that had been favoured for a century by many of the party's 'Grandees' towards one based on free market economics and wholesale wealth redistribution into fewer hands. The Conservative Party Board, which meets once a month, is the key decision-making body, although the organization is seen as remarkably decentralized with a number of split responsibilities. This decentralization makes for a political party that is prone to splitting into factions, but what unifies the party is its commitment to private enterprise and the defence of long-established practices and institutions. Thus, the British Conservative Party represents an organization whose name suggests a particular attitude to social change (Whiteley et al. 1994). Many parties of the right across the globe would subscribe to such values and their protection. Organizations designed to be protective of particular interests within the status quo and to have little interest in 'progressive' change would fit upon the surface of Face 3. Some organization theorists who subscribe to the views of Michels's 'iron law of oligarchy' (Michels 1923) might say that meant *all* of them.

Upon the plane of sedimentism lie organizations that are very hierarchical and elitist. Management prerogatives are held in the hands of a small clique of figures who are often there by birth rather than ability. Decision-making may well take place behind closed doors—sometimes in gentlemen's clubs to which women are not allowed direct access. Inheritance of position is as important as inheritance of wealth on this plane. The longer the 'pedigree' of the office holder the higher they are held in esteem. Aristocratic lineage is therefore crucial to many an organization found here, with a decided emphasis on tradition, honours, and ritual.

If its geometric positioning in the design cube is suggestive of anything, it points to the tensions in the current but old core Conservative party between those who feel that Keynesianism still has something to offer, those

Face 3

committed to the potlatch economics of huge expenditure on the military in the defence of what remains of empire, and the greening of the party that the present prime minister flirted with before coming to office (Bale 2011). Yet these tensions may be manageable when contrasted to the radical pull of Neo-Liberalism from the face of rupturism. That between-face tension is the one most dangerous to the British Conservative Party in terms of its integrity.

Face 3

The plane of rupturism

Rupturism's anti-historicism might be seen by some as representative of a *low* respect for the past. As such it is associated with the following cluster (or parts thereof) of assumptions. The 'past' is usually placed centuries ago, but can relate to the last decade. The past was a place of disease, brutishness, and death and was therefore inferior to the present on all (or nearly all) relevant dimensions. The past showed low understanding of science and technology, and by virtue of being 'past', bygone times demonstrate their low level of survivability and their inability to prosper. Forgetting the past allows progress to take place, and reason means the past is largely locked into myth, unreasonableness, and superstition. Technology, reason, and science require that the past is put firmly behind us. What follows is 'The Ascent of Man' (Bronowski 1973).

Rupturism is a plane marked out by the following four design corners as laid out in Figure 9.17.

In architectural and system design terms we have the following four extremities within which the plane is contained. The reader will note that this is a plane of the contemporary and the fashionable. It is not a plane that the Conservative Party is likely to inhabit willingly.

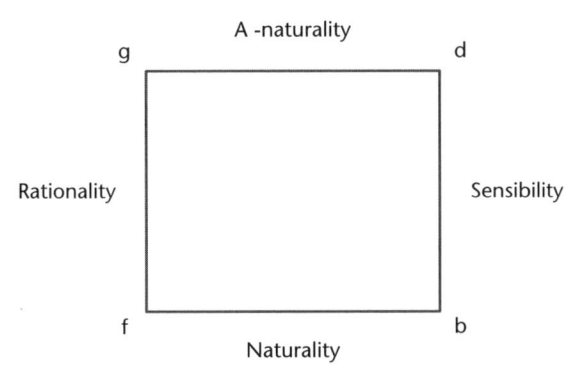

Figure 9.17 Face 3: The containment of the plane of rupturism

Planes of Agreement

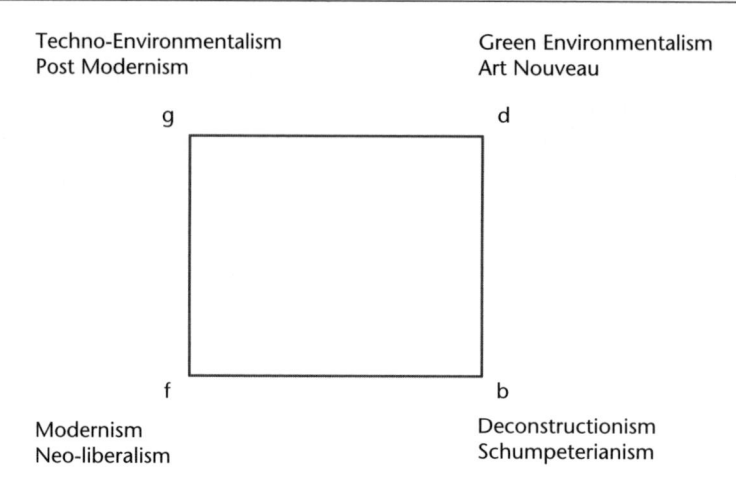

Techno-Environmentalism 　　　　　Green Environmentalism
Post Modernism 　　　　　　　　　　Art Nouveau

　　　　g　　　　　　　　　　　d

　　　　f　　　　　　　　　　　b

Modernism 　　　　　　　　　　　Deconstructionism
Neo-liberalism 　　　　　　　　　　Schumpeterianism

Figure 9.18 Face 3: The containment of social organization upon the plain of rupturism

Enval　　　　　　　　　　　　Zapatistas
　　　　g　　　　　　　　　　　d

　　　　　　British NHS

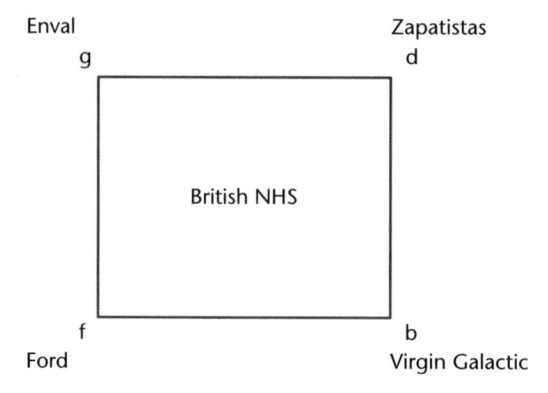

　　　　f　　　　　　　　　　　b
Ford　　　　　　　　　　　　　Virgin Galactic

Figure 9.19 Face 3: Rupturism and the organizational case of the British NHS

Figure 9.18 shows that these points mark out an area characterized by a celebration of newness, an unremitting love of technology, and an attitude of 'out with the old'. The attitude is scientistic as well as scientific, and may well be social revolutionary in terms of the pre-existing social order, perhaps. The Progressives in the USA are examples of just such a movement but their covert politics of anti-semitism hardly make them socially reformist in orientation. The plane of rupturism is for those who embrace the modern, who turn their back against the pre-modern, and who embrace change irrespective sometimes of what that contains. They positively embrace 'the shock of the new'.

What lies beneath the number 4 as an organization typical of such a central position on the plane of rupturism? Figure 9.19 shows that my answer is the British National Health Service.

The National Health Service

The British reader may spot here, before we do any analysis of the NHS, that, as an organization, it is pulled on the plane of rupturism in one direction by Fordist mass production, in another by high-technology investment in small-scale organizational forms, in yet another by huge vanity projects involving massive investments in, let us say, new computer systems and yet again by protection of 'national treasures'. It is an organization pulled in many design directions (Pettigrew et al. 1998; Pollock 2006; White 2010).

If we have looked previously at the rise of the warfare state in contemplating the six planes of the design cube, we must now turn our attention to the welfare state and the ways in which the UK, at least, has organized this provision. What we will see is an extremely large organization that has been subject to constant change over the years (White 2011). This is not only in terms of the structure of the system but in the technological possibilities opened up by new medical technologies and new drugs. Both drugs and technological kit, of course, can be extremely expensive. Roche UK, for example, is calling for the NHS to buy more of its products but it has been estimated that using ten new cancer drugs now being developed would alone cost the NHS £0.9 billion, such are the prices being charged by the pharmaceutical companies.

The National Health Service came into being in 1948 and is seen by many as a world-class system of free health care at the point of use. It is part of central government and is financed from general taxation from which the majority of health services are directly provided. Aneurin Bevan said that in order to win over the doctors to the scheme he had to 'stuff their mouths with gold'. By 2009 it was the third (or fifth) largest employer in the world, having a full-time equivalent staffing of 1.18 million employees, of which 0.13 million were doctors or clinical staff, 0.34 million were nurses, 0.13 million were scientists and technical staff, and 0.02 million ambulance personnel. The headcount is somewhat different (Bach and Kessler, *The Modernisation of the Public Services and Employee Relations: Targeted Change*, 2012: 19), with 1.58 million employees, 0.14 million doctors and 0.42 million nurses being recorded in 2009. Administration, which consists of approximately 0.58 million staff, makes up the rest. It is comparable to the Chinese army or the Indian railways in terms of its size and complexity. Its budget is around £130 billion per annum, of which 60 per cent goes on staff pay.

Since its inception it has been constantly subjected to processes of change (Pettigrew, Ferlie and McKee 1992). Bach and Kessler's subtitle to their book is 'Targeted Change'. These regular changes often involve the tension between privatization and public-service ethos, between centralization and decentralization, between all services being free at the point of use and only some services being available. So central is the issue of health to voters that most governments seek 'reform' of what has happened. Many attempts at cultural change have been attempted, most recently (in 2011) from being 'target driven' to offering 'patient care'. According to Pollock (2004: vii), the NHS 'has been progressively dismantled and privatised' and these are the dominant trends. Service users are no longer seen as 'pawns' patiently accepting the decisions of health care professionals but are 'active users' who express preferences (Le Grand 2007). They are no longer patients but are consumers. In addition, the Labour government introduced a performance regime within the NHS, characterized by Bevan and Hood (2006) as 'targets and terror' where senior managers' 'heads were on the block' if these targets were not met.

These have been attempts at radical top-down reorganization and fundamental changes in direction which have left many staff employed within the NHS feeling change exhaustion (Harris, Clegg and Hopfl 2011: 4–6). Put succinctly, in 1983 the Griffith Report argued for a major change programme and in 1988, the Thatcher government introduced 'the internal market'. In the 1990s the Labour government of Tony Blair replaced the internal market with the notion of 'integrated care' but the rising costs of new technology and drugs and an ageing population led the second Blair administration to turn to a target-driven internal market. Attempts at pay reform were made via the Agenda for Change (AfC) programme which was published as a paper in 1999 and was implemented in the period 2004–6. The Private Finance Initiative (PFI) was introduced at a cost to the public purse of many billions repatriated to PFI companies at hugely advantageous rates of return. A sum of £5.4 billion is owed to private capital at current prices but this is rising all the time. When we think of a British hospital it is difficult to know what comes to mind but it is not unlikely to be a PFI building.

The British Medical Association (BMA) sought a return to the ethos of public-sector care against the privatization that had been witnessed in the 1990s but a 'centralized performance audit regime' (Blackler 2002) was in existence by the start of the millennium that allowed senior clinicians very little role. According to Blackler they were mere conduits for the policies of state officials. Today, hospital staff are now (2011) faced with a coalition strategy of downright privatization wherein the Conservative/Lib Dem coalition of 2011 attempted the most radical change for decades, seeking to allow privatization of expensive areas of medicine and care and decentralization of power to general practitioners (GPs).

Over the past 25 years then, the NHS has faced six major reorganizations, coming on average at less than one every five years (the life of a typical British Parliament). It is for this reason that I place the NHS upon the plane of rupturism as *the* organization of change. D. J. Hunter (2005) calls this 'dynamism without change' because of the flip-flopping of options. Yet for those inside the NHS, it is an organization in constant flux.

In management terms, then, the emphasis on the plane of rupturism is for each and every manager to be a change agent, for the notion of 'the singular change agent is deeply embedded in modern consciousness' (Buchanan and Badham 1999: 23). Pettigrew and Whipp (1993) argue that change is essential in the face of international competition and a huge literature grew up on the back of the change imperative arising out of competitiveness. Notice that the discourse is decidedly not of cooperation between and within organizations but is predicated upon threat to survival. This plane is a place of constant harassment of managerial groups and possible survival comes at the cost of competition. Managers then live under threat and must make decisions that embrace change. In the face of this, many change management consultants encouraged game playing, impression management, and a certain disregard for existing staff of the organization. Change management is imbued with the whiff of testosterone. However, as Starbuck and Nystrom (1981: 9) tell us, radically new practices can often threaten the whole corporate edifice, yet in the 1990s major change programmes driven by BPR were undertaken across the globe, only for the originators to recant on their approach some years later (Hammer and Champy 1993). The plane of rupturism has been a plane upon which many managers a decade ago were forced to live. Some would argue that managerial groups are always upon this field—but they would be wrong, of course.

Here, then, as Figure 9.20 demonstrates, we have six organizations that 'fit', one would argue, nicely into the central ground of the planes identified. In the enforced absence of cases located at almost every point upon the planes, I have chosen to let these single organizations stand, metonymically, for their neighbours.

Also, I have presented them as opposing pairs to bring out differences, but clearly it is possible to see similarities between adjacent faces. Blackwater and the RAND Corporation sit upon Faces 5 and 6. Greenpeace and the NHS occupy the mid ground of Faces 1 and 4, and so on. And since these are adjacent faces, there is at least one line of commonality in the styles of

PLANE	CENTRALLY PLACED ORGANIZATION
Face 1: Naturality	Greenpeace
Face 6: A-naturality	Blackwater
Face 2: Sensibility	BBC Radio 1
Face 5: Rationality	The Rand Corporation
Face 3: Sedimentism	The Conservative Party
Face 4: Rupturism	The National Health Service

Figure 9.20 A summary chart of life upon the planes

Planes of Agreement

Face	Central Organization	Managerial issues
FACE 1 **Naturality**	Greenpeace	Volunteering, participative, utopian, arcadian
FACE 2 **Sensibility**	BBC Radio 1	Priestly, emotive, gut-feel Driven by fantasies of clerics
FACE 3 **Rupturism**	NHS	Change agents, constant shift in programmes' objectives, constant threat
FACE 4 **Sedimentism**	Conservative Party	Aristocratic, hierarchical, sexist, club based, traditional
FACE 5 **Rationality**	RAND Corporation	Research based, rational choice, maths, systems theory
FACE 6 **A-Naturality**	Blackwater	Height, control, Indenture, slavery, contract work. H and S concerns

Figure 9.21 The managerial and organizational parameters of each face

organizing. Upon these six planes, then, we can understand that those ideas that graze there share in common an intellectual territory marked out by its 2D assumptions.

Figure 9.21 attempts to outline the sorts of managerial issues and approaches that typify the centre of each of the planes.

What has been seen here in the present chapter is in the same general sort of enterprise as other approaches to laying out a field, such as the 'typology of systems of exchange' by Biggart and Delbridge (2004), or the presentation of 'The Four Elementary Forms of Human Relations' identified by Fiske (1991). These classification schemas have a utility. However, as I argued above, there is a need to develop a three-dimensional approach to our images of style. Planes are not enough in understanding design cubes and their complexity. These six planes pay little or no attention to the world above and beyond their ken. Face 1 cannot sympathize with Face 6 because they are worlds of misunderstandings and conflict. Each to the Other is the world upside down. Faces 5 and 2, and Faces 3 and 4 are worlds in opposition. So what I now intend to do in Part IV is to consider the voids or spaces within the design cube and the emplacement of particular schools of thought in organizing styles and designs across the four areas. We are moving away then from the planes to the depths and heights of styling.

Part IV
The Will to Form Content

10

Interior Design

In terms of our research agenda, what I am suggesting in this chapter is that organization theorists should look more carefully at fully rounded 'styles' and tastes in which the world organizes itself. I do not regard looking for symptoms with some underlying cause in the 'zeitgeist'—the spirit of the times—as a way forward. Zeitgeist is a description, rather than an explanatory notion—and it raises the issue of what is meant by the 'times'. We must be careful, then, about suggesting there are linear sequences to social constructions. 'There is a tidy and misleading analogy between history and human life which proposes that architectural movements are born, have youth, mature, and eventually die. The historical process which lead to the creation of . . . movements in architecture had none of this biological inevitability, and had no clear beginning which can be pinpointed with precision' (Curtis 1996: 21). The assumption is made here that styles can coexist in the same epochs, and whilst they may not be equally popular, their existence alongside each other continues. The design space is always filled with content—even if there is a very low population density for some of those who use a specific style of organizing.

Rather than seeking an explanation in the ever mobile zeitgeist, I am more interested in the possible existence of a *'problematique'* and the way in which activities, ideas, and problem-posing develop—and present themselves—in a patterned repetitive way. What problems are styles repeatedly seeking to address? So the repertoire of possible styles is not an infinite one, and there always will be resonances with the established lexicon of styles which pre-exist. Our task perhaps, is to become aware of these styles and what they came to represent, and to examine them closely to see if what they can still offer, and problematize, and avoid, gives us any clues to what organizational arrangements might come to look like in the near-to-medium-term future.

In seeking out clues, Turner (1994:2) has argued that: 'art has to be seen in a sociological and historical context and thus the aesthetic question becomes a sociological one: what set of cultural and social circumstances produces taste?'

In approaching his question, it is worth quoting Spotts at length. He analyses Hitler's attitude to 'taste' in order to comprehend the Fuhrer's evaluation of 'styles', wherein it is clear that ideology should be made materially manifest—*'Wort aus Stein'*, word in stone:

> Other past styles held no attraction. He strongly disliked Romanesque; its darkness, he believed, had contributed to the mysticism of the era. In gothic architecture he found something 'foreign and unnatural' and asked 'Why suddenly break up a naturally beautiful arch into an unnecessary, absolutely useless pointed arch? And why all the pointed towers and pinnacles that are only there for the sake of appearance since they are walled up and make entry impossible?'... Baroque was also not to his taste, but he welcomed its development out of the counter-reformation since it had moved architecture away from Gothic towards a style that he characterised as 'bright, open and light'. (Spotts 2002: 316)

The will to form in Hitler's hands, then, became an attempt to use 'style' in order to further his personal and political ends. He sought to impose his taste upon the world. So architecture, politico-economic systems, design, and organization theory were but parts of his project for a 1,000-year Reich. His one overweaning 'will to form' attempted to integrate the sciences, arts, and humanities to produce a particular form and content, and introduce them into the life of the German nation. Style, in the hands of the fascist, can be used as a mechanism for attempting profound social change and I shall discuss this below as an attempt by Hitler to undertake a 'deconstructionist monumentalism'. But is the very attempt to manipulate 'style' a far-right-wing endeavour? Of course this is *not* its only provenance. The manipulation of stylistic conventions goes on in many places at many points in time. My interest lies in *understanding* these issues by considering the design cube and the ways in which the void is filled by overarching 'styles'.

In seeking to fill in the void for the reader, three principles need to be remembered by your writer. First, there must be *recognition* of the style as discernible from all those features which are not part of that style. Second, the style must have features that demarcate it out from the background, allowing a *manifestation* of the style in a foregrounded sort of way. And third, the style must reflect a sense of *coherence* in that its features form a pattern which appears to hold together. Put simply, using a metaphor from the optician's world, the patterns I assemble must allow all but the colour-blind to perceive clear, differently coloured numbers on the page. These 'numbers' are made recognizable on the page by being manifested through colour and shade, and appear as coherent symbolic forms with shared meaning. This sort of pattern book, which most of us have seen when being tested for colour blindness, and where the numbers clearly stand out from the background colouration, is akin to what I seek to provide. Styles, in the same

Interior Design

way, are patterns, discernible within special colour plates, and these are what I seek to provide in the two concluding chapters.

As an 'interior designer' of sorts, one faces the challenge of designing a space—from the inside—in order to integrate several activities in ways which underline their common wealth. My approach is to start at the corners and work inwards. This goes against much thinking in interior design which starts from the centre, maybe with a focal point, and works outwards. Rather than seeking centrality and the view from the metropolitan middle, what I desire is the view from the extremities. Beginning the process in the corners introduces a certain 'edginess' which I seek, so it is an edgy extremism that infuses my filling of the void with content. My view is that the centre is a place of confusion, interruption, noise. It represents a polyglot melange of competing half styles and idioms. The central void of the design envelope is a large space and it is here within these confines that we sometimes find a wide variety of halfling and hybrid styles of organizing. They wheel around each other in relative anonymity. My argument is that taste comes from the edges. Juvenal, the Roman poet, said: 'Dare to do something worthy of transportation or imprisonment if you wish to be of consequence' (quoted in Vermorel 1997: v). Thus, the major colonization of this conceptual space is from the forces of the nomad, living life outside the city and the heartland. In the Marches, these styles have huge influence. It is only when their style of organizing leaves the provinces that its effect begins to loosen. By the time it has reached the metropolitan core its influence is notably lessened—as Figure 10.1 attempts to show.

My 'strategy of the void' (Koolhaus 1995: 603) is that these spaces are filled by all the logical possibilities, some more popular than others, of course, but nevertheless there is a population for each part of the void. What is produced below is an articulation of the volumes contained by three coordinates which, when seen collectively, give a number of self-contained spaces that are conceived here as emanating or radiating from the extreme corner point. The centre of the cube then is influenced by several of these forces. And so it is difficult to discern with any precision its particular style of organizing at one particular time. We must note that the arc of influence from any style does not succeed in totally colonizing the central spaces of the design cube. There is no one totalizing zeitgeist. None is strong enough to engulf the central spaces on their own, or even in small numbered combinations. Coexistence of styles in the centres of discourse is what one should expect, expressed in the form of competing problematiques. Figure 10.2 presents this competitive coexistence as a dense, dark, febrile, and hybrid core of competing perspectives.

But in this chapter I am only going to deal with *eight* of the more established of them.

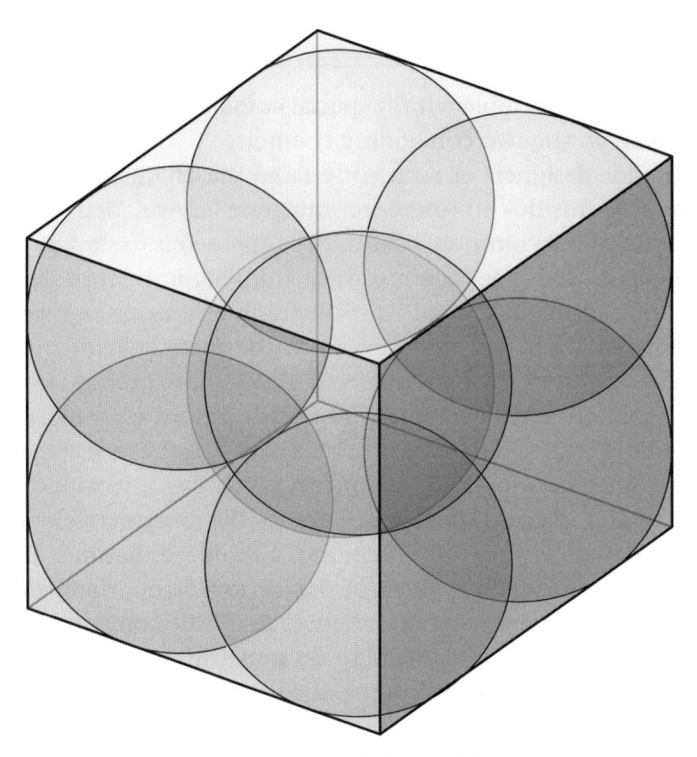

Figure 10.1 The colonization of the void from the provinces

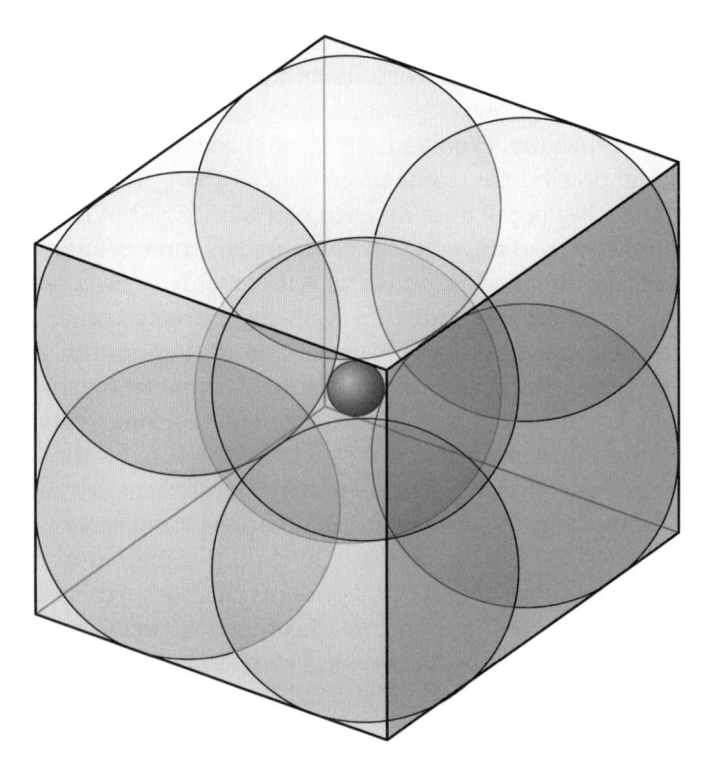

Figure 10.2 The febrile hybrid core of the design cube

The idea that styles should only number eight, all emanating from the corners, does not seem intuitively correct and of course there is more than an element of truth in this. For monstrous hybrids abound in the metropolitan centres. We saw in earlier chapters long lists of putative styles, some of which may seek to interbreed by virtue of their 'genetic' similarity. But a concentration upon eight major styles, each emanating from a corner of the cube, is enough to be getting on with, even if it is only a beginning for analysis rather than an end point. The detailed analysis of the stylistic melange of the centre will have to wait for another('s) effort—although I hope there are ideas herein of some utility in furthering that microscopic level of detail.

Styles of Organizing, then, is meant to be a book of repetitious patterns. Rather than 'anatomizing' the subject matter of four distinct and separable disciplines with a scalpel, perhaps the dominant metaphor (of many) used throughout the book is of weaving and stitching together an integrated fabric. Herein, strands from political economy, architecture, design studies, and organization theory all have a role to play in the warp and weft of the text. Chapter 10 is meant to represent *both–and* rather than *either/or* thinking. By moving away from the oppositional approach that has driven the majority of my narrative thus far, the attempt is made in this chapter (as in the previous one) to see connections between styles of organizing rather than only their differences. But as I have pointed out, it may be that individual instances of patterns do not resemble each other at first sight. The pattern may not be quickly and readily obvious. Careful handling, astute observation, and downright commitment may be required by the putative analyst. The voids, of which this chapter title speaks, are not empty but contain several separate styles, sometimes alongside each other but never in identical points in the design space and sometimes, of course, in directly opposite ends of the design cube. Their interrelationships are governed by a number of factors.

First, each style has to be understood not only in terms of what it represents but also what it does not represent. Indeed, it needs to be seen against what it opposed and what opposed it. Second, there is the question of whether style is an 'it' at all. It is a term, as we have seen, with many meanings for many users. The complexity of the elements of any 'style' is usually approached by seeking to capture it and rendering it immobile. But the fluidity of style is such that its contextualization has to be seen as something ever-changing and dynamic. Styles are part of the fluid vortex and do not render themselves up for analysis readily. The exact historical 'originary' location of any named style is an implacable opponent, for there are huge vested interests in changing its shape and rendering it safe for consumption through dragging it away from where it was born and gestated.

Interior Design

Yet, despite its apparent crudity, this reduction of the debates in the arena of style to three dimensions, and one cube, helps us to understand some of the debates in these fields which we, as management and business scholars, enter as neophytes. More importantly, however, it clarifies some issues in our *own* field of organization theory. My argument is that this move helps us understand underlying principles of organizing. Moreover, we are perhaps enabled by this schema to understand the conceptual locale of styles when this seems essential for making any sense of the issues one finds raised in the literature of the arts and humanities.

Filling the void with names

What names and concepts should we use? The labels I have used are not at all uncontentious but I will describe and analyse each of these eight suggested stylistic terms in turn, using terms from art history. I do not include, in Dempsey's terms (2004), new avant-garde attempts to comprehend the world. Styles are successful before the 20th century precisely because they eschew liberationary politics as best they can. They are paid for and bought by the owners of buildings who have disposable income and functions they wish to have performed. It is only in the 20th century perhaps that the *avant garde* arises fully as a notion of leading political change through artistic endeavour. So what I *do* seek to use are long-established terms in art history as the basis in this chapter to comprehend politico-economic systems, architecture, design, and organization. Precisely because they are so deeply entrenched in the humanities, I seek to use them as overarching notions within which to include concepts from within science and social science. The reader will note they are often profoundly conservative.

First, I need to give the reader some sense of location and placement of styles within particular parts of the void. In locating these architectural and design styles, one may be helped by imagining smaller *curved* spaces, contained within a fixed section of the overall design cube itself, described as follows within Figures 10.3 and 10.4:

> Faces 1, 2 and 4 radiating from Point A are the space of Romanticism
> Faces 1, 2 and 3 radiating from Point D are Art Nouveau
> Faces 1, 5 and 4 radiating from Point E are the space of Neo-Classicism
> Faces 1, 5 and 3 radiating from Point G are Postmodernism
> Faces 6, 2 and 3 radiating from Point B are the space of the Gothic
> Faces 6, 2 and 4 radiating from Point C are Deconstructionism
> Faces 6, 5 and 3 radiating from Point F are the space of Modernism
> Faces 6, 5 and 4 radiating from Point H are the space of the Baroque

Filling the void with names

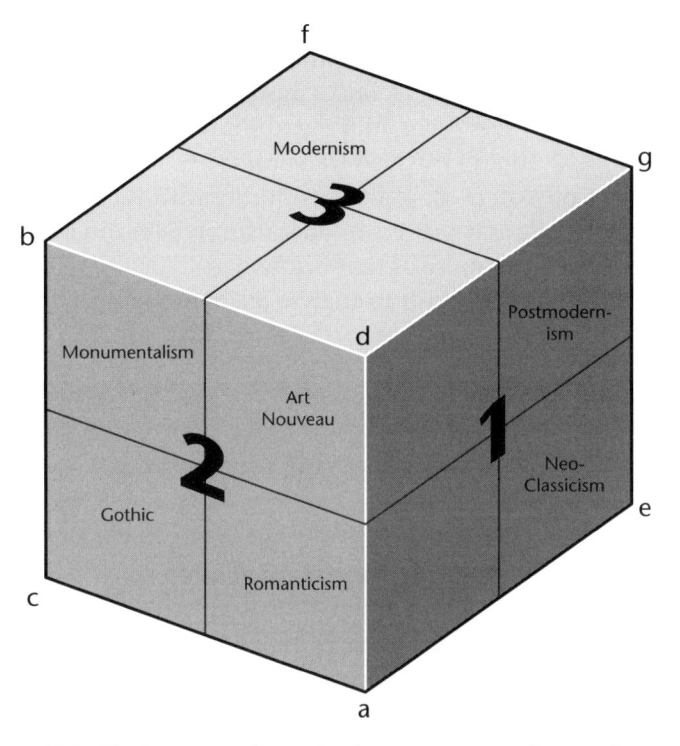

Figure 10.3 The location of specific designs orientated around Point A

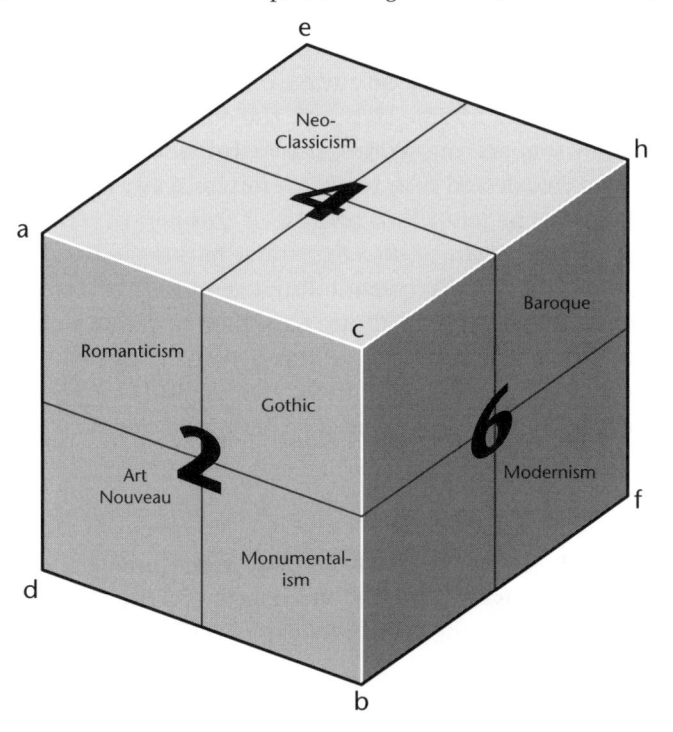

Figure 10.4 The location of specific designs orientated around Point F

This suggests that the stylistic assumptions of Romanticism (the space confined by the place where Faces 1, 2, and 3 meet) are totally antithetical to those of Modernism where Faces 4, 5 and 6 meet. Similarly, opposed to each other are the Gothic (6, 2, 3) and the Neo-Classical (1, 5, 4) as defined below. The notion that Art Nouveau (1, 2, 4) shares nothing with the Baroque (6, 5, 3) is somewhat problematic as is that Postmodernism (1, 5, 3) and monumentalism (6, 2, 4) are opposed, but more of that below.

Since the styles which we wish to analyse are here conceptualized as curved spaces, let me lay them out in that sort of form. I lay out each face in turn in Figures 10.5–10,10.

I shall deal with each style in turn, reflecting primarily on their approach to styles of organizing human life, but the reader will also be confronted by a little art history as well, of which I have already spoken in Chapter 4.

Art Nouveau and its organizational principles

At the Great Exhibition of 1851, it was commonly agreed that British furniture design was appallingly bad, compared to many other nation states. This economic interest in design meant that Art Nouveau, according to Jencks (1987: 197), 'was a definite industrial, urban and class phenomenon'. It was spurred onwards 'by a new form of communication, a new graphic means and a new urban audience'. It was to arise and remain as an eclectic influence on the rising bourgeoisie, yet it rode on a wave of major social change. It began as a result of an expanding middle class and the communications systems that they used. So newspapers, magazines, the metro, and the telegraph were all part and parcel of this design shift towards crafts and away from mass production. It resurfaced in the late 1960s because of this period's (partial) rejection of rationalistic productivism, and so Art Nouveau thereby became part of the counterculture emphasizing serpertine lines, tendrils, and tressels. Wrought iron and silver were the metals of choice to be used in gentle arabesque curves. Curiosities dredged from forests and seas replace conventional landscape vistas as the dominant imagery. Fecundity, decay, and rampant growth litter the artistry of Art Nouveau, newly awaked (or reawakened) to Freudian symbolism. The subconscious and the mystical were to become central to its interests. It was promoted by a German connoisseur, Seigfried Bing, in a French shop (*l'Art Nouveau*) from which it got its name. As a design style, it was very strong in Belgium too, newly wealthy from Congolese minerals, so its influence in France, Belgium, the UK, Germany, and the USA make it a truly international style. It developed into a form of 'lifestyle marketing' which is

Art Nouveau and its organizational principles

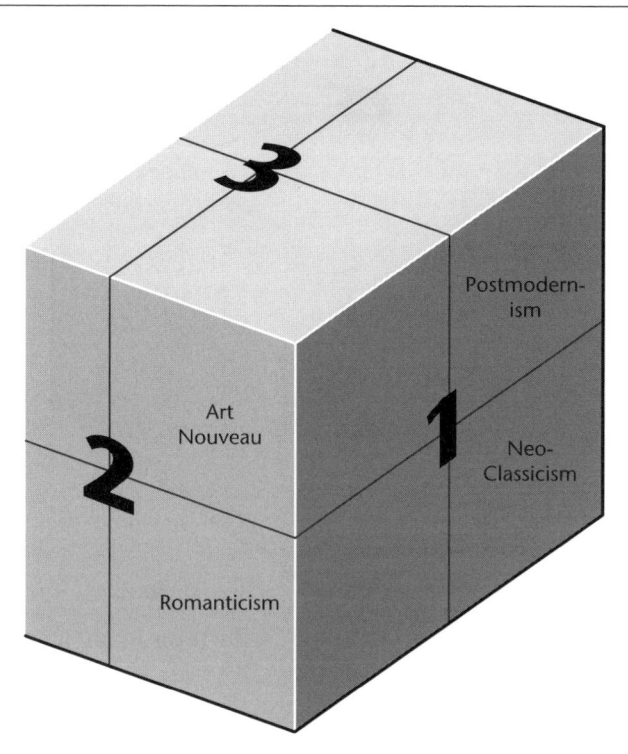

Figure 10.5 Face 1: Designs upon the plane of naturality

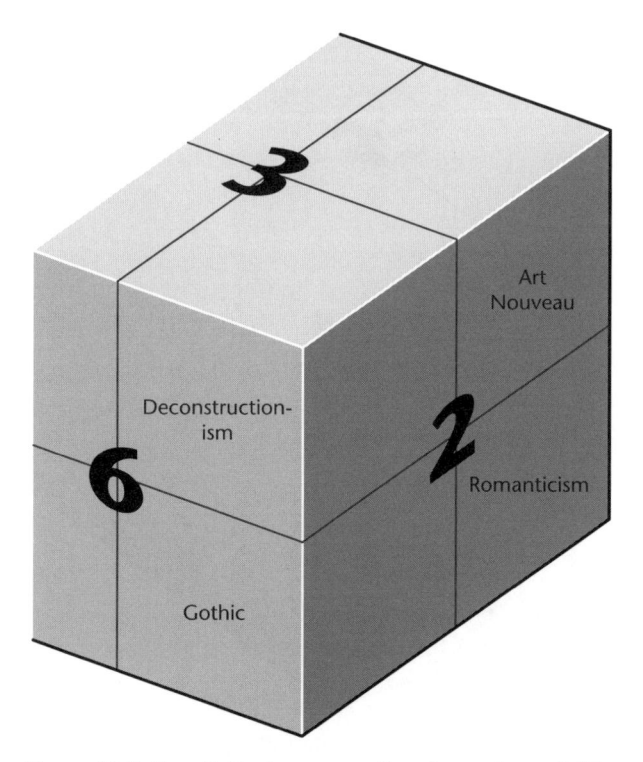

Figure 10.6 Face 2: Designs upon the plane of sensibility

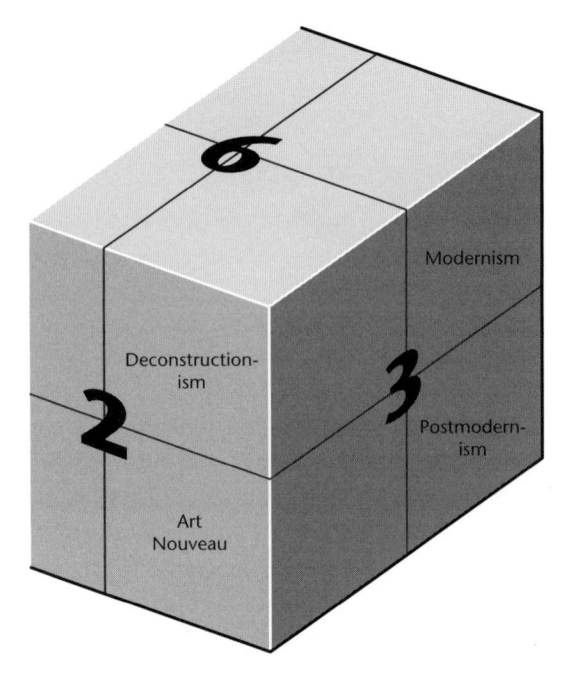

Figure 10.7 Face 3: Designs upon the plane of rupturism

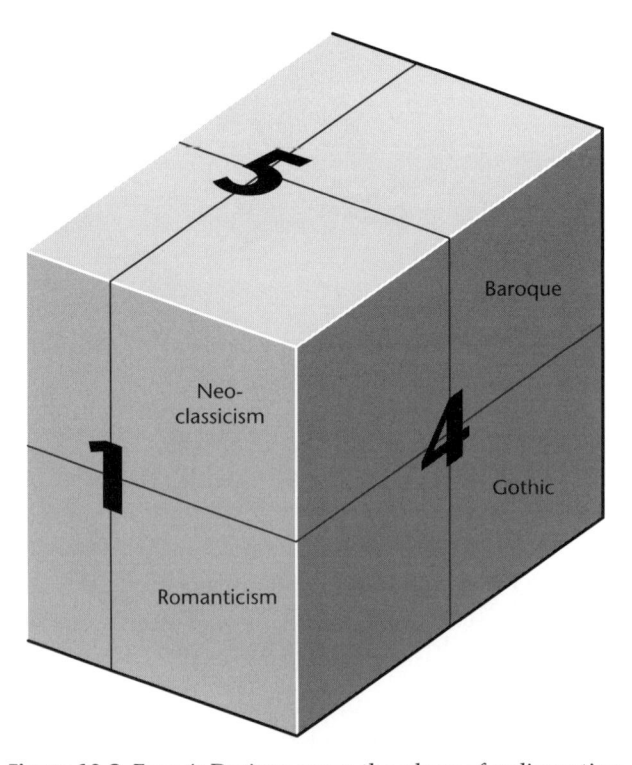

Figure 10.8 Face 4: Designs upon the plane of sedimentism

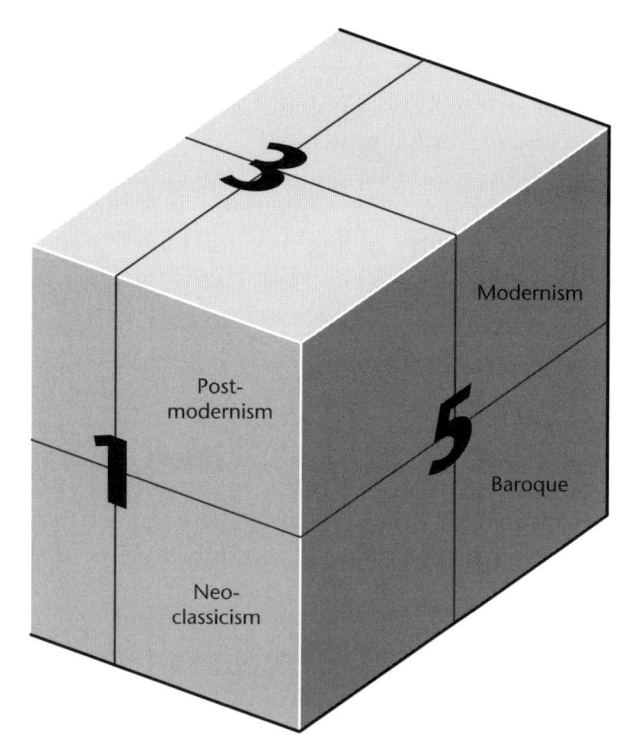

Figure 10.9 Face 5: Designs upon the plane of rationality

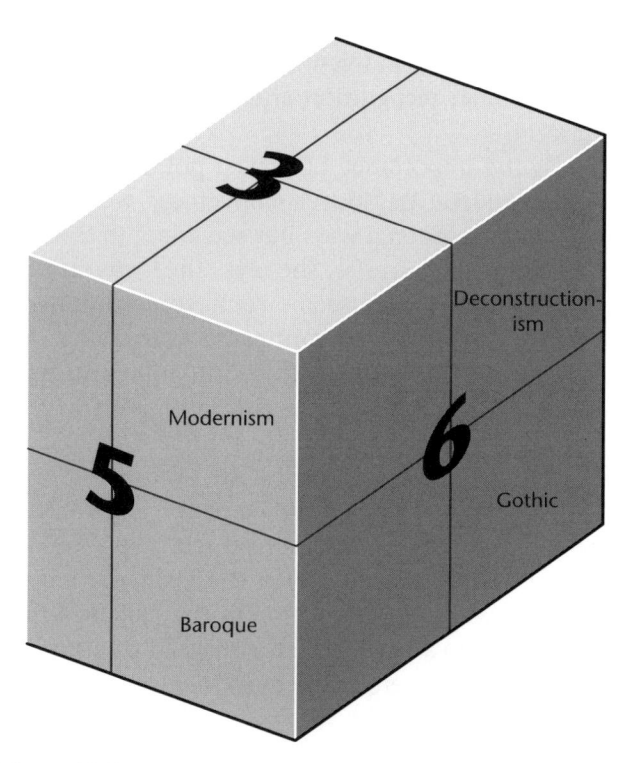

Figure 10.10 Face 6: Designs upon the plane of A-naturality

now found everywhere. It drew not upon historicism but upon a fusion of new technological and organizational principles.

Bing said of the USA, where he had just travelled, 'they do not, as we [Europeans] do, make a religion of...traditions. It is their rare privilege to make use of our aged maturity, adding to it the bursting energy of youth's prime' (quoted in de la Bedoyere 2005: 114). This is the sense of newness and novelty and energy that he wished to see in European art and architecture.

What organizational principles can we draw then from the Art Nouveau reaction to the 'age of change' and its focus upon the unruly aspects of the natural world? I have already given consideration to the Zapatistas who are attached to magical realism in which the magical, the bizarre, and the strange can be seen as opening up a window on reality. Fused with a belief in the power of irrationality and uncertainty, one can see that Art Nouveau has certain similarities with the Mayan cultural interests of the Zapatistas. Duritto, their revolutionary beetle who figures much in their cultural reflections, is not unlike several of the images found in the glass and jewellery objects made in western European workshops. A ceremony of allegiance to the organization is held in which seven objects are involved in an act of collective identity. They are the Mexican flag, corn, earth, and so on. The seven object-ideals are then connected to the seven major indigenous tribes that make up the Zapatista Movement. Yet there is also a call for a 'recognition of difference' in their 'war against oblivion' (Conant 2010). The Mexican state, with regard to indigenous peoples, had followed a strategy of assimilation rather than recognition and this had led to recurrent rebellion of a violent kind.

Also, of course, is the importance of gender politics in both approaches. Within the Zapatistas *and* the Art Nouveau movement, women were treated in a heavily gendered and traditional way. But according to those such as Mary McLeod (1996: 11), this is no surprise. She says: 'the focus on transgression in contemporary architecture circles seems to have contributed to a whole atmosphere of machismo and neo-avant-garde aggression. The theoretical language...is violent and sharp; the architecture milieu is exclusive—like a boy's club.' Since both approaches are associated with a certain level of violence, this does appear to be a germane comment. When we reconsider the way that women were portrayed in the Art Nouveau 'movement' of the 1890s and were treated as Nature personified, it resonates with the Zapatista experience throughout the 1990s. Widespread acceptance of Mexican machismo meant that even in the mid 1990s the state was obviously highly patriarchal. One of the early developments in the Zapatista movement was the 'Revolutionary Women's Law', which consisted of a dozen or so statements of women's 'rights' as seen by the movement:

Postmodernism and its organizational principles

When these laws, demanding equality and justice for women, were presented to the leadership committee of the Zapatista Army, they were ridiculed by many of the men present, but met with singing and applause from the women in the group. The laws were passed. It is apparent that, just as the Zapatistas have risen up against an unjust and subordinating government, the women Zapatistas have risen up against their own unjust and subordinating communities. In addition to fighting alongside the men in their challenge to the Mexican government, the women of the EZLN have chosen to challenge the men of the EZLN with their own ideology of democracy, justice and liberty for all people. However, when the men are confronted with the reality of no longer being allowed to hit their wives, sell their daughters, or treat women as virtual slaves, the men found that these standards are not so easy to live up to. (N. Krupskaya, 31 August 2009 on Facebook)

The pattern design features of Art Nouveau and the Zapatistas are to some extent shared ones. These commonalities relate to a 'naturalism' which shows itself in the symbolism used by the movements in their designs and their value systems. Land and land ownership figure highly in both. Another connection is their interest in marketing techniques so that their ideas (and products) might become more widely available for sale. Bing was a keen marketer, as are sections of the Zapatistas, apparently. The commodification of the designs is to be expected, one presumes, but it is a marked feature of both types of organizing that there is an interest in it. This leads to a use of 'modern' technologies of communication, media management, and public relations. Yet because of its closeness to other styles within the design cube, Art Nouveau's connections to Postmodernism and to Romanticism are worth noting, perhaps, especially where the Zapatistas have been claimed by both.

Postmodernism and its organizational principles

As the reader will know, much ink has been spilt on the issue of 'Postmodernism' and its relationship to 'Modernism'. The intention here is not cover this ground again but it is worth indicating perhaps the merest outline of these issues in what will look like a very brief section. In architecture, various currents of Postmodernism had been circulating within the deep pool of antagonism for the commercial architecture being produced by corporate architects for corporate clients. Whilst Mies's dictum that 'less is more' had driven much of this mundane, anodyne architecture, Robert Venturi's book *Complexity and Contradiction in Architecture* (1966) announced 'less is a bore' and he advocated the use of both–and rather than either/or thinking. This led to the rise of Postmodern architecture, where dullness was abhored. Richness in colour was to be brought back into the interior design of buildings and how they looked on the outside too. According to Glancey (2003: 199): 'At its worst it was a silly game for big kids who should have known better and led to a spate of candy-coloured buildings... that were pastiche confections of historic[al] and Hollywood styles pasted on to conventional and concrete framed buildings.' But Venturi stood out against the repetition and tedium of all buildings in whatever style and in 1973 published *Learning from Las Vegas*. This became a required text for 'pomo' architectural endeavour, at the same time as glass-reinforced plastic (GRP) became its material of choice. Soon, Pomo became the house style for fast-developing companies in the newly deregulated financial services sector. After this, the narrative shifts to the Derridean element of 'deconstructionism', which is supposedly reflected in the work of Gehry and others.

As I have indicated elsewhere (Burrell 2006), Postmodernism in social theory generally may be assumed to rest on four corner posts. These are Lyotard's book *The Postmodern Condition* (1984), the problematization of the issue of identity and the self, Derrida's articulation of 'deconstruction', and certain elements of the work of Michel Foucault. The effects of these writings upon organization theory is open to debate and for some there was no reason to take any notice whatsoever, for these non-readers lived comfortable lives of untroubled certainty. For some, Postmodernism was not a philosophical rethinking but was a descriptor of fundamental shifts in the organization of production. Stewart Clegg, in particular, (1990) has driven this interpretation of the notion of Postmodernism in the world of organizations. In a number of places he has compared and contrasted the world of organizations under Modernism with those under a Postmodern regime. Postmodernism here comes to mean the use of flexible specialization rather than Fordist mass production. Postmodernism in this sense becomes post-modernism, in that it is supposedly a stage in capitalism's development that has replaced what dominated previously. The post-modern organization, such as Benetton, reflects the attainment of more flexibility in its internal arrangements than hitherto possible. Elsewhere, others such as Warren (2005) have looked at Postmodernism's use of playfulness and in the search for *joussiance* have shown how games rooms and dress-down Fridays within an organization can or cannot liberate the energies required by the corporation. This discussion that attended the supposed rise of post-modernism resonated with Lash and Urry's highly dubious contention that the world was now a 'disorganized capitalism'. For organization theorists it was plain that a newish form of organizing was underway through globalization and the rise of new markets, but it was in no way disorganized. For the reader who wishes to read this decidedly pre-recession material, there are forest loads of paper upon which Postmodernism and post-modern organizations have been discussed.

Romanticism as a style of organizing

As we have also articulated above, there is something extraordinary within Romanticism for it is based on high respect for emotion, for nature, and for history (Schmitt 1991). There is a sense in which the origins of Romanticism lie in France with Rousseau and in Germany with Kant and Schelling amongst others, particularly with the *Sturm und Drang* movement of the 1770s. It spread across western Europe and into Russia at the end of the 18th century and into the early 19th century. Its origins lie in a reaction against Neo-Classicism, against rationalism and against mechanism. It transformed Western thought by returning to a respect for nature in the face of industrialization's apparent rape of the countryside and to a respect for the unconscious in the face of rationality's relentless emphasis on ratios, rations, and ratiocination. It emphasizes the feelings of humanity rather than the achievements of humanity (or Man as they would have said) and in some ways, in some places, foresees a different role for the artist or poet or architect. In place of the realization of demonstrable controlled human activity, it puts distancing, myth, fervour, and sometimes nihilism. Music, poetry, and art were seen more as an expression of the subjective psyche of the creative artist than as a craft or skill to amuse and entertain.

In architecture, however, Romanticism is a tendency that draws upon the 18th-century Picturesque movement, particularly as it was expressed in the English landscape tradition. This was the period in which 'Arcadia' was supposedly reborn. With images of peaceful animals wandering across immaculately manicured grasslands, tended by healthy, ruddy-faced peasants, Arcadian imagery suggested a countryside so unlike the emaciated gin-drinking workers of the industrializing cities where a fermenting social unrest terrified the aristocracy and the developing bourgeois classes. Having lost sight of its origins in the Dionysian excesses of the founding Greek Arcadia, for the Georgians their Arcadia was a notion that they had hijacked from a wilderness of violent animalistic Bacchanalian orgies, to simply mean a quiet, un-smoky rural idyll. Just as Virgil had done for the Romans in the turbulent politics of 44–38 BC, Arcadia became a retreat. It came to mean a place of plenty, peace, and pleasure.

Arcadia in its new form had a profound impact on architecture. Whilst many towns claimed the name across the globe the appearance of grass was deemed to be a sine qua non. Nikolaus Pevsner in the immediate post-World War period threw his considerable weight behind the Picturesque faction, fighting at the time to dominate British architecture and urban renewal. He also supported the Victorian revival that was part of this, as was the Festival of Britain. So Pevsner, born in Leipzig, espoused the virtues of 'Englishness' in what appeared, even at the time, as excessively parochial. Today this Arcadian vision still exists. David Pearson in *The Breaking Wave: New Organic Architecture* (2001: 72) outlined a set of rules for organic architecture and design known as the *Gaia Charter*:

Let the design:

- be inspired by nature and be sustainable, healthy, conserving, and diverse.
- unfold, like an organism, from the seed within.
- exist in the 'continuous present' and 'begin again and again'.
- follow the flows and be flexible and adaptable.
- satisfy social, physical, and spiritual needs.
- 'grow out of the site' and be unique.
- celebrate the spirit of youth, play and surprise.
- express the rhythm of music and the power of dance.

In 'alternative architecture' one sees much of the spirit of this charter. Rudofsky (1964), for example, speaks of the untutored vernacular style of adobe settlements in the USA which were seen to come from 'a golden past'. Earth shelters which offer good insulation being made from local turf, alongside attempts at self-build 'bricolage' structures, using local materials that happen to come to hand, both speak of 'Romanticism' too, where there is a distrust of professional architects and much more willingness to live in and through an historically based culture of rural self-reliance. In 2012, in Scotland, it is estimated that there are a thousand huts spread around the country but concentrated in places like Carbeth and Peebles. Here, 'hutters' seek to regain a way of life that has been close to extinction. Whilst this way of life has been retained in Scandinavia with 430,000 cabins in Norway alone, in Scotland its existence had been threatened by landowners. Hutting is claimed to promote low-impact, ecologically sound living that is good for rural regeneration (Carrell, *Guardian* 6 January 2012: 12–13). Hutting has faced the depradations of planning laws which have allowed expulsion from ancient lands and one community has been bulldozed by the local landowner. Carbeth hutters, formed by radical Clydeside political groups before World War II, began a rent strike 14 years ago and are now close to buying their communal land. So today, Romanticism is alive and well as a style of living amongst the organization of hutters in the boreal woods of northern Europe. It is alive and well in the Arts and Crafts Movement in design but also in terms of organizing.

Some in the Arts and Crafts Movement were avowedly socialist and saw the movement as progressive and supportive of the skilled working man and woman. By offering protection for craft skills, it was believed that the worst excesses of an alienating mass production could be held off. The protection of the guild mentality was thus central to the movement. Morris, for example, extolled the virtues of quasi-medieval life in which simplicity and the countryside were enough. The theme of the rural idyll was maintained and fed upon. Urban expansion and industrialization were the ghost at the banquet, of course, but Morris and his supporters wanted to use traditional building skills and crafts to solve the problems of modern life (Miele 1996). The vernacular styles of half timbering, the use of bricks, houses placed around village greens and within 'garden cities', and an overall simplicity in construction were the hallmarks of the movement.

George Orwell's valorization of this world of individualized privacy—of a world well understood by the Arts and Craft Movement—would have been shared by many post-war Britons. In *Nineteen Eighty-four* Orwell (1966: 81) describes Winston Smith's nostalgia for the pre-Big Brother world where 'It seemed to him that he knew exactly what it felt like to sit in a room like this, in an armchair beside an open fire with your feet on the fender and a kettle on the hob; utterly alone, utterly secure, with nobody watching you, no voice pursuing you, no sound except the singing of the kettle and the friendly ticking of the clock.' This is perhaps a classic representation of Romanticism in a British context with contemporary rafts of antique hunters seeking a nice copper kettle from the 1930s.

Romanticism is a term that has been used in organization theory in several places. Du Gay (2007: 137), for example, in his discussion of epochal change, quotes from Carl Schmitt's book, *Political Romanticism* (1991): 'The romantics transform... every instant into a historical moment... But they do even more than this. Every moment is transformed into a point in a structure... so every point is a circle at the same time, and every circle a point. The community is an extended individual, the individual a concentrated community.' This mirrors the discussion by Gergen (1992: 208) who sees Romanticism as a 'forestructure of understandings concerning the nature of human functioning'. According to Gergen, the Romanticist discourse reached its ascendancy in the 19th century, and affected poets, novelists, philosophers, composers, and architects. In his view, what was created was a sense of the '*deep interior*' and the need to develop an introspective sensitivity. The resources possessed by humanity to love, grieve, hate, create, and inspire—in other words, to find meaning in life—are seen as enormous. As for organizational analysts representing romanticism, Gergen nominates inter alia the Tavistock Institute, the Human Relations School, some Japanese management theory, and people like Cooperrider (part of the Taos Institute) who are interested in personal and organizational development (Cooperrider et al. 2008). These Romanticist approaches, says Gergen (1992: 210), allow people to live out their meaning systems in a more congenial way.

Now, I am not sure that Gergen here is strictly accurate in his portrayal of 'Romanticism', for he takes a narrow disciplinary stance towards the topic, drawing upon individualistic or social psychological definitions. This viewpoint affects his attitude to understanding Romanticism. Of course, his orientation is certainly resonant with a 'collapsing' theme that Schmitt's quote reflects, where under Romanticism, the individual stands for collectivity and vice versa within a collapsed understanding of both levels of analysis. But Gergen himself has collapsed a variety of non-modernist themes into one category and has sought to protect parts of social psychology by placing them in a safe box in a trichotomy of Romanticism, Modernism, and Postmodernism. Romanticism appears to be the 'other' to a debate then going on in organization theory, and functions as a repository for everything not being debated within the Modernism –Postmodernism exchange.

Nor is it clear to me that the Tavistock Institute, or human relations approaches, or the Taos Institute, reflect Romanticism in any real sense, yet there may be a commitment within them all, at one time or another, to the value of the hearth and the academical village. Certainly, if one is to look at the work on 'appreciative inquiry' by Cooperrider within the Taos Institute in New Mexico, one finds the following. The expression of the institute is through the medium of a romantic vision of the oldest continuously occupied township in North America with a maintenance of the values of the Pueblo peoples who occupied the area being said to be important to the work and life of the institute.

Romance is everywhere where there is an evacuation from home. Romanticism's contemporary vibrancy comes in the wave of church building now going on in other parts of eastern Europe. Imre Makovecz and Friedensreich Hundertwasser's work is what I have in mind here. It is perhaps easier to see the relevance of this approach if one compares it to the contemporary Autowerks of Volkswagen. Compare the straightforward glass-walled car production lines of Leipzig and Dresden with these Romanticist views, often involving a religious bent expressed in curves and an abhorrence of the straight line.

The organizing principles of Neo-Classicism

This was a style based on classical principles (i.e. in the architecture of Ancient Greece and Rome) in use supposedly from about 1715 until 1800, although it often reappears. It governed the architecture of the new United States in this period and has arguably been hugely influential thereafter. It first emerged in the work of the Scottish architect Colen Campbell, whose book *Vitruvius Britannicus* was published in 1715. It was based on the work of Andrea Palladio from whence it gets its name but other sources include Italian Renaissance architects and Inigo Jones who worked in the previous century. Lord Burlington was its most persuasive champion and it was he who developed the character of Neo-Palladianism, signalling a link between the virtues of Rome and Italy with the culture and burgeoning empire of the British nation. The Age of Reason found that perfection in form and proportion was much more important that curves and broken lines.

It is interesting how Neo-classicism has persisted throughout the 19th and 20th centuries as an enduring theme in design and architecture. The most respected architectural edifice of all time in Western eyes may well be the Parthenon. Many of the elements have been taken and mass-produced for factories and public housing. It has also been seen as a way of aiding upward social mobility in that the nouveau riche often bought Neo-Classical designed houses in order to associate themselves with the prestigious past. Many state governments in the Victorian age looked (as the USA had done in the 18th century) for ideas to build the state as a representation of powerful elegant edifices. Often it was Classicism to which they turned.

Architecture in many places was seen as requiring Neo-Classicism and had to obey classical rules—or it was not built or countenanced. In the United States, of course, the Lincoln Memorial by Henry Bacon in 1922 is in exactly the same style as that envisaged by Neo-Classicists everywhere. The espoused liberal democracy of that time does not fit well with any totalitarian drive but it would be facile to assume that Bacon did not see the potential for a concentrated statism in his edifice. According to Jencks (1987: 186), Neo-Classicism as a 'style reappears regularly on demand, every thirty years' and it is not hard to understand why, for 'Neo-Classical architecture has dominated both the form and style of parliament buildings, the layout of parliament buildings characterized by the great ceremonial spaces of the chamber, central hall and monumental entrance enclosed in a classical structure' (Sudjic and Jones 2001: 20). This style offers to the powerful a legitimation by harking back to the past accompanied by a sense that the powerful are those who are remembered by architecturally intimidating the population.

Today, Neo-Classicism is alive and well in Poundsbury and Celebration. Poundsbury is a village on the edge of the Prince of Wales's estate near Dorchester in Dorset. It is meant to represent an entirely 'new way of living'. Houses are built new to look old-fashioned within the village. The imagery is one where there would be no crime, no members of the working class, and no experimentation with other styles. The same is true regarding Disney's Celebration. By 2010, 20,000 inhabitants were to live in the company of decent law-abiding folk in white clapboard homes near Orlando in 4,900 acres of reclaimed swampland. It is not a 'gated town' but is integrated into the areas where four million urban Americans have retreated since the mid 1990s. Inside the compound, there are strict rules on regularly clipping the lawns, and curtains must all be white. Neo-Classicism is thus correctly associated with imperial demands from the population in exchange for peace and protection.

There is much discussion about the emphasis in Neo-Classical architecture on simplicity of form, stripped lines, and functionality. Charles Handy's borrowing of Harrison's Temple structure to describe bureaucracy is not incidental to this. There is something of Fordism in this caricature even though it might be much easier to make an argument for Fordism to be associated with Modernism. The Glass Factory at Dearborn had nice Doric columns evident in its four chimneys. We know that Ford himself liked 'chimneys' to exist within his corporation, of both a real and a metaphorical kind. Since there are those who describe the corporations of today as the new 'empire' (e.g. Hardt and Negri 2002), it is little to wonder that Neo-Classicism is still one design of choice for the corporate world. But Neo-Classicism has spread now into computer architecture.

Jon Postel set up the first attempt at organizing the Internet from the University of Southern California. This is known as ICANN and is based in Marina Del Ray, California. It is the only regulator of the Web and has been free from government control since 2006. There are 16 directors on the Board and it is a not-for-profit organization. It is mandated to organize its business in a 'bottom up, consensus driven, democratic' sort of way. However, these efforts have proved fruitless and democratic elections have not been forthcoming nor has the structure remained fluid. There are said to be few opportunities for public involvement, although the Internet Governance Forum was set up in 2005. It is alleged by free marketeers that ICANN does not allow market mechanisms full rein, which is what would serve the Internet best. The Berkman Center for Internet and Society at Harvard University conducted an inquiry into ICANN's transparency, accountability, and participation by the public. Thereafter, the Internet Governance Forum was set up via the UN in order to 'harness' the potentialities of the Internet for 'all peoples of the world'. The structures they seek to encourage are Neo-Classical in form, believing that the architecture of the Web is akin to a shambles of cross-cutting cyber alleyways. The obvious enticement for the powerful is the search for control of this architecture and the rendering up of it to simplicity and hierarchical control. The use of specified 'portals' as the term of access is not an innocent one, and much effort is being expended at controlling entry into the system through the use of other Neo-Classical imagery, building upon columns and headstones. The 'Internet Governance Project' which consists largely of academics, wrote a provocative piece in 2010 entitled 'Building a New Governance Hierarchy' in which they talk of 'resource public key infrastructure' (RPKI). They say;

> Implementation of security technologies are never neutral in their impact...RKPI is no exception...As the price of its security benefits, RKPI could reduce the autonomy of internet service providers and centralise authority of internet resources...It is attracting the attention of law enforcement agencies. (Mueller, Kuerbis and van Eeten 2010: 7)

The possibility is of a centralized, strictly hierarchical model, supporting regulatory authority over users. The optimal, eventual RPKI configuration, they maintain, may well consist of a 'single trust anchor' but they realize the existence of much opposition to this project of building a Neo-Classical structure of order, regularity, and enlightenment. Yet, if one is to look at the California-based 'Internet Library' which, it is claimed, is electronically copying every book ever published, and creating (in five minutes) a hard copy of it too, one sees a particular logo. The company has chosen via its impression management strategy to present itself as the classic Greek temple with columns and a pediment. The Internet is becoming Neo-Classicist in style.

Modernism and its organizational principles

The work by Adolf Loos published in 1908 entitled 'Ornament and Crime' (and referred to above) argued that there was a fundamental opposition between degenerate and anachronistic decoration on one hand and cultured plainness on the other. Decoration harked back to the historical past. All ornament should be stripped away to give favour to contemporary cultural honesty. It was this pamphlet that paved the way for the fully fledged modern movement in architecture to develop. Freedom from ornamentation was the sign of an uncorrupted mind possessed most notably by the peasantry and by engineers. To build like an engineer is to build 'without style'. The rise of almost pure engineering structures, such as the factories of Albert Kahn in both the USA and the Soviet Union, as well as those of Buckminster Fuller where wall and roof were as one in his 'anticipatory design', can be seen as reflective of Loos thinking. Some have seen his concern for anti-design to have also influenced the 'brutalism' of the 1950s.

Modernism's respect for history, its respect for sensibility, and its respect for nature are all at a very low level. This, of course, is what precisely makes it attractive to many across the planet who see in Modernism the future, and what is more, a future untrammelled by the past and its mistakes, by the dead hand of emotion and fear, and by concern for a dangerous and always threatening natural world. According to Jencks (1987: 372), Modernism has been a term of praise in architecture since at least 1460. His definition is more limited in scope than this but still remains extensive. He says:

Briefly defined, Modern architecture is a *'universal' international style stemming from the facts of the new constructional means, adequate to a new industrial society, and having as its goal the transformation of society, both in its taste, or perception and social make-up.* (italicized in original)

At one time, Modernism was avant-garde because Modernism was meant to lead a sluggish population to a new stage of social and economic development, indeed into a new stage of existence. Modernism stood both against consumer society and as an alternative to mass culture. It was originally utopian. It is concerned with social amelioration in a machine age. Architects like Le Corbusier certainly saw their designs as having transformatory possibilities across Europe and beyond. Le Corbusier's dictum that houses are 'machines for living in' and the rise of architectural modernism, originally stemming out of grain silo design, was the attempt to capture the imagination of decision-makers. The idea of function leading to purity of form led to an aesthetic and commercial impetus through which a whole infrastructure for an environment for living was to be developed (Leach 2007).

However, the phrase 'Meis means money', used by developers and senior executives in New York and Chicago in the 1950s, came to signal the end of the utopian dream, and Modernism became the house style of corporate capitalism. At this point one confronts the material construction of space and how it has been produced by ideas from within the organization of production. Modernism's embrace of new systems for human manipulation meant that 'The Efficiency Movement' and 'Scientific Management' ideas were seen as crucial in the early 20th century. As we have seen, Guillen (1997: 683) argues that Modernists were highly influenced by Taylorism and that Gropius, Mies van de Rohe, and Le Corbusier all saw in Fordism and Taylorism 'beauty with technical, economic and social efficiency'. Yet, whilst Guillen's piece is one of the few to deal with the links between organization theory and architectural styles, there are a number of serious problems with it (Dale and Burrell 2003: 163–7), not least of which is the enthusiasm the European Modernists had for these new organizational systems based on about a dozen grainy photographs. The one-way lines of influence across the Atlantic that Guillen identifies do not seem to be borne out by actual events and timings.

In the 'office', however, the indigenous American influence predominated. 'The United States created not only the technology of the office but also its aesthetic. Scientific Management and work studies pioneered by Taylor and the Gilbreths [were] combined with the architecture of the skyscraper, pioneered in the 1880s in Chicago and sophisticated later in New York' (Duffy 1982: 6). Whilst some of these buildings to house modern organizational technologies were speculative, others were constructed as palaces to glorify the company that built them. The Union Carbide Headquarters built in New York City in 1959 (and designed by SOM) reflected the full insertion of corporate values into design. It was conceived of as a total system of coordinated parts with the modular division of space into differential areas to reflect hierarchy. It became the model for corporate office design for perhaps four decades.

On the other hand, when we think of modern organizations we could do worse than begin with Gareth Morgan's (1986: 19) discussion of 'organisations as machines'. He begins by talking of 'office factories' where paper is processed in the form of insurance claims, tax returns, bank cheques, or where fast food is prepared and delivered. Within these buildings one expects to find ranks and uniforms, the use of standardized equipment, systematic training through drill and written rules, the fragmentation of tasks and their recombination in planned measured ways, and a strict division of labour that is represented in space so that managers inhabit different places from those employees of subordinate status.

This led to an extreme form of functionalism in which everything had to be rationally planned and placed. The construction of the 'daylight factories' of Alfred Kahn and the glass office blocks of Skidmore, Owings and Merrill represent ways in which architecture has addressed the needs of its corporate clients (Ghirardo 1996). Kahn undertook work for Packard, Ford, and Stalin, producing almost 20 per cent of the design and construction of all US factories up to World War II whilst being responsible for almost all factory construction in Stalinist USSR in the early 1930s. He was responsible for designing edifices that 'built' the factory worker, producing huge areas under concrete, brick, and glass within which Fordist mass production could fully function.

Today, these factories still exist and they are still 'building' the industrial worker. They happen to be in other parts of the 'developing' world. The largest free trade Exporting Processing Zone (EPZ) in the Philippines is Cavite, 90 miles from Manila. It was famously studied by Naomi Klein for her book, *No Logo*. There are 207 factories on a 682-acre site producing goods for export. Rationality here takes the form of giant sheds—windowless workshops—each with a gate and a guard. Ventilation is an open door between the aluminium sheets that make up the factory's walls and roof. It is, says Klein (2001: 204), 'a tax-free economy, sealed off from the local government of both town and province—a miniature military state inside a democracy'. Here there are no taxes, no duties, low rents, low wages, and low costs. Management is military style, workers tend to be young women, the work is low skill and monotonous, contracts are short and unlikely to be renewed, and the workforce is often migrant, and of course, non-unionized. The denizens of the EPZ could be moved anywhere at any time to some cheaper location. They are sometimes called 'swallows' because of their ability to flit from continent to continent.

Yet there are strong blockades to stop the unwanted members of the local populace (including police and welfare officials) from entering the EPZ. Klein (2001: 208) tells us that 'In Cavite, the zone is a kind of futuristic industrial suburbia where everything is ordered; the workers are uniformed, the grass manicured, the factories regimented.'

As for a contemporary machine sensibility, Volkswagen claims that its Wolfsburg factory, with 1,140 robots, is the largest auto plant in the world. There are 46 miles of streets within the Autostadt and it employs 23,000 people. According to the park's official guide, 'the Principality of Monaco would fit into the halls alone'. Visitors to the *Volkswagenfabrik* are offered a *WerkTour* in 'panorama trains' to see the daily production of 4,000 Golfs and other models. Also designed by Dr Gunter Henn is the Dresden 'Transparent Factory' or *Glaserne Manufaktur*, which produces the Phaeton luxury model for VW. The production facility is L-shaped and is next to a studio where Phaeton customers may see options for their car, as well as their model being assembled in front of them.

Outside the factory and office, Scientific Management and Modernism appear in some places to triumph in the private domestic home, and particularly its kitchen. What is found in the home today, some 80 years on, are also the trappings of Taylorist work. Whilst the home has always been an important place of work (Felstead et al. 2005: 42–3) for doctors, dentists and lawyers, as well as skilled manual workers in a variety of artisanal trades, clearly industrialization and professionalization reduced the numbers of adults working in paid employment from home. Of course, domestic labour continued unabated along with inequality, violence, and uncertainty. But for professional and managerial staff, the home has been reasserted as a key workplace. Academics outside the laboratory sciences have known this for some time and often perceive benefits in this 'freedom'. Work tasks using ICT are the obvious example of this incursion 'back into' the home of work practices. The 'wiring' of the home to make it PC friendly is a sine qua non of managerial-level domestic work. 'New' routines and routes therefore are rendered accessible to capital as we humans learn to develop tacit understandings of these ways of incorporating us into a system of habituation.

In factory, office, and home, then, we cannot escape the designs of Modernism. It is the organizing principle par excellence of the contemporary world, yet it is not all that there is. The closeness of Modernism, in patterning terms, to Postmodernism, the Gothic, and the Baroque means that we should not be surprised by various crossovers in which the difference between Postmodernism and Modernism disappears in the hands of some commentators; where Baroque reason is seen as close to the full-blooded rationality of Modernism and where Gothic skyscrapers pit their embellished selves against the stripped-down forms of Modernist office blocks.

Organization in the style of deconstructionist monumentalism

The term used here of 'deconstructionist monumentalism' implies that monumental structures are designed and built to rupture the society asunder from what it was before. Here, my focus is not upon memorials for that which has passed but remains valued. Rather it is upon innovative symbolic manipulation in seeking to transcend the past and its realities, and replace them with an invented future. Monuments seek to create rather than reflect value(s). Here, we confront Huyssen's (2003) argument that monumental architecture is the basis of 'memory politics'. This not only refers to the symbolic intentions of the commissioning 'authors' but it also includes what others then do to, and with, those intentions. Giza and Stonehenge are many thousands of years old and both have been heavily involved in 'memory politics', and not only in their own national territories either. By 'monumentalism', then, I mean the construction of very large edifices with an obvious and espoused political function. And often this function is the preservation of hierarchy.

Hierarchalism as a design principle for capitalist organizations reached a peak perhaps with the Ford Foundation's building in New York, completed in 1968. This was designed with a paradisical theme in mind, where the foundation's top executives lived as close to a life of hedonistic perfection as was possible in an office building. An open court is overlooked by a lush interior garden, signalling relief from the urban world outside. The designer claimed that the garden was a living room for the whole foundation, 'the spatial expression of their common organizational aim' (Klein 1982: 168). Materials used are expensive and luxurious, with mahogany and bronze being the major components of the desks. For the first time, 'trimphones' with push-button dials were commissioned and above every desk was placed individual lighting. The building itself mirrored the organization's hierarchy, with senior executives occupying the top floors and the auditorium and boardroom just below. It was an organizational and architectural design to show that certain executive lives could be 'effortless, unpredictable and free' (Klein 1982: 168).

Whilst this sort of lifestyle for 'Masters of the Universe' may have some appeal to deans and vice-chancellors, and even for deluded organization theorists, Glancey (2005) describes this sort of architecture as 'the architecture of ogres', saying it is designed not only to impress but to crush the human spirit. How many of us have had our spirit crushed as we enter the main administrative building of our institutions, gazing upon the deep white carpets along 'mahogany row' on our weary way for a bollocking? More seriously, Albert Speer tells us that Hitler liked to say that the purpose of his building was to transmit his time and its spirit to posterity. Ultimately, all that remained to remind men of the great epochs of history was their monumental architecture, he remarked. Architecture, even when ruined, provides a 'bridge to tradition' to future generations. It was meant to outdo the glories of Rome and produce massive buildings whose ruins would last for a thousand years of the Reich which had given them birth. Fascist architecture reached its high point in the remodelling of Berlin which was to become known as Germania. An avenue six times the length of the Champs Élysées was to connect north and south railway termini. A Great Hall was to be passed on the way down this triumphal avenue, which was to be 1000 feet tall and hold 16 times the volume of St Peter's Cathedral in Rome.

But Hitler was by no means alone in this fetishized view of memory. We see such a drive to monumentalism throughout history. In Bucharest, Rome, and in East Asia examples from the last century come quickly to mind. In Italy, the monument to fascism is perhaps the railway stations but little is left of Mussolini's attempts at 'decadent monumentalism'. In France, elements of monumentalism are to be rendered visible in the subterranean worlds of the Maginot Line. Here, on the Franco-German border, massive earthworks connected 'Earthscrapers' and communication tunnels into a complex defensive network. The Maginot Line gives the appearance of being a stout and fixed fortification against German expansion and was derided as being a static, defence wall to fight World War I all over again. However, its design facilitated movement, flows of personnel, equipment, and communications, yet it became a monument to a war already fought. The extensive underground railways of the Maginot Line are today used for tourism where the monumentalism of the project, and the francs it consumed, are still visible. Other attempts at monumentalism might take the form of the Atlantic Wall in France, which Paul Virilio (1994) has studied since his youth. Raw concrete is often used in times of tough budgetary constraint and the Brutalism which developed in the post-war UK is sometimes seen as a monumentalism to the survival of the state throughout a long war between 1939 and 1945. Glancey sees the array of Brutalist buildings on the South Bank of the Thames in London as 'urban mountains' more than architecture. They are monuments to British survival through the Second World War.

If the slogan of deconstructionist monumentalism is 'Big is good, enormous is better,' then Ceausescu's regime in Romania demonstrates this approach dramatically. After attempting to develop a personality cult in which he took titles upon himself such as 'The Genius of the Carpathians', had a royal sceptre made for himself, always had imagery of himself aged in his 40s used in the media, and never allowed his lack of height to be obvious, he sought to retain power in his family's hands. This was described by opponents as leading to 'socialism in one family'. They lived in an immense palace that Ceausescu had built. The Palace measures 270 metres long by 240 metres wide and is 86 metres high, made up of 12 storeys. There is an underground area, consisting

Organization in the style of deconstructionist monumentalism

of four levels, some 92 metres deep, and it is so large that the *Top Gear* team from the BBC staged car races within it. It has two underground parking garages and 1,100 rooms. The floor space is some 340,000 m² (3,700,000 square feet). The building is constructed almost entirely of materials of Romanian origin. It is estimated that it includes one million cubic metres of marble, 3,500 tonnes of crystal used for 480 chandeliers and a multitude of mirrors, 700,000 tonnes of steel and bronze for doors and windows, almost one million square metres of indigenous wood, 200,000 square metres of woollen carpet, and curtains embroidered with silver and gold. The principles of monumentalism then revolve around building your family in your own image, constructing a cult of the personality with attention to personal appearance and being very image conscious, manipulating the media so that the message is controlled and constructing buildings that will dominate important spaces and places.

What are often forgotten in the focus on political monumentalism are the business organizations of the 21st century that seek to be raised as monuments to entrepreneurs. Now this can be in the form of the great philanthropic foundations, where fortunes are deposited in order that the name of the business person will live on, long after their death, as a monument to their memory and to their achievements. Anywhere where there is a named building (e.g. the Stata Building at MIT) or a foundation, or an entrepreneurial charity, one sees the attempts at monumentalism in action. Buildings come and go but they tend to last longer than an endowment that depends on good financial advice and a lack of legitimate or illegitimate embezzlement, and of a charity where the behaviour of one's children can bring a reputation crashing to the ground. The Gates Foundation, aided by large donations from Warren Buffett, has guaranteed to spend all its reserves by 50 years after the death of the last trustee. Buffett has insisted that the foundation spends all of his donation within the next ten years. This has led to the appointment of 900 staff, some of whom have been questioned about their attitude to donations to Africa and to vaccination programmes, not least by 'grantees' who, in a 2011 survey, claimed in a ratio of 3:1 that in the distribution and management of funds, they had been badly mistreated. This is an example of a new 'philanthro-capitalism' where governments, NGOs, and corporate sponsors act together. The timing of 50 years before the end of the foundation seems to go against the 'monumentalism' of which I speak, but of course, many foundations lose the public eye and peter out in a slow decline towards inactivity. Buffett and Gates will both know that there is a big bang (an 'explosive alteration') to be had in the quick release of monumental funds in the coming decades.

Foundations of bricks and mortar tend to outlast organizations. That is perhaps why these organizations call themselves foundations. Some buildings attempt to awe the entrant to their monumental nature. The Judge Institute, like many buildings in Cambridge University, makes this effort, as does BMW headquarters in Munich, using the four pistons as a durable reflection of power, prestige, and product. Readers will be able to nominate their own example of monumentalism in their own organizations. In the UK, buildings are named after vice-chancellors, lecture theatres after famous alumni, scholarships after dead students and the spouses of the donors. The search for remembrance, for an acknowledgement of our existence, goes on and it is all around us in organizational life. Some just seek bigger headstones than others. I have nominated the Virgin Galactic organization as an example of monumentalism even though the owner is still alive. But of course the whole point of monumentalism is that the powerful are keen to achieve it before their successors get anywhere near the project. It is said that Branson spends much time worrying about threats to his control of the organization and that therefore (like Ford) he is a great believer in the building of organizational chimneys in his empire and encouraging competition between divisions. With such a view of one's colleagues, it should not surprise us that monumentalism would be undertaken by the chief executive themself. And in stylistic terms, of course, the verticality of the Gothic and the emphasis upon feelings and sentiments of the Romantic are very close by.

Baroque and its organizational principles

The Baroque 'period' arose from the Counter-Reformation, from Catholic anxiety at the growing power of Protestantism, from the rise of Absolutism in the face of the ever-more challenging mob, and from economic crises and failures of management (Tilly 1994; McAdam et al. 2001). The Baroque 'style' was a response to crisis and anxiety on a very large scale in religious, political, and economic life. 'The Baroque movement...has been associated with the Catholic Counter-Revolution and with monarchical absolutism. Essentially it was a power movement' (Hillier 1998: 13). Techniques for deceit and deception were developed. Key forms of this rendering of the visible invisible were the masqued ball, the use of *trompes l'oeil*, the cultivation of labyrinths in the garden, hidden exits, and entrances by which the monarch might make a sudden appearance or disappearance only to turn up elsewhere at some distance from the hidden opening. This obscuring of the real location of the king, of course, is a way of securing his power.

The contextual factors that were essential for the original formulation of the style centred on the ascent of Absolutism, and Leibnitz's defence (satirized by Voltaire) of it as 'all's for the best in the best of all possible worlds'. Theodicy, that is the vindication of divine providence in the very existence of evil, fits in

Baroque and its organizational principles

very well with the rise of the Counter-Reformation. The problem of getting Catholics back into church, and at the same time developing power plays which used deception and trickery against disruptive social forces (Turner in Buci-Glucksmann 1994: 8–9) are also key social forces. In the Baroque period, the Church self-consciously resorted to seduction to win back the masses. Loyola's role in this was to suggest an aggrandizement of the eye of the beholder within newly built churches.

Buci-Glucksmann (1994: 39) argues that reason under the Enlightenment was different from reason under the Counter-Reformation. 'For baroque reason, with its theatricization of existence and its logic of ambivalence, is not merely another reason within modernity. Above all it is the *Reason of the Other,* of its overbrimming excess.' Regarding excess, Hyde Minor (1999: 73) tells us that 'the monarchies of the seventeenth and eighteenth centuries were assertive, repressive, inefficient, and crisis-ridden ... and the arts were firmly incorporated into the cultures of the age'. Arts were taken in hand for the specific purpose of creating *'la gloire'* of the monarch and were marshalled with great success. The *theatre* was crucial in these developments as demonstrated by Brockett (1968: 358). We find theatricalized splendour of the courts of Frederick the Great and of Louis XIV. At Versailles there were 'Tournaments, fetes, princely entries, firework displays, masques and water spectacles' (Jay 46). There was a desire for grandeur, allowing a claim by Lacan that the Baroque is 'the regulation of the soul through corporeal scopics' (quoted by Buci Glucksmann 1994: 139).

The science of the Baroque was military, but more than this, it was cabbalistic and secret and Masonic in many senses. The Baroque was also a period of conspicuous consumption undertaken by the aristocracy at court, led, of course, by the sovereign. Colbert developed the 'National Manufactory of Gobelins' to provide furnishings and tapestries for the royal palaces, creating in the process an art *'industry'* (Hyde Minor 1999: 62). The organizational implications of this development of sophisticated customers dealing in a 'market' for high-cost luxury items should not be underestimated because economic changes have nearly as much to do with aristocratic fashion and taste as they do with corn prices and agricultural wages. The 'top' end of the market, for customers who have almost everything, but not yet enough tulip bulbs (Schama 1994), allows 'form to swallow function'. The concern in the Baroque for the horizontal more than the vertical marks it off from previous architectural styles in the late Renaissance where verticality was celebrated as closeness to God. The open parkland and fields of Versailles stand against the Gothic cathedrals, as each style takes a different approach to what in nature needs to be controlled and subordinated. Conquest in the Baroque was meant to be of (humanist) horizontal space and not of the vertical heavens in a dangerous rivalling of God.

Today, we may not live under absolutism as conventionally understood but there is a sense in which the reign of capitalism is virtually unquestioned. According to Baudrillard (1998: 72), 'this is, at least tendentially, the total dictatorship of the order of production'. Control-freakery emanating from our politicians today is reminiscent of earlier political systems, especially the Baroque. The technologies of celluloid and pixel clearly differentiate the current world from the Baroque, but the *trompes l'oeil* in the form of CGI special effects in Hollywood mirror the use of stage design by some of the most creative artists of the Baroque. Las Vegas is a town which uses all the range of sensory controls to produce a control of imagery and environment which Versailles could only dream of. There are no clocks in the gambling halls. Food and drink are free within their confines. Bedrooms in the hotels have very poor air conditioning whilst the gambling areas have the lowest and most comfortable temperatures. The phantasmagoria of the visual spectacle and the array of 'top' performers on show nightly all attract the gambler into the venues in the first place. The importance of the dazzling brightness of the phantasmagoria used to sell products is obvious. The use of colour, texture, and anamorphosis in creating contemporary images and brands by large commercial organizations is quite well understood.

The importance of display in the organizational world is well recognized, of course, and 'impression management' is the usual term to describe this sense of needing to offer a performance, irrespective of the sense of the 'real person'. Organizations that seek to appear responsive to the needs of their staff have installed 'dress-down' days where appearance is seen as less rigidly controlled (at least if one is male). But there is the counter perspective here to take into consideration—the hiding of appearance. The enclosure of space for purposes that outsiders should not see or be aware of is apparent in rise of secure rooms and the emphasis on crypts/labyrinths. The 'secure room' at (the former) Arthur Andersen which had lead-lined walls is a good recent example of the search for invisibility. Here, top decision-makers sat in the boardroom, sure in the knowledge that laser-borne listening devices, operated from overlooking buildings, could not pick up the words of their executives. Counter-surveillance is a Baroque concern, stemming from the openness and transparency of the horizontalization of space.

The Baroque horizontalization of space is also evident in talk of globalization where the old 'level playing field' in international trading relations tries to make concrete an absence of 'superiority' between players. Talk of space and the global consequences of actions reinforce the proffering of openness and the de-verticalization of social relationships. The use of corporate parkland has become very noticeable in the last 25 years for research and development activity. At the time when universities were encouraged or even forced to look more and more like businesses, businesses, particularly in the high-technology industries, began to look more and more like universities. Hewlett Packard's research centre on Nine Mile Ride in Berkshire was but one example of this tendency. There is the eschewing of height in favour of horizontal expansion. Square footage of area rather than volume became important as heating and ventilation bills grew. This conquest by the horizontal of the vertical can be vastly overemphasized, of course, but architectural firms like Skidmore, Owings and Merrill designed such buildings in the high-tech sectors almost for off-the-shelf use. The use of bridges between the very high tower blocks in the Petronas Tower is an example, for some, of the move away from a crude verticality in organizational life.

In the rhetoric of openness, and decline in hierarchy, grand entrances were not designed to awe the visitor but were supposedly designed for the climber to be energized by accessing the site. This suggests, of course, that the inside of the building contains much more dynamism that what lies without, but this aside, it does allow for certain technologies of surveillance to be enhanced. Single-width escalators in the Hong Kong and Shanghai Bank on Kowloon, for example, could be closely monitored by cameras. Being the only entrances into the building, such technologies of ingress ensured that every person could be clearly seen and noted. So whilst it looks like a monument to verticality, a building such as this retained some notion of horizontality.

In short, the Baroque could be argued to be all around us, as a different form of reason—as a different organizing of organization. It is a design style which has been resurrected because of the absolute powers which it confers on those who control the dominant *trompes l'oeil* within a Society of the Spectacle.

The organizational principles of the Gothic

At the end of the 12th century, England remained firmly feudal, and grand architecture was dominated by its dukes and their imposing castles that were coming to resemble palaces. Elsewhere in Europe, however, the development of trade meant that it was the commercial burghers of the trading towns and cities that produced grand civic architecture. Filarete first used the term 'modern' in 1461 to describe an architectural style, when he used the epithet negatively to describe the then current fashion for Gothic architecture (Jencks 1987: 407). 'Gothic' stood for everything that was barbarous and rude, particularly as a critique in the hands of Vasari. It was tantamount to saying it was the architecture of the vandal. The pointed arch, flying buttresses, tracerie windows, and pinnacles all characterize the style. The aim was to produce structures which dominated a town and indeed the local area, and would be by far the biggest structures that the local inhabitants had ever seen. Tall spires and turrets were commonplace. There is great emphasis on verticality with attempts being made to stop the eye of the observer moving sideways and to force it upwards. Gothic architecture is also known for its valorization of light, and the architectural designs used allowed structures to be much more open than before. The mathematical and geometrical arrangement of these buildings in the Gothic period was meant to show that the glory of God is in order. The loftiness was to convey the great magnificence of God. 'Creation' was signified in the statues and symbols adorning these ecclesiastical edifices. Often the decoration was highly coloured—as appears to have been forgotten by contemporary purveyors of the Gothic as being in a permanent state of gloomy darkness (Parker 2005).

A Gothic revival began in the United Kingdom in the 1830s in the face of the success of Nonconformism, and it was seen by many as an attempt by the High Church to fight back through a revival of the old ways. Gothic styles were associated with monarchism and the traditional ways of doing things. Neo-Classicism on the other hand was associated with Republicanism and Liberalism, so it is little wonder that Gothic became the key style for the ecclesiastical expansion in church building, associated with the rise of the newly industrializing cities of the Midlands and the North. In 1840 it was announced that there was a plurality in styles which had got out of hand. This led to the 'Great Style Debate' in which the major protagonists were Neo-Classical and Gothic orientations fighting across a Political terrain as well as politically (Hill 2007; Frankl 2001). Key to proselytizing the latter was A. W. N. Pugin, the title of whose book *Contrasts; or a parallel between the noble edifices of the 14th and 15th centuries and similar buildings of the present day* speaks of the volume's contents very well. He argued that this medieval gothic was the only true Christian style and should serve as an image for the future. He advocated the rejection of 'sham' and each piece of architecture should express its purpose both symbolically and practically. This architecture then was to be moral in tone and often went back to the Age of Chivalry and the notion of *noblesse oblige* wherein the peasantry were quiescent and the nobility enlightened to the point of benevolence. Drawing upon a labour theory of value, Ruskin claimed the superiority of the Gothic style because of all the long hours of skilled labour that had to go into the mason's traceries.

Pugin mounted an attack upon the 'linear and abstract' style of 'Greek' and 'New Square Style'. He claimed that there was a purer truth in the Gothic style. In the 1830s after a fire had destroyed the Houses of Parliament, Pugin succeeded in convincing the decision-makers that Gothic represented the quintessence of Britishness and that he should be given the commission for the New Palace of Westminster. Who exactly was responsible for the design of the biggest Gothic revivalist building in the world—whether it was Barry or Pugin—is not clear but it represented the triumph of the Gothic style in its use of verticality.

The organizational principles of the Gothic

Beyond architecture, 'Gothic', then, becomes a word that is used widely and without much sensitivity. It can mean horror, vampires, and the cult of Dracula. The rise of the genre of the Gothic novel is associated with Horace Walpole and was furthered by Mary Shelley's *Frankenstein*. Martin Parker (2005) has dealt with the importance of Gothic to the world of organizations and we shall turn to that issue in a moment.

As we have already seen, according to Owings (1973: ix), SOM used 'the master builder system based on the anonymous Gothic builders of the Middle Ages'. It was to be 'a multi-disciplinary service competent to design and build the multiplicity of shelters needed for man's habitat' designed as a modern 'Gothic Builders Guild' in which the strategy was to be 'to work we must have volume' and thereafter 'volume meant power' (Owings 1973: 66). And SOM did become very powerful indeed. For Parker (2005: 161) 'it was precisely the contemporary ubiquity of (a) demonology of the corporation that interested me in tracing some of the antecedents of contemporary gothic'. He goes on to say (Parker 2005: 161) that 'the figure of the corporate tycoon conspiring at the top of their skyscraper; the organization as a place where monsters are spawned; and the visualisation of work as incarceration' are common nowadays. Thanem (2011) has also spoken of the 'monstrous organization' in very similar terms, focusing upon bodies. When he suggests (Thanem 2011: 3) that 'it may be argued that the very act of organizing is an act of taming, killing and excluding the monstrous', no doubt Parker would immediately claim that he was a Gothicist. Parker would embrace Vacchani (2009) into that category too. True, he does deal with the Gothic as an issue in dress style, in movies, and in literature, but as with Gergen's treatment of the 'Romantic', the term 'gothic' (whether capitalized or not) becomes an omnibus, in which all comers are taken on board. However, for me, there are limits to the legitimate use of the term 'Gothic' and I am sure that everything that is grotesque or melodramatic (Parker 2005: 162) is not 'Gothic' (e.g. Garrick and Clegg 2000).

Indeed, Parker himself points out that often what he addresses is a confection of horror, melodrama, and the grotesque. And it is a confection in my view of quite different styles. Despite Parker's everyday notion that revolutionary romanticism is anti-Gothic, it might not be. Nor does Gothic always stand for darkness, disorder, and transgression. The Gothic cathedrals (in comparative terms) were highly ordered places of great colour and light. Nor are the cave and the subterranean necessarily 'Gothic'. As we have seen, it is more Baroque than Gothic in thematization. In other words, Parker seems to place in the coffin marked 'Gothic' almost everything that is not Modernist or Classical. It is as if organization theory can only manage three categories at any one time. I wish to keep 'Gothic' alive for a little longer as a separate entity and decidedly not as one of the 'undead'.

The Neo-Gothic work of Yamasaki in his Consolidated Gas Building of Detroit is characterized by Jencks (1987: 196) in the following way: 'Gothic fretwork, crown of thorns, the eternal blue flame of consolidated gas. Here is the attempt to transform urban realities into a nostalgic dream of a classical past; the forms are univalent, simple and applied. This is failed seriousness at its best, most horrible.' Alongside this is a quote from the actual architect of this Gothic pile himself: 'An architecture to implement our way of life and reflect it must recognise those human characteristics we cherish most: love, gentility, joy, serenity, beauty and hope, and the dignity and individuality of man. This idea is in its essence is the philosophy of humanism in architecture.' Gothic sees itself as offering this humanism to those who fall under its sway.

For me, there is little about the Gothic style of charity and gentility. It is 'most horrible'—but politically and not aesthetically. The Gothic is a style of nationalism and is part and parcel of political moves to reinforce the nation's strength and authenticity. It harks back to days of yore and tales of knightly and courtly etiquette but where Christianity was unquestioned. It is about aristocratic privilege. And it is here where Norbert Elias may prove useful. Although he does not use the term 'gothic', Elias (1974) does talk of 'the Court Society' prior to his discussions of 'The Civilising Process'. For him, court society was an historically significant form of social organization, being one of the last non-bourgeois features of our own society (Van Krieken 1998: 86). It was to the familial households of European royalty that Elias turned in seeking to understand today's social organization. But there is some conflation in Elias's orientation, because some of his early discussion is about a Baroque regime centred on Versailles, whilst in *The Civilising Process* the search goes back further into European history and to different places. He starts from the Middle Ages, where 'social control is mild. Manners, measured against later ones, are relaxed in all senses of the word...One must only refrain from falling on the dish like a pig, and from dipping bitten food into the communal sauce' (Elias 1994: 87). Courtly figures untrammelled by self-control, engaged in acts of ferocity, murder, torture, sadism, and destruction. Unlike the usual depiction of a caring nobility, the behaviour of medieval knights was perhaps better characterized by Bernard de Caznac, who plundered churches, attacked pilgrims, and mutilated the innocent—especially women. For Elias, all this was 'socially permitted pleasure'. For me, this ferocity ties in much better with the origins of the notion of 'the monstrous' that surfaces in the 'Gothic'. Gothic organizations are about ferocity and fear, as we might see from Libeskind's biography. And today they are fearsomely fecund.

The violence that one expects from and within organizations is paralleled by violence to and upon that organization. The ferocity with which any organization competes within a marketplace, or within the international 'arena' (sic) is matched by the attacks upon itself. So organizations build protective defences, at the same time as constructing a better armoury of aggressive weaponry. Like the Venice Arsenale, happy is the organization that thinks of war in times of peace. So in thinking of the collapsing tower, typically seen as one of the Tarot cards, the usual way of addressing this is through the notion of humanity rivalling (the) god(s). It is on this tarot card of the 'tower' where a lightning bolt, emanating from the heavens and produced by a cry from the Fool, brings the magnificent tower, with its high, arrogant inhabitants all convinced of their righteousness, down. For me, then, the Gothic is about fear of the tower being brought down by aggressive and violent action from 'the Other', the competitor, the enemy. And whilst it stands, the ferocity of the tower's inhabitants against those of the 'Other' sometimes knows no bounds. The evil Gothic master atop the citadel, and so often drawn in movies and novels, is best seen as originating in Bernard de Caznac. And we all know of Gothic knights like that who are alive and well in the penthouse suites of London, New York, and Hong Kong.

In the next and final chapter, I shall try and bring these cases—my casuistry—together and, in the face of the flying axes of the medieval knights, sew them up into a fabric of warmth and comfort. There I shall attempt to engage in embroidering upon the 'materiality of ideas' (Braidotti 1994: 126).

Conclusions: The Face of the Other

In the Preface to this book, I suggested that the following symbols acted as a useful indicator of the reader's design preferences.

Design patterns for organization theorists
   (*pace* Morgan 1986)
A. Sinuous intertwined leaves
F. Decorationless perfection
B. Explosive alteration
E. White-painted picket fence
C. The collapsing tower
G. Geodesic domes
D. Sunlit poppies
H. The hidden grotto

It is time to uncover the reasoning behind this claim. This book began by proclaiming itself as an offering in the spirit of Foucault's search for the order of things. Just as he ambitiously sought to span science, the arts and humanities, and the social sciences, I sought a more ordinary escape from the sclerotic narrowness of organization theory's tendency for dealing in footnotes. In the search for something more expansive in and for organization theory, I have sought to construct a space that opens up, rather than closes down, debates. An expanding of conceptual space may be thought of in many ways, and may be seen, quite legitimately, as producing something plastic, amorphous, miasmic, and shapeless. Yet the will to form abhors and thus resists astructuration. So in this book the space of forms has been presented as geometrical, well ordered, and constrained. The cube is often held up to be the most regulated void, all 'fair and square' in shape and appearance. However, it also can be seen as the 'iron cage' of rationality from which no escape is held to be possible. Cuboids, indeed, might be thought to be *the* geometric shape of control.

The Face of the Other

However, cubism was not a shaper of control. I am struck by instances in this book of resonances with Italian Futurism. Key notions to this artistic approach in painting were 'lines of force' to be demonstrated through 'pictorial dynamism' and the 'interpenetration of planes'. And when fused with cubism in the hands of Russian painters and sculptors, a hybrid form was created, called Cubo-Futurism. Whilst this had some short-lived impact on the Bolshevik Revolution, Futurism in its 'purer' form became central to Mussolini's Fascist movement because its Italian proponents sought in their work to glorify war and patriotism in the context of enthusiasm for machinery and speed. Here is a Futurist vision (Jencks 1985) of how they, as a group, expected to be treated:

> They'll storm around us, panting with scorn and anguish, and all of them, exasperated by our proud daring, will hurtle to kill us, driven by a hatred the more implacable the more their hearts will be drunk with love and admiration for us.
> Injustice, strong and sane, will break out radiantly in their eyes.
> Art in fact can be nothing but violence, cruelty and injustice. (quoted in Hollis 2009: 268)

The Futurists expected to be vilified and attacked, reminding us that any embracing of art is fraught with danger. In the book, I have sought to avoid the reader's violence, cruelty, and injustice but will be accused myself perhaps of perpetrating violence, cruelty, and injustice against my material. The act of cutting up bodies of literature with a sharp stylus leaves blood on the floor, even if one invites the reader to only remember how one has sutured parts back together again.

Using a cuboid form to suture disciplines and literatures, I have presented a design envelope which is the closed space of all possibilities in styling organization. It is meant to speak to all those interested in studying the processes of organizing because of its particular aims.

The Aims of the Design Envelope were to:

1. Demonstrate the importance of the 'will to form' to organization theory
2. Show that the generalized 'will to form' a safe material and ideational house is expressed differentially in distinct 'styles of organizing'
3. Argue that these styles operate right across the human sciences and erupt from particular solutions to particular problems of an enduring kind
4. Maintain that styles are connected rhizomatically—through their intra-actions, not least of which is their tautological definitional base—to produce isomorphic forms in widely diverse areas of human knowledge
5. Indicate how these styles are recognizable, manifest, and coherent.

The elements of style I have chosen to elaborate upon are as below. First, there are politico-economic systems, each of which has solutions to abiding human problems, but approached in different ways. This leads to the philosophical framework found in each style, where attitudes to nature, humanity, self, space, and time all reside, awaiting solutions. This rudimentary framework also exists within each architectural/design style which is tied intimately to philosophy and politics and economics. To understand architecture and design, one needs a degree in PPE. Buildings therefore express style with the possibility of some coherence in the exterior and interior embellishments, whilst inside, management practices also tend to reflect the same stylistic issues. Styles are last, but by no means least, discernible in organizational structures and processes, some of which serve as exemplars of extreme forms of styles of organizing.

As for the very broad-based content of 'styles' with which I am operating, I face, of course, the issue of forcing such much material into 'a procrustean bed' where it may scream and groan. Indeed, the reader may well have screamed and groaned at some of my content in the chapters of this book. My solution to this major issue is *'commensuration'*, which Espeland and Stephens (1998) describe as 'a process of transforming disparate forms of value into homogenous units', thereby leading to 'information reduction, uncertainty absorption, and simplification of decision making'. This life jacket of commensuration makes survival in a world of difference possible.

Building upon very simple geometry and using the notion of commensuration for analysing material, both presented in the context of 'the casuistry of individual cases' (du Gay 2007), the book then sought to create a design envelope which is conceived of as a cube. Put schematically, the characteristics of the design cube are:

— It is a conceptual 'void', conceivable as a containing envelope, the size and shape of which is constrained by the answers given to specific fundamental questions. It is formed by points, lines, and faces.
— This envelope constrains politico-economic systems, design, organizing, and architecture, by enabling and encouraging some content to be placed in specific areas and not in others.
— Thereby it suggests that distinctive 'pattern books' exist for different parts of the cube wherein a regularity of similar solutions has become recognized and prioritized. Choice exists but is not large.
— It points to the occurrence of regular 'style wars' between differing assumptive positions, the existence of which offer explanations for opposition and conflict.
— It is indicative of the fact that we might not like the style of our containment at all—and there is a choice—if we but had the freedom of movement...
— Your choice speaks of your preferred 'style of organizing'.

The Face of the Other

The problematic nature in dealing with different elements of commensuration should be obvious, but key to the process of 'transforming disparate forms of value into homogeneous units' are the lines of fight I have chosen. These lines are the key to your choice of styles of organizing

Sensibility	...	Rationality
Sedimentism	...	Rupturism
Naturality	...	A-naturality

These three lines, consisting of a myriad of points of possibility, produce a three-dimensional space if placed at right angles to each other. A plethora of intermediate points is available on each of the lines where classic orthodox positioning is easily found—as in the case of 'evolutionism', for example. These points, lying intermediately between extremes, can be plotted and permit the drawing of grids or even a map of the cubic surfaces and interior. Obviously, the design cube itself is offered in the tradition of 'the will to form' as an interdisciplinary positioning device. If the mapping analogy works, then, what shall we label the continental spaces that are made evident?

The following set of labels is offered alongside your choice of favoured design. But please note, my interpretation of each of these design metaphors is characterized by a singular portmanteau term into which much meaning must drop. Sometimes the label chosen is a well-recognized aesthetic term, sometimes a well-recognized economic term, sometimes a mixture, and sometimes a neologism. Each label is meant to reflect the *dominant* ideational set within the style and this is not straightforwardly predictable.

- A. Sinuous intertwined leaves—'Romanticism'
- F. Decorationless perfection—'Neo-Liberal Globalization'
- B. Explosive alteration—'Computer generated Schumpeterianism'
- E. White-painted picket fence—'Heritage Protectionism'
- C. The collapsing tower—'Potlatch politics'
- G. Geodesic domes—'Techno-Pragmatism'
- D. Sunlit poppies—'Red Revolution'
- H. The hidden grotto—'Keynesian Statism'

Let me explain what lies behind this. As yet, for the reader, there may be no recognition, manifestation, or coherence of these patterns, but I shall do my best to create this set of responses as we move on. These eight terms present styles of organizing as very particular expressions of the will to form. As a design, it predicts the presence of *isomorphs* within and across the four disciplines in any given location of a given major style. Indeed, I have spent time in previous chapters attempting to demonstrate the presence and nature of these isomorphic forms. However, it must be noted that styles of organizing do not inhabit closed-off worlds as isolated niches, but these worlds open up into shared communal spaces. Romanticism is opposed to Neo-Liberal globalization but shares common interests, for example, with Potlatch politics on the plane of sensibility, and with Heritage Protectionism on the plane of Naturality. Red Revolution is opposed to Keynesian Statism, but shares interests, for example, with Techno-Pragmatism on the plane of Naturality and computer-generated Schumpeterianism on the plane of Rupturism. In other words, certainly more than one style might appeal to us as organization theorists because of the openness, to varying degrees, of each style to other influences.

This takes us to the middling positions upon the lines of fight. I have not said much about these intermediate locales, preferring to concentrate upon extremities in order to bring the discussion into starker focus. Only Chapter 9 looked in any detail at such positioning. It will not need saying but much work needs to be done in this part of the spectrum of styling organization.

As already explained, the internal ground at the centre of the cube is a melange of these cross-cutting currents, producing hybrids of hybrids. So just as in the febrile minds of Hollywood producers one can conceive of singular horror-comedy-science-fiction-cowboy movies, in the labyrinthine city centres of organizational design, monstrous stylistic chimeras are possible. But these tend not to survive. Hybrids are often unable to reproduce themselves and die out after an experimental attempt at survival in the maelstrom of 'flows'. In Ovid's *Metamorphoses* (2004), the theme is clearly 'transformations', by which he seeks to unify Greek and Roman mythology. It is the articulation of the titular 'form which morphs' that his set of poems concentrates upon, in 'spinning a thread' from the beginning of the world to his own life time. The Roman Empire is presented as living through a time of flux in which even its own existence will end. And characters in mythology are seen as living through changes in their identity which can transform them from deity into human, human into vegetable, and deity into animal. The maelstrom of flows is exactly what Ovid depicts. The point that I want to make here is that whilst this diachronic perspective excites and pricks our understandings, a more synchronic persistence of isomorphic forms is what *Styles of Organizing* is about. It is the 'will to form' rather than the will to 'transform' that represents the thread of this particular argument.

Transformations in taste are difficult to manage (Aldrich 1979; Carroll 1984). As Hannan and Freeman (1977) showed in the 'population ecology' of their research field, restaurants, perhaps what we now call 'fusion' food is likely to create problems for organizational survival. Organizations are driven towards safe, well understood 'isomorphs'. Styles of cuisine which are recognizable and enduring tend to be key to restaurant survival. They follow recipes quite carefully whether concerning their food or their formal features.

The interweaving of threads

What I have attempted to do is weave four discrete areas of intellectual endeavour together, through the interrelated and overarching notions of the will to form, wherein 'styles' are seen to be a product of the 'production of organization' and the organizing of organization. The will to form creates a defined and controlled intellectual shape through patterning, mapping, and regular rerecording. Thus conjured into existence is a design space which represents the same design constraints and opportunities for all four academic endeavours. Within each pattern of organizing inside the design space, we find, first, those material elements which relate to how emplacement of human beings is undertaken represent 'structures'; second, individual examples of how the enactment of processes is conceptualized and designed, creating particular 'formats'; and third, 'embellishments' as those 'enchanting' elements of materiality which adorn structures, but which do not change the structure or the format. These are analytical terms, then, allowing comparisons to be made via each element, on a case-by-case basis.

One has found cases where all of the structural, formatting, and embellishing features of specific *architecture and organizations* show some identity. The autistic organization of Wittgenstein's house, designed and constructed between 1927 and 1928 (Leitner 2000) has an isomorphic identity with Ford's factories of exactly the same period. Similarly, at the level of organizations and designs that inhabit the midst of the planes, and not the extreme corners of the cube, one might return to one of organization theory's favourite cases, the Tennessee Valley Authority. One can see the elements of structure, formatting, and embellishment of this organization line up very nicely in a relatively seamless isomorphic way with architectural modernism. Emplacement, enactment, and enchantment within the TVA positively drip modernism. The architecture of the huge projects undertaken was chosen by its designers to reflect the structure of the authority itself. A command economy produced both organizational and architectural forms which reflected each other. The embellishments within the TVA also reflected both organizational and architectural structures and their formatting (Huxley 1942). However, this clear correspondence of all three levels of patterning in organization design and in architecture is by no means common. But it does suggest that many business and state organizations are creatures first and foremost of Modernism and, in many of their buildings, embrace zero architecture (Banham 1980).

Where, then, do organization and *political economy* match up closely to architecture and design? The protectionism evident in organizations, defensive of their competitive position and eager to regulate competition, is characteristic of empires. Against competition from the novel and the innovative, heritage serves so many functions in a realm of protectionism. And the architecture of choice for the imperial urge is Neo-Classicism, with its imagery of longevity, elegance, and its production by slave labour from conquered peoples. As noted earlier, this architecture and organizational form are the style of choice for those who seek to control the great unwashed in the e-sphere. Authority over the Internet, because of its lack of control and command structures, is often presented as requiring hierarchical, column-based structures where surveillance and lines of command are clear and obvious. The examples I gave of the search for pillars and columns under Neo-Classical organization theory is not easy to see in the architecture of the Internet, always assuming one knew how to access this. Yet, the 'Empire of the Gaze' requires imperial measures and imperial architecture. Greco-Roman portals to the Internet are the way forward for many of a regulative bent.

However, a passing glance at the design cube might suggest that it is Modernism, the Baroque, and Monumentalism which are the three styles with which the organizational world is most at ease. For there is little discrepancy between architectural/design and organizational/political economy approaches to emplacement, enactment, and enchantment under these three stylistic regimes. Now this may come as no surprise to the reader. All are associated with styles that are comfortable with power in the 21st century.

Previous chapters also indicate that Postmodernism in architecture/design and Postmodernism in organizational life may bear little relationship to each other. The answer to this discrepancy may well come from the different uses put to the term 'Postmodern' and its articulation as 'post-modern' with the all-important hyphen. Here, in the hands of Clegg and others, the term has come to mean something in the world of organizational theorizing and something very different in the world of design thinking. Also in this unfortunate category of misunderstandings is the Gothic. As I have indicated already, the use of Gothic by analysts such as Parker has meant that the identity of (organizational) gothic with (architectural/design) Gothic has not been achieved. Indeed, the terms have come to have an opposing character. One route from this particular difficulty might be to legislate against the sloppy use of terms by one's colleagues—but that's never going to happen!

Similarly, romanticism in organizational life is often hidden because these examples are contained within very small-scale, often community-based, voluntary organizations. Again, accessing these is not easy for typical organization theorists, comfortable as they are in their business schools, where the name on the tin ('business') means something. Romanticism in the 21st

The Face of the Other

century remains largely hidden underground and much research will be necessary by my colleagues to uncover these cases.

In summary, as we can see from Table 11.1 on the facing page, originating from the very distinctive outliers at the extreme points of the cube are the applicable elements of style.

The will to form and the identical subject-object

In this final section I wish to discuss not the casuistry of individual cases but their underlying foundations. Upon what are our constructions of, and within, styles of organizing laid? 'Uncovering' what lies hidden in the foundations of all that we undertake leads us to the importance of excavation. My contentment with the notion of rhizomes perhaps indicates a keenness for the subterranean. And in the final section of the book, I shall give this darkness full force.

On the surface, this is a book written by an organization theorist about architecture, aesthetics, political economy, design, and artwork, and their relationship to 'organizing'. But beneath that is an attempt to resolve some intellectual puzzlement that has occupied my attention for many years. It is the search for some thing, some grouping, some idea, some material object, some place, some time, from which to view the *'identical subject-object'*. This is seeking a position from which one can deal 'fairly and squarely' (not innocent terms, of course) with some major issues in social philosophy and social science. That is, this text seeks out a location where one might stand and see that the material and the ideational were both recognized as equal in importance; where mind and body coexist in a partnership of equals. A place from whence structure and process, solidity and liquidity, stasis and movement, repetition and change could all be seen and recognized in their equivalence. A theoretical home where order and conflict, conservatism and revolution, peace and war were seen as worthy of investigation in an equitable way is what is desired here. If one could find the identical subject-object, perhaps it would be possible to see economics, design, architecture, and organization theory simultaneously, through the same lens—without going blind in the process. In other words, by using 'both–and' thinking rather than 'either/or' approaches, this final section seeks to look upon the face of the Other.

The word combination 'will to form' may help us here. The identical subject-object cannot be achieved where human subjectivity is either all-powerful or is devoid of any impact. The 'will to form' fortunately is made up of two interlocking components which each resonate with one particular side of the duality, rather than the other. Let us deal with them in turn.

Table 11.1 Elements of style

Cube positioning system	Politico-economic system	Management	Art	Architect	idiograph	Organizational exemplar	Summary stylistic term
A Sensibility Sedimentism Naturality	Green Environmentalis	Participative, volunteering, green objectives, seasonal non-capitalist	Romanticism	Gaudi	Excessively imaginative adornment	National Trust	Romanticism
F Rationality Rupturism A-naturality	Neo-Liberalism	Globalization, shareholder value, zero architecture, accounting for cost reduction	Modernism	Wittgenstein	Decorationless perfection	Ford Motor Company	Neo-liberal Globalization
B Sensibility Rupturism A-naturality	Schumpeterian Creative Destruction	Entrepreneur, risk taking, firm based pro-capitalism	Deconstructionism	Gehry	Explosive alteration	Virgin Galactic	Computer-generated Schumptererianism
E Rationalism Sedimentism Naturaliity	Heritage economics	Marketing, protectionist, impression management, localist	Neo-Palladian	Jefferson	New World Order	Tilting Community	Heritage protection
C Sensibility Sedimentism A-naturality	Potlatch economics	Management as servant of capital' defensive of authority, magnificence	Gothic surrealism	Gothic builders, SOM	Collapsing tower	Freedom Tower, NY	Potlatch politics
G Rationalism Rupturism Naturality	Techno-environmentalism	Management as expertise, problem solving through technique	Dymaxion	Buckminster Fuller	Doing more with less	Enval SME	Techno-pragmatics
D Sensibility Rupturism Naturality	Pol Potism	Twin circulations, anti-expertise, anti-management	Art Nouveau	Horta	Art as freedom	Zapatistas	Red Revolution
H Rationalism Sedimentism A-Naturalism	Keynesianism	Employment, creative accounting, economic management	Baroque	Louis XIV	*Trompes l'oeil*	Enron	

A *'will'* suggests a force of human consciousness in which the mind has an idea of what it wishes to project into the future. It may not achieve that projection but it may well continue to seek an achievement of its objectives by repetition, time after time. If a 'will' is the active seeking of a desired objective by a subjective entity, the second term, a *'form'*, is perhaps best conceptualized as an objective entity which may well represent an outcome desired by designers, but may also be independent of any human design. This independence of an objective material form (like the universe) means that humanity may well recognize that it must seek to exert its will on an entity which is a pre-existing object that has both its own form and content. Entwined within the identical subject-object, then, are both 'will' and 'form'. The 'will to form' which this book has sought to elaborate upon perhaps offers a small key to unlocking some of the mystery of the identical subject-object.

Three major points are worth making.

In discussing the identical subject-object as a way forward for many strands of social science, one confronts many problems. First is the question of German Idealism, a tradition which is somewhat at odds with the Positivism developed by Comte and finely honed much further west of the Rhine. German Idealism is associated most clearly with the work of Hegel, the 19th-century philosopher with whom most social science has to deal with at one time or another—whether it wants to or not. Reality was to be understood not only as 'substance, but as subject'. The role of the mind in creating our reality, rather than simply apprehending it, was to be raised to be *the* principle of human thought's relationship to the world. At Jena, Hegel had had an epiphany and had seen the 'identical subject-object' riding a white horse through the streets. This apparition, of course, sat astride Marengo, was Napoleon, who, in all his victorious pomp, at that time was associated with radical and positive change across the face of Europe. Many were to change their minds about Bonaparte in later years—but the key words here are the importance of 'their minds'. How was this approach to mind, to ideas, to consciousness, which was so different from that being developed in the natural sciences, to be comprehended after Hegel? One route was taken by Georg Lukacs, who, in raising again the issue of the identical subject-object, showed his thinking to resemble that of Hegel's in the crucial aspect of elevating consciousness to a primary role (Lukacs 1971: 39). In this Idealist context, Lukacs had attacked Engels's famous exposition of the 'Three Laws' of dialectics—the unity of opposites, the transformation of quantity into quality, and the negation of the negation—because Engels had embraced a positivist epistemology rather than one reflective of Idealism. Says Lukacs of Engels:

> He does not mention the most vital interaction, namely the dialectical relation between subject and object in the historical process...Yet without this factor dialectics ceases to be revolutionary...thought remains contemplative and fails to become practical. (Lukacs 1971: 3)

Lukacs's first solution as to who was the 'personage' now occupying the role of identical subject-object, was the proletariat. The working class offered itself as the exemplification of the identical subject-object, in its capacity to understand and change the world in which humans live. However, it was to be subsequently acknowledged by Lukacs (1989) that: 'the proletariat seen as the identical subject-object of the real history of mankind is no materialist consummation that overcomes the contradictions of idealism. It is rather an attempt to out-Hegel Hegel.' In other words, for a Lukacs more concerned to embrace a Soviet-led Europe in the mid 1960s, 'materialism' was necessarily de rigueur. The subjective idealism of his writings on 'the identical subject-object' did not fully embrace the material world and he 'regretted' this in his later work. Nor had the proletariat been overly visible, through an experiential understanding of capitalism, in a role of creating a new post-capitalist world.

Because of this perhaps, Adorno differed fundamentally from the early Lukacs in two ways: he sought to deny the possibility or even the desirability of reconciling subject and object in the Lukacsian manner, and he rejected the equivalent reconciliation between theory and practice. Since the object could not be collapsed into the subject, and theory should not be dissolved into practice, both had to remain independent to allow a developing critique and a developing praxis. The role of the workers in leading this developing critique, and developing praxis alongside it, was not obvious to the patrician Adorno.

Zizek, in a more contemporary vein, has been 'accused' of embracing Idealism in resurrecting a version of the 'identical subject-object'. Boucher (2009) in *The Charmed Circle of Ideology* has said that 'there is an impossible desire to resurrect the doctrine of the "identical subject-object of history" in Zizek's Lacanian dialectics', and that 'This condemns Zizek to lurch between these antinomic poles' (2009: 166). Subject and object are presented by Boucher as polar antinomies, incapable of reconciliation, just as Adorno did.

In brief, then, these are some of the painful difficulties faced by those who wish to take forward the notion of the identical subject-object. Suffice it to say here that if we are to develop the identical subject-object as a notion for understanding styles of organizing we have our work cut out so as to variously avoid: any romantic notion that it is a 20th-century 'proletariat' who will do the job for us; lurching between antinomies; believing that anything with the title '*subject*-object' rather than the obverse '*object*-subject' can be fair to both in equal measure; and that its intellectual roots in German Idealism will go down well with audiences from west of the Rhine (or the Atlantic). The solutions posited to this nice set of conundrums lie further ahead—but the reader should note that they still involve some geometry.

The identical subject-object as the middle

In searching for the identical subject-object, I am not seeking the middle ground as advocated by Deleuze and Guatarri, for they do not seem able to 'realize', to bring into being through a becoming, this middle place in their method. Nor is this location to be confused with the diplomatic notion of the 'mid-ground', a locus in between philosophical disputes where polite negotiations might take place in the anodyne language of diplomacy. It is not the notion of a 'golden mean', beloved of liberal negotiators, that I am looking for, but a position of transcendence wherein one enters a third dimension, that of verticality, from whence the debate is clearer and more transparent than if one is in its midst. But 'loftiness', as evidenced in the stance of Adorno, for example, is always a difficult vantage point. The attitude that comes from altitude is a heady one, as at least one of the tarot cards shows.

The place of the identical subject-object is a rather difficult location to find but it is *not* to be found in the middle of the design cube. Here is a stylistic melange of many competing styles, idioms, designs, and patterning. Starting as I have done from the corners of the cube, I have been keen to emphasize difference, distinction, and differentiation. But, as the major styles coagulate into an engorged central location, making distinctions more and more difficult, we should not seek out the identical subject-object here. This is the anomic place of a uniformity of separate idioms, not style.

In a world of 3D possibilities, the identical subject-object may hover above the battleground where antinomies fight it out. So it may not be a place at all in the sense of a fixed destination but rather it may require a pursuit, as it moves constantly and permanently, from which its trace will be recognized. It may be rendered accessible, perhaps, through noting its shifts and trails rather than through uncovering its locus. Many attempts have been made to find this ideal vantage point, variously through dialectical materialism, the theory of morphogenesis, structuration theory, configuration theory, and so on. But these are rather large and unwieldy beasts and, being themselves in search of ordered fixity, are slow to move in finding a place or (series of) places where the identical subject-object temporarily lives. But if 'big theory' such as these cannot provide a lingering glimpse of the identical subject-object, how are organization theorists to approach it?

What if we were to approach this task through a number of smaller ideas—ideas of the middle range—that dealt with specific dilemmas in the social sciences, which allowed us to see the different 'faces' of the identical subject-object? In other words, in seeking to understand and pacify these philosophical antinomies, perhaps we should not look for one solution in a grand unified theory (GUT) of everything but be content to deal with each *'plane'*, each arena of contestation, in its own terms and on its own merits (Deleuze and Guattari 1988: 265–6). And when planes exist alongside each other, perhaps it is best to see them as operating in three dimensions, not just two. Here we reconfront simple 3D geometries as the second major foundational issue.

The identical subject-object as cubist

Throughout the book, I have attempted to use several other notions—derived from outside geometry—in building up a multifaceted, somewhat 'cubist', picture of the identical subject-object. Through accessing the different faces of the identical subject-object we might find, not common ground, not a more rounded understanding, but a 3D appreciation of a structured set of processes. This cubism might allow us to approach that impossibility to perspectivalist thinking—an all-round understanding of a fluid, yet solid, three-dimensional volume. So, for the author, *Styles of Organizing* was designed to provide rounded 3D imagery of a complex 'surface' of aesthetic design styles and their contextual placement, whilst dealing *at the same time* with a 'depth' of philosophical dilemmas. The mediating concept which links these layers together is 'organization'. Organization holds both surface and depth in an interplay, anchoring one above the other for the most part, but influencing moves both ways. This book therefore has also been about how all of these deep dilemmas and the partial solutions to them are central to organizing our lives for us—and how in turn we organize them. Here we come to 'the face of the Other'.

The identical subject-object as the 'face of the Other'

I am going to borrow a term, 'the face of the Other' and place emphasis upon the term as suggestive of seeking, knowing and responding to the side of the Other, whilst being ethical about it.

Given the usual importance attached to understanding the 'other' side of an argument, a skill which universities, upon the plane of rationality, are supposed to take very seriously indeed, one recognizes the mundane difficulties in doing this. Merleau Ponty (1962) shows how, because of our embodied position within an enfleshed skeleton, we are limited in what we can see of solid objects, including our own bodies. For example, have you ever seen your own

The Face of the Other

back in the fullness of its nature? 'Does my bum look big in this?' is not an innocent question, because it reveals the human difficulty in seeing more than one side of oneself. Normally, we need someone else to tell us of our other side. Someone we trust provides the face of the Other. So whilst there are ways of achieving 'positions of exteriority' to viewing our own backsides, these involve heavily partial use of strategically placed mirrors, or more usually photographs taken by others, with or without our knowledge. When we see these photographs we can gain some sense of whether our backsides look big or not and the view from the 'Other'. But it is difficult to focus with two sides in play at any one time. The face of the Other can never be fully known to us, for photographs of our backs, taken in the brief light of a momentary flash, once seen, then slip out of memory. Just as concerns for the Other, so central to us in a brief flash of interaction and empathy, give way to the mundanities of tending to our own psychological and physiological needs. We need to feed our own faces.

Meanwhile, the faces of the design cube are homes for many people. So too are the nooks and crannies of the voids. Their places and spaces for work, play, and sleep are well known to them and shape the conditions of possibility for their lives. Just as these conditions of possibility create the styles for designing our lives, they too are created by everyday human interactions in a way which sediments human habits and regularities into stylistic isomorphs. Each of these styles, of course, is itself constrained by the lines of fight we identified in earlier chapters. And because they involve contestation and struggle, we must expect that this human attachment to the face of possibilities will be tenacious and rendered possible through our use of strong ideational ropes and crampons. This suggests that our willingness to abandon the face upon which we are most comfortable is not likely to be high. Added to this is the lowish possibility of ever escaping from the face we know and love. The possibility of human beings de-facing themselves in order to understand the place of the Other on another face is not high. It involves discomfort, pain, and no little danger.

Nevertheless, it is possible. Adrenalin seekers, explorers, colonists, indeed adventurers of all sorts may seek to leave their face and go in search of the Other. But what they will take with them is their own style of organizing—their own prejudices about what functions well, what is beautiful and what is grotesque. Even for the adventurers who swing to another face, it is difficult to see what is happening in what they used to call their home. Once on another face, the full view of home is lost. It was Foucault who said there were 'no positions of exteriority to power' and this is the issue here. As we have seen in previous chapters, we must constantly ask how far it is possible for someone to be in a position of exteriority to the 'style of organizing' in which they exist. Does life there not constantly seduce one to the 'one best way', the 'right and

The identical subject-object as the 'face of the Other'

proper way', and towards organizational 'isomorphism'? This is what style is about—establishing the conditions of possibility for some but not other structures, processes, and behaviours. Yet, some conditions of possibility surely allow one to escape stylistic constraint and to become, in some way or another, avant-garde.

The term *avant-garde* refers to the advance guard of an army, better known in English as the vanguard, and usually contains 'shock troops'. That is, the soldiers in this body are meant to attack with vigour at the forces of the opponent. But this sense of opposition and contestation has since become lost and now means artists who are unconventional. Followers of Saint Simon in 19th-century France saw changes in the arts as a key way of bringing about cultural, political, and economic reform, thereby placing the arts at the centre of contemporary political debate. Today, however, avant-garde ideas are sometimes seen as repetitive reinventions of notions from the early 20th century (Schwartz 1996) and as commercialized as anything that mainstream business would invoke in selling products. The debate about mass culture and the reproduced kitsch which it produces stands opposed to the idea that the avant-garde can be a force of destabilization and innovation. A transcendental overview may not be, in fact, even what the avant-garde seeks, nor conceives of as even possible. My view, for what it is worth, is that the notion in its original guise as politically motivated is well worth investigating.

Raised here is the question of the possibility of distancing oneself from *all* the faces, and finding some external place that offers a transcendental picture of the whole edifice, or at least develop an imaginary of the totality—as if one could look from the outside. Some will argue that this is precisely what I am claiming for myself, but I have been keen to show that the internal style that would appear closest to my own leanings is the boxed hedge of utopiary. But to develop any externalist perspective one would need to think through in detail what a distant view of the solid body would show. And even assuming this totality is viewable from a place and space outside it—a point of transcendence—there is still the issue of dynamism and change. How to fully appreciate the solidity of the structure is a task of Herculean proportions.

My argument throughout this book has been that, so far as styles are concerned, we can conceptualize there being *six* sides of the argument in play simultaneously. Simon Eling's two photographs, shown in a previous chapter, demonstrate the plurality of faces that is constantly in play in considering one dice, even in a settled position. It is the same in comprehending the organizing of our built environment. Multiple 'orientations' (from facing east to pray, so having to know where one is in relation to the east) are possible. Now when Simon sent me the pictures of each face and the faces nearest to it, of course they were in the form of separate and statically oriented images. But as one scrolled through them, they came into motion. Just as a movie is made up of still pictures moving fast through a lens, and the human eye does the work of imbuing these images with movement, as I leafed through pictures of dice, they set about *rotating*. And serendipitously this seemed a way forward in my search for some understanding of the identical subject-object's role in the will to form. For this 'thing' is not a place, but it is a process, emerging out of the forming of something recognizable, manifest, and coherent.

Respect for the face of the Other means that one would actively seek out their company. What is on offer here to the reader, then, is the notion that speedy rotation around the cube of design is in fact a way *forward*. This is because movement *de-forms*. One knows that looking out of a speeding train window deforms the view outside. Deformation of existing structures may well accompany rapid rotation, allowing the viewer new vistas. So we might appreciate the value of constant movement, constant fluidity in seeking the new vista of the identical subject-object. In a piece by Ambrose King published in 1977, the principle of rotation is brought to the fore. Here one finds a discussion of the style of organizing advocated by Mao and carried out by the Red Guard during China's period of the Cultural Revolution. Mao advocated in his Red Book the principle of inversion, whereby workers and peasants swapped roles with bureaucrats and professionals. This was to be done regularly, giving a process akin to rotation. Crop rotation has been understood since the Neolithic revolution. In the Maoist era it stood for the rotation of human beings in roles, expenditure of manual labour and relative levels of power. It supposedly meant that elements of a highly complex society understood the lives and problems of other sections of that same society. All members of Chinese society came, it was argued, to understand the faces and fates of each other.

The Ise Inner Shrine in Ujiyamada, Japan is also an example of social rotation. Every 20 years or so, the wooden Ise Shrine to Amaterasu, the Sun Goddess of Shintoism, is moved to another location within the grounds of the temple. In Shintoism this practice is meant to reflect changes within the world and its ongoing dynamism—yet also its underlying rotation of forces bringing life into a flux of predictability and understanding. This is a reflection of kami, the sacred power found in the vicissitudes of nature. The shrine looks very much as it would have done 1,300 years ago when it was first built. It is a simple timber-and-thatch construction and resembles a storehouse raised above the ground on stilts (Glancey 2000: 107). In general, all Shinto shrines are reconstructed every 20 years in a way which goes against Western notions of environmentalism. Yet it reflects the nomadic existence of the imperial family in the years before AD 710 when they finally settled. The wooden beams used in each reconstruction are all straight, whereas the fashion for centuries has been for upwardly curved beams as in the upper of two beams upon the

The identical subject-object as the 'face of the Other'

well known *tori* symbol. And of course, wood was chosen in part because of its properties in being able to deal with earthquakes and a Nature which was typically violent. The work of the Japanese architect Tadao Ando is relevant here, for it is deeply respectful of nature. His reverential attitude to the natural world is said to be typical of Japanese traditionalism and he produces buildings which arise out of the earth in a 'poetry of vertical movement'. He seeks to produce oases where people can gather in peace to sense art and the surrounding environment. So a nice, quiet oasis might have been the best place and space for you to end this contemplation of style and organization and the search for the identical subject-object.

Yet... if you do sit in your oasis of choice, designed by others for your comfort, you should have your dice in your hand. Throw it in the air. Watch it carefully and keep throwing it. Understanding the 'face of the Other' will never be easy, for there are many idiosyncratic and individuated assumptions that we make as we negotiate our way around reality. Understanding the face of the other side of the design cube will send your head spinning. But it is this search for movement in space, the desire to be nomadic, which is the best hope for academic endeavour and the understanding of Others. Certainly, I prefer the nomadic life to Ando's oasis of contemplation. So, in *Styles of Organizing*, I would not claim to have produced a quiet place of reflection, because I rather hope that colleagues and students will look afresh at the world of organizing and organizations, with their eyes upward, searching for details of design as they proceed 'careering' into the far distance.

It is also my hope that this approach to organization theory, which seeks out connections with the arts and science of architecture and design, opens new doors (so to speak) for my discipline. And of course, there was my very dicey adventure into the realm of politico-economic theorizing. Shall we *all* go there? As organization theorists we should appreciate that there is much to be learnt from the face of those Others. So long, of course, as they do not spit in ours.

In conclusion then, as we bring the book to a final close, much work needs to be done to assess 'middling' design patterns pertaining to organizations on a case-by-case basis. All I have tried to put in place is a synthetic fabric into which some material of relevance might fall.

Yet... that last sentence was only one more possible closure to the book. Ending on the warp and weft of a fabrication unfortunately hides the one true function of design. The organizing of organization is derivative of a will to form which produces a cosy shelter in which we, organization theorists and the population both, hide from Chaos. It is the will to form which stops us—whether organization theorists or not—from peering helplessly into the pitch-black fathomless abyss. Deep down there, as you plummet, a dice is useless.

References

Abbott, EA 1992 *Flatland: A Romance of Many Dimensions* Dover Thrift, London
Abrahamson E 1996 'Technical and Aesthetic Fashion' in Czarniawska B and Sevan G (eds) *Translating Organizational Change* de Gruyter, Berlin, pp 117–37
Adler P 2010 (ed.) *The Oxford Handbook of Sociology and Organization Studies* Oxford University Press, Oxford
Aldrich H 1979 *Organizations and Environments* Prentice Hall, Englewood Cliffs, NJ
Alexander C, Ishikawa C, Silverstein M 1979 *A Pattern Language: Towns Buildings, Construction* Center for Environmental Structure Series, Berkeley
Althusser L 1969 *For Marx* Penguin, Harmondsworth
Aristotle 1998 *The Metaphysics* Penguin, Harmondsworth
Bach S and I Kessler 2012 *The Modernisation of the Public Services and Employee Relations: Targeted Change* Palgrave, Basingstoke
Bachelard G 1964 *The Poetics of Space* Orion, New York
Bale T 2011 *The Conservative Party* Polity Press, Cambridge
Ball P 2009 *Universe of Stone* Vintage, London
Banham R 1972 *Theory and Design in the First Machine Age* Architectural Press, London
Banham R 1986 *Concrete Atlantis* Architectural Press, London
Barbalet J (ed.) 2002 *Emotions and Sociology* Blackwell, Oxford
Barley S and Kunda G 1992 'Design and Devotion' *Administrative Science Quarterly* 37: 363–99
Barnes Julian 2009 *Flaubert's Parrot* Vintage Books, London
Barthes R (trans. A Lavers) 2009 *Mythologies* Vintage, London
Barzeley M and Estrin S 2011 'Design Science as a Reference Point for Management Research' in Morsing M and Rovira AS (eds) *Business Schools and their Contribution to Society* Sage, London, pp 85–94
Baudrillard J 1998 *The Consumer Society* Sage, London
Baudrillard J 2005 *The System of Objects* Verso London
Bauman Z 1989 *Modernity and the Holocaust* Polity Cambridge
Bauman Z 1991 *Modernity and Ambivalence* Polity Cambridge
Bauman Z 1995 *Life in Fragments* Blackwell Oxford
Beaton E 2006 *Mrs Beaton's Book of Household Management* Wordsworth Reference, Ware
Becker M and Knudsen T 2009 'Schumpeter and the Organization of Entrepreneurship' in Adler P (ed) *The Oxford Handbook of Sociology and Organization Studies* Oxford University Press, Oxford

References

Bell D 1973 *The Coming of Post-Industrial Society: A Venture in Social Forecasting* Penguin, Harmondsworth

Benjamin W 1999 *The Arcades Project* Harvard University Press, Cambridge Mass

Benko G and Strohmayer U (eds) 1997 *Space and Social Theory* Blackwell, Oxford

Bergson H 1912 *Creative Evolution* Macmillan, London

Bethell L 1984 *A Cambridge History of Latin America* Cambridge University Press, Cambridge

Bevan G and Hood C 2006 'What's Measured is What Matters' *Public Administration* 84(3): 517–38

Biggart N and Delbridge R 2004 'Trading Worlds: A Typology of Systems of Exchange' *Academy of Management Review* 29: 28–49

Bircham E and Charlton J 2001 *Anti-Capitalism: A Guide to the Movement* Bookmarks, London

Blackler F and Kennedy A 2004 'The Design and Evaluation of a Leadership Programme for Experienced Chief Executives' *Management Learning* 35: 181

Boas F 1897 *The Social Organization and the Secret Societies of the Kwakiutl Indians* Elibron, New York

Boisot M 1998 *Knowledge Assets* Oxford University Press, Oxford

Boje D, Gephart M, and Thatchenkery D 1996 (eds) *Postmodern Organizations* Sage Thousand Oaks

Bosworth RJB 2011 *Whispering City: Rome and its Histories* Yale University Press, Conn

Boucher G 2009 *The Charmed Circle of Ideology* Re Press, London

Bourdieu P 1984 *Distinction: A Social Critique of the Judgement of Taste* Harvard University Press, Cambridge, Mass

Bragg M 2002 'In Our Times' Radio 4 3 January 2002

Braidotti R 1994 *Nomadic Subjects* Columbia University Press New York

Braverman H 1974 *Labor and Monopoly Capital* Monthly Review Press, New York

Brissenden R 1974 *Virtue in Distress* Harper and Row, New York

Brockett O 1968 *History of the Theatre* Allyn and Bacon, Boston

Broudehoux AM 2007 'Spectacular Beijing: The Conspicuous Construction of an Olympic Metropolis' *Journal of Urban Affairs* 29: 4, 383–99

Bronowski J 1970 *The Ascent of Man* BBC Books, London

Bryman A and E Bell 2007 *Business Research Methods* Oxford University Press, Oxford, 2nd edn

Buchanan D and Badham R 1999 *Power, Politics and Organizational Change* Sage, London

Buci-Glucksmann C 1994 *Baroque Reason* Sage, London

Buckley P and Casson M 1993 'Economics as an Imperialist Social Science' *Human Relations* 46: 9, 1035–52

Burrell G 2004 'Twentieth Century Quadrilles' *International Studies of Management and Organizations* 32: 2, 25–50

Burrell G 2006 'Foucault and Postmodern Approaches to Work' in Korcynski M, Hodson M, and Edwards P (eds) *Social Theory and Work* Oxford University Press, Oxford, pp 155–81

Burrell G and Morgan G 1979 *Sociological Paradigms and Organizational Analysis* Ashgate, Hants

Burrell G and Dale K 2002 'Utopiary' in Parker M (ed) *Utopia and Organization* Sage, London, pp 106–27

Butler R and Carney M 1986 'Strategy and Strategic Choice' *Strategic Management Journal* 7: 2 161–77

Byatt AS 2011 'Ragnorok: the Doom of the Gods' *Guardian* 5 August 2011

Campbell C 1715–25 *Vitruvius Britannicus; Or, The British Architect* Three Volumes

Campbell R 2007 'Three Years Later: Does Gehry's Strata Center Really Work?' *Architectural Record* 30 May

Carr A and Zanetti L 2000 'The Emergence of the Surrealist Movement and its Vital Estrangement effect on Organization Studies' *Human Relations* 53: 7, 991–1020

Carrell S 2012 'Scottish Campaigners Set out to Revive Hutting' *Guardian* 6 January 2012: 12–13

Carroll G 1984 'Organization Ecology' *Annual Review of Sociology* 10: 71–93

Castells M 1997 *The Rise of the Network Society* Blackwell, Oxford

Castoriadis C 1987 *The Imaginary Institution of Society* Polity, Cambridge

Chandler A 1977 *The Visible Hand: Managerial Revolution in American Business* Harvard University Press, Mass

Chaney D 1993 *Fictions of Collective Life* Routledge, London

Chevalier J and Gheerbrant A 1996 *The Penguin Dictionary of Symbols* Penguin, Harmondsworth

Chia R 1998 'From Complexity Science to Complex Thinking' *Organization* 5: 3, 341–69

Chia R (ed.) 1998a *In the Realm of Organization* Routledge, London

Chia R (ed.) 1998b *Organised Worlds* Routledge, London

Child J 2009 'Challenging Hierarchy' in Alvesson M, Bridgman T, and Willmott H (eds) *The Oxford Handbook of Critical Management Studies* Oxford University Press, Oxford, pp 501–14

Ching Francis 1996 *Architecture: Form, Space and Order* Van Nostrand Reinhold, New York

Clark Kenneth 1969 *Civilisation: A Personal View* Harper and Row, London

Clegg S 1990 *Modern Organizations* Sage, London

Clegg S and Dunkerley D 1980 *Organization, Class and Control* Routledge, London

Clegg S and Kornberger M 2006 *Space, Organization and Management Theory* Liber, Copenhagen

Clegg S, Harris M, and Hopfl H (eds) 2011 *Managing Modernity: Beyond Bureaucracy* Oxford University Press, Oxford

Cole E (General Editor) 2003 *A Concise History of Architectural Styles* A and C Black, London

Conant J 2010 *A Poetics of Resistance* AK Press, London

Cooke B 2003 'The Denial of Slavery in Management Studies' *Journal of Management Studies* 40: 8 1895–1918

Cooley M 1987 *Architect or Bee: Human Price of Technology* The Hogarth Press, London

Cooper R 1989 'Modernism, Postmodernism and Organizational Analysis: The Contribution of Jacques Derrida' *Organization Studies* 10: 4, 479–502

Cooper R 1992 Formal Organization as Representation in Reed M and Hughes M (eds) *Rethinking Organization* Sage London, pp 254–72

References

Cooper R 1998 'Epilogue' in Chia R (ed.) *Organised Worlds* Routledge, London, pp 131–81

Cooper R and Burrell G 1988: 'Modernism, Postmodernism and Organizational Analysis: an Introduction' *Organization Studies* 9: 1, 91–112

Cooper R and Law J (1995) 'Organization: Distal and Proximal Views' *Research in the Sociology of Organizations* Vol 13 JAI Press Greenwich 237–74

Cooperrider D, Whitney D, and Stavros J 2008 *Appreciative Enquiry Handbook* Crown Custom, Brunswick Ohio

Cragoe CD 2008 *How to Read Buildings* Ivy Press, Lewes

Cresswell T in Benko G and Strohmayer U (eds) 1997 *Space and Social Theory* Blackwell, Oxford

Cronin AM 2006 'Advertising and the Metabolism of the City' *Environment and Planning D* 24, 4, 615–32

Crossley P 2000 'Introduction' to P Frankl *Gothic Architecture* Yale University Press, New Haven

Curtis W 1996 *Modern Architecture Since 1900* Phaidon, London

Czarniawska B 1997 *Narrating the Organization* University of Chicago Press, Chicago

Czarniawska B 2003 'The Styles and Stylists of Organization Theory' in Tsoukas H and Knudsen C (eds) *The Oxford Handbook of Organization Theory* Oxford University Press, Oxford

Czarniawska B 2011 'Introduction to Special Themed Section on Fashion in Research and Management' *Organization Studies* 32: 5

Czarniawska B and Sevan G (eds) 1996 *Translating Organizational Change* de Gruyter, Berlin

Daft R 1989 *Organization Theory and Design* West, St Paul

Dale K 2001 *Anatomising Embodiment and Organization Theory* Palgrave, Basingstoke

Dale K 2005 'Building a Social Materiality' *Organization* 12: 5, 649–78

Dale K and Burrell G 2003 'Aesthetics and Anaesthetics' in Hancock P and Carr A (eds) *Art and Aesthetics at Work* Palgrave Basingstoke

Dale K and Burrell G 2008 *Spaces of Organization and the Organization of Space* Palgrave, Basingstoke

Dale K and Burrell G 2010 'Reading the Ruins' *Culture and Organization* 17: 2 107–21

David P 2008 'The Historical Origins of Open Science' *Capitalism and Society*, 3(2), article 5

Davenport-Hine A 1998 *Gothic: Four Hundred Years of Excess, Horror, Evil and Ruin* Fourth Estate, London

Day R 2001 'Ethics, Affinity and the Coming Communities' *Philosophy and Social Criticism* 27: 21–38

de la Bedoyere C 2005 *Art Nouveau* Flame Tree, London

Debord G 1996 *Guy Debord presente potlatch* Gallimard Education, Paris

Deleuze G and Guattari F 1988 *A Thousand Plateaus* Athlone, London

Deleuze G 1993 *The Fold: Leibnitz and the Baroque* Athlone, London

Dempsey A 2004 *Styles, Schools and Movements* Thames and Hudson, London

Derrida J 1978 *Writing and Difference* University of Chicago Press, Chicago

Dicks B 2000 *Heritage, Place and Community* University of Wales Press, Cardiff

References

Dickson D 1974 *Alternative Technology and the Politics of Technical Change* Fontana London

Diggins JP 1999 *Thorstein Veblen: Theorist of the Leisure Class* Princeton University Press, Chichester

Donaldson L 2008 'Statistico-Organizational Theory' in Barry D and Hansen H (eds) *New Approaches in Management and Organization* Sage, London, pp 135–45

Dow S 1985 *Macroeconomic Thought: A Methodological Approach* Blackwell, Oxford

du Gay P 2007 *Organizing Identity* Sage, London

Duffy F 1982 'Introduction' to Klein J 1982 *The Office Book* Frederick Muller, London

Eco U 1986 *The Future of the Book* University of California Press, Berkeley

Edensor T 2005 *Industrial Ruins: Space, Aesthetics and Materiality* Berg, Oxford

Elias N 1984 *The Court Society* Wiley Blackwell, Oxford

Elias N 2000 *The Civilising Process* Blackwell, Malden MA

Elias N (with Mennell S and Jephcott E) 2005 *The Court Society* University College Dublin Press, Dublin

Espeland W and Stevens M 1998 'Commensuration as a Social Process' *Annual Review of Sociology*, 24: 313–43

Etzioni A 1988 *The Moral Dimension: Towards a New Economics* Macmillan, New York

Eyerman R and Jamison A 1989 'Environmental Knowledge as an Organizational Weapon' *Social Science Information* 28: 1, 99–119

Featherstone M 1991 *Consumer Culture and Postmodernism* Sage London

Felstead A, Jewson N, and Walters S 2005 *Changing Spaces of Work* Palgrave, Basingstoke

Fiske AP 1991 *Structures of Social Life: The Four Elementary Forms of Human Relations* Collier Macmillan, London

Flyvbjerg B 2002 *Making Social Science Matter* Taylor and Francis, London

Ford H 1931 *Moving Forward* Heinemann, London

Ford H 1926 *Today and Tomorrow* Heinemann, London

Foucault M 1986 'Spaces, Knowledge and Power' in Rabinow P (ed) *Michel Foucault Beyond Structuralism and Hermeneutics* Penguin Harmondsworth

Foucault M 1992 *The Order of Things: An Archaeology of the Human Sciences* Routledge, London

Fox A 1985 *Heritage and History: Social Origins of the British Industrial Relations System* Harper Collins

Frankl P 2001(Introduction by P Crossley) *Gothic Architecture* Yale University Press, New Haven, Conn

Frederick M 2007 *101 Things I Learned in Architecture School* MIT Press, Cambridge Mass

Galbraith J 1973 *Designing Complex Organizations* Addison Wesley, Reading Mass

Galbraith JK 1989 *A History of Economics* Penguin, Harmondsworth

Gamma E, Helm R, Johnson R, and Vlissides J (1994) *Design Patterns* Addison Wesley, Boston

Garfield S 1999 *The Nation's Favourite: The True Adventures of Radio 1* Faber and Faber, London

Garrick J and Clegg S 2000 'Organizational Gothic: Transfusing Vitality and Transforming the Corporate Body' in Symes C and McIntyre J (eds) *Working Knowledge* Open University Press, Buckingham

References

Gehry F 2011 (interviewed by J Glancey) *The Guardian* G2, 6 July: 21
Gergen K 1992 'Organization Theory in the Postmodern Era' in Reed M and Hughes M (eds) *Rethinking Organization* Sage London, pp 207–26
Gerth H and Mills CW 1991 (eds) *For Max Weber* Routledge, London
Ghirardo D 1996 *Architecture after Modernism* Thames and Hudson, London
Giddens A 1984 *The Constitution of Society* Polity, Cambridge
Giddens 1989 'A Reply to my Critics' in Held D and Thompson J (eds) *Social Theory and Modern Societies: Anthony Giddens and his Critics* Cambridge University Press, Cambridge
Giedion S 1967 *Space, Time and Architecture* Oxford University Press, Oxford
Glancey J 2000 *Twentieth Century Architecture* Carlton Books, London
Glancey J 2003 *The Story of Architecture* Dorling Kindersley, London
Golding W 1964 *The Spire* Faber and Faber, London
Goodchild P 1996 *Deleuze and Guattari* Sage, London
Gordon A and Suzuki D 1991 *It's a Matter of Survival* Harvard University Press, Cambridge Mass
Granovetter M and R Swedberg (eds) 2001 *The Sociology of Economic Life* 2nd edn Westview, Boulder, Col Greenpeace official website
Gregory D 1989 'Presences and Absences: Time-space Relations and Structuration Theory' in Held D and Thompson J (eds) *Social Theory and Modern Societies: Anthony Giddens and his Critics* Cambridge University Press, Cambridge
Gregory D, Martin R, and Smith G 1994 *Human Geography: Society, Space and Social Science* Macmillan London
Grosz E 1995 *Space, Time and Perversion* Routledge, London
Guillen M 1997 'Scientific Management's Lost Aesthetic' *Administrative Science Quarterly* 42: 4, 682–715
Guillen M 2006 *The Taylorized Beauty of the Mechanical* Princeton University Press, Oxford
Gustafsson B 2006 *Democracy in Science Education* Working Paper, School of Technology and Design, Växjö University
Guthey E, Clark T, and Jackson B 2009 *Demystifying Business Celebrity* Routledge, Abingdon
Hall Peter A 1993 'Policy Paradigms, Social Learning and the State' *Comparative Politics* 25: 3, 275–96
Hammer M and Champy J 1993 *Re-engineering the Corporation* Nicholas Brearley, New York
Hammer and Champy J 2001 *Re-engineering the Corporation; A Manifesto* Harper Collins, New York
Handy C 1985 *Understanding Organisations* Penguin, Harmondsworth
Hannan M and J Freeman 1977 'The Population Ecology of Organizations' *American Journal of Sociology* 82: 171–86
Hannan M and J Freeman 1989 *Organizational Ecology* Harvard University Press, Cambridge Mass
Harbison R 2000 *Reflections on Baroque* Reaktion Books London
Hardt M and Negri A 2002 *Empire* Harvard University Press, Cambridge, Mass
Harries S 2011 *Nikolaus Pevsner: the Life* Chatto and Windus, London

Harris M, Clegg S, and Hopfl H 2011 'Introduction' to Clegg S, Harris M, and Hopfl H (eds) 2011 *Managing Modernity: Beyond Bureaucracy* Oxford University Press, Oxford, pp 1–10

Harrison R 1972 'How to describe your Organisation' *Harvard Business Review,* May/June

Harvey D 2007 Neo-liberalism as Creative Destruction *Annals of the American Academy of Political and Social Science* March, 610: 1, 21–44

Harvey D 2003 *Paris: Capital of Modernity* Routledge, London

Hatch MJ (with A Cunliffe) 2006 *Organization Theory* Oxford University Press, Oxford

Haveman H 2010 'The Columbia School and the Study of Bureaucracies' in Adler P 2010 (ed.) *The Oxford Handbook of Sociology and Organization Studies* Oxford University Press, Oxford, pp 585–606

Hay C 2004 'Restating Politics, Re-politicising the State' *The Political Quarterly* 75: 38–50

Held D and Thompson J (eds) 1989 *Social Theory and Modern Societies: Anthony Giddens and his Critics* Cambridge University Press, Cambridge

Henley S 2009 *The Architecture of Parking* Thames and Hudson, London

Hill R 2007 *God's Architect* Penguin, Harmondsworth

Hillier B 1997 *Space is the Machine* Cambridge University Press, Cambridge

Hillier B and McIntyre K 1998 *The Style of the Century* Herbert Press, London

Hillier J 2008 'Plan(e) speaking: A Multi-planar Theory of Spatial Planning' *Planning Theory* 7: 1, 24–50

Hix WM 2003 (ed.) *Rethinking Governance of the Army's Arsenals* RAND, Issue 1651, Santa Monica

Hollis E 2009 *The Secret Lives of Buildings* Portobello, London

Hoskin K 1995 'The Viewing Self and the World We View' *Organization* 2: 1, 141–62

Hübsch H 1992 *In What Style Should We Build* University of Chicago Press, Chicago

Hudgins E (ed.) 2002 *Space: The Free Market Frontier* Cato Institute, Washington, DC

Hughes R 1991 *The Shock of the New: Art and the Century of Change* Thames and Hudson, London

Hunter DJ 2005 'The National Health Service 1980–2005' *Public Money and Management* 25: 209–12

Huxley J 1943 *TVA: Adventure in Planning* The Architectural Press, London

Huyssen A 2003 *Present Pasts: Urban Palimpsests and the Politics of Memory* Stanford University Press, California

Hyde Minor V 1999 *Baroque and Rococo: Art and Culture* Lawrence King, London

Illich I 1973 *Tools for Conviviality* Fontana London

Ingold T 2000 *The Perception of the Environment* Routledge London

Ingold T 2007 *Lines: A Brief History* Routledge, Abingdon

Jefferson Thomas 1984 (ed. by Peterson M) *Writing, Auto-biography, Notes on the State of Virginia* Library of America

Jeffries S 2002 'A Dwelling for the Gods' *Guardian* Saturday, 5 January

Jencks C 1987 *Modern Movements in Architecture* Penguin Harmondsworth

Jenkins S 2011 'Sir George Gilbert Scott, The Unsung Hero of British Architecture' *The Guardian* July 8: 35

Jenks C 1998 (ed.) *Core Sociological Dichotomies* Sage, London

Jonsen AR and Toulmin S 1988 *The Abuse of Casuistry* University of California, Berkeley

References

Judd D 1965 *Specific Objects* Arts Yearbook 8
Julier G 2000 *The Culture of Design* Sage, London
Kemp K 2007 *Destination Space* University of Virginia, Virgin Books
Kemp C 2008 The Discovery of Structural Form *Proceedings of the National Academy of Sciences* 105: 31
Kiernan B 2004 (2nd edn) *How Pol Pot Came to Power* Yale University Press, New Haven
Kiernan B 2008 *The Pol Pot Regime: Race, Power and Genocide in Cambodia* Yale University Press, New Haven
Kilduff M 1993 'Deconstructing Organizations' *Academy of Management Review* 18: 13–31
Klamer A 2007 *Speaking of Economics* Routledge, Abingdon
Klee Paul 1961 *The Thinking Eye: The Notebooks of Paul Klee* First Thus Edition, London
Klein J 1982 *The Office Book* Frederick Muller, London
Klein N 2001 *No Logo* Flamingo, London
King A 1977 'A Voluntarist Model of Organization: The Maoist Version and its Critique' *British Journal of Sociology* 28: 3, 363–74
Koolhaus R 1994 *Delirious New York* Monacelli Press, New York
Kornberger M, Kreiner K, and Clegg S 2011 'The Value of Style in Architectural Practice' *Culture and Organization* 17: 2, 139–53
Krupskaya N 2009 Zapatista Gender Relations http://www.facebook.com/pages/Nadezhda-K-Krupskaya/130438732255 Accessed 31 August 2011
Lasch C 1982 *The Culture of Narcissism* WW Norton and Co, New York
Lash S and Urry J 1994 *Economies of Signs and Space* Sage, London
Lash S and Urry J 1987 *The End of Organized Capitalism* Sage, London
Latham Y and Dale K 2012 Paper Presented to EGOS, Helisinki, July
Law J (1986) 'On the Methods of Long Distance Control' in Law J (ed) *Power, Action and Belief Sociological Review Monograph* 32: 234–63
Leach N (ed.) 2007 *Rethinking Architecture* Routledge, Abingdon
Le Carre J 2011 *Tinker Taylor Soldier Spy* Sceptre, London
Le Grand J 2007 *The Other Invisible Hand* Princeton University Press, New Jersey
Leitner B 2000 *The Wittgenstein House* Princeton Architectural Press, New York
Leitner B 1976 *The Architecture of Ludwig Wittgenstein* Princeton Architectural Press, New York
Lefebvre H 1991 *The Production of Space* Basil Blackwell Oxford
Levi Strauss C 1969 *The Elementary Structures of Kinship* Penguin, Harmondsworth
Levinas E 1998 *Entre Nous: Thinking of the Other* Athlone, London
Libeskind D 2004 *Breaking Ground* Hodder, London
Linstead S and Pullen A 2008 'Un-gendering Organization' in Barry D and Hansen H (eds) *The Sage Handbook of New Approaches in Management and Organization* Sage, London, pp 540–51
Loos A 1998 *Ornament and Crime: Selected Essays* Ariadne, London
Lowenthal D 1985 *The Past is a Foreign Country* Cambridge University Press, Cambridge
Luhrmann B 2001 *Moulin Rouge!* Twentieth Century Fox/Bazmark Production
Lukacs G 1971 *History and Class Consciousness* MIT Press, Boston

References

Luke T 1992 'New world order or neo-world orders' *Theory, Culture and Society 10th Annual Conference* Champion, Penn
Lury C 1996 *Consumer Culture* Polity, Cambridge
Lyotard JP 1984 *The Postmodern Condition* Edinburgh University Press, Edinburgh
MacGregor N 2010 *A History of the World in 100 Objects* Penguin, Harmondsworth
Marcus S 2008 *The Other Victorians* Transaction Publishers, London
Marshall P 1993 *Demanding the Impossible* Fontana, London
Martin J 1992 *Cultures in Organizations* Oxford University Press, New York
Martin J 2005 (3rd edn) *Organizational Behaviour and Management* Thomson, London
Marx K 1976 *Capital Volume 1* Penguin, Harmondsworth
Mauss M 1954 *The Gift* Free Press, Glencoe
McAdam D, Tarrow S, and Tilly C 2001 *Dynamics of Contention* Cambridge University Press, Cambridge
McKinley W 2007 'Managing Knowledge in Organisation Studies through Instrumentation' *Organization* 14: 123–42
McKinley W 2010 'Organization Theory Development: Displacement of Ends?' *Organization Studies* 31: 47
McLean B and Eckland P 2006 *Enron: the Smartest Guys in the Room*
McLeod M 1996 'Everyday and "Other" Spaces' in Coleman E, Danze E, and Henderson C (eds) *Architecture and Feminism* Princeton Architectural Press, New Jersey, 1–37
McLeod MJ 2004 Book Review *Journal of Latin American Studies* 36: 3, 588–90
Mellin R 2003 *Tilting: House Launching, Slide Hauling, Potato Trenching and Other Tales from a Newfoundland Village* Princeton Architectural Press, New York
Merleau Ponty M 1989 *Phenomenology of Perception* Northwestern University Press, Evanston Ill
Meyer M 1990 'The growth of public and private bureaucracies' in *Structuring Capital* ed. by S Zukin and P Di Maggio Cambridge University Press, Cambridge, pp 152–72
Michels R 1949 *Political Parties* Free Press, Glencoe
Miele C 1996 *William Morris on Architecture* Sheffield Academic Press, Sheffield
Milliard T 2003 Overcoming Post Colonial Myopia *Military Law Review* Vol 176: 5, 1–70
Mintzberg H 1979 *The Structuring of Organizations* Prentice Hall, New York
Mintzberg H 1992 *Structuring in Fives: Designing Effective Organizations* Prentice Hall, New York
Mitchell T 1991 *Colonising Egypt* University of California Press, Berkeley
Mitford N 1994 *The Sun King* Penguin, Harmondsworth
Moholy-Nagy L 1947 *Vision in Motion* Paul Theobald and Co, London
Morgan B 1978 *Monetarists and Keynesians* Macmillan, London
Morgan G 1986 *Images of Organization* Sage, London
Mueller B, Kuerbis M, and van Eeten M 2010 'Building a New Governance Hierarchy' Internet Governance Project, UN ICT Task Force, New York
Mumby D and Putnam L 1992 'The Politics of Emotion' *Academy of Management Review* 17: 456–86
National Trust for Historic Preservation in the United States, 2012, Preservation Press, Washington DC

References

Nietzsche F 2003 *Writings from the Late Notebooks* Cambridge University Press, Cambridge

Nietzsche F 1993 *The Birth of Tragedy* Penguin, Harmondsworth

Nonaka I and Takeuchi H 1995 *The Knowledge Creating Company* Oxford University Press, New York

Nyathi N 2008 *The Organizational Imagination in African Post-Colonial Thought* University of Leicester, School of Management PhD thesis

Orwell G 1966 *Nineteen Eighty-four* Penguin, Harmondsworth

Ovid 2004 *Metamorphoses* Penguin, Harmondsworth

Owings NA 1973 *The Spaces In Between* Houghton Mifflin, Boston

Parker M 2002 *Against Management: Organization in the Age of Managerialism* Polity, Cambridge

Parker M 2005 'Organizational Gothic' *Culture and Organization* 11: 3, 153–66

Parker M 2009 'Capitalists in Space' in Bell D and Parker M (eds) *Space Travel and Culture* Wiley Blackwell, pp 83–97

Parkinson CN 1957 *Parkinson's Law* Penguin, Harmondsworth

Parsons T 1971 *The System of Modern Societies* Prentice Hall, New Jersey

Pearson D 2001 *The Breaking Wave: New Organic Architecture* University of California Press, Berkeley

Perrow C 1990 'Economic Theories of Organization' in *Structuring Capital* ed by S Zukin and P Di Maggio Cambridge University Press, Cambridge, pp 121–52

Peters T and Waterman R 1982 *In Search of Excellence* Warner Books, New York

Peters T 1987 *Thriving on Chaos* Macmillan London

Pettigrew A, McKee L, and Ferlie E 1988 'Wind of Change Blows through NHS' *Health Service Journal* 3: 1, 296–8

Pettigrew A, Ferlie E, and McKee L 1992 *Shaping Strategic Change* Sage, London

Pettigrew A and Whipp R 1992 *Managing Change for Competitive Success* Blackwell, Oxford

Pevsner N 1964 *Outline of European Architecture* Penguin, Harmondsworth

Pevsner N 1975 *Pioneers of Modern Design* Penguin, Harmondsworth

Pfeffer J 2008 'Organization Studies is (and should be) different from Economics' in Barry D and Hansen H (eds) *The Sage Handbook of New Approaches in Management and Organization* Sage, London, pp 148–9

Pick D 1993 *The War Machine* Yale University Press New Haven

Pixley J 2002 'Emotions and Economics' in Barbalet J (ed) *Emotions and Sociology* Blackwell, Oxford

Plato 2006 *Plato's Dialogues* Read Books, London

Plumwood V 1993 *Feminism and the Mastery of Nature* Routledge, London

Pollock A 2006 *The New NHS: A Guide* Routledge, Abingdon

Porritt J 1984 *Seeing Green: The Politics of Ecology Explained* Wiley-Blackwell, London

Princen T, Finger M, Clark M, and Manno J 1994 *Environmental NGOs in World Politics* Routledge, London

Pugin AWN 2009 *Contrasts; or a parallel between the noble edifices of the 14th and 15th centuries and similar buildings of the present day* London

Pullman P 2011 *Northern Lights: His Dark Materials* Scholastic, London

References

Recht R 2008 *Believing and Seeing: The Art of the Gothic Cathedral* University of Chicago Press, London

Reed M 2005 'Beyond the Iron Cage' in Du Gay (ed.) *The Values of Bureaucracy* OUP, Oxford

Reed M 2010 'Bureaucratic Theory and Intellectual Renewal in Contemporary Organization Studies' in Adler P 2010 (ed.) *The Oxford Handbook of Sociology and Organization Studies* Oxford University Press, Oxford, pp 559–84

Rowlinson M 1997 *Organizations and Institutions* Macmillan, Basingstoke

Rudofsky B 1964 *Architecture without Architects* MOMA, New York

Sahlins M 1960 (ed) *Evolution and Culture* University of Chicago Press, Illinois

Salingaros N 2000 The Structure of Pattern Languages *Architectural Research Quarterly* 4: 149–61

Salingaros N 2007 *Anti-Architecture and Deconstruction* Umbau-Verlag, Berlin

Sardar Z 1998 *Postmodernism and the Other: The New Imperialism of Western Culture* Pluto, London

Sawyer M 1989 *The Challenge of Radical Political Economics* Harvester, Hemel Hemstead

Scahill J 2007 *Blackwater: The Rise of the World's Most Powerful Army* Serpent's Tail, London

Schama S 1988 *The Embarrassment of Riches* Fontana Press, London

Schama S 1995 *Landscape and Memory* Fontana, London

Schein E 1984 'Coming to a new awareness of Organizational Culture' *Sloan Management Review* 25: 3–16

Schmitt C 1991 *Political Romanticism* MIT Press, Cambridge

Schumpeter J (orig 1942) 2010 *Capitalism, Socialism and Democracy* 2nd edn, Pober Publishing Company, New York

Schwartz H 1996 *The Culture of the Copy* Zone Books, New York

Scott M 2008 *Harley-Davidson Motor Company* Greenwood, Conn

Scott W 1995 *Institutions and Organizations* Sage, Thousand Oaks

Selznick P 1949 *The TVA and the Grass Roots* University of California Press, Berkeley

Selznick P 1950 *The Organizational Weapon: A Study of Bolshevik Strategy and Tactics* RAND report 201

Sennett R 1994 *Flesh and Stone* Faber and Faber London

Sennett R 2008 *The Craftsman* Penguin, London

Shapiro M 1999 'Triumphalist Geographies' in Featherstone M and Lash S (eds) *Spaces of Culture* Sage London, pp 159–74

Shelley PB 1994 *The Collected Poetry and Prose of Shelley* Wordsworth Edition, London

Shenhav Y 1995 'From Chaos to Systems: The Engineering Foundations of Organization Theory' *Administrative Science Quarterly* 40: 557–85

Simmel G 1994 'The Sociology of the Meal' *Food and Foodways* 5: 4, 333–51

Simon H 1950 'Modern Organization Theories' *Advanced Management* 15 October 2–4

Sinha P, Inkson K, and Barker J 2012 'Committed to a Failing Strategy: Celebrity CEO' *Organization Studies* 33: 2, 223–46

Skidelsky R 2004 *John Maynard Keynes 1883–1946* Pan Books, London

Smith A 1775 (1976) *The Wealth of Nations* University of Chicago Press, Chicago

References

Smith RW and Bugni V 2006 'Symbolic Interaction Theory and Architecture' *Symbolic Interaction* 29: 2, 123–55

Spencer J and Rugg K 2004 *Space Tourism: Do you want to go?* Apogee Books, Ontario, Canada

Spender JC 1989 *Industry Recipes: The Nature and Source of Management Judgement* Blackwell, Oxford

Spotts F 2002 *Hitler and the Power of Aesthetics* Random House, London

Starbuck W and Nystrom P 1981 'Why the world needs organizational design' in Nystrom P and Starbuck W *Handbook of Organizational Design* Oxford University Press, Oxford, pp iv–xxii

Steffen AN 2003 *Worldchanging: A User's Guide for the 21st Century*

Steffen AN 2006 'The Next Green Revolution' *Wired*, May Issue

Stern R and Dietsch D 2002 *Architecture for Dummies* Wiley, London

Sterne L 2001 *A Sentimental Journey* Penguin Classics, London

Stevens H 1998 *Dutch Enterprise and the VOC* Walburg Pers, Amsterdam

Strati A 1999 *Organization and Aesthetics* Sage London

Sudjic D and Jones H 2001 *Architecture and Democracy* Glasgow

Sutton I 1999 *Western Architecture: From Ancient Greece to the Present* Thames and Hudson, New York

Swartz M and Watkins S 2004 *Power Failure: the inside story of the collapse of Enron*

Swift J 1991 *Swift's Irish Pamphlets* Colin Smythe, London

Taylor FW 2011 *Principles of Scientific Management* Create Space, New York

Teerlink R and Ozley L 2000 *More than a Motor Cycle* Harvard Business School Press, Cambridge, Mass

Thanem T 2011 *Monstrous Organizations* Palgrave, Basingstoke

Till J 2009 *Architecture Depends* MIT Press, Cambridge Mass

Tilly C 1994 *Coercion, Capital and European States AD 990–1992* Wiley, New York

Tonnies F 2011 *Community and Society* Dover Publications, New York

Townley B 2008 *Reason's Neglect: Rationality and Organizing* Oxford University Press, Oxford

Tsoukas H 1998 'Chaos, Complexity and Organization Theory' *Organization* 5: 3, 291–313

Tsoukas H and Chia R 2002 'On Organizational Becoming: Rethinking Organizational Change' *Organization Science* 13: 567–82

Turner B 1994 'Introduction' to Buci-Glucksmann C 1994 *Baroque Reason* Sage, London

Urry J 1990 *The Tourist Gaze* Sage, London

Urry J 1995 *Consuming Places* Routledge, London

Urry J 2003 *Global Complexity* Polity Cambridge

Urry J 2011 *Climate Change and Society* Polity Cambridge

Van Krieken R 1998 *Norbert Elias* Routledge, London

Veblen T 1899 (1953) *Theory of the Leisure Class* Mentor Books, New York

Venturi R 1977 *Learning from Las Vegas* MIT Press, Cambridge, Mass

Venturi R 1984 *Complexity and Contradiction in Architecture* (2nd edn) MOMA, New York

Vermorel F 1997 *Fashion and Perversity* Bloomsbury, London

Virilio P 1994 *Bunker Archaeology* Princeton Architectural Press, New York

References

Vogel R 2012 'The Visible College of Management and Organization Studies' *Organization Studies* 33: 8, 1015–44

Ward LF 2012 *Dynamic Sociology* Lightning Source, London

Warner Bros *The West Wing* 2000 Burbank, California

Warren S 2005 'Creating Creativity' *Pink Machine Working Papers* No 9

Webb S 2004 *Out of this World* Copernicus Books, New York

Weber M 1947 *Theory of Economic and Social Organization* Routledge, London

Weik E 2011 'In Deep Waters: Process Theory Between Scylla and Charybdis' *Organization* 18: 5, 655–72

Welsch W 1997 *Undoing Aesthetics* Sage London

Wexler R 2004 *Greenpeace* Raincoat Books, Rodale

White T 2010 *A Guide to the NHS* Radcliff, Abingdon

Whiteley P, Seyd P, and Richardson J 1994 *True Blues: The Politics of Conservative Party Membership* Oxford University Press, Oxford

Willmott H 2011 'Back to the Future: What does studying Bureaucracy tell us?' in Clegg S, Harris M, and Hopfl H (eds) 2011 *Managing Modernity: Beyond Bureaucracy* Oxford University Press, Oxford, pp 257–95

Wilson B 1970 (ed.) *Rationality* Blackwell, Oxford

Wittfogel K 1961 *Oriental Despotism* Yale University Press, New Haven

Woodward K 2002 *Social Sciences: The Big Issues* Routledge, Abingdon

Woolgar CM 1999 *The Great Household in Late Medieval England* Yale University Press, New Haven

Wright EO 1989 in Held D and Thompson J (eds) *Social Theory and Modern Societies: Anthony Giddens and his Critics* Cambridge University Press, Cambridge

Yeats WB 2000 'Under Ben Bulben' part 4 in *The Collected Poems of WB Yeats* Wordsworth Press, London

Zald M 1987 'Review Essay: The New Institutional Economics' *American Journal of Sociology* 93: 3, 701–8

Index

Abbott E A 47, 261
aesthetics 27, 33, 38–9, 41, 59, 60, 65–6, 73, 88, 98, 102, 250, 264, 265, 272, 273
Aldrich H 247, 261
Alexander C et al 11, 86, 261
Amsterdam 84, 89, 178–9
anaesthetics 66, 98, 264
angst 4, 9
A-naturality 99, 112–13, 118, 122, 179–85, 251
animals 4, 6, 96, 100, 103, 111, 112, 131, 147, 161, 221
antinomies 38, 65, 96, 98, 253–5
Apple Inc 87
Arcadia 8, 158, 175, 221–2
architects 6–7, 13, 19, 27, 40, 43, 47–9, 69–72, 79–87, 98, 130, 136, 138, 140, 165, 219, 222, 223, 224, 228, 271
aristocrats 97, 134, 180, 196, 202, 235, 240
Aristotle 10, 261
armies 90, 108, 182–3, 192
Arras Town Hall 76–7
arsenals 128, 181–3, 191–2, 241, 267
Art Nouveau 80, 132, 139, 144, 161, 171, 198, 214–8, 251
Arts and Crafts Movement 69, 86, 222
Austria 124, 128, 132–4, 144
autism 96, 117, 132, 134, 144, 148, 151, 248
'Autostadt' 75, 230
avant-garde 69, 212, 218, 257

Bach S and Kessler I 199, 261
Bachelard 7, 16, 261
Bale T 195, 197, 261
Banham R 151, 248, 261
Barnes J 60, 261
Barthes R 13, 261
Barzeley M and Estrin S 64, 261
Battle of the Styles in 1858 85–6
Bauhaus 29, 79, 80
Bauman Z 13, 45, 108, 181, 192, 261

Beauvais Cathedral 137, 164–6, 169, 171, 180, 186, 195
Becoming 10, 32–7, 97, 254, 272
Being 10, 34–6
Benjamin W 67, 262
Bergson H 96–7, 262
Bevan G and Hood C 200, 261
BBC Radio 1 187–9, 201, 202, 265
Biggart N and Delbridge R 202, 262
bike sheds 83–4
Bing S 214–5, 218–9
Bircham E and Charlton J 159, 262
Blackler F 200, 262
Blackwater (Xe) 181, 182–5, 192, 201, 202, 271
Boisot M 38, 51, 262
Boje D 35, 262
Bosworth R 67–8, 262
bounded rationality 99, 103
Bourdieu P 82, 262
Braidotti R 241, 262
brane 48–9, 97
Branson R 153–4, 170, 234
Braverman H 9, 262
Bright Green Environmentalism 123, 127, 144, 166, 170
Brissenden R 186–7, 262
Brockett O 235, 262
Bronowski J 197, 262
Brutalism 227, 232
Bryman A and Bell E 22, 262
Buchanan D and Badham R 201, 262
Buckley P and Casson M 22, 262
Buci-Glucksmann C 163, 235, 262
bureaucracy 23–5, 52, 60–1, 90, 128, 154–5, 173, 181, 226, 263, 271
Burrell G 10–11, 24, 37, 38, 65–6, 78, 86–7, 109, 135, 140, 146, 150, 161, 220, 228, 262–3
Burrell G and Dale K 10, 13, 263
Burrell G and Morgan G 37–8, 262
Business Process Re-Engineering (BPR) 188, 201
Byatt A S 5, 263

Campbell C 224, 263
Canada 139, 150, 155–7

Index

capitalism 82, 104, 109, 110, 127–8, 144, 152–3, 170–1, 181, 192–3, 220, 228, 233, 236, 251, 253
carparks 75–6
Carr A and Zanetti L 46, 263
Carrell S 222, 263
Carroll G 247, 263
Cartesianism 22, 73, 102
Castells M 45, 82, 109, 159–61, 263
Castoriadis C 4, 263
casuistry 119, 145, 241, 245, 250, 267
Ceausescu Family 232–4
Celebration, Florida 225
Chandler AD 17, 263
Chaos 4–6, 17, 117, 135, 170, 259, 270, 271, 272
Chevalier J and Gheerbrant A 51–2, 96, 263
Chia R 3, 35, 109, 263
Chicago 76, 228
Child J 73, 263
Childs D 165
China 70, 126, 129, 258
Ching F 28–40, 50, 263
Chomsky N 5, 135
churches 9, 30, 81, 84, 85, 89, 102, 103, 105, 193, 224, 235, 238, 240
circulations 23, 32–3, 129, 144, 251
cities 13, 14, 15, 67, 129, 150, 221, 223, 237, 238
Classicism 85, 88, 132, 137, 225
Clark K 72, 263
Clegg S 24, 35, 68, 72, 97, 128, 200, 220, 239, 249, 263
cluster 26, 29, 31, 88, 189
coherence 14, 15, 65, 208, 246
Cole E 70, 263
computer aided design (CAD) 39, 49–50, 155
Conservative Party (UK) 195–7, 201, 202, 261, 273
commensuration 245–6, 265
Cooley M 9, 263
Cooper R 3, 10, 16, 35, 37, 88, 109, 114, 263–4
Cooper R and Burrell G 10, 109, 264
Cooperrider D 223, 224, 264
Cragoe C 27, 264
creative destruction 123, 127–8, 134, 136, 143, 152, 170, 251, 267
Cronin AM 67, 264
Crossley P 60, 264
'crushing the human spirit' 231–2
cube positioning system 116–9, 251
cubes 41–57, 120–142, 250–259
cultivation 13, 66, 155, 158, 234
culture 25–6, 61, 63, 65, 89, 101, 235, 269
Curtis W 69, 207, 264
Czarniawska B 13, 41, 261, 264

Daft R 23, 34, 35, 264
Dale K 10–13, 34, 64–6, 73, 86–7, 135, 140, 146, 150, 161, 165, 263, 264
Dale K and Burrell G 44–5, 78, 87, 140, 228
Darwinism 6, 101
Day R 37, 264
death 17, 21, 43, 60, 102, 109, 132, 151, 192, 197, 233
de Caznac B 240–1
deconstructionism 134–6, 143, 171, 198, 212, 220, 251
deconstructivist monumentalism 231–4
'decorationless perfection' 134, 169, 246, 251
Deleuze G and Guattari F 36–7, 43–4, 50, 77, 96, 98, 254–5, 264, 266
Dempsey A 69–70, 212
Derrida J 37, 220, 263, 264
design envelope 27, 95, 115, 138, 146, 148, 172, 176, 209, 244
design geometries 26
Design School 17, 64
'desire to divide' 16
Detroit 150, 240
de Troyes G 43–4
dice 52–5
Dicks B 157, 264
Dickson D 124, 265
di-visions 14, 17, 37
Donaldson L 42, 265
Dow S 22–3, 265
Dresden 224, 230
drives 6
Duffy F 228, 265
du Gay 43, 72, 119, 245, 265, 271
Dunga people 8
Dutch economy and culture 88–9, 192
dymaxion 138–9, 144, 170, 171, 175–6, 190, 251

Eco U 59
economics 19, 22–3, 67–8, 71, 81, 95, 99, 101, 113, 122–3, 125–9, 133–4, 138–9, 144, 170–2, 180, 186, 190–1, 195–7, 244–5, 250–1
Elias N 82, 240, 265, 272
embellishment 12, 87, 90, 113, 146, 147, 148, 151, 155, 158, 160, 161, 163, 168, 176, 179, 184, 245, 248
empires 63, 85–7, 88–91, 128, 166, 181, 197, 225–6, 247, 249, 266
emplacement 8, 31, 86, 146, 148–9, 152–3, 155, 157, 160, 161–2, 163, 165, 166, 167–8, 176, 177–8, 183–4, 248, 249
enactment 32, 45, 87, 146, 147, 150–1, 154–5, 157–8, 160–1, 162–3, 165–6, 168, 176, 178, 184, 248, 249
Engels F 80, 252

Index

Enlightenment 7, 15–16, 89, 101, 103, 141, 227, 235
Enron 161–3, 169, 171, 181, 185, 191, 195, 251, 269, 272
entrepreneurs 125, 127–8, 143, 151–5, 182, 192, 233
Enval 166–9, 170, 171, 176, 191, 198, 251
EPZ (Exporting Processing Zones) 229–30
Espeland W and Stevens M 245–6, 265
Etzioni A 22–3, 265
Euclid 22, 46
evolutionism 99, 109, 110, 246
Eyerman R and Jamison A 177, 265
extremities 99, 118, 119, 121, 123, 130, 143, 151, 168, 170, 174, 197, 209, 247

factories 17, 34, 72, 127, 139, 226, 229–30, 235
Featherstone M 67, 271
ferocity 240–1
feudalism 137, 237
Flyvbjerg B 190, 265
Fiske AP 202, 265
Frankl P 3, 6, 60, 97–8, 238, 264, 265
Frederick M 32, 71–2, 84, 265
Freedom Tower 164–9, 181, 188, 195, 251
Freud S 6, 134, 214
Ford, Henry 108, 127, 139, 148, 151, 152, 265
Ford Motor Company 148–51, 171, 181, 185, 190, 191, 198, 229, 251
formatting 12, 32, 144, 147, 148, 150, 151, 163, 248
forms of organizational structure 24–7, 29–32
Foucault M 3, 15, 19, 34, 65, 99, 119, 220, 243, 256, 262, 265
Foundations (e.g. Ford, Gates) 190, 231, 233
Fuller, Buckminster 79, 138, 166, 227, 251
Futurism 244

Galbraith J 64, 265
Galbraith K 68, 265
Gamma E 12, 265
gardening state 13, 45, 108, 181, 192, 261
Garfield S 189, 265
Gaudi 80, 131–2, 144, 146, 148, 169, 171, 175–6, 186, 194–5, 251
Gehry F 49, 134–6, 143, 151, 170–1, 180, 186, 220, 251, 263, 265
Genesis 4
geometry 9, 21–40, 41–55, 86, 91, 95–97, 118, 133, 245, 254–5
Gergen K 223–4, 239, 266
German Idealism 6, 252–3
Gerth H and Mills CW 16, 266
Ghirardo D 229, 266
Giddens A 10, 35, 43, 106–8, 110, 266, 267
Giedion S 45–6, 266

Glancey J 49, 81–3, 135, 138, 219, 231, 232, 258, 266
Golding W 138, 164–5, 266
Gothic 3, 40, 69–70, 85–7, 97, 137–8, 143, 164–6, 169, 193, 194, 208, 212, 214, 230, 234, 237–41, 249, 266
Greece 5, 9, 22, 25–6, 34, 40–1, 66, 100, 136, 221, 227, 238, 247
grids 14, 15, 26, 31, 61, 246
Green environmentalism 123, 124, 127, 131, 143, 169, 171, 175, 186, 195, 198
Greenpeace 176–9, 201, 273
Gregory D 15, 107, 266
Grosz E 65, 266
Guillen M 83, 228, 266
Gustafsson B 10, 266

Hall P 22, 266
Hammer M and Champy J 188, 201, 266
Handy C 25–7, 158, 226, 266
Hannan M and Freeman J 43, 266
Hardt M and Negri A 181, 226, 266
Harley-Davidson 24, 271
Harris M 200, 267
Harrison R 25–7, 226, 267
Harvey D 14, 125, 153, 155, 267
Hatch MJ 27, 78–9, 267
Hegel 38, 252–3
Heidegger M 7, 35
height 83, 136, 137–8, 154, 166, 179, 180, 202, 232, 237
Henley S 75–6, 267
heterotopia 28, 66, 78
hierarchy 32, 72–3, 95, 171, 189, 226, 229, 231, 237, 263, 269
Hill R 238, 267
Hillier B 27, 183, 267
historicism 107–8, 193–4, 197, 218
Hitler A 62–3, 80, 208, 231–232, 272
Hix WM 181, 192, 267
Hollis E 41–2, 45, 244, 267
horizonality 29, 30, 96, 235–7
Horta V 140, 251
Hoskin K 33, 267
households 16–7, 22, 126, 240, 273
Hubsch H 193–4, 267
human body 34–6, 39–40, 102, 115
humanism 6, 100, 240
Hunter D 200–1, 267
'hutters' 222
Huxley J 104–5, 248, 267
Huyssen A 231, 267
hybridization 12, 18, 182, 209–11, 224, 247
Hyde Minor V 235, 267

IBM 87
ICANN 226–7, 269

277

Index

Identical subject-object 99, 250–9
identity 84, 100–1, 220, 247, 265
idioms 14, 59, 90, 132, 139, 209, 254
Illich I 82, 124, 267
impression management 15, 170, 201, 227, 236, 251
India 63, 70, 85, 88–9, 192, 199
individualism 6, 14, 22, 26, 43, 67–68, 83, 101, 108, 117, 125, 180, 223–4, 240
Ingold T 9, 16, 22, 96, 267
Internet 26, 160, 161, 226–7, 249, 269
intra-actions 18–19
intizam al-manzar 14–5
iron cage 23–4, 27–9, 52, 243, 271
isomorphs 246, 247, 256, 257

Japan 64, 70, 79, 223, 258–9
Jefferson T 136–7, 155, 158, 171, 175, 194, 251, 267
Jencks C 70–1, 79–81, 83, 214, 225, 227, 237, 240, 244, 267
Jenks C 65, 267
Julier G 82, 128, 268

Kahn A 227, 229
Kahn H 191
Kiernan B 129, 268
Keynes J M 22–3, 123, 129–30, 140, 142, 144, 171, 180, 190, 195, 196, 246–7, 251, 269, 271
Kilduff M 37, 268
King A 258, 268
Klamer A 23–4, 133, 134, 268
Klee P 28, 268
Klein J 231, 268
Klein N 229–31, 268
Kornberger M, Kreiner K and Clegg S 64, 268

labour 6–7, 9, 17, 19, 23, 77, 80, 81, 108, 110, 125, 137, 182, 185, 229–30, 238, 249, 258
Lasch C 101, 268
Lash S and Urry J 43, 220, 268
Las Vegas 236, 272
Latham Y and Dale K 64, 268
Latin America 69, 160, 262, 269
Law J 88–9, 264, 268
Le Carre J 7
Le Corbusier 72, 80, 139, 228
Lefebvre H 15, 268
Le Grande J 200, 268
Leitner B 132–4, 248, 268
Leonardo da Vinci 30, 34
Levi-Strauss C 15
Lincoln Cathedral 83, 225
linearity 28, 33, 38, 86, 96, 102
liquidity 42, 44, 45, 109, 250
Louis XIV 61, 76, 140–1, 180, 235, 251, 269

Loos A 134, 227, 268
Lowenthal 71, 268
Lukacs G 38, 252–3, 268
Luke T 109, 269
Lury C 67, 269

MacGregor N 62–3, 269
Maginot Line 232
'magnificence' 126, 169, 235
Maison du Peuple 140, 171, 175, 186
management 16, 23, 25, 26, 36, 38, 43, 51, 64, 68, 72–3, 82, 122–30, 131, 143–4, 147 169–72, 188, 193, 196, 201, 212, 223, 227–30, 234, 245, 251
management of change 43, 188
manifestation 14, 15, 65, 208, 246
mapping 14–15, 38, 51, 119, 145, 246, 248
Martin 23, 25, 269
Marx K 6–7, 142, 261, 269
masons 44, 137–8
materialism 253–4
materiality 27, 33, 45–6, 60, 73, 96–7, 241, 264, 265
mathematics 22, 102, 117, 132, 135, 179, 193, 238
MBAs 43, 167, 189
McAdam D et al 234, 269
McKinley W 42–3, 269
McLeod M 65, 159, 218, 269
medieval history 16, 43, 85, 137, 138.186, 194, 222, 238, 240, 241, 273
Mellin R 158, 269
Melville H 15
membrology 97
memory politics 231
Merleau-Ponty 255, 269
Mesopotomia 4, 63
metropolitan 14, 66–7, 111, 209, 211
Mexico 140, 160
Meyer M 193, 269
Michels R 196, 269
middles 36, 44, 98, 99, 109, 173, 247, 259
Miele C 223, 269
Mies van de Rohe 72, 228
Milliard T 183, 269
Mintzberg H 17, 23–4, 64, 269
Modernism 69, 72, 144, 169, 171, 192, 198, 212, 214, 219, 220, 224, 226, 227–30, 248–9, 251, 263, 266
Moholy-Nagy N 72, 269
monumentalism 62, 76, 80, 109, 208, 231–4, 249
Morgan G 1, 34, 37–8, 60, 229, 243, 262, 269
Morgan B 130, 269
Morris W 86, 159, 222–3, 269
mosques 30, 39, 51
'Moulin Rouge' 84–5, 268

Index

Mrs Beaton 16
music 22, 84, 134, 158, 188, 221, 222
Mussolini 232, 244

N-dimensions 47–8
Napoleon 252
National Health Service 198–202
National Trust 145–8, 171, 188
Naturality 99, 111–2, 116, 174–9, 202, 215, 251
natural science 12, 55, 112, 252
Neo-Classicism 76, 144, 212, 224–7, 238, 249
Neo-Gothic 71
Neo-liberalism 22, 23, 71, 123–5, 132, 144, 154, 169, 171, 180, 183, 190, 198, 246–7, 251, 267
Neo-Palladianism 136, 144, 225, 251
New World Order 144, 251, 269
New York 79, 165, 169, 228–9
Nietzsche F 5–6, 13, 270
Noailles Road 141
Nonaka I and Takeuchi H 38, 270
Non-Governmental Organizations (NGOs) 177, 179, 223, 270
Nyathi N 101, 270

office design 228–30
organizational culture 25, 271
organization studies 3, 35, 42, 109
organizing of organization 10, 13
organization theory 4, 11, 19, 21, 28, 31, 36, 38, 40, 42–3, 46, 47, 59, 68, 71, 78, 82–3, 95, 104, 105, 109, 174, 177, 181, 208, 211, 212, 220, 228, 239, 243, 249, 250, 264, 265, 271
organon 34
Orwell G 23, 270
Owings N 8, 72, 76, 165–6, 169, 171, 229, 237, 239, 270
over-codings 77

Paris 14–5, 67, 106, 141, 267
Parker M 151–2, 189, 238–9, 249, 262, 270
Parkinson's Law 27, 270
parkland 88, 235, 236
pattern books 11–12, 17, 41, 91
pattern language 11, 86, 261
patterns 1, 5, 11, 17, 19, 31–2, 42, 55, 69, 77, 105, 107, 144, 208–9, 211, 244, 246, 259
Pearson D 222, 270
peasantry 28, 129, 160, 221, 227, 238, 258
periodization of styles 68–73
Perrow C 68, 270
Peters T 25, 43, 158, 270
Pettigrew A 199, 201, 270
Pevsner N 8, 83, 221, 266, 270
Pfeffer J 68, 270

philanthro-capitalism 233–4
Picturesque movement 70, 146–7, 221
Planck thickness 48
Plato 9, 270
planes 28, 29, 44, 46, 50, 51, 84, 91, 95, 116–9, 173–203, 244, 248, 255
Plumwood V 13, 270
Pollock A 199–200, 270
Pol Potism 123, 129, 139, 140, 144, 171, 175, 186, 251
population ecology 42, 247, 266
potlatch economics 123, 125–7, 137, 138, 144, 169, 171, 180, 186, 195, 197, 246, 247, 251, 264
Poundsbury, UK 225
privatization 108, 125, 162, 199, 200
problematique 90, 209
production of organization 248
professions 13, 17, 19, 24, 27, 39, 79, 81–2, 101, 136, 144, 157, 196, 200, 222, 230, 258
proletariat 7, 142, 252–3
property 63, 104, 108, 125, 129, 147, 167, 183, 195
Proteus 41–2, 44–5
protogeometry 44
Progressivism 17, 108, 127, 150–151, 198
psychology 101, 187, 224
Pugin AWN 85, 238, 270
Punk 84, 90
pyramids 23, 27, 29, 42, 44, 51, 60–1, 83

RAND Corporation 190–4, 201, 202, 271
rationality 16, 17, 21, 24–5, 44, 96, 99, 101–5, 142, 189–93, 217, 229, 272, 273
Recht R 97, 271
Reed M 82, 104, 263, 266, 271
recipes 14, 15–16, 61, 248, 272
recognition 14, 15, 65, 208, 246
rhizome 19, 244, 250
riparianism 44–5
Romanticism 112, 129, 131, 148, 193, 212, 214, 219, 221–4, 239, 246, 247, 249, 251, 271
rotation, principle of 258
Rowlinson M 68, 271
Royal science 43–4, 96
Rudofsky B 72, 222, 271
rupturism 99, 108–110, 114, 117, 122, 171, 197–202, 251
Russia 64, 153, 244

Salingaros N 135, 271
Sardar Z 14–15, 271
Scientific Management 228–30
security 7–9, 11, 33, 107, 144, 165, 183
sedimentism 99, 105–10, 114, 117, 122, 123, 193–7, 201, 251

279

Index

separation of home from work 16–17
sensibility 69, 99–105, 121, 144–5, 148, 151–4, 175, 180, 185–9, 201, 215, 227, 230, 246–7, 251, 262
sewing 12, 36, 37
Schama S 88–9, 112–3, 271
Schopenhauer 6
Schumpeterianism 82, 123, 127–8, 134, 143, 152, 170, 171, 180, 186, 198, 246, 247, 251, 262, 271
Schwartz R 257, 271
Scott GG 85–6, 267
Scott W 24, 68, 271
Sennett R 7–8, 10, 15, 16, 34, 271
shelter 7–9, 28, 77, 222, 239, 259
Shenhav Y 17, 68, 271
shops 67, 81, 146–8, 214
signature artists/architects 82, 130, 137, 168
Simmel G 67, 271
Sinha P 154, 271
Sidelsky R 142, 271
Skidmore, Owings and Merrill 8, 76, 165, 169, 171, 229, 237
socialism 80, 127, 132, 152, 170, 176, 232
skyscrapers 39, 112, 228, 230, 239
software 11–12, 39, 49
Speer A 62, 231
Spencer J 154, 272
Spender JC 16, 38, 272
Spotts F 208, 272
squares 22, 27, 29–32, 42, 238, 243, 250
stabilizing practices 9–10, 29
standardization 14, 17
Starbuck W 64, 201, 272
Stata Building, MIT 134–5, 155, 233
state 13, 16, 23, 25, 39, 43–4, 60–1, 64, 66, 77, 79, 80–1, 85, 88, 90, 97, 101, 104, 108, 112–3, 125–9, 141–2, 144, 152–3, 157, 159, 162, 166, 171, 181–5, 192, 199–200, 211, 214, 218, 225, 229, 232, 248
statistico-organizational theory 42, 265
Stern R and Dietsch D 39, 272
Stewart R 14
Stevens H 88–9, 272
'strategy of the void' 209
Strati A 66, 272
structuration theory 10, 65, 106–7, 243, 254, 266
stylus 12, 37, 59–60, 244
Sutton I 83, 272
symbolism 132, 214, 219
synthetic cubism 45–7

Taos Institute 223–4, 264
Tavistock Institute 223–4
Taylorism 83, 228, 266
telos 5, 6, 110

Tennessee Valley Authority (TVA) 104–5, 139, 248, 267, 271
termes 13, 14, 18–9, 130
Thanem T 239, 272
three-dimensional (3D) 28, 31, 38–9, 46, 47–50, 52, 117–18, 202, 246, 255
Till J 46–7, 272
Tilly C 234, 272
Tilting, Fogo Island 155–8, 169, 170, 171, 176, 191, 195, 251, 269
tourism 128–9, 146, 153, 232, 272
towers 1, 29, 30, 70, 72, 75–7, 113, 135, 137–9, 143, 164–6, 169, 171, 181, 188, 195, 208, 224, 237, 241, 243, 251
Townley B 101, 272
trompes l'oeil 163, 172, 234, 236, 237, 251
Tsoukas H 5, 35, 109, 264, 272
Turner B 208, 235, 272
two-dimensional (2D) 38–40, 41, 47, 49, 52, 54, 117, 172, 202

unemployment 129, 168
uniformity 52, 84, 90, 123, 229, 230, 254
Urry J 43, 111, 129, 166, 220, 268, 272
Utopia 8, 14, 81, 132, 155, 158–9, 176, 202, 228, 257, 263,
utopiary 13–14, 257, 263

Vacchani 239
Van Krieken R 240, 272
variable geometry 24, 273
Venturi R 219–20, 272
Vermorel F 84, 209, 272
Versailles 140–1, 144, 163, 171, 180, 190, 195, 235, 236, 240
verticality 29, 30, 32, 73, 85, 87, 149, 234–8, 254, 259
villages 66, 101, 136–7, 151, 156–7, 223, 224, 225, 269
Virgin Galactic 88, 151–5, 169, 171, 181, 185, 188, 198, 234, 251, 268
Virginia, University of 136–8, 170, 171, 190, 195
Virilio P 45, 232, 272
VOC 88–9
Vogel 3, 273
voids 29, 51, 203, 256
volumes 29, 51, 209
vortex 10, 109, 211

Ward LF 112, 273
Warren S 220, 273
Webb S 48, 273
Welsch W 65–6, 273
Wilson B 101–2, 273
Wittgenstein L 132–5, 144, 148, 151, 169, 171, 180, 248, 251, 268
Weber M 16, 23, 44, 52, 104, 182, 192, 266, 273

Index

White T 199, 273
Whiteley P 196, 273
Wittfogel K 16, 61, 273
Woodward K 63, 273
Woolgar CM 16, 22, 273
writing 14, 16, 61, 264

Zald M 64, 273
Zapatistas 158–61, 169, 170, 171, 176, 188, 198, 218–9, 251
zeitgeist 9, 22, 45, 71, 83, 91, 207, 209
'zero architecture' 151, 169, 248, 251
Zikek S 38, 253